Foreword

Welcome to the second edition of *The Customise* ... ve collectors guide to all GB stamp/label stamp she ... ce source for collectors of these customised stamp sl ... on was published in February 2007 by Graham Howard and Chris Potts, interest in this branch of stamp collecting has continued to grow with many new products emerging from Royal Mail, Isle of Man Post and Universal Mail. I have now expanded this guide to include all these additional entrants and the number of sheets illustrated has more than doubled in the second edition.

Acknowledgements

The author wishes to thank and acknowledge the following individuals and organisations for their continued help, advice and encouragement in the compilation of this work. My sincere thanks go to:

- Chris Potts for co-authoring the first edition of this catalogue in 2007 and for his helpful advice, support, contribution and friendship over the years.
- Royal Mail for their support and encouragement and providing access to Royal Mail archives for some of the illustrated material used in this catalogue; and to
- The specialist business customised stamp sheet producers for giving permission to illustrate their products in this catalogue. These include: Gerald Moore at Benham, Adrian Bradbury, Tony Buckingham, Steven Scott at the Strand Stamp-Centre; John Chapman and Terry Mitchell at Bletchley Park Post Office, Graham Jones at Planet Prints, and to
- Glenn Morgan for his help, support and for his many splendid articles featuring these sheets which have appeared in British Philatelic Bulletin from time to time; and to
- Mike Shepherd for his knowledge, help and assistance, particularly for the issue notes information and for his critical and helpful comments in reviewing the first edition of this catalogue; and to
- The many contributors to the on-line Smilers News blog at www.smilers-info.com who, since the first edition appeared in February 2007 have helped identify a number of key varieties and printing differences which have all helped to expand this reference work; and to
- Truprint for providing images of the publicity material featured in Appendix C and to
- John Vincent, Robert McRitchie, Mike Czuczman, Allan M. Grant and many others too numerous to mention, who have helped get this work to publication.

You know who you are and for your support and help, my sincere thanks.

Graham Howard
Moscow, February 2010

Copyright Notice

Publishing History

First Edition - 2007

ISBN: 978-0-9555249-0-5

Second Edition - 2010

ISBN: 978-0-9555249-1-2

Published by : Ridgewood Publications, Ridgewood, Pine View Close, Haslemere, Surrey, GU27 1RT

Printed and bound by: Pardy and Son Printers Limited, Ringwood, Hampshire

www.smilers.co.uk

Exclusive Designs by Adrian Bradbury

Dear Adrian
Just a note to let you know how much your stamp sheets are appreciated. As an historian, I can see how much research goes into the sheets and that, in turn, produces superb designs and information. They easily outclass other sheet producers and are a joy to have.

A G BRADBURY 3 LINK RD Stoneygate LEICESTER LE2 3RA

Introduction

This guide provides a comprehensive listing of all Customised Stamp Sheets issued by Royal Mail, Isle of Man Post and other commercial organisations up to the end of January 2010. It is issued as a reference work for the customised stamp sheet collector. Each sheet is given a unique reference number with a prefix corresponding to the section the sheet is listed under. Whilst every effort has been made to ensure the details contained in this catalogue are accurate, corrections to this listing are welcomed and encouraged.

This catalogue is not a sales list. The prices shown are intended as a guide to market prices but please be aware that this is a relatively new area of stamp collecting and prices are subject to change. There has been strong interest in this branch of stamp collecting since the First Edition of this catalogue was issued and we would like to think that this has been due in part to the sharing of information that this publication has promoted. This catalogue is divided into nine chapters. A brief description of each Chapter now follows.

Chapter 1 - The Smilers Story

The Smilers Story traces the evolution of the early greetings stamps, issued in 1989, to the present day smilers stamps and their various incarnations along the way. It documents Royal Mail's earlier attempts to introduce customised mail which in hindsight was truly ground breaking in the world of postal authorities and years ahead of its international peers. It examines the development of generic Smilers sheets, Customised Smilers sheets, Business Customised stamp sheets through to the recently introduced Commemorative Stamp Sheets and Smilers Packs, featuring the Smilers for Kids range of products.

Chapter 2 - Generic Stamp Sheets

Generic Stamp Sheets comprise small sheets of 10 or 20 stamps plus photo-tabs set within a border with a generic sheet/tab design commemorating or celebrating an event or theme and sold at a premium above the face value of the actual stamps. Generic Stamp Sheets may be obtained directly from Royal Mail at Tallents House, Edinburgh. Since 2000, the public have been able to personalise the photo-tabs of some of these Generic Smilers sheets by sending their own images to Royal Mail Tallents House and the cost of these Customised Stamp Sheets, branded *Smilers* by Royal Mail, is higher than the standard Generic sheets.

Chapter 3 - Customised Stamp Sheets

Customised Stamp Sheets or *Smilers* are a variant of the Generic Stamp Sheets. Since the original Stamp Show 2000 the public have been able to have their photos printed alongside the stamps in place of the generic tabs. This service, initially available only from booths at events such as Stamp Show 2000, has been extended and is now available to the public by post or by ordering on-line from the Royal Mail at **www.royalmail.com/smilers.** These sheets were available from the Royal Mail at a premium above the normal price of the Generic Stamp Sheets. Appendix B provides a pictorial summary and listing of all the stamps used by Royal Mail in its series of Smilers. Royal Mail adopted the trademark *Smilers* after Australia Post took exception to their use of *Personalised Stamps,* which had earlier been adopted and registered by Australia Post.

Chapter 4 - Business Customised Sheets

Business Customised Sheets are similar to Generic Stamp Sheets in that they contain generally the same Royal Mail stamps but the borders and photo-tabs are designed by Philatelic and other commercial organisations to promote a theme, anniversary or event. Generally these sheets are produced in much smaller quantities and are sold at a much higher premium than the Generic Stamp Sheets.

Chapter 5 - Themed Sheets and Covers

Chapter 5 comprises a listing of what we have termed **Themed Customised Stamp Sheets**. These are essentially Customised Stamp sheets (Smilers) which have been produced not for personal use on mail but for the philatelic market. Since the advent of the definitive-sized Smilers sheets late in 2005 there has been keen interest in extending the concept of Customised Stamp Sheets into special event or themed sheets, created by Smilers sheet enthusiasts

Chapter 6 - Commemorative Stamp Sheets

Commemorative Stamp Sheets were introduced by Royal Mail in 2008 and are in all respects similar in format and design to Business Customised Stamp sheets but are produced directly by Royal Mail to commemorate or mark anniversaries of national importance which didn't quite make it into the annual stamp programme.

Chapter 7 - Smilers for Kids Packs

Royal Mail introduced another Smilers innovation in 2008 in the form of Smilers-for-kids packs. The concept was to print A5 sized, sheets of 10 stamps and generic-tabs targeted at children, or perhaps more correctly the parents of children, supplied in a pack containing other activity-based material in support of the pack theme, including colouring, letter-writing activities etc., designed to attract the attention of Royal Mail's younger customers. The Smilers for Kids packs as they were branded by Royal Mail illustrated certain well known children's characters such as the Flower Fairies, Noddy and Friends, Mr Men and Little Miss and the World of Beatrix Potter.

Chapter 8 - Isle of Man Customised Stamp Sheets

Early in 2008, the Isle of Man Post Office issued a series of three stamp/tab sheets remarkably similar in style to Royal Mail's Generic Smilers sheets which caught the attention of the Smilers collectors . These were quickly followed by the issue of a stamp/tab combination produced by AG Bradbury thus giving the Isle of Man its equivalent of the Customised Stamp Sheet collectibles.

Chapter 9 - Universal Mail Customised Stamps

During 2006, the government passed new laws de-regularising some of Royal Mail's 160 year-long monopoly on handling certain UK postal items including business mail and overseas bound post. As yet no competitor exists to challenge Royal Mail's dominance on the domestic front but there are companies emerging who have their eyes firmly fixed to the lucrative business and overseas markets. One such company is Universal Mail, a New Zealand based company who provide similar services to Business users in the UK and who from mid-2008 provided customised stamps for use on overseas mail. This chapter provides an illustrated listing of all varieties issued to date.

Appendix A - Smilers Dealers List

Appendix A provides a list of Stamp dealers, their names, addresses, e-mail and contact numbers is provided together with a commentary on their activity with respect to selling Smilers related sheets, packs, covers etc., to help the new collector build his/her collection.

Appendix B - Smilers Stamps

Appendix B provides a summary and listing of the Smilers stamps used by Royal Mail to date, as referenced in its Smilers publicity material.

Appendix C - Smilers Publicity

Appendix C provides a convenient reference collection of various Royal Mail produced and other Smilers publicity leaflets, which are referenced throughout the catalogue.

Finally, a word on indexing...

In any work such as this, finding what you are looking for is all important so we have tried to make it as easy as possible for you. The index that follows lists the contents of each of the chapters previously described, in a sequential manner. Each chapter can be easily identified and located by noting the colour at the top of the indexed listing and turning to the matching colour coded tabs at the vertical edge of the chapter pages.

Remember, whatever your interest in these issues ...

... keep Smi)ing!

Chapter 1 - The Smilers Story

Chapter 2 - Generic Stamp Sheets

Chapter 2 - Generic Stamp Sheets

Chapter 2 - Generic Stamp Sheets

Chapter 3 - Customised Stamp Sheets

Chapter 3 - Customised Stamp Sheets

Chapter 3 - Customised Stamp Sheets

Chapter 4 - Business Customised Sheets

Chapter 4 - Business Customised Sheets

Chapter 4 - Business Customised Sheets

Chapter 4 - Business Customised Sheets

Chapter 4 - Business Customised Sheets

Description **Page**

Chapter 6 - Commemorative Stamp Sheets

Chapter 7 - Smilers For Kids

Chapter 8 - Isle of Man Stamp Sheets

Chapter 9 - Universal Mail Customised Stamps

Chapter 1 - The Smilers Story

The Bear Facts

The issue of a new book of stamps in 1989 heralded a shift in Post Office stamp-selling policy. The stamp-booklet in question was the 1989 *Greetings* booklet and, for virtually the first time, it contained stamps which could not be regarded as either *definitive* or *commemorative*. The first *definitive* was the 1d Black of 1840 and, as the name implies, these tend to be unchanging in design and available over a long period.

Commemoratives were first introduced in 1924 and were only issued to *commemorate* important events or anniversaries and, from 1966 (with the *Landscape* issue), *themes* of relevance to Britain or British culture. Some exceptions can be noted – the Charity issue of 1974, and a few stamps of relevance to international themes or anniversaries, but they are few and far between. The stamp designs used in the *Greetings* booklet stamps, together with their accompanying generic tabs can be seen as the forerunners to the Smilers sheets that followed in 2000.

1989 ***1991*** ***2005***

The first Greetings booklet featured a series of five stamps depicting images (a teddy bear, Cupid, etc) which permitted a form of 'personalised' expression (or choice) dependant upon the stamp image used. Between the period 1989 to 1997, a total of ten Greetings booklets were to be issued, utilising variations on the Greeting theme. Perhaps the most significant was the set which first appeared in 1990, a set of 10 stamps depicting famous "smiles". Whilst these were again re-issued with non-value indicators in 1991, the set re-appeared again as part of a souvenir stamp sheet issued to coincide with the International Stamp Show 2000. Many of the *Greetings* series of stamp-booklets were also supplied with a set of special labels bearing greetings messages which, together with the stamps, could be combined to add a personalised message – does this sound familiar?

Occasions or Smilers?

What stamp collectors have affectionately come to term as *Smilers* stamps and sheets could have perhaps more appropriately, been called *Greetings* or *Occasions sheets*, after the stamps used by Royal Mail in the production of the early Smilers stamp sheets. However, the ability to have your photograph alongside a Royal Mail stamp was new for the British public and what was needed was an identity distinct from the *Greetings* stamps that would promote this as a fun thing to do. The selected brand *Smilers* is therefore perhaps best described as an evolution, rather than a revolution, having its roots in the earlier Greetings/Occasions stamp issues by Royal Mail.

Royal Mail A4 Grille Cards

Post-a-Photo

From about the early 1990's the Post Office/Royal Mail embarked on a series of marketing initiatives, designed perhaps to broaden their customer base but always with a philatelic theme. The Post Office had sold crockery at a Stampex event in the late 70's depicting the *Wildlife* series from that period. The introduction of the Post-a-Photo service is an important development in the Smilers Story and provides a clear link between the early Greetings stamps of the 80's and 90's to the Smilers sheets of the new millennium.

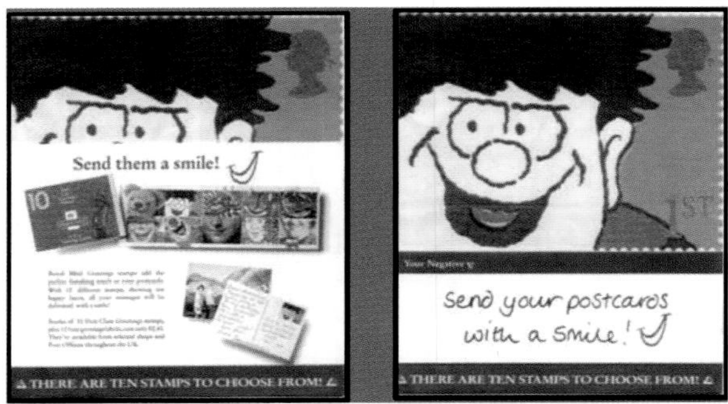

During 1992 Royal Mail introduced a personalised postcard service called Post-a-Photo. Initially the subject of a Royal Mail promotion, Royal Mail customers were invited to submit a negative and 4 x 1st class stamps to Royal Mail who in return agreed to supply 20 personalised postcards using the negative provided. Royal Mail may have underestimated the popularity of this product, or perhaps the manufacturer was unable to fulfil all the orders, but shortly afterwards Royal Mail apologised for the initial delay in providing the postcards and subsequently its cancellation of some orders. The Post-a-Photo promotion was subsequently cancelled completely by Royal Mail as the text of the following letter and postcard describes. A complimentary book of stamps issued January 1992 was supplied to all disappointed Royal Mail customers.

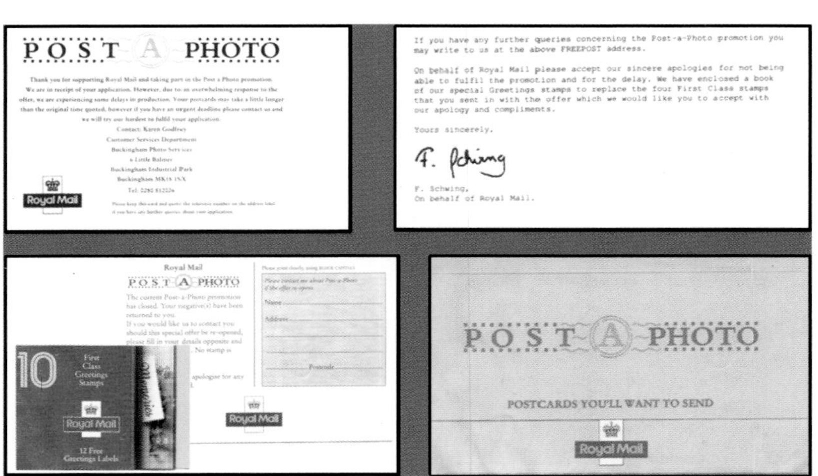

POST A PHOTO

Thank you for supporting Royal Mail and taking part in the Post a Photo promotion. We are in receipt of your application. However, due to an overwhelming response to the offer, we are experiencing some delays in production. Your postcards may take a little longer than the original time quoted, however if you have an urgent deadline please contact us and we will try our hardest to fulfil your application.

Contact: Karen Godfrey
Customer Services Department
Buckingham Photo Services
Buckingham Industrial Park
Buckingham MK18 1SX

Royal Mail

If you have any further queries concerning the Post-a-Photo promotion you may write to us at the above FREEPOST address.

On behalf of Royal Mail please accept our sincere apologies for not being able to fulfil the promotion and for the delay. We have enclosed a book of our special Greetings stamps to replace the four First Class stamps that you sent in with the offer which we would like you to accept with our apology and compliments.

Yours sincerely,

F. Schwing

F. Schwing,
On behalf of Royal Mail.

Royal Mail
POST A PHOTO

The current Post-a-Photo promotion has closed. Your negative(s) have been returned to you.
If you would like us to contact you should this special offer be re-opened, please fill in your details opposite and ... No stamp is ... apologise for any ...

Name
Address
Postcode

Royal Mail

10 First Class Greetings Stamps
Royal Mail
12 Free Greetings Labels

POST A PHOTO
POSTCARDS YOU'LL WANT TO SEND
Royal Mail

Post-a-Photo (continued)

Following the initial Post-a-Photo promotion, Royal Mail did appoint another postcard manufacturer because by November 1992 customers were again being contacted to supply their negatives by 6th November 1992, the closing date for the re-launched service.

As part of that effort, two postcards were issued to disappointed customers by Royal Mail which featured two of the smilers stamps. The first "Bear with us ..." advises customers of a problem. The second "Hurry along now!" advises customers of the closing date for the service.

...we're hard at work, searching for a new manufacturer who can turn your favourite photograph into 20 high-quality postcards.

It's taking a little longer than we first thought, as we want to be sure you'll be delighted with your new postcards.

At the moment we're talking to potential manufacturers, and we'll be writing soon to let you know where to send your negatives. If you plan to move house before then, please let us know your new address or go into your local Post Office and ask them to redirect any post to your new home.

Thank you for being so patient.

Warm regards,

Franziska Schwing,
On behalf of Royal Mail.

If you have any queries, please contact me at: Post-A-Photo, Customer Care, FREEPOST KE 8330, LONDON EC1B 1TA

HQ SERIAL 2222 POSTAGE 1 PAID

MR J WALSH
23 BOYNE ROAD
BUDLEIGH SALTERTON
DEVON
EX9 6SE

Royal Mail

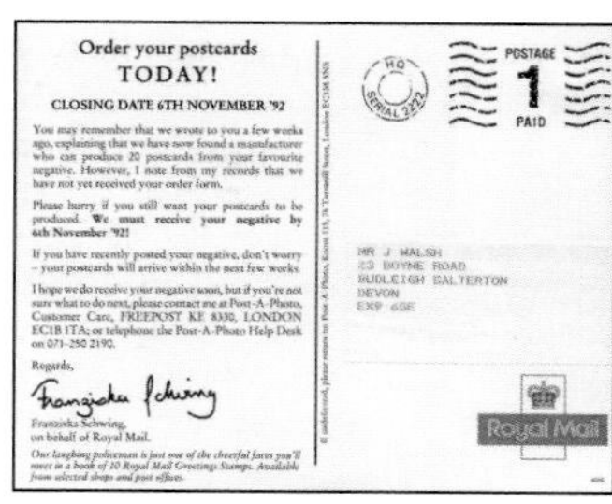

Order your postcards
TODAY!

CLOSING DATE 6TH NOVEMBER '92

You may remember that we wrote to you a few weeks ago, explaining that we have now found a manufacturer who can produce 20 postcards from your favourite negative. However, I note from my records that we have not yet received your order form.

Please hurry if you still want your postcards to be produced. **We must receive your negative by 6th November '92!**

If you have recently posted your negative, don't worry – your postcards will arrive within the next few weeks.

I hope we do receive your negative soon, but if you're not sure what to do next, please contact me at Post-A-Photo, Customer Care, FREEPOST KE 8330, LONDON EC1B 1TA; or telephone the Post-A-Photo Help Desk on 071-250 2190.

Regards,

Franziska Schwing,
on behalf of Royal Mail.

Our laughing policeman is just one of the cheerful faces you'll meet in a book of 10 Royal Mail Greetings Stamps. Available from selected shops and post offices.

HQ SERIAL 2222 POSTAGE 1 PAID

MR J WALSH
23 BOYNE ROAD
BUDLEIGH SALTERTON
DEVON
EX9 6SE

Royal Mail

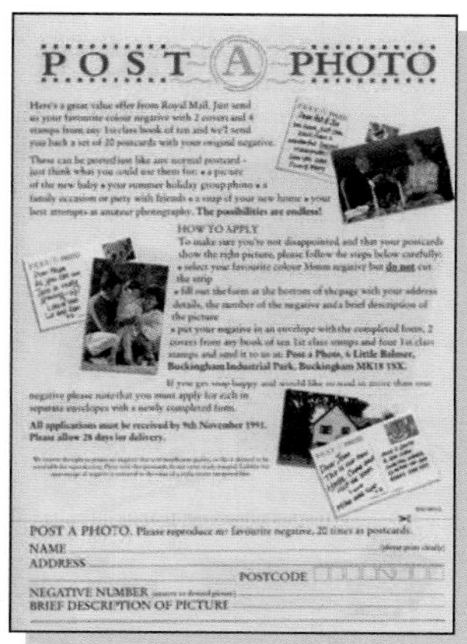

Generic Smilers

Following the success of the Stamp Show 2000 sheet and 2000 Christmas sheets, The Post Office issued five different Customised Smilers sheets in May 2001 featuring the Hallmark stamps of the previous February. The Hallmarks Generic Smilers sheet did not appear until 5th June 2001 and whilst it is not clear why this sheet was delayed it was a welcomed move by Royal Mail. Until then the only way collectors could obtain a set of Hallmark Smilers stamps and generic-tabs was to buy a set of five customised sheets. Over sixty sheet designs have now been released, averaging about six per year. The early ones are hard to find in unblemished condition – many have minor bends/creases from handling, or have been folded in half in the case of sheets supplied by post from Edinburgh. As with normal commemorative issues, the generic sheets are usually available from philatelic counters for 12 months (this was extended to 13 months for one issue, GS-015) unless sold out earlier.

The Stamp Show 2000 sheet sold just fewer than 52,000 copies, but the sales figures for subsequent sheets have never been released. Bearing in mind the premium over face most sales are likely to be philatelic, but commercially used singles can be found in kilo-ware, particularly of the Christmas issues. Even so, sales of GS-001 were lower than any regular GB commemorative issue (the closest, the £1 PUC of 1929 sold 61,000 copies). Interest in the early sheets tailed off rapidly after GS-001, before picking up at the end of 2002. Some are quite scarce, notably the 2001 Christmas pair.

Commemorative and definitive releases are normally publicised in Post Office outlets by means of A4 coloured illustrations – the so-called 'grille' cards, see page 1-1. Apart from the initial issues (Xmas 2000) none of the Generic Smilers sheets have been publicised in this way, but the designs are normally illustrated in the Royal Mail 'preview' brochures well in advance of issue using artists mock-ups. The issued versions often show modifications when actually released and in at least two instances the original printings have been issued in error alongside the revised versions, notably the 2003 Occasions sheet and the 2005 ITV sheet, refer page 2-7 and 2-13.

Customised Smilers

The Post Office introduced 'Smilers' sheets as a way of 'personalising' postage stamps at the London International Stamp Exhibition in May 2000. The A4 sized sheets contained ten (later, twenty) stamps se-tenant with an unprinted photo tab which could be customised with a photograph. The service was quite expensive. The initial cost for a single sheet of ten personalised stamps was £5.95 (£5.00 each for two or more sheets, a premium of £4.80 on the cost of twenty stamps). The current cost is £13.50 per personalised sheet of twenty first-class stamps (a premium of £5.70 over face), though this falls to £12.50 for two or more sheets. The Post Office, subsequently renamed Consignia plc (2001), then Royal Mail Group plc (2002) and currently Royal Mail Group Ltd (2006), intended the *Smilers* trademark to apply to personalised stamp sheets only, but at the same time a sheet with printed tabs was made available at a lower price (£2.95 – a 35p surcharge on the cost of the stamps). The Post Office used to refer to these simply as *generic* sheets, but now call these *Generic Smilers™ Sheets*. Since 2005 this has changed on all sheets to *Generic Smilers® Sheets*. In a more recent development (from late 2006), Royal Mail have now started omitting the word *Smilers* from those generic sheets not available in personalised format, e.g. the *We Shall Remember Them* sheet , *Wembley* and *Machin* sheets have the brand *Smilers* omitted. Whilst somewhat confusing all generic sheets are sold under the banner of the *Generic Smilers Sheets* via Royal Mail's on-line order facility but not all sheet are available in personalised format. It has become even more confusing with the recent release of the Castles series of Generic Smilers Sheets all of which are branded Smilers but are not available in personalised formats! Stanley Gibbons initially announced that since Smilers sheets were not available at face they would be relegated to the status of catalogue footnotes, and this, coupled with the cost (over single-set new issues) and unwieldy sheet sizes, led to a steady decline in sales of the subsequent sheets until interest took off in late 2002. Royal Mail released a dedicated album for the series in 2003 and Gibbons eventually listed the generic versions in the 2004 GB 'Concise' catalogue, which further fuelled demand.

The personalised sheets are footnoted by Gibbons in the GB 'Concise', but not illustrated. In contrast to the generic series, they have received scant attention in the philatelic literature – to the extent that many collectors have never seen them. To date about sixty basic designs have been released: some are almost identical to the generic versions, but most contain unique border designs and/or stamp combinations. Several were produced by a different printer to that responsible for the generic issue, resulting in recognisably different stamps. The print runs of 'blanks' for personalisation are much lower than for the generic sheets and some have been subjected to (unannounced) reprints. Royal Mail has strict guidelines as to the type of image that can be reproduced in the blank tabs: these are displayed on Post Office publicity brochures and on the website. It is believed that the first issue was only available with photographic portraits, but all subsequent issues could be customised with pictorial images. These are scarce on the early sheets - examples are illustrated below for Xmas 2000, sold to raise funds for New Marnoch Church in Aberchirder, Scotland.

The very first Themed Smilers featuring New Marnoch Church in Aberchirder

Given the interest expressed by collectors, philatelic sales of these sheets would appear to have been small (the first issue apart) until interest was again renewed late 2005. Early Smilers sheets are difficult to find intact, either having been broken up for postage or gathering dust as sentimental keepsakes. On the plus side, when they occasionally do surface they can often be bought for less than the generic equivalents! Their relative scarcities do not parallel the generic series – the 2000 and 2001 Christmas issues are among the 'easier' personalised sheets. Paradoxically, commercially used personalised singles crop up in kiloware more frequently than do singles from the generic sheets, so demand from the public has clearly been high enough for Royal Mail to justify the service. Most sheets available after late 2005 are much easier to find, though there are some exceptions, such as the ITV sheet (CS-026) which was withdrawn unexpectedly in mid-2006.

The period of sales of these sheets has been difficult to establish: they usually become available on the same date as the generic versions, but withdrawal dates are rarely announced. Some, such as the Stamp Show 2000, were available for just a few weeks while some, such as the 'Moving Home' Occasions sheet, had been on sale continuously since introduction in 2002 up until 2006. Some are 'seasonal' – the Xmas 2002 sheet could be ordered from October to December each year until the end of 2004, but not in the intervening months. The only reliable way of keeping track is by phoning the 'Smilers helpline' periodically and enquiring which are still available.

Instant Smilers

Visitors to The Stamp Show 2000 were, for the first time in Britain, able to purchase a sheet of postage stamps with their own image printed on photo-tabs adjacent to the stamps and create their very own personalised souvenir covers. Customers completed an order form, had their photographs taken and the resulting image was printed onto sheets containing blank photo-tabs. The whole process took about 10 minutes. The exhibition attracted 55,000 visitors and this innovation proved popular with visitors – a Post Office survey dated July 2000 cited 23% of those surveyed intended to buy the personalised stamps. The resulting personalised Smilers Sheet was presented to the customer in an attractive red folder with a distinctive *Smile* cut-out, very reminiscent of the cover of the 1990 *Greetings* stamp-booklet which had used the same stamp images as the personalised *Instant Smilers* sheet. Visitors to the show could re-order additional copies of their personalised Smilers Sheets by sending a special re-order form to *Royal Mail Smilers, House of Questa, Byfleet* at a cost of £5 each.

SS-2000 *Instant Smilers* Order Form

Stamp Show 2000 *Instant Smilers*

Stamp Show 2000 *Instant Smilers* Re-Order

Regional Instant Smilers

The *Instant Smilers* service was again tested at six regional Post Offices which had a Philatelic Counter (Bristol, Cambridge, Canterbury, Edinburgh, London and Manchester) between October 2001 and January 2002. Whilst widely publicised in the Post Offices where these booths were located, and within the philatelic press, it was not widely known to the general public and consumer uptake was reportedly 'negligible'.

An *Instant Smilers* Photo Booth

The *Instant Smilers* facility surfaced again as a single booth at Stampex in Autumn 2005 and has also appeared at various trade-related Royal Mail product launches and subsequent Stampex events. A single booth also operated at the London Boat Show in January 2006. The 2006 Boat Show customers were also offered an option of customising sheets with the Boat Show logo, instead of a personal photo. Whilst it is understood that the *Instant Smilers* sheets printed with the show's logo on the photo-tabs were never officially sanctioned or approved by Royal Mail, it is probably true to say that the recent philatelic interest in Themed Customised Smilers sheets since that event can be traced back to the excitement generated by the pair of Boat Show Smilers sheets, see also page 5-11

Smilers by Post/On-Line

The mail-order personalisation service operated (intermittently at first) from October 2000, in which the customer posted photographs to Edinburgh, and from 29th November 2002 images could be submitted on-line in digital format. The Royal Mail website www.royalmail.com/portal/rm/shop is easy to use and payment is by credit or direct debit card. The ordering process can take up to two weeks at times of peak demand (the Christmas period), but can be much faster, in a matter of days.

From July 2003 the sheets were given 'SM' codes to facilitate orders. This was after release of the 'Multiple Choice' sheet, but before the 'Cartoon Crossword' sheet. The apparent random assignation of SM codes from SM1 (Hello) to SM11 (Christmas 2002) may reflect the popularity of the sheets available at the time; they then become sequential from SM12 (Crosswords). A new 'DS' series code was introduced for the self-adhesive stamps in definitive format issued in October 2005. From 2008 Royal Mail again revised their Smilers stamp coding system reverting to a system using a SM prefix. Please refer to *Appendix B* for a fuller description of Royal Mail SM and Smilers stamp coding.

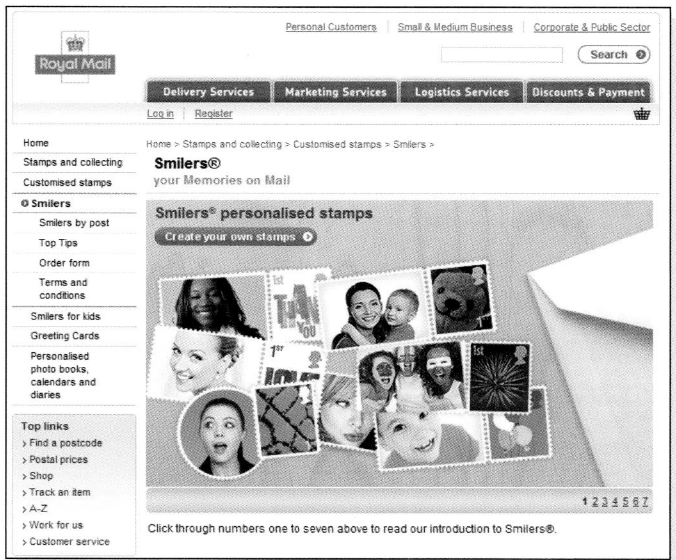

Screenshot of Royal Mail's on-line Smilers web portal

Business Customised Sheets

Royal Mail introduced this service in December 2002. It was aimed at customers willing to place an order of 100-6000+ sheets, the customer being able to add its own design to both photo-tabs and border according to their requirements. At present these have to be ordered by posting a digital CD containing artwork to Tallents House; a brochure can be downloaded from the Royal Mail website www.royalmail.com/smilers. choose the *Business Customised* option.

The current (2010) cost of this service varies depending on the type of sheet required (gummed or self adhesive) and the number of stamps per sheet (10 or 20). The 10 stamp sheet starts at £17.50/£24.50 (gummed/self-adhesive) per sheet for the minimum order (100), falling to £4.25/£4.50 per sheet for 6000 or more sheets. Sheets of twenty start at £21.25/£28.25, falling to £7.75/£8 for 6000 or more sheets. For a small premium the sheets can be numbered, to cater for limited-edition collectors. To date the service has primarily been used by those catering to the memorabilia and collecting market, resulting in a plethora of limited edition sheets commemorating topics as diverse as military anniversaries, sports teams and science-fiction characters. About two-hundred and fifty sheets have appeared so far, with print runs from as little as 100 sheets extending right up to about nearly 15,000 sheets.

Depending on the stamp (s) chosen, se-tenant combinations unavailable from other sources can be created. The sheets have attracted a relatively strong interest and, as the print runs are miniscule compared to the generic ones, may well be the rarities of tomorrow.

Royal Mail evolves the range of stamps for customisation by this service and many designs offered at the outset are no longer available. Furthermore, in some cases the printer employed is different to that employed for production of the normal issue and Smilers sheets, resulting in recognisably different stamps. Most sheets, targeting the philatelic market, are readily available, but several are very scarce.

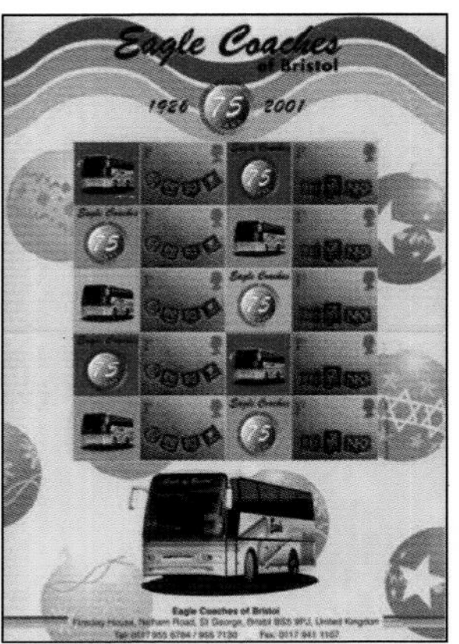

The *Eagle Coaches* Business Customised Stamp Sheets

A set of two prepared for Eagle Coaches (Bristol), generally accepted as the first issue released, sold for £2240 in August 2006. Other rarities worthy of note are the Benham 'Red Arrows' sheet (BC-056) of 2005 and the Westminster HRH The Queen - 80th Birthday Sheet (BC-085) of 2006.

Charity Smilers

In 2003 Cancer Research UK became the first organisation to lend their name to a set of charity Business Customised stamps featuring various individuals who have either been affected by the disease or contributed significantly to research or fundraising.

The four label designs were all printed on a single Smilers sheet of ten resulting in 4 x 4 blocks of 1 x strip of two stamps from each sheet.

The Cancer Research charity customised stamp sheet

The majority if not all the sheets printed (we have never seen a whole sheet other than that in the Royal Mail archives) were broken up as blocks or pairs and given away free in special presentation packs in exchange for a minimum donation of £5 to further the work of the scientists trying to find a cure for cancer. These are much sought after and exchanged hands for c. £500 in 2006.

It has been suggested, based upon conversations with Cancer Research employees dating back to 2004, that Cancer Research may not have received whole sheets from Royal Mail. It has been suggested that Royal Mail broke up the sheets and made up the Presentation Packs themselves, supplying these directly to Cancer Research. We may never know the full story!

- Pair one comprises: Bobby Moore perhaps England's most famous footballer, who led his country to victory in the 1966 World Cup final at Wembley. Bobby sadly died of bowel cancer and his wife helped launch this Business Customised Stamps promotion. Hannah Tonkin representing one of the 1,450 children in Britain that is annually diagnosed with cancer. Hannah lost an eye to the disease, but is now a happy and healthy young girl.

- Pair two comprises: Sir Paul Nurse CEO of Cancer Research UK and Dr Tim Hunt, responsible for Cell Cycle Control, who were jointly awarded the Nobel Prize for Medicine and Physiology in 2001 for their major discovery work. The final label depicts Stuart Calder, Ernie Arbery, Phyllis Black and Lisa Costley all of whom are fundraisers and promoters for the charity.

There are at least two variants of this presentation pack. Type 1 has the stamps conventionally positioned at the bottom and Type 2 has the stamps at the top. Whilst these appear to be different presentation packs, they are in fact the same card folded "inside-out". The stamps come from a single Smilers sheet and presentation packs in this author's possession include both pairs and blocks of four of the four-stamp/label combinations.

Chapter 1 - The Smilers Story

Since the arrival of Smilers sheets the potential of the media as a force for good has been recognised by a number of organisations and individuals including the folks at Ridgewood and a number of Business Customised and Themed Smilers stamp sheets have been produced to raise funds for charities. Apart from the Royal Mail inspired Cancer Research presentation pack as described above, as far as we know

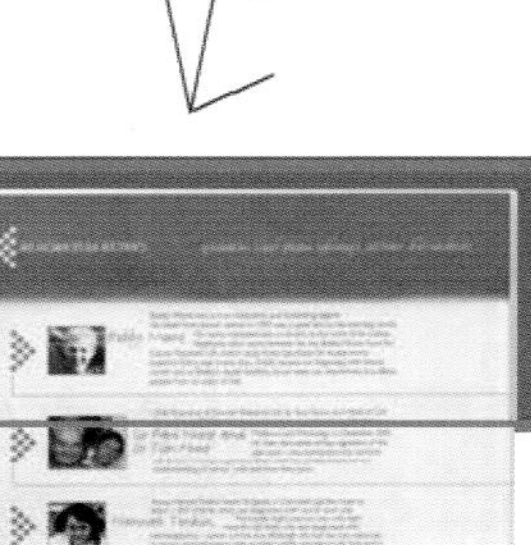

Type 1 - Panel at Top

Type 2 - Panel at Bottom

The Westminster Collection can lay claim to being the first organisation to identify the potential of smilers media as a means to raise money for charity. Buckingham covers followed a year or so later and have produced a number of attractive sheets. Even Ridgewood Publishing have produced a coupe of themed smilers sheets to raise money for Red Nose Day and Children in Need.

Finally, a London based promotions company, Shine Communications, can probably lay claim to raising the most interest in their Mothers Day/Fathers Day series of autographed smilers sheets all featuring images of various celebrity's children.

The following table lists those charity smilers sheets which have done their bit in raising money for charity.

Sheet No.	Description	Date Issued	Charity	Sheet Producer
BC-055	Route to Victory	07 Apr 2005	British Legion	The Westminster Collection
BC-086	England Winners 1966	06 Jun 2006	Bobby Moore	The Westminster Collection
BC-097	The Snowman	30 Oct 2006	Child Line	Buckingham Covers
TS-124	Red Nose Day	01 Mar 2007	Red Nose Day	Ridgewood Stamp Sheets
TS-135	Penny Lancaster (1)	01 Apr 2007	Woman's Aid	Shine Communications
TS-136	Penny Lancaster (2)	01 Apr 2007	Woman's Aid	Shine Communications
TS-137	Penny Lancaster (3)	01 Apr 2007	Woman's Aid	Shine Communications
TS-138	Penny Lancaster (4)	01 Apr 2007	Woman's Aid	Shine Communications
TS-139	Penny Lancaster (5)	01 Apr 2007	Woman's Aid	Shine Communications
TS-140	Penny Lancaster (6)	01 Apr 2007	Woman's Aid	Shine Communications
TSL-019	Helena Christianson (1)	07 Mar 2008	Woman's Aid	Shine Communications
TSL-020	Helena Christianson (2)	07 Mar 2008	Woman's Aid	Shine Communications
TSL-021	Helena Christianson (3)	07 Mar 2008	Woman's Aid	Shine Communications
TSL-022	Helena Christianson (4)	07 Mar 2008	Woman's Aid	Shine Communications
TSL-023	Helena Christianson (5)	07 Mar 2008	Woman's Aid	Shine Communications
TSL-024	Helena Christianson (6)	07 Mar 2008	Woman's Aid	Shine Communications
BC-169	Lest We Forget	23 Sep 2008	British Legion	The Westminster Collection
TS-323	Children In Need	15 Oct 2008	Children In Need	Ridgewood Stamp Sheets
TSL-117	Elizabeth Hurley	21 Jun 2009	Woman's Aid	Shine Communications
TSL-118	Jasmine Guinness	21 Jun 2009	Woman's Aid	Shine Communications

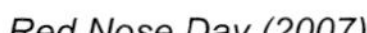
Red Nose Day (2007)

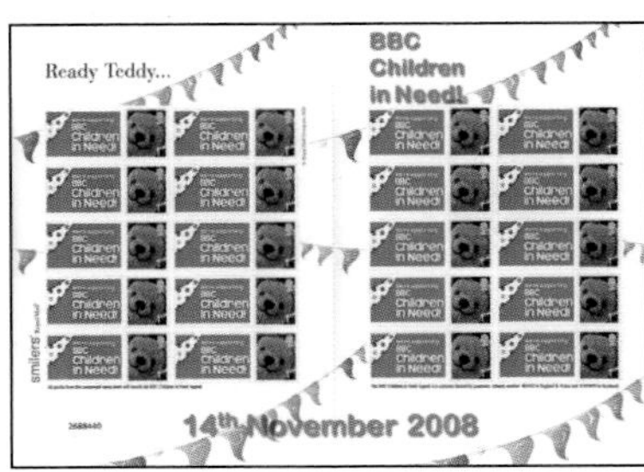

Children In Need (2008)

A shining example...

In March 2007, Shine Communications, a promotional company based in London offered, via an on-line auction site, the opportunity to buy a set of six charity Smilers sheet, raising money for the domestic violence charity, Woman's Aid. Royal Mail and Shine Communications produced a number of autographed and non-autographed sets of charity smilers featuring the photographs of famous celebrities children, to coincide with Mothers Day, under the theme of *Motherhood* and it is understood an autographed set sold for c. £1,000. Unsigned sets were sold at around £300.

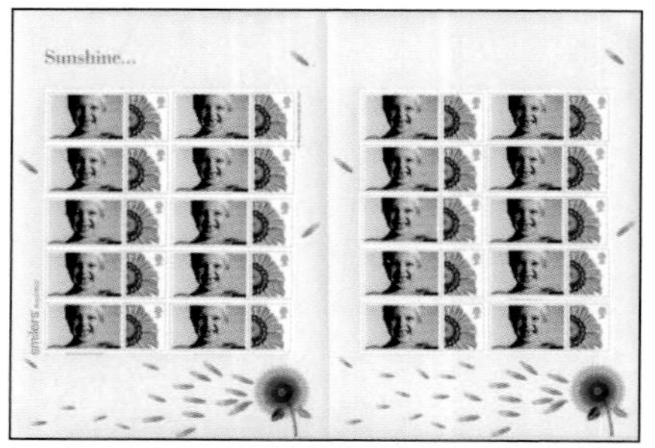

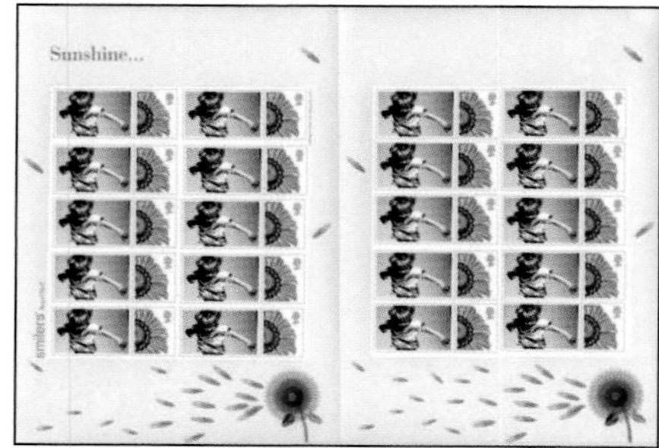

Two of the six celebrities Charity Smilers Sheets sold in 2007

Building on this success, in March 2008 Shine Communications again offered 5 (subsequently 6) autographed celebrity smilers. Helena Christensen donated images of her son to raise money for the same charity, Woman's Aid, again under the theme of Motherhood to coincide with Mothers Day. The set of six sheets eventually sold at an on-line auction for a surprising £511, much lower than the previous signed set.

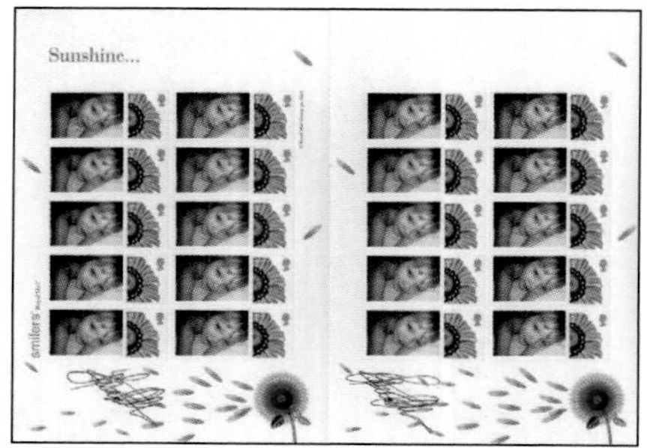

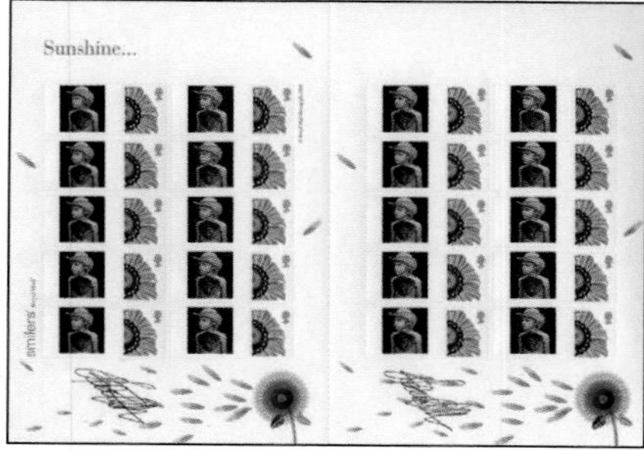

Two of the six celebrities Charity Smilers Sheets sold in 2008

In 2009 Shine Communications offered for sale by auction five pairs of signed charity smilers, the third year in a row that they had sold charity smilers to raise money Woman's Aid. Like the two previous years, the theme was based around Motherhood and the sheets were issued to coincide with Mothers Day. However, unlike the previous two years the general media got to hear about the promotion and it received much coverage in national celebrity press and newspapers. The pair of smilers sheets featured donated images of Damien Hurley, son of Elizabeth Hurley, model and actress, and Steve Bing. The other image was of Elwood Guinness, son of Jasmine Guinness, also a model and heir to the Irish brewing family's fortune. The sheets were signed by Elizabeth Hurley and Jasmine Guinness respectively.

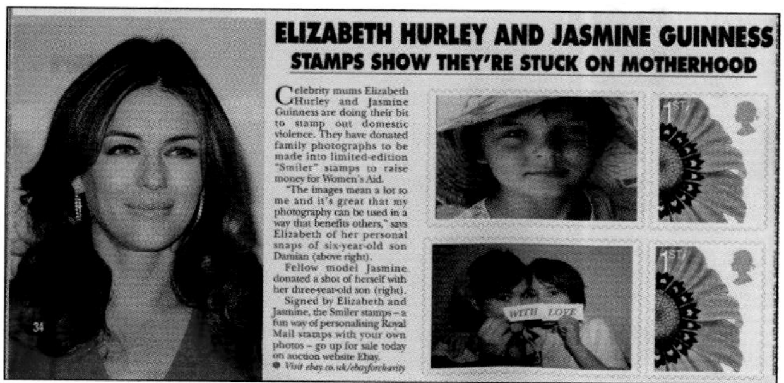

ELIZABETH HURLEY AND JASMINE GUINNESS
STAMPS SHOW THEY'RE STUCK ON MOTHERHOOD

Celebrity mums Elizabeth Hurley and Jasmine Guinness are doing their bit to stamp out domestic violence. They have donated family photographs to be made into limited-edition "Smiler" stamps to raise money for Women's Aid.

"The images mean a lot to me and it's great that my photography can be used in a way that benefits others," says Elizabeth of her personal snaps of six-year-old son Damian (above right).

Fellow model Jasmine donated a shot of herself with her three-year-old son (right).

Signed by Elizabeth and Jasmine, the Smiler stamps – a fun way of personalising Royal Mail stamps with your own photos – go up for sale today on auction website Ebay.

● *Visit ebay.co.uk/ebayforcharity*

Media coverage of the 2009 Motherhood Coverage (Hello magazine)

The pair of 2009 Celebrity Charity Smilers Sheets

Themed Smilers

These are essentially Customised Smilers sheets which have been produced primarily for the philatelic market. Since the advent of the definitive-sized Smilers sheets in 2005 there has been a growing trend to extend the concept of Customised Smilers Sheets into the production of relatively low print numbers (typically 10-100) of special event or themed sheets, many of them created by Smilers sheet enthusiasts. There are now over 500 different sheets identified by the authors, and these are listed in Chapter 5.

Example of an overprinted Themed Customised "Smilers" sheet

Some of the sheet designs produced are almost unrecognisable as customised stamp sheets due to overprinting of the border areas by the sheet producer, dramatically changing the appearance of the customised stamp sheet produced by Royal mail beyond recognition. We have noted that in recent years, the customised Smilers sheets produced by Royal Mail have considerably more border art and decoration than their earlier equivalents and in the opinion of the author the development of Themed Smilers sheets has had an influence over the selection of customised sheet designs by Royal Mail.

....whilst sheet production is impressive, the anniversaries are sometimes puzzling!

Circular Smilers

In January 2008, Royal Mail introduced a further innovation of their Smilers product in the shape of stamp sheets with circular photo-tabs. As far as we are aware, a world first, which has not been replicated elsewhere. The sheet formats (circular photo-tabs and staggered stamps) may have evolved as a result of Royal Mail's designs for the Smilers For Kids range of stamp sheets which also appeared in 2008 (October). The concept behind the circular label design was to provide an alternative label format more closer resembling a persons face than the rectangular label designs. The choice of stamp designs - Union Flag, Hello, Love - were (reportedly) the most popular in Royal Mail's range of Personalised stamps. The format was replicated for the Smilers For kids issue and Christmas issue issued in October/November 2008 and the 2nd issue Smilers for kids issue from April 2009. However they were dropped for the Christmas 2009 issue which may indicate that their appeal was rather short lived.

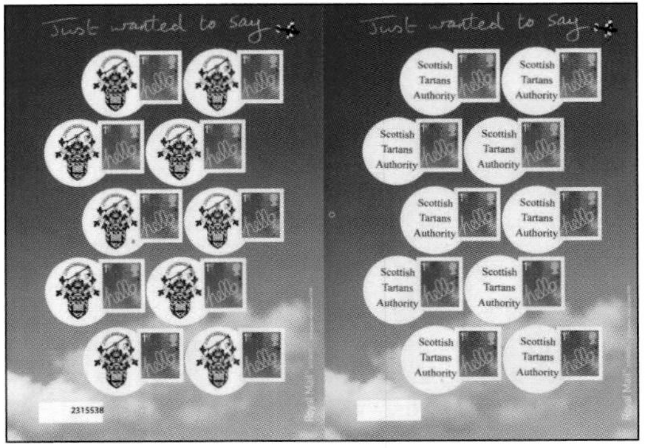

an example of a dual-label circular smilers sheet

Commemorative Stamp Sheets

Commemorative Stamp Sheets were introduced by Royal Mail in 2008 and are in all respects similar in format and design to Business Customised Stamp sheets but are produced directly by Royal Mail to commemorate or mark anniversaries of national importance which didn't quite make it into the annual stamp programme.

The retail price of these sheets is currently competitively priced with the Business Customised sheets at £13.50 each and although sold at a premium over face they could have been called *Smilers Presentation Packs* since they are accompanied by a printed card stiffener containing many more facts about the event being commemorated and the sheet and its informative stiffener are encapsulated in a protective clear sleeve.

When the first Commemorative Stamp Sheet appeared Royal Mail announced that the range of existing customised stamps would be used to produce these new format sheets. This policy seems to have lasted eighteen months until the arrival of the first 2012 Olympic stamp issue in October 2009, which was also accompanied by a special commemorative sheet pack featuring the new range of Olympic stamps.

2012 Olympics First Issue 2012 Olympics First Issue

Smilers For Kids Packs

Smilers For Kids are A5 sized Smilers sheets sold in sealed packs and aimed primarily at the younger generation (under 12's). The packs consist of a sheet of 10 stamps and corresponding round generic tabs, with other materials designed to appeal to youngsters, or perhaps their parents or grandparents!

When these packs first appeared in October 2008 they retailed at £7.95 each, some £4.35 over face value of the stamps. As a result the reaction from the philatelic trade was "predictable" to say the least. Bowing to pressure from the souvenir cover trade who had no need for the pack contents (various children's activities, letter writing material, paper, envelopes etc.,) or external packaging for that matter, Royal Mail hurriedly revised their plans and brought out generic smilers sheets comprising 20 stamps/generic-tabs in similar, but modified, designs to the Smilers For Kids A5 sheets. The Smilers for Kids Packs are designed to be displayed/sold on racks as a retail item much in the same way that some stamps were sold in the 90's in newsagents, WH Smith. It is believed that they were only available from the Philatelic Bureau at Tallants House, Edinburgh.

Smilers For Kids Pack

Smilers For Kids Generic Sheet

Generic Stamp Sheets

Generic Stamp Sheets are designed and produced by Royal mail and comprise small sheets of 10 or 20 stamps plus attached labels/tabs set within a border design commemorating or celebrating an event or theme and sold at a small premium above the face value of the actual stamps, generally via Royal Mail's Philatelic Bureau.

These sheets have collectively become known as or Smilers® sheets after the use of the Smiles/ Occasions stamps in the very first sheet issued in 2000.

Smilers® is a registered trade-mark of Royal Mail who protect their trademark with vigour. We wanted to call this catalogue the Smilers Catalogue (or Smilers Cat for short) but this was declined by Royal Mail. We think this is a shame as these sheets have become to the stamp collector what "Hover" is to the vacuum cleaner market, a brand name to describe a generic product.

Sheets which appear similar to Generic Stamp Sheets but with personalised photo-images on the label/tabs are known as personalised or customised stamp sheets. Since 2000, the public have been able to order customised stamp sheets by sending their own photographs or label designs to the Royal Mail Philatelic Bureau. The cost of these photo-image label/tab customised stamp sheets is higher than the standard Generic Smilers sheets and are covered in some detail in Chapter 3.

GS-001

The Stamp Show 2000

2000 (22 May), Photo by Questa, Perf 15 x 14,
Initial selling price: £2.95

GS-001 .... £ 25.00

GS-001a Overprinted *"5th Anniversary"*...... £ 50.00

Issue Notes: Britain's first generic-tab stamp sheet comprising 10 x 1st class *Smiles* stamps plus generic tabs. The sheet was issued to coincide with the London International Stamp Exhibition, 22-28 May 2000. As the first generic Smilers sheet it had novelty appeal, coupled with the Post Office promotion as an exhibition souvenir. However, the sheet format created storage/display problems owing to its size and is quite hard to find free of handling bends.

Known varieties: GS-001a is a privately produced overprint sold privately in 2005 to commemorate the 5th Anniversary of Smilers Sheets.

GS-001a

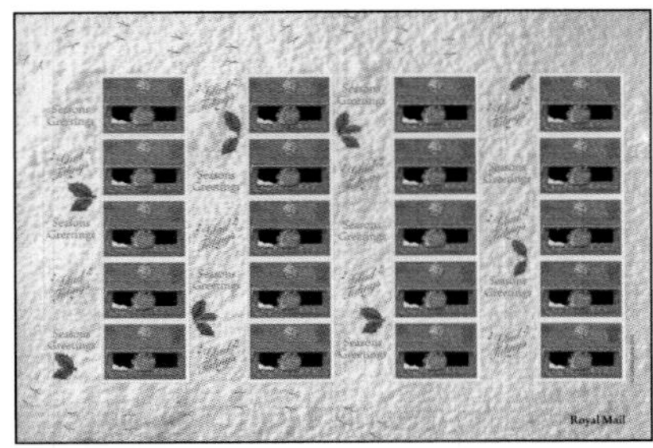

GS-002

GS-003

Christmas 2000

2000 (3 Oct), Photo by Questa, Perf 15 x 14,
Initial selling price: £3.99 (GS-002) £2.95 (GS-003)

GS-002 ....£ 125.00

GS-002a Printer's Trial (see notes) .... £ 3,500.00

GS-003 .... £ 125.00

GS-003a Phosphor bands inset left 2mm... £ 175.00

Issue Notes: 20 x 19p Robin-in-Letterbox stamps plus generic tabs set in a plain decorative border (GS -002) and 10 x 1st Santa and Cracker stamps plus generic tabs set in a decorative Christmas cracker border design (GS-003). The 19p design first appeared as part of the 1995 Christmas issue. The 1st design first appeared as a part of the 1997 Christmas issue, both were originally printed in gravure by Harrison. Withdrawn 2nd October 2001. Both designs were also available in customised label formats (see Chapter 3).

Known varieties: At least two whole sheets are thought to exist of the 19p value, completely blank apart from the Queen's head and value printed in red (silver was used on the issued sheets).

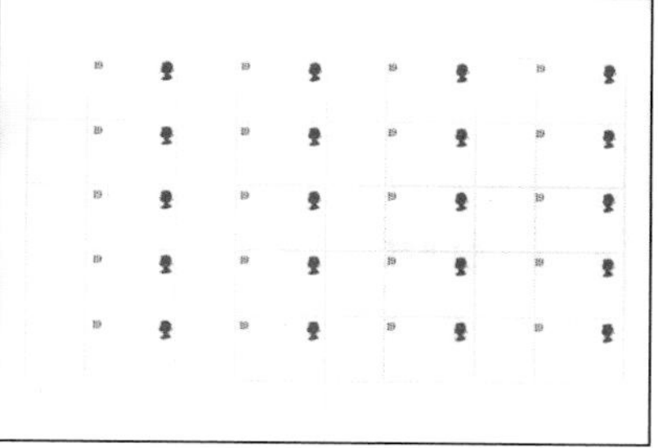

GS-002a

Another sheet was broken up to singles, pairs and blocks. These have been variously proposed to be proofs or test sheets for the personalised stamp printing process. Gibbons were retailing single 'stamps' for c. £250 in 2005. A whole sheet was purchased in 2008 for c. £3,500 from a dealer in Hampshire.

The 1st Class sheet (GS-003) is also known with inset phosphor bands to the left c. 2mm. These sheets will command a small premium over normal sheets.

GS-004

Occasions 2000

2000 (5 Jun), Litho by Questa, Perf 14½ x 14 , Initial selling price: £2.95

GS-004 .... £ 200.00

GS-004a Shade variety (see notes) .... £ 250.00

Issue Notes: Comprising 10 x 1st Hallmarks stamps, and generic tabs in a decorative border. The Generic sheet is actually a modification of the Customised Smilers sheets which were issued five weeks earlier. In the border, the Customised sheet banners have been replaced by 'Occasions', but the space at the bottom left for the customer code is still strangely present. The Queen's head, border and generic tabs are printed in silver on the Generic sheet (as in the regular issue, released 6th February 2000), whereas the head and border vary to dull grey in the Customised Smilers sheets. This was the first Generic sheet to bear the new 'Consignia' imprint following the Post Office re-branding exercise of 26th March 2001. Withdrawn from sale on 4th June 2002 (unconfirmed).

Known varieties: At least two distinct shades exist for this issue, probably from different printings. The shade difference is distinguishable by comparing the stamp background colour and the fineness of the lettering in the border areas. The original printing (GS-004) is quite pinkish in its overall appearance. By contrast the shade variety looks much darker and less pink.

Generic

Original and Shade variety

Differences also exist in the intensity of the border printing in silver. In the original printing the lettering is sharp and fine whereas on the darker shade variety it is thicker and less fine.

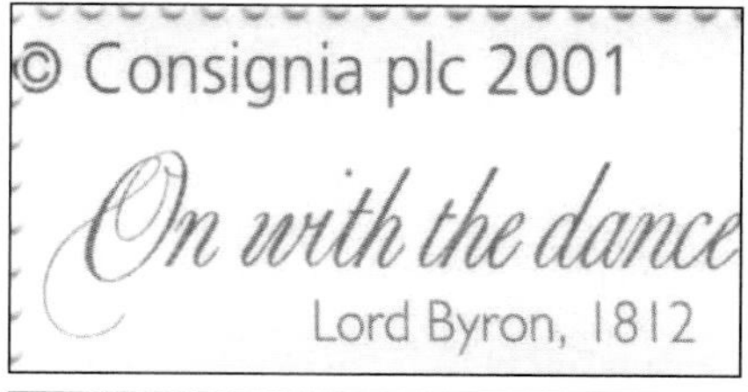

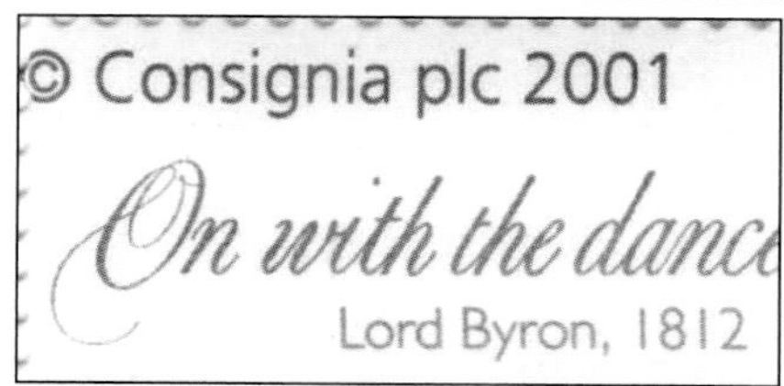

Difference in lettering colour in the border area

GS-005

Greetings - Smilers

2001 (3 Jul), Litho by Questa, Perf 14½ x 14 ,
Initial selling price: £2.95

GS-005 ....£ 150

Issue Notes: Comprising 10 x 1st class Smilers stamps and generic tabs with an appropriate text message. Although apparently similar to GS-001, with different generic tabs, this sheet differed in several respects. Printed by Questa in litho rather than by Harrison in photo, with a new perforation gauge, & bearing the 'Consignia' imprint. It was probably sufficiently similar in appearance to GS-001 to persuade many collectors to skip the issue, hence its relative scarcity. Some good shades exist. Withdrawn July 2002.

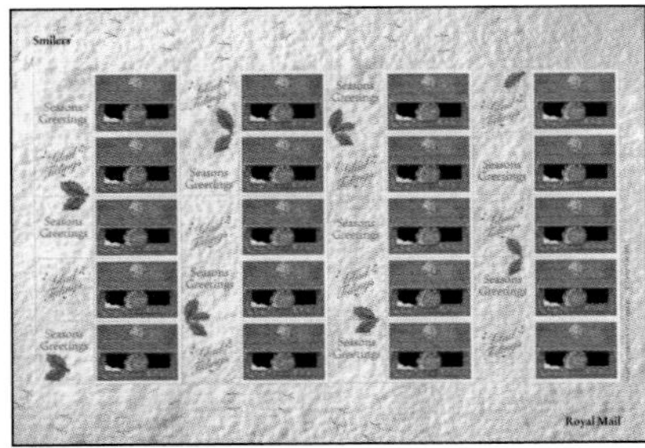

GS-006

GS-007

Christmas 2001

2001 (9 Oct), Photo by Questa, Perf 15 x 14,
Initial selling price: £3.99 (GS-006) £2.95 (GS-007)

GS-006 ....£ 450.00
GS-007 ....£ 450.00

Issue Notes: Comprising 20 x 19p Robin-in-Letterbox (GS-006) & 10 x 1st Santa and Cracker (GS-007). As with GS-005, Royal Mail showed little innovation with this issue, utilising essentially the same designs as for the previous year. The two sets can be told apart by differences in the sheet border inscriptions – the word *Smilers* has been added to the top left corner of both sheets, and the lower right inscription has been changed to *Consignia plc*. The 1st class stamps can be distinguished from the 2000 (GS-003) issue in that the phosphor bands are weaker, noticeably on the Queen's head. The scarcest of the Generic series: as with GS-005, it appears many collectors did not identify the differences with the 2000 set. An unblemished pair of sheets will set the buyer back about £900.

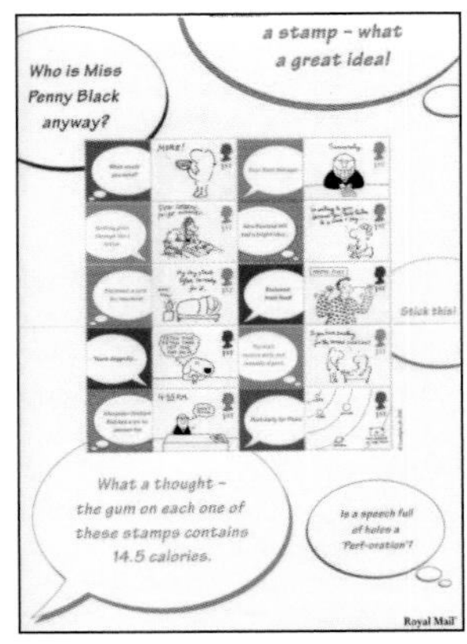

GS-008

Occasions (Cartoons)

2001 (18 Dec), Litho by Questa, Perf 14½ x 14 , Initial selling price: £2.95

GS-008 ....£ 35.00

Issue Notes: 10 x 1st class Cartoons (GS-008) It is understood that this sheet sold out early in 2002 and was reprinted but there would appear to be no difference between the two printings. Withdrawn 17th December 2002.

Known Varieties: None

GS-009

Occasions (2002)

2002 (23 Apr), Litho by Questa, Perf 14½ x 14 , Initial selling price: £5.95

GS-009 ....£ 45.00

GS-009a shade variety (see notes) .... £ 75.00

Issue Notes: Comprising 4 x 5 se-tenant x 1st Occasions stamps (different designs). The sheet sold out c. October/November 2002, It is believed to be the only Generic Smilers sheet to sell out prior to the official withdrawal date. The early sell-out prompted a resurgence of interest in the earlier sheets – one of which (GS-008) was still on sale – hence the relatively high numbers of GS-008 available.

Known Varieties: Two printings (at least) are thought to have been made of this sheet with the second printing distinguishable from the first in that the background has more of a pinkish hue than the original printings.

Occasions shade varieties

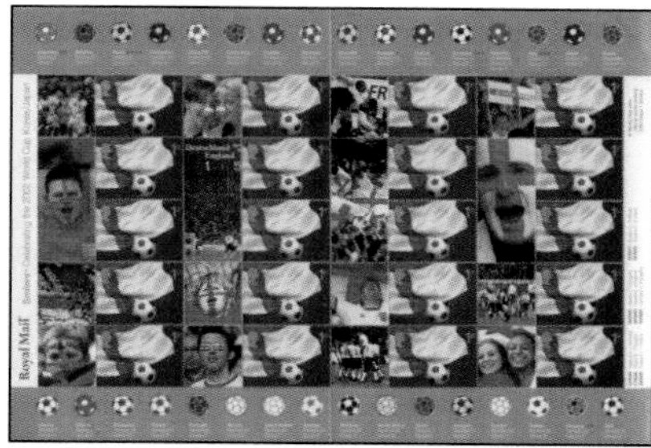

GS-010

World Cup 2002

2002 (21 May), Litho by Questa, Perf 14½ x 14 , Initial selling price: £5.95

GS-010 ....£ 20.00

Issue Notes: 20 x 1st class (GS-010). This sheet featured an unusual perforation format, containing four double-sized vertical generic tabs and twelve normal-sized ones. Sheet withdrawn 20th May 2003.

Known Varieties: The sheet is known with a 4 mm phosphor band shift upwards causing the printed bands to extend into the top border design and this is clearly visible with the naked eye.

The error sheet was sold by Ian Lasok-Smith in late 2007 on eBay, This variety may be a one-off (unlikely) or more widely-spread.

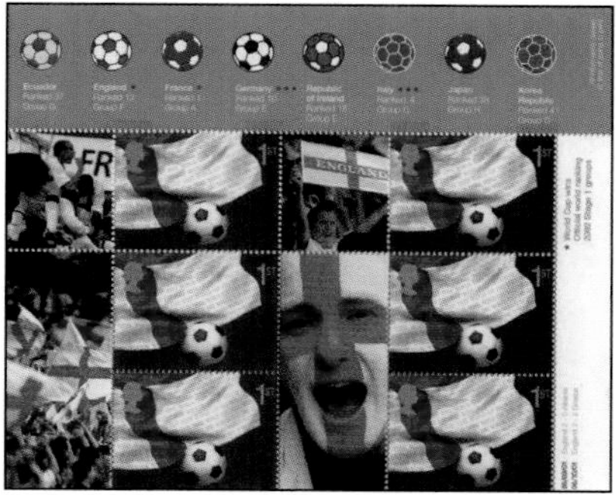

Phosphor Bands shifted up by 4mm

Generic

GS-011

Knock! Knock!

2002 (1 October), Litho by Questa, Perf 14½ x 14 , Initial selling price: £5.95

GS-011 .... £ 20.00

Issue Notes: 20 x 1st class (GS-011). The sheet still bears the 'Consignia' imprint – either an oversight, or they were printed prior to June 2002.

GS-012

Christmas 2002

2002 (1 October), Litho by Questa, Perf 14½ x 14 , Initial selling price: £5.95

GS-012 .... £ 20.00

GS-012a Off-set Gold Head on reverse ...... £ 75.00

Issue Notes: 20 x 1st class (GS-012). The sheet features the Father Christmas design used in the Christmas Smilers of 2001 and 2002, but this time printed in sheets of twenty by litho rather than gravure. The phosphor bands are wider than those on stamps from 2001 and 2002, the perforation gauge is also different and the Queen's head is a darker shade of gold. As with GS-011 (issued on the same date), it has the 'Consignia plc' imprint. Sheet withdrawn 30th September 2003.

Known Varieties: The sheet exists with a weak off-set of the gold head on the reverse in the right-hand row: Several were bought while on general release from the Strand PO and have since been seen on eBay (it sold for £50). Sheet withdrawn 30th September 2003.

GS-013

Flowers

2003 (21 January), Litho by Questa, Perf 14½ x 14 , Initial selling price: £5.95

GS-013 ....£ 20.00

GS-013a Constant Speck Flaw .... £ 30.00

GS-013b "CE" Speck Flaw .... £ 30.00

GS-013c Phosphor Shift 2 mm Left .... £ 75.00

GS-013d Phosphor Shift 16 mm Left .... £ 1000.00

Issue Notes: 20 x 1st class (GS-013). This design was first introduced in a 'Greetings' booklet released in 1997. Perhaps one of the most attractive sheets released to date, and one of the few issues outside Christmas which appear to have been commercially used in quantity. Sheet withdrawn 20th January 2004. This is the first generic sheet to bear the imprint **Royal Mail Group plc .**

Known Varieties: This sheet exists in an least two different shades, which may be due to a second printing of the sheet. The majority of sheets show the floral background in soft tones, whilst the second is more distinct and less-soft.

This sheet has also been seen with what look like constant inking flaws. We have seen a number of these sheets with at least two constant inking flaw. The first appears as a circular "speck" flaw in the lower gold frame above "classified". Thought to have appeared in some later sheets only and could be an inking flaw or a 2nd printing flaw. All sheets from the Croydon area had this flaw. (Ex-Croydon Stamp shop). A similar flaw appears on the 2nd printing sheets in the form of a "CE" flaw in top gold frame below FLOWERS.

The Generic sheet is also known with various misplaced phosphor bands, perhaps the most striking is one with phosphor bands misplaced 16 mm to the left, each stamp has a single centre band and the adjoining generic tabs have a slightly off-centre band. A whole sheet with this error sold privately for £850 in September 2006 (ex: Mike Holt).

This was from the initial print run as these phosphor shifts have been seen on First Day covers.

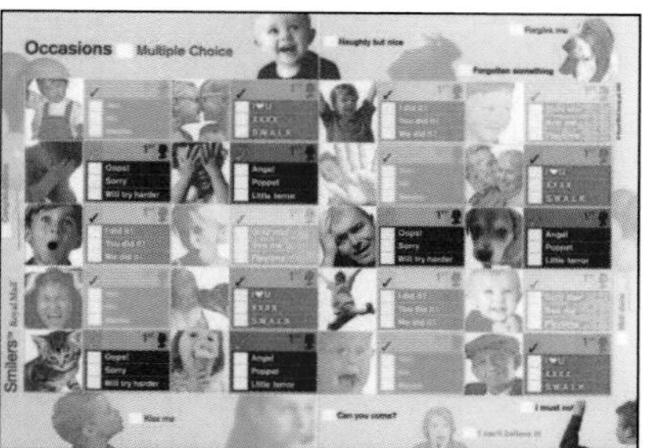

GS-014

GS-014a

Occasions (2003)

2003 (4 Feb), Litho by Questa, Perf 14½ x 14 , Initial selling price: £5.95

GS-014 ....£ 20.00

GS-014a .... £ 2500.00

GS-014b Phosphor on gummed side .... £ 750.00

Issue Notes: 20 x 1st class (GS-014). The individual stamps differ slightly in shade to the regular issue which is a reddish purple as opposed to purple).

Sheet withdrawn 3rd February 2004.

Known Varieties: An interesting variety has emerged: Royal Mail pre-release images differed from the version actually issued, the wording 'Multiple Choice' at the upper left border is shown in pale green rather than red as-issued. Four copies of the variant (GS-014a) surfaced amongst normal stock whilst on general sale. The first (no.1), found in Northants, was apparently included in a bulk order of normal sheets from Edinburgh. The second (no. 2) was bought on the day of issue from the main Post Office in Northampton and sold on by Mark Sargent, the third and fourth were bought from the same Post Office in Northampton area (no. 3 and no. 4), one of which sold on eBay in March 2004.

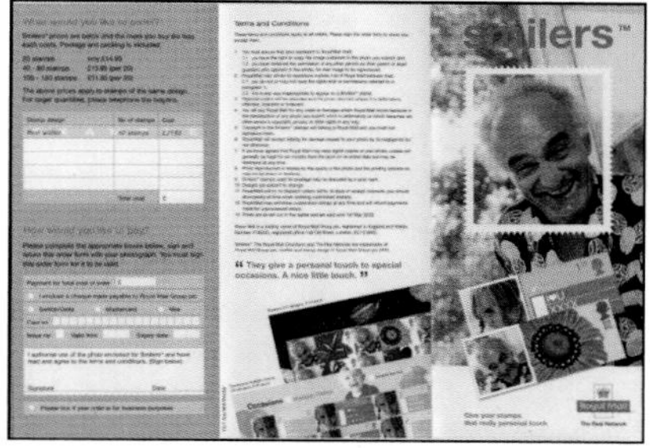

Royal Mail Publicity Showing Green Lettering

Apart from the inscription, the shade of green is completely different to that in GS-014 and SG 2340 (lime instead of emerald).

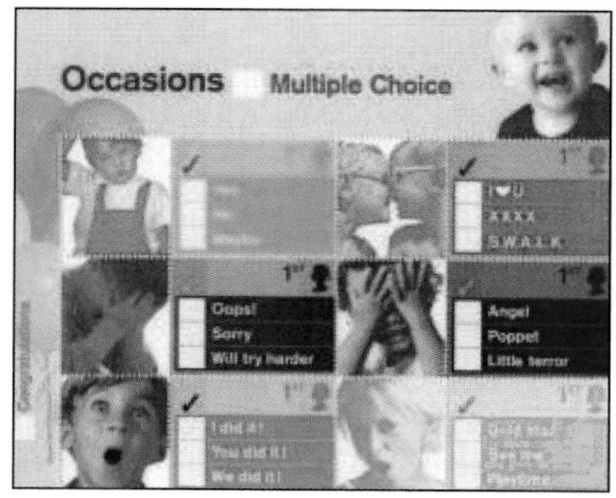

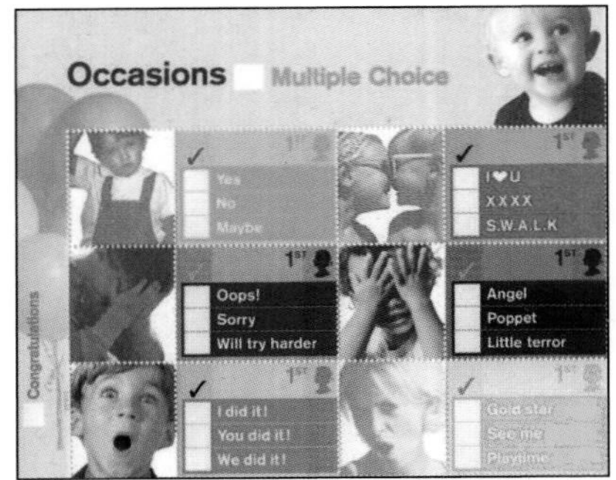

Shade varieties between GS-014 and GS-014a

Tom Pierron, in his 'GB Errors' catalogue, suggests that they are trials which should not have been released. A contributor to this work, had an opportunity to compare sheet no.1 with sheet no. 3 and reports that they show minor differences in the intensity of the other colours between the two. The conclusion reached was that they came from a substantial printing run.

The purchaser of the two sheets from the Northampton area spoke to the printers who denied their existence but did confirm that they were printed in sheets of four and then cut. It is likely that at least one of the printers sheets of four were distributed with the released sheets, probably in error.

One theory is that originally the wording Multiple Choices was printed in green but Royal Mail rejected a proof printing (GS-14a) as not meeting colour matching specifications with the green shade from ordinary sheets of the same set. If a reprint was ordered, Royal Mail may well have decided to change the 'multiple choice' wording to red, providing a more striking colour contrast between the title and the sheet border. We may never know the true story!

In December 2008 one of the four known sheets came up for auction at Warwick and Warwick and was purchased by one lucky collector for under £2,000. Another of the four known sheets changed hands in early 2009 for c. £3,000. The estimate is based on a well publicised auction realisation .

A nice phosphor variety is known on this issue. In July 2007 a complete sheet was sold at auction (Harmers) with phosphor bands printed on the gummed side in error. One eagle-eyed collector noted that Harmer's had included a lot in the July auction described as a *2003 Occasions (Multiple Choice) Post Office Label Sheet with Phosphor applied on the rear.*

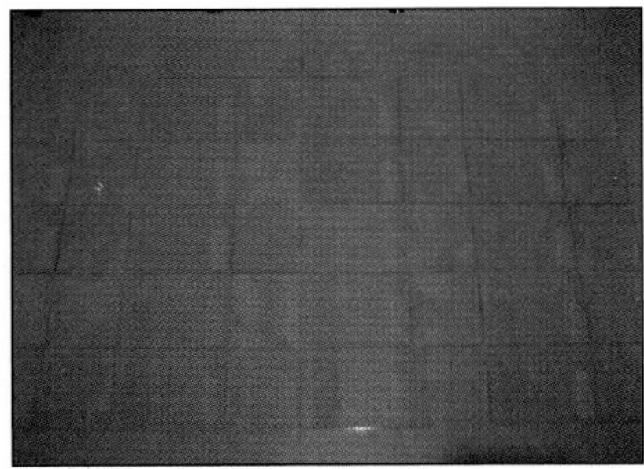

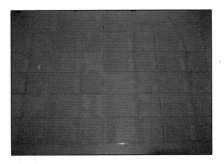

What it did not say is that the phosphor coating had been omitted from the front. Assuming this sheet was discovered in legitimate Royal Mail stock, and we have no reason to doubt this, at least three other sheets must also exist as Smilers sheets are printed in larger printers panes of four and then guillotined into four sheets.

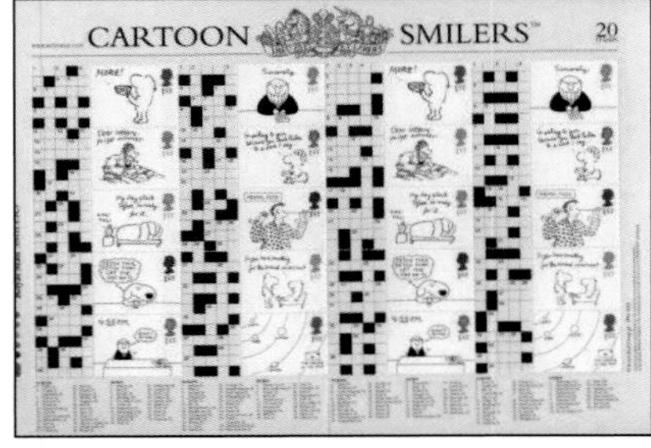

GS-015

Crosswords

2003 (29 Jul), Litho by Questa, Perf 14½ x 14 ,
Initial selling price: £6.15

GS-015 ....£ 20.00

GS-015a Missing Phosphor £1,000.00

Issue Notes: 20 x 1st class Cartoon Smilers (GS-015). For some reason the period of sale of this sheet was extended by one month over the usual twelve month period. The mauve and purple colours of the Queen's head were markedly deeper in sheets on sale towards the end of the release period . Sheet withdrawn 28th August 2004.

Known Varieties: Six copies of this sheet were discovered in 2005 with phosphor omitted. At least one sheet was split into two halves. Whole and half sheets were sold by Mike Holt (whole sheets £600 half sheets £325).

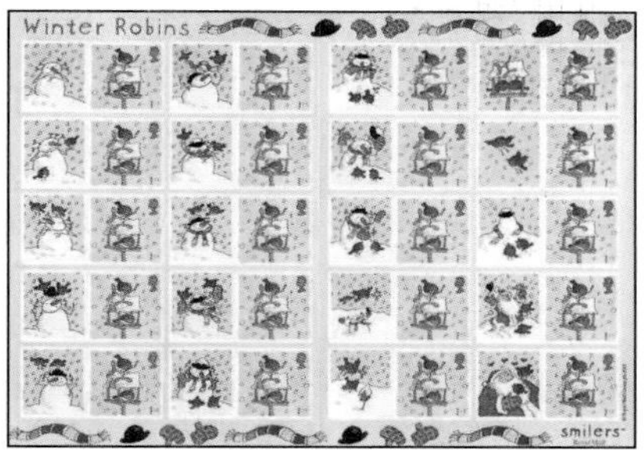

GS-016

Winter Robins

2003 (30 Sep), Litho by De La Rue, Perf 14½ Die Cut
Initial selling price: £6.15

GS-016 .... £ 20.00

GS-016a Misplaced Die-Cut Perfs. £2,000.00

GS-016b 2nd Printing (see notes) .... £ 50.00

Issue Notes: 20 x 1st class (GS-016). This sheet has the distinction of being the first to be printed on self-adhesive paper with die-cut simulated perforations, and in a new format. Although officially printed by De La Rue, this followed the take-over by De La Rue of the House of Questa earlier in the year.

The sheet went on sale alongside the traditional Christmas stamps and associated Smilers sheets and offered an alternative look to celebrating Christmas. The sheet was withdrawn 29th September 2004.

Known Varieties: At least one sheet exists misperforated (by 8mm, the phosphor band is offset by the same distance) and mis-cut such that the left margin is very short. Brandon Galleries were offering the variety at £1500 in late 2005 and the sheet was eventually sold at STAMPEX (September 2006) for £1200.

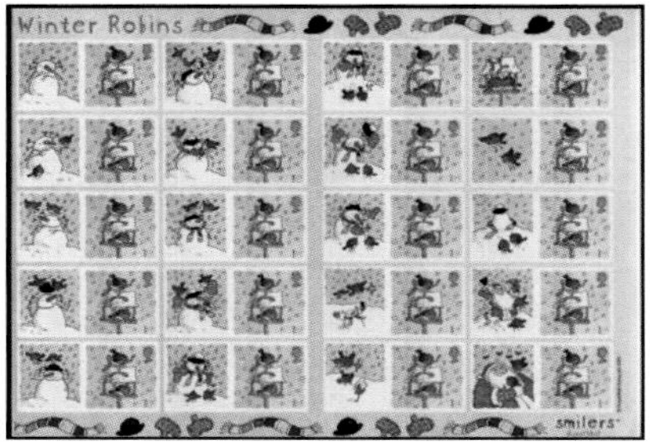

GS-016a

There are also clearly two printings of this sheet as the later printing shows the Queens head an orange-red rather than the deeper red of the first printing.

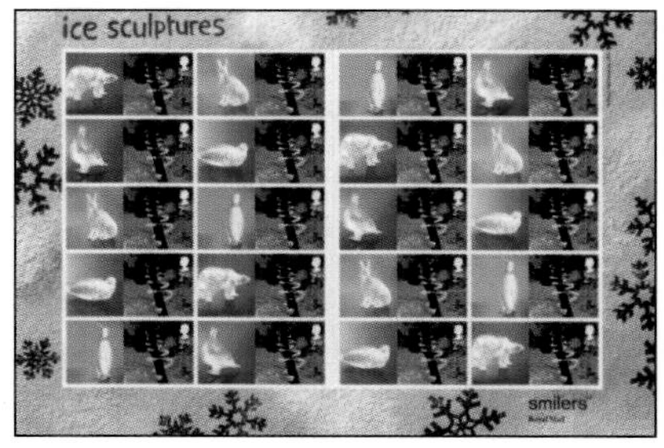

GS-017

GS-018

Ice Sculptures - Christmas 2003 Issue

2003 (30 Sep), Litho by De La Rue, Simulated Die-Cut Perforations 14½ x 14.
Initial selling price: £4.20 (GS-017) £6.15 (GS-007)
GS-017 .... £ 15.00
GS-018 .... £ 17.50
GS-018a Phosphor shift to right by 10mm ... £ 500.00

Issue Notes: Generic Sheets of 20 x 2nd class (GS-017) and 20 x 1st Class (GS-018) utilising the Ice Sculptures designs from the Christmas 2003 stamp set but printed in Litho not Gravure. Sheets withdrawn 3rd November 2004.

Known Varieties: There is reported to be a wide spectrum of shades on the second class sheet (GS-017) from violet-blue to Prussian blue, more obvious on the customised versions of this sheet.

The 1st class sheet (GS-018) is also known to have a double phosphor printing with the second application shifted to right by 10mm causing 3 of the 4 vertical rows of generic tabs to be printed with phosphor bands. A sheet with this variety was sold by B. Alan for £200 in 2006. We have not seen others sold since .

GS-019

Hong Kong Stamp Expo

2004 (30 Jan), Litho by Walsall, Perf 14½ x 14.
Initial selling price: £6.15
GS-019 .... £ 12.50

Issue Notes: 20 x 1st class HELLO stamps (GS-019), similar in layout and design to the Smilers Customised sheet CS-008a (ex-Occasions 2002 series). Apparently this sheet was only available by mail-order from Tallents House and was not distributed to Philatelic counters at Post Offices. The sheet was withdrawn 29th January 2005.

This sheet was issued as part of Royal Mail's participation at the *Hong Kong Stamp E*xpo and features the banner "Hello from the Royal Mail". It seems to have been hastily conceived as it was released with little advance notice, perhaps adopting the previously available customised HELLO sheet design from 2002 for that reason, to which it is strikingly similar apart from the ribbon colour which was changed from red to green. This sheet design has been used for similar philatelic exhibition sheets (see also GS-026 and GS-032)

As the sheet was primarily intended to publicise the Royal Mail's participation at the Hong Kong International Stamp Expo, no Customised version was available for this issue. It is perhaps interesting to note that despite Royal Mail's Smilers product line, they did not provide an 'instant Smilers' service at the show in Hong Kong.

Known Varieties: None

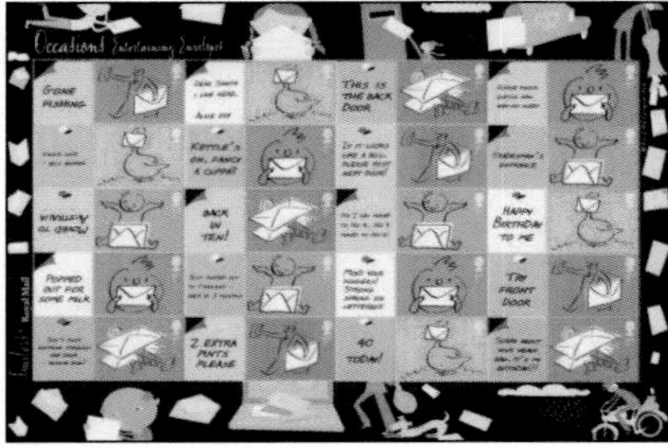

GS-020

Entertaining Envelops (Occasions)

2004 (3 Feb), Litho by Walsall, Perf 14½ x 14.
Initial selling price: £6.15
GS-020 .... £ 12.50

Issue Notes: 20 x 1st class Entertaining Envelopes issue (GS-020). Sheet withdrawn twelve months later.

Known Varieties: None

GS-021

Royal Horticultural Society Bicentenary

2004 (25 May), Litho by Walsall, Perf 14½ x 14.
Initial selling price: £6.15
GS-021 .... £ 12.50

Issue Notes: 20 x 1st class (GS-021). withdrawn 24th May 2005.

A Customised sheet (CS-019) was also available from the same date as GS-021 and withdrawn one year later. There is no discernable difference between CS-019 and GS-021 apart from the inclusion of a white oblong code box in the bottom left hand corner.

Known Varieties: None

GS-022

Rule Britannia

2004 (27 Jul), Litho by Walsall, Perf 14½
Initial selling price: £6.15
GS-022 .... £ 12.50

Issue Notes: 20 x 1st class Union Flag stamps (GS-022). This sheet was a re-issue of the Union Flag stamp first issued in 2001 as part of a flags mini-sheet. The border artwork for this sheet depicts a Union Flag with what look like on first inspection prominent scratches all round, however these are believed to denote stitching although it is not clearly shown.. Sheet withdrawn 26th July 2005

Known Varieties. None

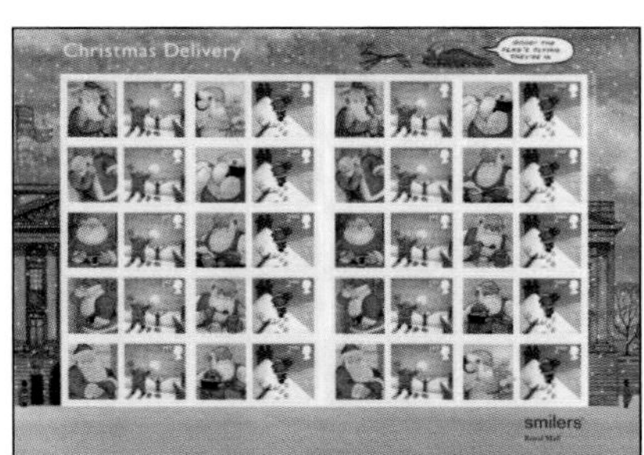

GS-023

Christmas Delivery - Christmas 2004

2004 (2 Nov), Litho by De La Rue, printed on self adhesive paper with simulated die-cut perfs 14½ x 14, Initial selling price: £5.40

GS-023 .... £ 12.50

Issue Notes: 10 x 1st class and 10 x 2nd Class stamps combined in one sheet (GS-023). This was the first sheet to contain two different value stamps. This sheet also contains an unusual error. The illustrated generic tabs se-tenant to the 2nd class stamps at the right of the sheet are out of sequence – the top label has been transposed to the bottom of the strip. One can only assume that if Royal Mail spotted the mistake prior to issue, it decided it did not merit a reprint.

Interestingly, the sheet design featured in Royal Mail preview Number 137 (November 2005) depicts a pre-issue illustration with a slate grey border and not blue, as issued. Perhaps a late change by Royal Mail means that proof copies with a greyish background may exist.

Known Varieties: None

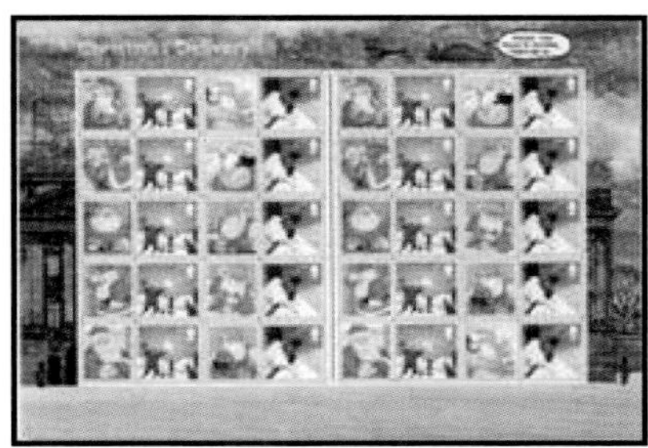

Pre-Issue Illustration ex RM Preview No. 137

GS-024

Farm Animals

2005 (11 Jan), Litho by Walsall, printed on self adhesive paper with simulated die-cut perfs 14½.
Initial selling price: £6.15

GS-024 .... £ 12.50

Issue Notes: 20 x 1st class farm animal stamps (GS-024). This issue was criticised at the time, but works well in this sheet format set against a farm-yard scene. The sheet was withdrawn 10th Jan 2006.

Known Varieties: None

Generic

GS-025

Magic Circle Centenary

2005 (15 Mar), Litho by Walsall, perfs 14½.
Initial selling price: £6.15

GS-025 .... £ 12.50

Issue Notes: 20 x 1st class stamps (GS-025). Sheet withdrawn 14th March 2006.

Known Varieties: None

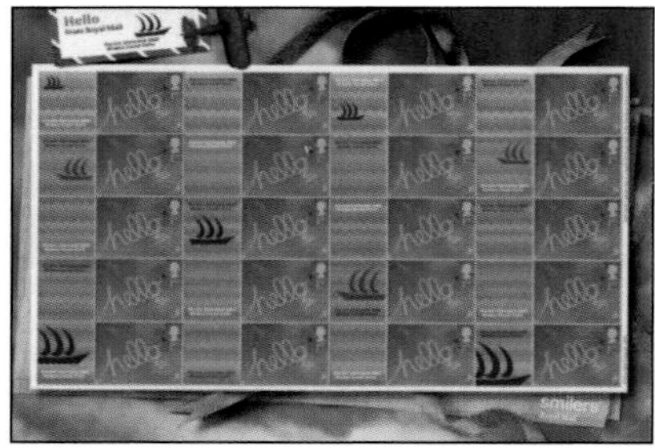

GS-026

Pacific Explorer Expo

2005 (21 Apr), Litho by Cartor, perfs 14½. x 14
Initial selling price: £6.55

GS-026 .... £ 12.50

GS-026a Weak phosphor wash............... £ 50.00

Issue Notes: 20 x 1st class HELLO stamps (GS-026). Apparently only available by mail-order from Tallents House. Sheet withdrawn 20th April 2006.

As with the earlier Hong Kong Stamp Expo sheet (GS -019) the sheet was issued to support Royal Mail's participation at the International Stamp Expo held at Sydney, Australia. This issue confirmed a trend adopted by Royal Mail to utilise previously used designs in connection with its participation at international philatelic exhibitions.

No Customised version of this sheet was available for this issue. Royal Mail did not provide an 'instant Smilers' service at the show in Sydney. However, the 'Instant Smilers' stand at all Stampex events in 2005 and 2006 displayed a Customised A2 mock-up of this sheet, despite the sheet never having been available from the Royal Mail.

Known Varieties. The sheet exists with a weak phosphor wash ("wibbly wobbly" bands) covering some stamps on the right and bottom of the sheet – B. Alan sold the variety for c. £25/sheet in 2005.

Weak phosphor spill to right of sheet

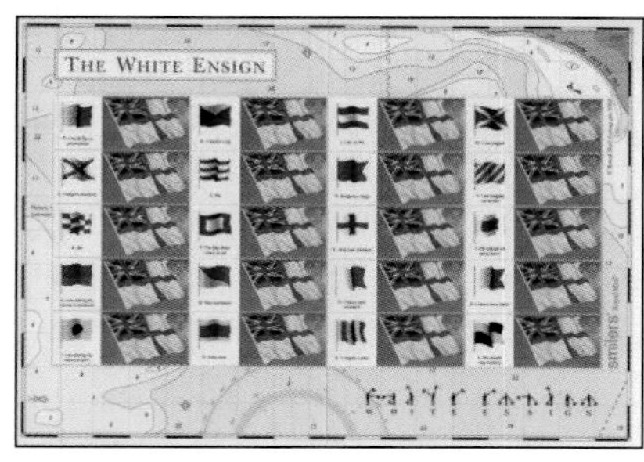

GS-027

The White Ensign

2005 (21 Jun), Litho by Cartor, perfs 14½. X 14
Initial selling price: £6.15

GS-027 .... £ 12.50

GS-027a All-over phosphor wash .... £ 150.00

GS-027b Extended Phosphor Bands ...... £ 250.00

GS-027c 2nd Printing .... £ 25.00

Issue Notes: 20 x 1st class "White Ensign" stamps (GS-027). Sheet withdrawn 20th June 2006.

Known Varieties. Over twenty sheets were discovered on the day of issue with a strong all-over phosphor wash covering the three left-hand columns of stamps and generic tabs. The right hand column was partially affected, the phosphor bands on the stamps still being visible. B. Alan Ltd. retailed the variety for £125 per sheet, and FDC's (single stamp + label) have appeared on eBay for about £20. Lesser extremes exist, with the wash affecting the left-hand first two columns. Reports of this stamp existing non-phosphor are in error, referring to the same variety. The sheet went "off-sale" on 20th June 2006.

In December 2008 eight sheets were discovered in a large private collection of Smilers sheets for sale by auction (Warwick and Warwick) with extended phosphor bands in the bottom border (GC-027b). The first three rows of stamps were affected.

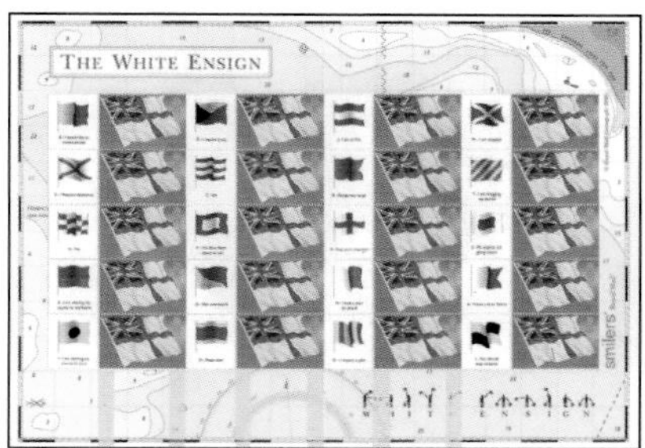

GC-027b - Extended Phosphor Bands

At least two printings of the generic sheet exist and these are relatively easy to identify. The difference in the printings can be easily identified by comparing the green colours in the top right hand corner.

The re-print (GS-027c) is a brighter more yellow green than the original printing, There are also notably differences in the reds on the flags.

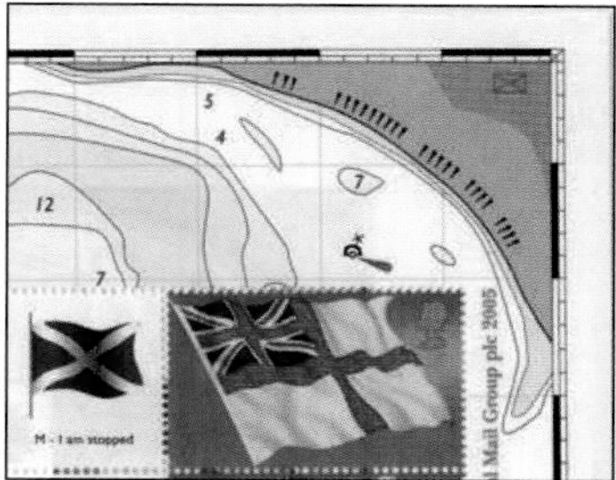

Original Printing—Dull Green

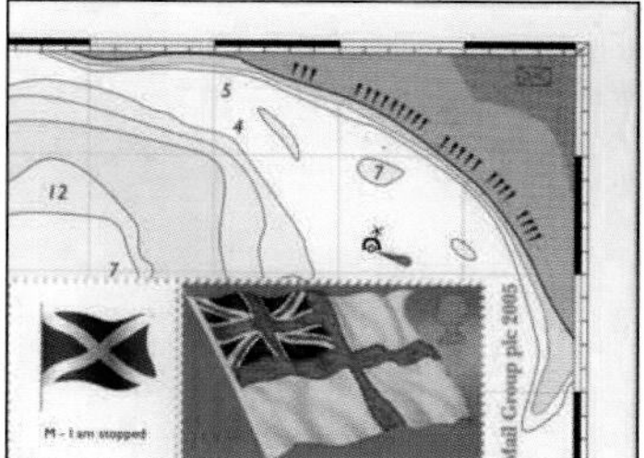

Re-Print - Yellow -Green

GS-028

GS-028a

Generic

50th Anniversary of ITV

2005 (15 Sep), Litho by (see notes), perfs 14½. X 14
Initial selling price: £6.15

GS-028 .... £ 12.50

GS-028a Cartor Printing (See Notes)..... £ 1000.00

Issue Notes: 20 x 1st class EMERDALE stamps (GS-028). depicting a 50's style station identification screen and TV Times programming. The issue was spiced up by a late error/design change (GS-028a). In total there are three different printings of the generic sheet. The first, by Cartor, was withdrawn prior to issue and has characteristically darker pinks and greys than the Walsall issued printing. In 2006 the sheet was re-printed again by Cartor. We are not aware of any visible differences between the two official "issued" printings. Withdrawn 14th September 2006.

Known Varieties. The Royal Mail printing contract for these sheets was placed with Cartor. The sheets were printed and distributed to Key Account customers and Post Office outlets when several textual errors were discovered in the generic tabs, se-tenant to the stamps.

The errors, described in the philatelic press, concerned the 3rd label in the 1st column (which had an incorrect date '22 September 1965' instead of '22 September 1955') and the 2nd label in the 4th column (which had an additional '10.00 ITV News at Ten' sandwiched between the '10.30 ITV News' and the '11.15 Film – Octopussy continued' headings). Stocks were recalled prior to release, and a new printing ordered from Walsall. In addition to the errors described by the Philatelic press there are differences in two other generic tabs – the 5th label in column 3 and the 3rd label in column 4 have 'am' after some of the early morning schedule times. These illustrations will help identify this error sheet.

GS-028 - 3rd label in the 1st column

GS-028 a - 3rd label in the 1st column

GS-028 - 5th label in the 3rd column

GS-028a - 5th label in the 3rd column

GS-028 - 2nd label in the 4th column

GS-028a - 2nd label in the 4th column

GS-028 - 3rd label in 4th column

GS-028a - 3rd label in 4th column

Finally, the following illustration is taken from Royal Mail *Preview* which shows additional differences to the Cartor and Walsall sheets.

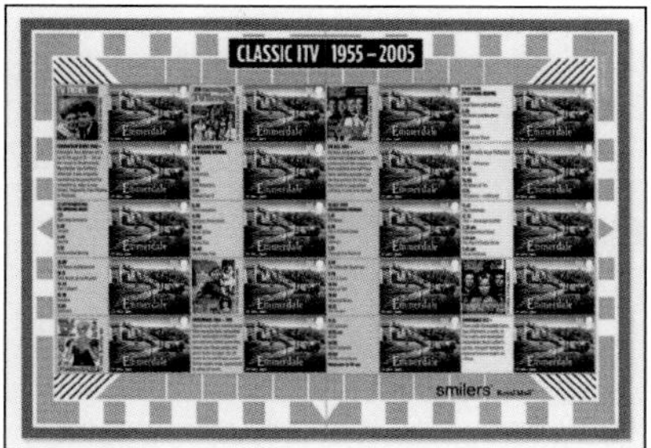

The 5th label in column 4 has the final word printed on a different line!

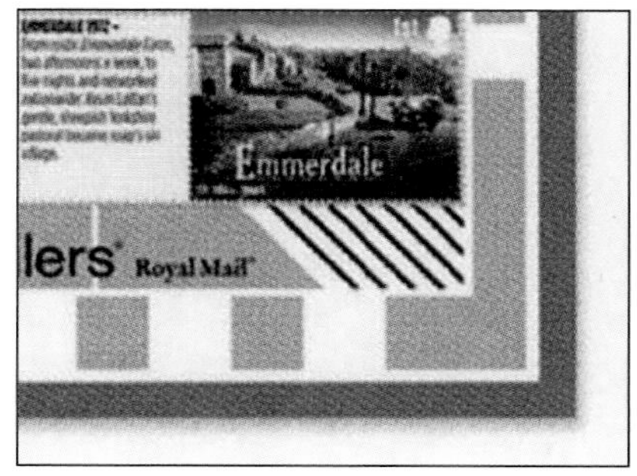

Detail - Royal Mail Preview

Either this is an artist mock-up of the sheet or there was an original Cartor printing which differs from the recalled version. As a result, the Generic sheet had at least one (and possibly two) withheld printings prior to the issued version.

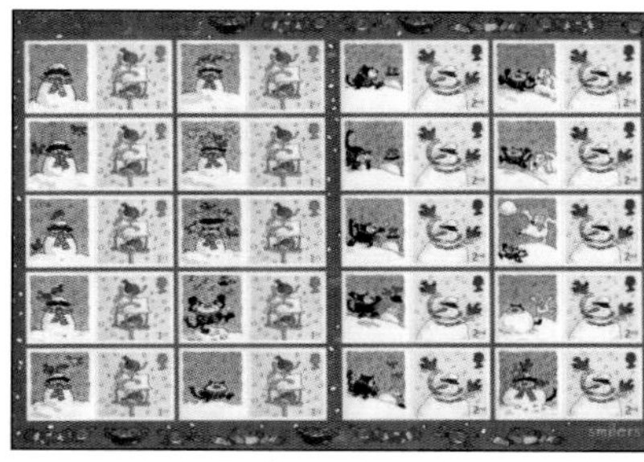

GS-029

Christmas Robins - Christmas 2005

2005 (1 Nov), Litho by Cartor , printed on self adhesive paper with simulated die-cut perfs 14½ x 14, Initial selling price: £5.60

GS-029 .... £ 12.50

Issue Notes: 10 x 1st class and 10 x 2nd Class stamps combined in one sheet (GS-029). Sheet withdrawn 31st October 2006.

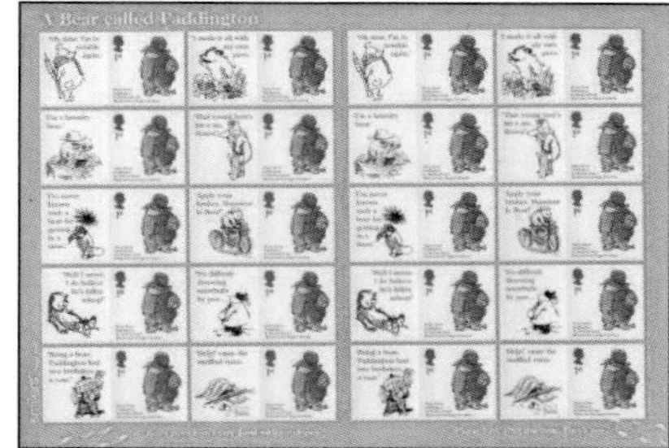

GS-030

A Bear Called Paddington

2006 (10 Jan), Litho by Cartor , printed on self adhesive paper with simulated die-cut perfs 14½,

Initial selling price: £6.55

GS-030 .... £ 12.50

Issue Notes: 20 x 1st class Paddington Bear stamps (GS-030) The sheets have a micro-graphed date '2006' in the value tablet of each stamp.). Sheet withdrawn in January 2007.

GS-031

Fun Fruit and Veg

2006 (7 Mar), Litho by Cartor , printed on self adhesive paper with simulated die-cut perfs 14½. Initial selling price: 6.55

GS-031 .... £ 12.50

Issue Notes: 20 x 1st class Paddington Bear stamps (GS-030). The sheets have a micro-graphed date '2006' in the value tablet of each stamp. The Fun Fruit and Veg designs protruded (without perforations) from the top and bottom of the stamp design. Around the border of the generic sheet were additional stickers that could be used to further customise the stamps/generic tabs e.g. Mr Potato Head. The Sheet was withdrawn on 6th March 2007.

Known Varieties: None

GS-032

Washington Stamp Expo

2006 (25 May), Litho by Cartor , perfs 14½ x 14 . Initial selling price: £6.55

GS-032 .... £ 12.50

Issue Notes: 20 x 1st class HELLO stamps (GS-032). The sheet was issued to mark Royal Mail's participation at the World Philatelic Exhibition held in Washington DC, USA between the 27 May and 3 June 2006. The design is similar to GS-019 and GS-026 except that the ribbons have been omitted and the plane redrawn and resized. No Customised version of this sheet was made available. The sheet was withdrawn from sale on 24th May 2007.

Known Varieties: None

GS-033

England's Finest Hour

2006 (6 Jun), Litho by Cartor , perfs 14½. Initial selling price: £6.95

GS-033 .... £ 15.00

Issue Notes: 20 x 1st class England Winners stamps (GS-033) set in an attractive if not simple sheet design with the 20 generic tabs providing a photographic and chronological record of England's last major football sporting triumph – 40 years ago in 1966. Somewhat strangely released to coincide with the World Cup championships held in Germany rather than the actual 40th Anniversary of that football victory on 31st July 2006. No Customised sheet was made available for this issue. The sheet was withdrawn from sale on 5th Jun 2007.

It is thought that the original design concept was for this sheet to be issued to coincide with the opening of the new Wembley Stadium (see also GS-041).

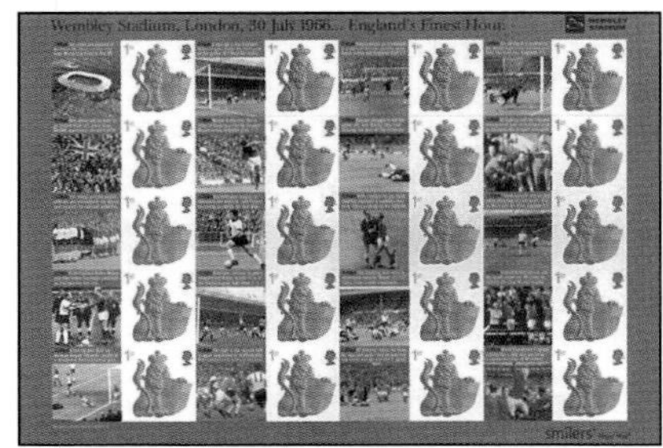

Un-issued Wembley Stadium Generic Sheet

Owning to on-going construction delays the sheet design was modified and the original stamp replaced with the World Cup 1st class value, presumably to coincide with the World Cup event.

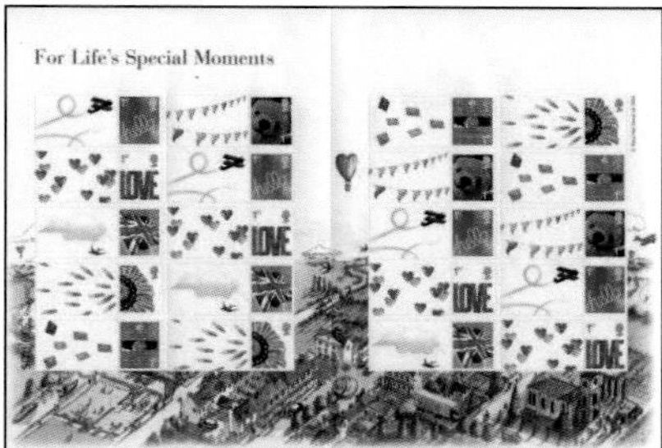

GS-034

Life's Special Moments

2006 (4 July), Litho by Cartor , printed on self adhesive paper with simulated die-cut perfs 15 x 14½
Initial selling price: £6.95

GS-034 .... £ 12.50

Issue Notes: 20 x 1st class definitive sized (DS) Smilers stamps (GS-034). set in an attractive *village-life* border design. Issued rather ironically on the US independence day, 4th July 2006. The DS smilers stamps originally appeared in self-adhesive booklet form, printed by Walsall and issued on 4 Oct 2005.

They are in effect adaption's of various larger sized Smiler stamp designs that have appeared in earlier sheet designs (see GS-002, GS-009 and GS-011) with the LOVE stamp being closest to a new design, although even this has similarities to the LOVE stamp ex GS-009.

This sheet contained between 3 and 4 of each of six adapted designs using the smaller definitive-sized Smilers format and may thus may be considered as the 2005 Occasions set.

These stamps differ from the booklet versions printed by Walsall in gravure in that they were printed in litho by Cartor but appear identical to those issued in Customised Smilers sheets issued in October 2005 (See Chapter X, CS-026a—CS-026f) The original Customised Smilers issue had attracted a good deal of bad press as collectors were being asked to spend nearly £80 to obtain a set of 6 x 1st class stamps with the new printing variety. Needless to say this sheet went someway to meet the demands of Royal Mail's critics.

Known Varieties: None

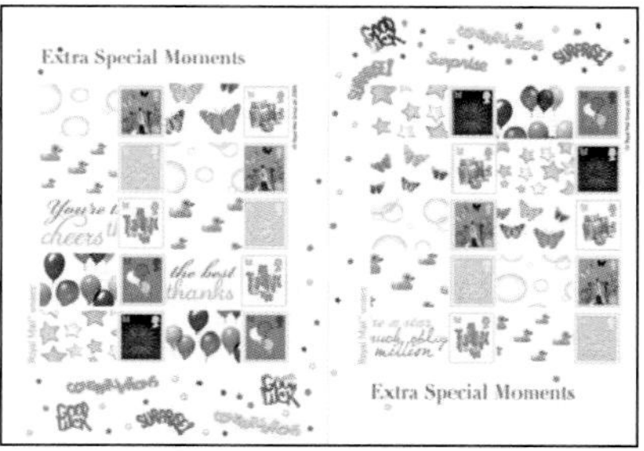

GS-035

Extra Special Moments

2006 (17 Oct), Litho by Cartor , printed on self adhesive paper with simulated die-cut perfs 15 x 14½
Initial selling price: £6.95

GS-035 .... £ 12.50

Issue Notes: 20 x 1st class definitive sized Smilers stamps (GS-035) with the stamps set in an explosion of mixed messages incorporated within the border design and showing more than a passing resemblance to GS-034. This sheet contains between 3 and 4 of each of 6 definitive size Smilers stamps previously released in self-adhesive booklet format.

Royal Mail appear to have intentionally "filled-in" most of the previously non-printed areas, presumably in an effort to thwart the over-printer's efforts in adding to the sheet design border detail.

Known Varieties: None

GS-036

Christmas Issue 2006

2006 (7 Nov), Litho by Cartor , printed on self adhesive paper with simulated die-cut perfs 15 x 14½
Initial selling price: £6.00

GS-036 .... £ 12.50

Generic

Issue Notes: 10 x 2nd class and 10 x 1st class definitive sized (DS) Christmas Smilers stamps (GS-036) featuring a Snowman (2nd) and a seated father Christmas (1st). The sheets were withdrawn from sale in January 2007 but reappeared again in the run -up to Christmas 2007 and were made available alongside the 2007 Christmas Smilers sheet which had a religious theme.

Known Varieties: None

GS-037

We Will Remember Them

2006 (9 Nov), Litho by Cartor , perfs 14½.
Initial selling price: £6.95

GS-037 .... £ 12.50

Issue Notes: 20 x 1st class Lest We Forget (2007) poppy stamps (GS-037) which also appeared in a mini-sheet issued on the same day. Royal Mail announced that this sheet would be the first of three sheets to be issued in successive years to honour the dead of the 1st World War. Royal Mail omitted their branding of *Smilers* from this sheet and in so doing clarified the term for future use by Royal Mail. This would only be used in connection with sheets that were also available in customised formats.

Known Varieties: None

GS-038

Belgica 2006 Stamp Expo

2006 (14 Nov), Litho by Cartor, perfs 14½. x 14
Initial selling price: £6.95

GS-038 .... £ 12.50

Issue Notes: 20 x 1st class full size HELLO stamps (GS-038). The Belgica sheet was issued two days before the show start date, unlike Pacific Explorer where the stamp was issued on the first day of the show. The generic tabs on the sheet show various thematic : royalty, birds, sport, animals and transport.

Known Varieties: None

GS-039

Glorious Wales

2007 (1 Mar), Litho by Cartor, printed on self adhesive paper with simulated die-cut perfs 15 x 14½
Initial selling price: £6.95

GS-039 .... £ 12.50

Issue Notes: 20 x 1st class Welsh definitive stamps (GS-038). Royal Mail extended the Smilers range by making the national Country 1st class stamps available for personalisation. The generic sheet featured 10 pictorial generic tabs showing Welsh scenes set against the background of the Welsh flag.

The Glorious Wales sheet was the first in a series of four sheets to feature the constituent parts of the United Kingdom and was issued on 1 March, St David's Day.

Known Varieties: None

GS-040

Glorious England

2007 (23 Apr), Litho by Cartor, printed on self adhesive paper with simulated die-cut perfs 15 x 14½
Initial selling price: £6.95

GS-040 .... £ 12.50

GS-040a Error Sheet (See notes) .... £ 250.00

GS-040b Overprinted "Curious Mistake"...... £ 30.00

GS-040c "Inglorious England" Labels £100.00

Issue Notes: 20 x 1st class English definitive stamps (GS-040). Closely following the Glorious Wales sheet the Glorious England sheet has been nick-named the *In-glorious England* sheet because of a notable Royal Mail howler!

Known Varieties: Just prior to the planned issue of this sheet Royal Mail recalled all the Glorious England Smilers sheets previously distributed to dealers and agencies. At the eleventh hour it was discovered that the sheet contained an unfortunate error on one particular label depicting The Needles at the Isle of Wight. In an inexplicable moment, Royal Mail renamed the island the *Isle of White* and as a result were somewhat red-faced - at least both colours are in keeping with the Smilers sheet theme!

Although the error was well publicised in the national and local press prior to the day of issue a few Glorious England error sheets appear to have been sold in error by Post Office counter staff. It is estimated that c. 100-200 error sheets are probably in circulation and whilst initial demand for this error sheet was high with prices fetching c. £500 they soon dropped to c. £200-300 due to a flood of sheets coming from the Edinburgh region.

At least two privately produced sheets were produced which highlighted the error. GS-040b was overprinted "Curious Mistake". Te second was an ingenious production from 10 different customised sheets each with a fabricated error label which were combined to produced a whole sheet of error labels.

GS-041

Memories of Wembley Stadium

2007 (17 May), Litho by Cartor, perfs 14½. x 14
Initial selling price: £7.35

GS-041 .... £ 12.50

GS-041a Error Sheet (see notes)............. £ 250.00

GS-041b Phosphor Wash (see notes)........ £ 100.00

Issue Notes: 20 x 1st class Lion and Shield stamps (GS-041) are combined with snap shots of some of Wembley's most magical moments. The 1948 Olympics, Henry Cooper v Cassius Clay and Live Aid are just a few of the events featured. As with the previous issue a rather unfortunate error crept into one of the generic tabs and like its predecessor had to be withdrawn and reprinted.

Known Varieties: The sheets were originally printed and distributed to Royal Mail philatelic trade customers and Royal Mail agencies around the world with a curious spelling error on the 1948 label - *Emil* was incorrectly spelt *Emile*. The error was spotted by Royal Mail before the official release date and Royal Mail duly arranged a re-print of these sheets with the correct spelling.

Royal Mail issued a recall notice to all key account holders to return the error sheets and they were subsequently supplied with the re-printed sheets. That is all key account holders except NEW YORK who, for some reason did not receive the recall notice. We understand New York were supplied with c. 400 sheets and these were spotted by a local dealer who purchased around 40 sheets before Royal Mail's recall notice arrived. He in turn sold these on eBay and to dealers in the UK. Another dealer picked up c. 15

sheets during a visit from the UK to New York and a further quantity are believed to have been distributed to Smilers collectors in the USA with standing orders and who to this day are probably completely unaware of the error sheet in their collection. The remainder were returned to Royal Mail for destruction. It is estimated that c. 100 Wembley Error sheets exist from various sources, perhaps some less than kosher!

The sheet is also known with a phosphor wash error apparent on columns 1 and 4. Phosphor wash errors can occur when the phosphor ink is re-charged during the printing process and such errors can appear as all over phosphor, in streaky lines or adjacent to certain printed phosphor lines as in this case.

GS-042

40th Anniversary of the Machin Definitive

2007 (5 Jun), Litho by Cartor, perfs 14½.
Initial selling price: £7.35

GS-042 .... £ 12.50

Issue Notes: 20 x 1st class Machin commemorative stamps (GS-042) which were also issued in mini-sheet format on the same day. The stamps incorporated within the Machin Generic sheet differ in a number of significant ways to those released in the min-sheet. The colour of the stamp is different; they are printed in Litho rather than gravure; and the stamps are not embossed.

The Generic sheet was designed to look like an album page of any avid Machin collector, the Generic Sheet features 20 First Class Machin definitive's, each in a different colour. Early publicity images of this sheet had the label in the bottom left-hand corner showing the £1 value. This was later changed in the final artwork and the value eliminated so as to avoid the label being used as valid postage, all other values being pre-decimal. The sheet has an interesting error that was not spotted by Royal Mail - a hat trick for Royal Mail.

Known Varieties: There have been reports that sheets with the £1 value in the lower right label have been purchased over the counter

GS-043

Harry Potter

2007 (17 Jul), Litho by Cartor, printed on self adhesive paper with simulated die-cut perfs 15 x 14
Initial selling price: 7.35

GS-043 .... £ 12.50

GS-043a *Harri Potta* Handstamp .... £ 75.00

Issue Notes: 20 x 1st class Hogwarts house stamps (GS-043) also issued in mini-sheet format on the same day. Unlike the mini-sheet the Generic sheet stamps were printed on self adhesive paper with simulated die-cut perfs. Alongside the stamps sit twenty generic tabs, each one featuring a magic spell from the Harry Potter books. Thermo-chromatic ink used in the printing process means that the secret of the spell is revealed (as if by magic!) when the mysterious label is warmed by hand.

Known Varieties: An interesting variety exists on some sheets cancelled on the first day of issue bearing a withdrawn first-day-of-issue hand-stamp.

The story behind this withdrawn hand-stamp concerns the licensing of the Harry Potter name. First Day Cover producers experienced extreme delays in finalising licensing arrangements for special hand-stamps. One enterprising individual decided to use

Generic

phonetics as a way round the licensing laws.

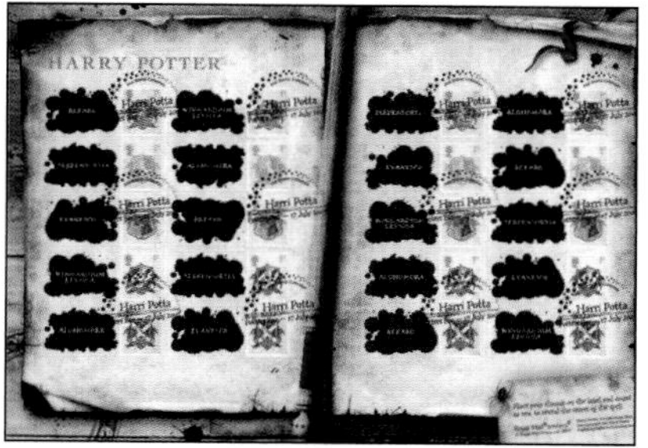

GS-043a

The postmark was approved but withdrawn within hours of the issue of the sheets by Royal Mail to limit the damage to their reputation. Portsmouth Stamp Shop prepared between 50 and 100 sheets stamped with this withdrawn hand-stamp and these are thought to be the only examples of this postmark in existence.

GS-044

Christmas Issue 2007

2007 (6 Nov), Litho by Cartor , printed on self adhesive paper with simulated die-cut perfs 15 x 14½
Initial selling price: £7.35

GS-044 .... £ 12.50

Issue Notes: 8 x 2nd class, 8 x 1st class and 4 x overseas rate (76p) definitive sized (DS) Christmas Smilers stamps (GS-044) featuring Angles with a background scene of a carols being sung in a village centre. The sheets were withdrawn from sale in January 2008 but reappeared again in the run-up to Christmas 2008 and were made available alongside the 2006 and 2008 Christmas Smilers sheets.

Sheets of individual stamps designs (20 of each) were available only via the Royal Mail personalised smilers service.

Known Varieties: None

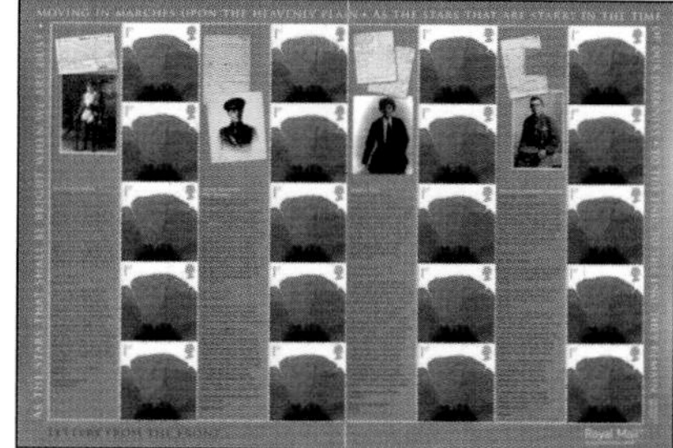

GS-045

Letters From The Front

2007 (8 Nov), Litho by Cartor, perf. 14½
Initial selling price: £7.35

GS-045 .... £ 12.50

Issue Notes: 20 x 1st class Poppy (2007) stamps plus generic tabs illustrating World War 1 soldiers and their letters home (GS-045). The second of three planned Remembrance sheets (See also GS-037 and GS-057). Also issued in mini-sheet format on the same day, printed in Litho by De La Rue.

Known Varieties: None

GS-046

Glorious Scotland

2007 (30 Nov), Litho by Cartor , printed on self adhesive paper with simulated die-cut perfs 15 x 14½
Initial selling price: £7.35

GS-046 .... £ 12.50

Issue Notes: 20 x 1st class definitive sized (DS) Scotland stamps first issued in 1999 with elliptical perfs plus generic tabs featuring various well known landmarks of Scotland set against a the Scottish St.

Andrew's flag (GS-046). The third Smilers sheet to be issued in the "Glorious" countries series (see also GS -039, GS-040, GS-048 and GS-051).

Known Varieties: None

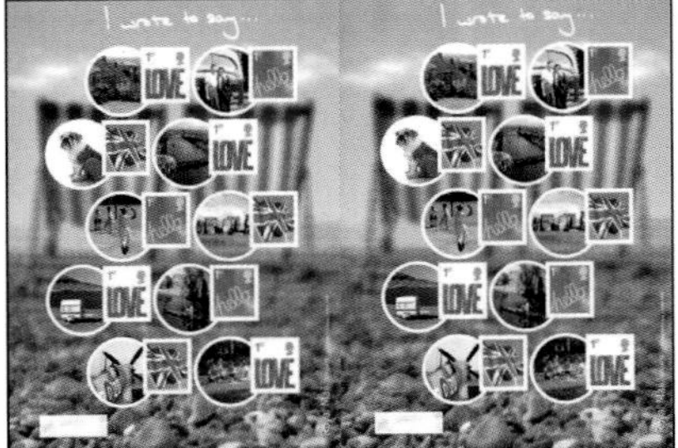

GS-047

I Wrote to Say .....

2008 (15 Jan), Litho by Cartor , printed on self adhesive paper with simulated elliptical die-cut perfs 15 x 14. Initial selling price: £7.35

GS-047 .... £ 12.50

Issue Notes: 20 x 1st class definitive sized Smilers stamps originally issued in Smilers format in the 2006 Life's Special Moment's sheet (GS-034) comprising 6 x Hello, 8 x Love and 6 x Union Flag DS stamps. For the first time these stamps appeared with simulated elliptical perforations. Also for the first time the Stamps were printed adjoined to circular generic tabs. The sheet was clearly intended for the holiday letter writing market but the format was a curious choice by Royal Mail. The other rather strange feature is the presence of the two white boxes at the foot of the sheet. These appear to be a mistake or perhaps the generic sheet was a last minute addition to the original concept of customised versions of this sheet. They exist as place holders to record the Royal Mail Order reference number. In the opinion of the author their inclusion in the design of the generic sheet detracts from the overall aesthetic appeal of this sheet.

Known Varieties: None

GS-048

Glorious Northern Ireland

2008 (11 Mar), Litho by Cartor , printed on self adhesive paper with simulated (elliptical) die-cut perfs 15 x 14. Initial selling price: £7.35

GS-048 .... £ 12.50

Issue Notes: 20 x 1st class definitive sized (DS) Northern Ireland stamps which first issued in 1999 with elliptical perfs plus generic tabs featuring various well known landmarks from Northern Ireland set against a background image of the Devil's Causeway (GS-048). The absence of an accepted Northern Ireland Flag makes this sheet unique in the "Glorious" countries series (see also GS-039, GS-040, GS-046 and GS-051)

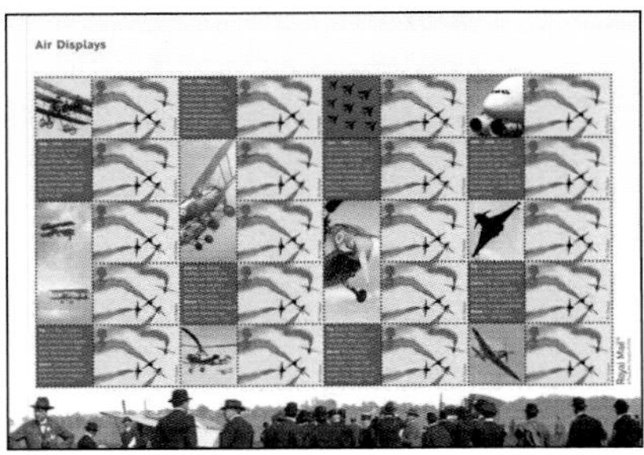

GS-049

Air Displays

2008 (17 Jul), Litho by Cartor , perfs 14½.
Initial selling price: £7.75 (new rate)

GS-049 .... £ 12.50

Issue Notes: 20 x 1st class Red Arrows Air Displays stamps plus generic tabs featuring images of Air Displays past and present (GS-049). The sheet was released to coincide with the 50th Anniversary of the first Air Show held at Farnborough in 1958.

Known Varieties: None

GS-050

Beijing International Stamp Expo

2008 (5 Aug), Litho by Cartor , perfs 14½.
Initial selling price: £7.75

GS-050 .... £ 12.50

Issue Notes: 20 x 1st class "Hello" Occasions/ Smilers stamps plus generic tabs featuring Chinese lateens issued to coincide with the Beijing International Stamp Exhibition and Fair held in Beijing during the 2009 Olympics event (GS-050). This sheet design follows the now familiar design established by Royal mail to mark their participation in various International Stamp exhibitions (see also GS-026, GS-032 and GS-038).

Known Varieties: None

GS-051

Glorious United Kingdom

2008 (29 Sep), Litho by Cartor, printed on self adhesive paper with simulated (elliptical) die-cut perfs.15 x 14. Initial selling price: £7.75

GS-051 .... £ 12.50

Issue Notes: 20 x 1st class regional definitive stamps (4 x Wales, 4 x Northern Ireland, 4 x England and 4 x Scotland) which first appeared in 1999 together with generic tabs featuring various well known landmarks from the four countries set against a background of the Union Flag (GS-051). This is the last in a series of five stamp sheets in the "Glorious" countries series and brings together the four previous stamps in one sheet. It is the first sheet to feature the Welsh, English and Scottish stamps with elliptical perfs printed in litho by Cartor. (see also GS-039, GS -040, GS-046 and GS-047). Although clearly marked "Smilers" this sheet was not available in customised format - a departure from the then current branding of Smilers by Royal Mail.

Known Varieties: None

GS-052

GS-053

GS-054

GS-055

Smilers For Kids (1st Issue)

2008 (28 Oct), Litho by Cartor, printed on self adhesive paper with simulated (elliptical) die-cut perfs 15 x 14. Initial selling price: £7.75

GS-052 .... £ 12.50

GS-053 .... £ 12.50

GS-054 .... £ 12.50

GS-055 .... £ 12.50

Issue Notes: 20 x 1st definitive-sized Smilers stamps (three different designs used) which first appeared in Smilers format in 2006 in the *Extra Special Moments* (GS-034) and *For Life's Special Moments* (GS-035). These sheets represents a new direction for Smilers sheets which, for the first time, were being specifically targeted at the younger market. The original design concept of the Smilers for Kids (S4K) sheets was to issue customised Smilers in sheets of 10 stamps with circular generic tabs featuring children's characters in a cellophane pack to include letter writing and other activity goodies. The price of each stamp/label combination effectively doubled in the process with the S4K packs retailing at £ 7.50 per pack. Whilst this may have appealed to children (doubtful) it definitely did not appeal to the philatelic cover producers who appealed to Royal Mail to make these stamps available to the philatelic market without all the trimmings. These sheets were the result (issued on the same day as the packs). There were four sheets issued:

GS-052- Flower Fairies (Almond Blossom)

20 x 1st definitive sized "Flower" (DS05) stamps

GS-053 - World of Beatrix Potter (Peter Rabbit)

20 x 1st definitive sized "New Baby" (DS09) stamps

GS-054 - Noddy and Friends (Noddy)

20 x 1st definitive sized "Balloons" (DS11) stamps

GS-055 - Mr Men and Little Miss (Mr Happy)

20 x 1st definitive sized "Balloons" (DS11) stamps.

Known Varieties: None

GS-056

Christmas Issue 2008

2008 (28 Oct), Litho by Cartor, printed on self adhesive paper with simulated (elliptical) die-cut perfs 15 x 14. Initial selling price: £8.85

GS-056 .... £ 12.50

Issue Notes: 8 x 2nd class, 8 x 1st class and 4 x overseas rate (81p) definitive sized (DS) Christmas Smilers stamps (GS-056) featuring Pantomime characters with a background scene of a traditional Pantomime. The sheets were withdrawn from sale in January 2009. Sheets of individual stamps designs (20 of each) were available only via the Royal Mail personalised smilers service.

Known Varieties: None

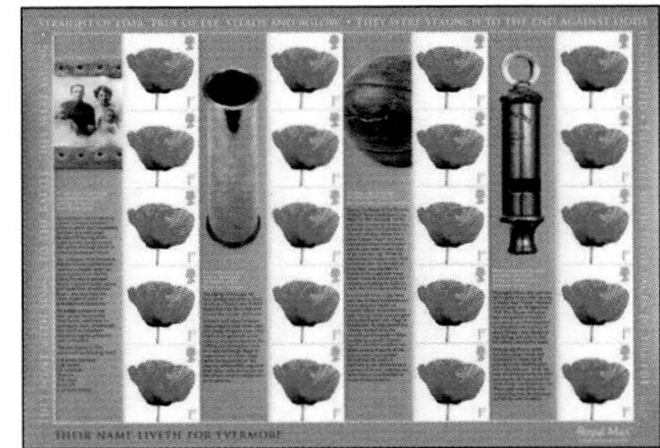

GS-057

Their Name Liveth for Evermore

2008 (6 Nov), Litho by Cartor, perfs 14½ x 14. Initial selling price: £7.75

GS-057 .... £ 12.50

Issue Notes: 20 x 1st class Lest We Forget (2008) Poppy stamps plus generic tabs - the second of three planned Remembrance stamp sheets (See also GS-037 and GS-045). The generic tabs show images of trench art and souvenirs from the front including a whistle carried by 2nd Lt Montague Moore, VC, 15th Batt, Hampshire Regiment; a decorated shell case by Bombardier T E Knights of the RFA; a football used by Capt William Percy Nevill, East Surrey Regiment and a picture frame carved from Army Ration Biscuits by Sgt M Herring, RASC (GS-057). The border incorporates a verse from the poem "For the Fallen" by Laurence Binyon.

"They went with songs to the battle, they were young. Straight of limb, true of eye, steady and aglow. They were staunch to the end against odds uncounted: They fell with their faces to the foe."

Issued also in mini-sheet format on the same day printed in Litho by De La Rue.

Known Varieties: None

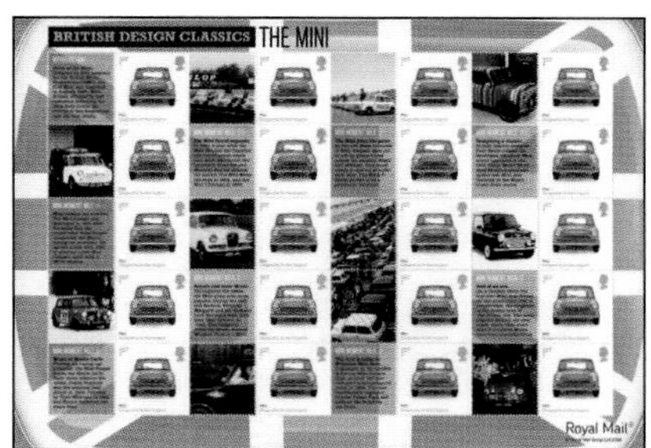

GS-058

British Design Classics - The Mini

2009 (13 Jan), Litho by Cartor, perfs 14½ x 14. Initial selling price: £7.75

GS-058 .... £ 12.50

Issue Notes: 20 x 1st class Mini stamps plus generic tabs - the first of two sheets to feature stamps from the British Design classics set issued on the same day (see also GS-059). The generic tabs show various images of this iconic car's history.

Known Varieties: None

GS-059

British Design Classics - Concorde

2009 (3 Mar), Litho by Cartor, perfs 14½ x 14. Initial selling price: £7.75

GS-059 .... £ 12.50

Issue Notes: 20 x 1st class Concorde stamps plus generic tabs - the second of two sheets to feature stamps from the British Design classics set issued on the 13 Jan 2009 (see also GS-058). The sheet was issued to coincide with the 40th Anniversary of Concorde's first test flight in 1969 and unusually has the stamps to the right of the generic tabs, the first time this format has been used by Royal Mail.

Known Varieties: None

GS-060

Castles of Northern Ireland

2009 (17 Mar), Litho by Cartor, printed on self adhesive paper with simulated (elliptical) die-cut perfs 15 x 14. Initial selling price: £7.75.

GS-060 .... £ 12.50

Issue Notes: 20 x 1st class definitive sized (DS) Northern Ireland stamps which first appeared in Smilers format in 2007 but without elliptical perfs. (GS-034). The sheet features images of Northern Ireland Castles in what is a new series of Smilers sheets fea-

Generic

turing castles of the United Kingdom.

The Castles shown in columns 1 and 3 are: *Monea Castle, Belfast Castle, Carrickfergus Castle, Dunluce Castle and Enniskillen Castle*. In column 2/4 they are: Dungiven Castle, Killyleagh Castle, Narrow Water Castle, Killymoon Castle and Gosford Castle.

Known Varieties: None

GS-061

Castles of England

2009 (23 Apr), Litho by Cartor, printed on self adhesive paper with simulated (elliptical) die-cut perfs 15 x 14. Initial selling price: £8.35.

GS-061 .... £ 12.50

Issue Notes: 20 x 1st class definitive sized (DS) England flag stamps which first appeared in the celebrating England mini-sheet issued in 2008 (GS-060). The sheet features images of well-known English Castles and this is the second sheet to be issued in a new series of Smilers sheets featuring castles of the United Kingdom. The Castles shown in columns 1 and 3 are: *Warwick, Orford, Bolsover, Dover* and *Framlingham*. The castles in Columns 2 and 4 are: Carlisle, *Windsor, Bamburgh, Kenilworth* and *Bodiam.*

Following a general Royal Mail Tariff rise on 1st April all Royal Mail products increased in price. From 1st April 2009 the Generic Sheets increased in price from £7.75 to £8.35.

Known Varieties: None

GS-062

GS-063

GS-064

GS-065

Generic

Smilers For Kids (2nd Issue)

2009 (30 Apr), Litho by Cartor, printed on self adhesive paper with simulated (elliptical) die-cut perfs 15 x 14. Initial selling price: £8.35

GS-062 .... £ 12.50

GS-063 .... £ 12.50

GS-064 .... £ 12.50

GS-065 .... £ 12.50

Issue Notes: 20 x 1st definitive sized "Smilers" stamps (three different designs used) which first appeared in Smilers format in 2006 in the *Extra Special Moments* (GS-034) and *For Life's Special Moments* sheet (GS-035). Four new sheets in Royal Mail's Smilers For Kids (S4K) 2nd issue.. The format and content are similar to the S4K 1st issue (see GS-052 to GS-055). There were four sheets issued:

GS-062 - Flower Fairies (Wild Cherry)

20 x 1st definitive sized "Flower" (DS05) stamps

GS-063 - World of Beatrix Potter (Jeremy Fisher)

20 x 1st definitive sized "Hello" (DS03) stamps

GS-064 - Noddy and Friends (Big Ears)

20 x 1st definitive sized "Balloons" (DS11) stamps

GS-065 - Mr Men and Little Miss (Little Miss Sunshine)

20 x 1st definitive sized "Balloons" (DS11) stamps

Known Varieties: None

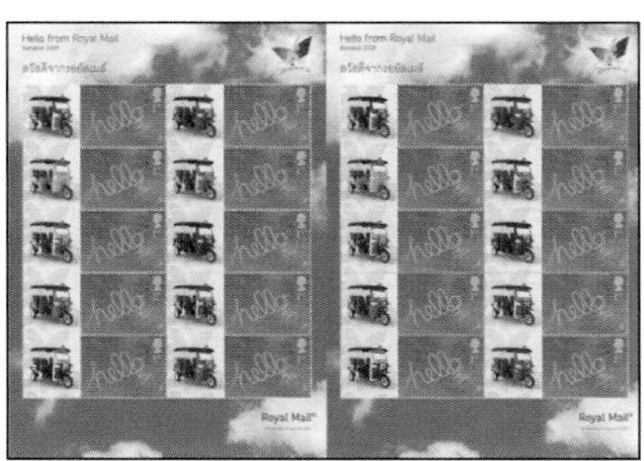

GS-066

THAIPEX - Bangkok Stamp Expo

2009 (3 Aug), Litho by Cartor , perf 14½.
Initial selling price: £8.35

GS-066.. £ 12.50

Issue Notes: 20 x 1st class "Hello" Occasions/ Smilers stamps plus generic tabs. Issued to coincide with the International Philatelic Exhibition THAIPEX held at Bangkok, Thailand. The sheet was available in A5 sized sheets of 10 generic tabs/stamps at the show and in A4 sheets of 10 stamps/generic tabs from Philatelic Bureau in Edinburgh.

Known Varieties: None

GS-067

Wall Boxes

2009 (18 Aug), Litho by Cartor , perfs 14 x 14.
Initial selling price: £8.35

GS-067.. £ 12.50

Issue Notes: 20 x 1st class "Wall Boxes" stamps (from the miniature sheet of the same name) plus generic tabs. The sheet depicted various wall mounted post boxes on the generic tabs and the stamps.

GS-068

Italia 2009 - International Stamp Expo

2009 (21 Oct), Litho by Cartor , perf 14½..
Initial selling price: £8.35

GS-068 .... £ 12.50

Issue Notes: 20 x 1st class "Hello" Occasions/ Smilers stamps plus generic tabs. Issued to coincide with Italia 2009—The International Festival of Stamps

Generic

held in Rome in October 2009. The sheet was available in A5 sized sheets of 10 generic tabs/stamps at the show and in A4 sheets of 10 stamps/generic tabs from Philatelic Bureau in Edinburgh.

Known Varieties: None

GS-069

Christmas Issue 2009

2009 (3 Nov), Litho by Cartor, printed on self adhesive paper with simulated (elliptical) die-cut perfs 15 x 14. Initial selling price: £9.00

GS-069 .... £ 11.50

Issue Notes: 8 x 2nd class, 8 x 1st class, 2 x 50p and 2 x overseas rate (81p) definitive sized (DS) Christmas Smilers stamps (GS-069) adjacent to generic tabs featuring details from stained glass windows. The sheet also features some verses from the Gospel according to Luke. The image on the right hand side of the Generic Sheet features a window depicting The Adoration of The Magi by Guillaume de Marcillat. The generic sheet was designed by Russell Warren-Fisher to look like an open book. The sheet was withdrawn from sale in January 2010. Sheets of individual stamps designs (10 or 20 of each) were available only via the Royal Mail personalised smilers service.

GS-070

Castles of Scotland

2009 (30 Nov), Litho by Cartor, printed on self adhesive paper with simulated (elliptical) die-cut perfs 15 x 14. Initial selling price: £8.35.

GS-070 .... £ 10.00

Issue Notes: 20 x 1st class definitive sized (DS) St. Andrews flag stamps which first appeared in the celebrating Scotland mini-sheet. The sheet features images of well-known Scottish Castles and is the third sheet in the series of Smilers sheets featuring castles of the United Kingdom. The Castles shown in columns 1 and 3 are: Edinburgh; Culzean, South Ayrshire; Stirling, Stirlingshire; Eilean Donan, Highland; Blair, Perthshire. The castles in Columns 2 and 4 are: Balmoral, Aberdeenshire; Castle Stalker, Argyll & Bute; Caerlaverock, Dumfries & Galloway; Kilchurn, Argyll & Bute; Cawdor, Highland.

GS-071

MonacoPhil International Exhibition

2009 (4 Dec), Litho by Cartor, perf 14½.
Initial selling price: £8.35

GS-071 .... £ 10.00

Issue Notes: 20 x 1st class "Hello" Occasions/ Smilers stamps plus generic tabs. Issued to coincide with Monaco International Stamp Exhibition held between the 3-6 December in Monaco. The sheet was available in A5 sized sheets of 10 generic tabs/ stamps at the show and in A4 sheets of 10 stamps/ generic tabs from Philatelic Bureau in Edinburgh.

Known Varieties: None

GS-072

For All Occasions

2010 (27 Jan), Litho by Cartor, printed on self adhesive paper with simulated die-cut perfs 15 x 14 (with two elliptical perforations). Initial selling price: £9.70.

GS-072 .... £ 12.50

Issue Notes: 2 x 10 x 1st class DS "For All Occasions" Smilers stamps plus generic tabs. Ten new Smilers stamps designs were incorporated in this sheet design and were also issued in gummed format in a miniature sheet available from the same day. These designs were designed to supplement the existing range of customised stamps, four of the new designs (Birthday Present/Birthday Cake designed by Annabel Wright and Europe/Worldwide designed by Lucy Davey) which were available for the personal Smilers service and six of which were made available via the Business Customised stamp sheet service.

Known Varieties: None

GS-073

Castles of Wales

2010 (1 Mar), Litho by Cartor, printed on self adhesive paper with simulated (elliptical) die-cut perfs 15 x 14. Initial selling price: £8.35.

GS-073 .... £ 10.00

Issue Notes: 20 x 1st class definitive sized (DS) Welsh flag stamps which first appeared in the celebrating Wales mini-sheet. The sheet features images of well-known Welsh Castles and is the fourth and final sheet in the series of Smilers sheets featuring castles of the United Kingdom. The Castles featured are: Caernavfon, Carreg Cennen, Biwmares (Beaumaris), Cricieth, Harlech, Cas-Gwent (Chepstow), Dinefwr, Dolbadarn, Dolwyddelan and Conway,

Customised Stamp Sheets

Customised Stamp Sheets are a variant of the Generic Stamp sheets described in Chapter 2.

Since the International Stamp Show held in London in 2000 the British public have been able to have their photos printed alongside stamps in place of the generic label designs. This service, initially available only from booths at events such as Stamp Show 2000, has been extended and is now available to the public by post or by ordering on-line from Royal Mail at www.royalmail.com/smilers.

These sheets were available from the Royal Mail at a premium above the normal price of the Generic Stamp Sheets. The Royal Mail Smilers stamp reference number (SMXX) quoted in this catalogue identifies the Royal Mail Tallents House reference number used in the order process of Smilers sheets, as these appeared in the Royal Mail Smilers publicity material. These are described in more detail in *Appendix B*.

Since the introduction of definitive sized Smilers stamps in 2005 there has been a growing interest (particularly from Smilers collectors) in extending the concept of Customised Stamp Sheets into special event or themed sheets, created by Smilers enthusiasts and dealers. We are calling this variant of Customised Stamp Sheets *Themed Customised Stamp Sheets* to distinguish between those produced for personal use and those produced for commercial reasons.

Please refer to Chapter 5, for a non-exhaustive listing of *Themed Customised Stamp Sheets* known to the author which have been made available commercially to collectors. Theses sheets are in all respects similar to the customised stamp sheets listed in this chapter except that they have been produced as commercially available commemorative sheets often embellished with border overprinting or decoration which arguably enhances their appearance. In some cases they are completely unrecognisable as customised stamp sheets and for many collectors prefer these as collectibles rather than the purest customised stamp sheets listed here.

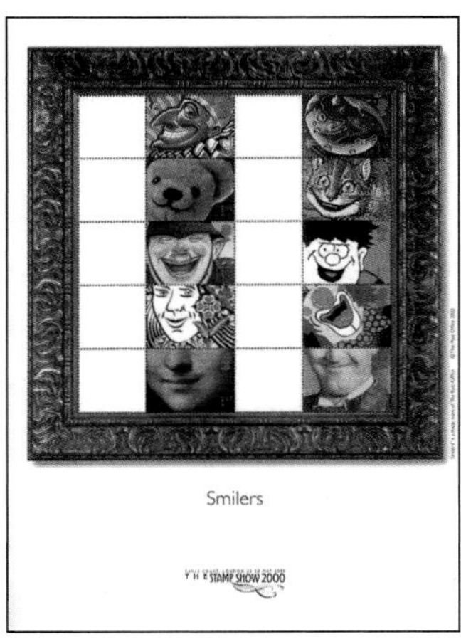

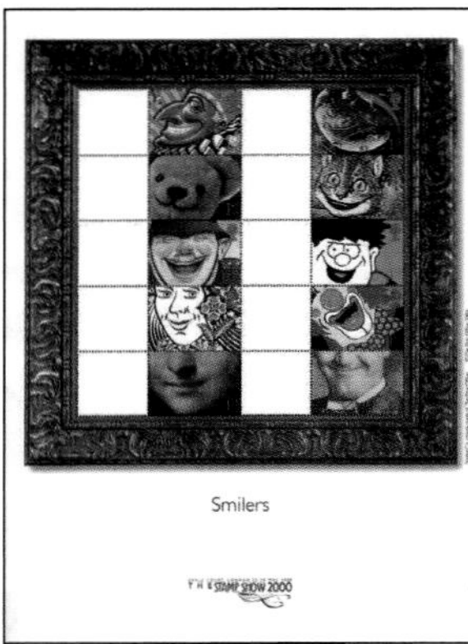

CS-001

The Stamp Show 2000

2000 (22 May), Photo by Questa, Perf 15 x 14, Initial selling price: £5.95

CS-001 .... £ 25.00

Issue Notes: Britain's first personalised stamp sheet comprising 10 x 1st class *Smiles* stamps plus photo tabs set in a guilt frame on white border,. The stamps first appeared in booklet form printed by Questa, and released in 1991. The sheet was issued to coincide with the London International Stamp Exhibition, 22-28 May 2000. A personalised or customised version was available via 'instant Smilers' photo-booths for the duration of the show (7 days) and by post for repeat orders from the Royal Mail Philatelic Bureau for a further two months, until 26th June 2000. There were at least 4 booths and possibly as many as 8 at the show, and turnover on the first day was steady. The procedure took no more than 10 minutes.

These are among the most common of the Customised Smilers sheets, but are still scarce in comparison with any of the Generic Smilers sheets (with the possible exception of Christmas 2001).They were supplied in a red A4 presentation folder inscribed 'Smilers' on the front, with a cut-out 'smile', modelled on the booklet cover for the original release of the stamps in 1991.

The folder makes an interesting front piece to a collection of these issues, but is more difficult to find than the sheet itself. A customer reference serial code was printed at the top left of my sheets of type 5466/8 (large font). The first number is the customer reference number/Royal Mail sales reference. The second number may refer to the booth operator - numbers from 1 to 12 have been seen indicating possibly three operators per booth.

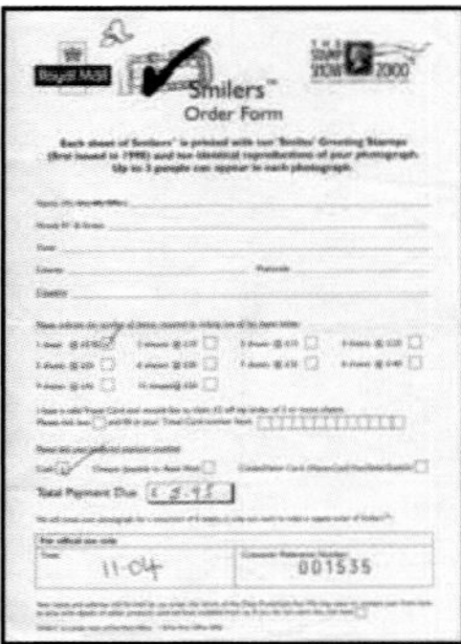

Royal Mail

Smilers™

Order Form

Total Payment Due £5.95

11-04

001535

The smilers order form makes an interesting distinction between the actual stamps and the stamp sheet, terming them "smiles" and "smilers" respectfully. The price per sheet ranged from £5.95 for one copy to £5 for 2 or more sheets.

Smilers™

EXCLUSIVE OFFER

Royal Mail

Order Form

Supplied with each sheet was a re-order form enabling the customer to purchase additional sheets directly from the printer (House of Questa) at Byfleet, Surrey. This Smilers re-order offer was valid up to 26th June 2000. The check code and font is likely to be different on re-ordered sheets emanating directly from Byfleet.

Known varieties: none.

Publicity material: Known to exist, but not seen. It shows the stamps in a different order. It is believed that this was just publicity material and there is no evidence that any sheets with this arrangement exist.

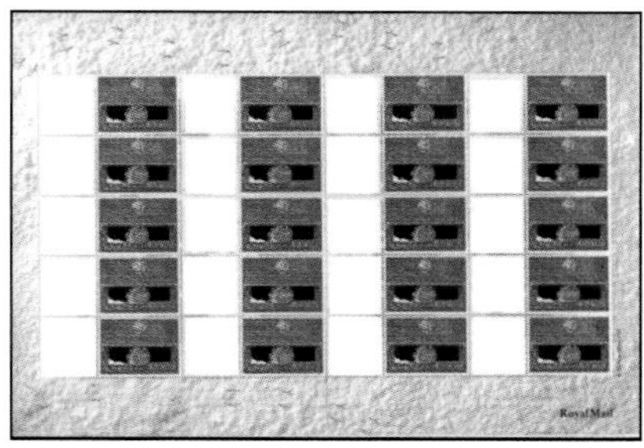

CS-002

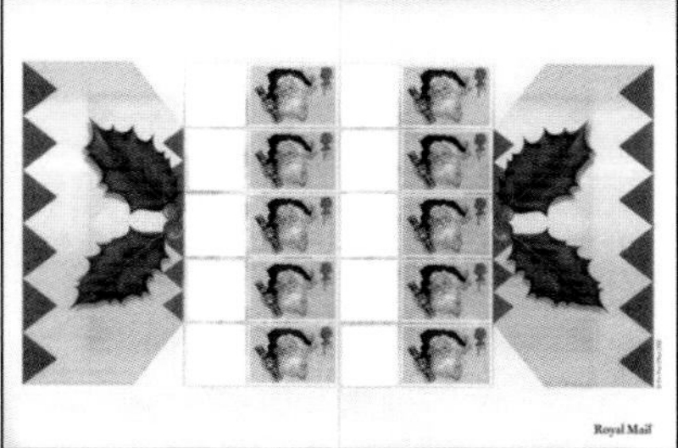

CS-003

Christmas 2000

2000 (3 Oct), Photo by Questa, Perf 15 x 14,
Initial selling price: £7.99 (CS-002) £5.95 (CS-003)

CS-002 ....£ 200.00

CS-003 ....£ 200.00

Issue Notes: 20 x 19p Robin-in-Letterbox stamps plus personalised photo tabs set in a plain decorative border (CS-002) and 10 x 1st Santa and Cracker stamps plus personalised labels set in a decorative Christmas cracker border design (CS-003). The 19p design first appeared as part of the 1995 Christmas issue. The 1st design first appeared as a part of the 1997 Christmas issue, both were printed Photo by Harrison. Withdrawn 2nd October 2001. Both designs were available in generic label formats.

Customers who ordered 'instant' sheets at SS2000 were sent Royal Mail promotional material advertising the two new customised sheets. The two sheets could be ordered from 3rd October 2000 until 29th December 2000. The sheet borders are identical to the Generic ones, but were overprinted in the lower left corner with a customer reference code. Two types of code: a large font (as used for SS2000 - this is rare, and may be for customers solicited by mail using stored photographic images from the show) and a small one (also used for subsequent sheets). Large font: 0000233 3 0 (identical for the Robins & Santa sheets); small font 5880658-20-00F, 5922457-02-02S. For the small fonts, F designates First Class, S Second Class, and the second and third numbers are presumably the order size (Santa, then Robins).

Known varieties: None known.

Publicity material: See page Appendix C, page C-1 - September 2000, no date or print code. The brochure has a reply-paid envelope attached and features the 2000 Christmas sheets. The Post Office participated in several promotional exercises in collaboration with newspapers, magazines and the BBC, offering pairs of 1st class sheets as prizes.

Themed Sheets: The Christmas Sheet designs were used to produce the first *Themed Smilers* sheets *(see Chapter 5)*. The first examples were original produced to raise funds for the Marnoch Church community association and the idea was to sell covers featuring stamps and photo tabs on matching covers, not as stamp sheets. The number of sheets printed was minimal (10 sheets of 1st Class and 8 sheets of 2nd Class). Nevertheless, a number of whole sheets (did survive and these are now highly collectible.

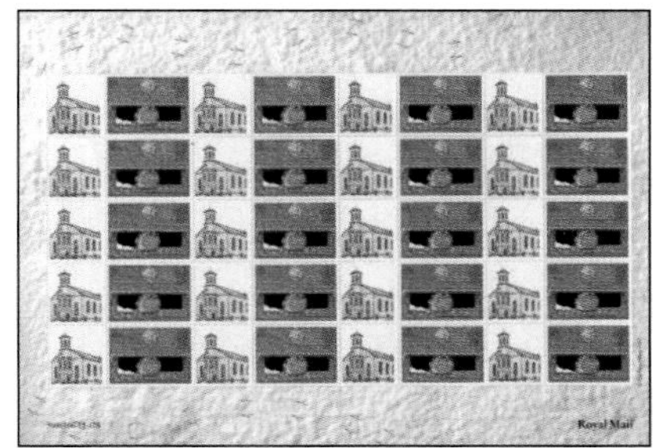

TS-001

TS-002

Occasions 2000

2001 (1 May), Litho by Questa, Perf 14½ x 14 ,
Initial selling price: £11.95

CS-004a .... £ 200.00

CS-004a/a Reprint (see notes) .... £ 250.00

CS-004b .... £ 250.00

CS-004c .... £ 250.00

CS-004d .... £ 250.00

Issue Notes: Four sheets of 20 x 1st class Occasions stamps with different border designs, in various combinations. The "Hallmark" Occasions stamps first appeared as a set of five stamps on 2nd February 2001 printed in Gravure by Joh. Enschedé. A generic sheet featuring all five stamps with generic tabs was issued 5th June 2001 some five weeks after the Customised Smilers sheet versions, also printed in Litho by the House of Questa. The Smilers sheets are the only source of this litho printing variety for this issue.

Four sheet variants were released: *Celebrations & Thanks* (CS-004a), featuring 10 x Cheers & 10 x Thanks, while the remaining sheets - *New Baby* (CS-004b), *New Home* (CS-004c) and *Love & Romance* (CS-004d), had 20 each of the appropriate design. The single-design sheets were probably withdrawn by the end of 2001 (latest May 2002), but *Celebrations & Thanks* was still available until mid-December 2004 (though potential customers were probably unaware of this – it was dropped from promotional material after September 2002). The late *Celebrations & Thanks* sheets have the head and border inscriptions printed in dull light grey, whereas all the initial printings were much closer to the silver of the Generic issue. At £11.95 per sheet, a set of four would have set a collector back almost £50 at the time of issue: the three single-design sheets are rare, and the *Celebrations & Thanks* sheet is scarce. A pictorially-Customised *Celebrations & Thanks* sheet realised £411 in May 2006 at an on-line auction. Commercially used singles are also difficult – the *New Home* stamp in particular. Codes – initially of the form 647316-CAT2-LAR2-NWB2-NWH2 (the number indicates the order size for each sheet), then from 2003 (C&T) 25909SM10/Cheers And Thanks. In the later codes the first number does appears be a dedicated 'Smilers' customer reference, the 'SM' code is the Tallents House sheet reference, and the order size is no longer revealed.

Known varieties: The re-printed CS-004a sheets

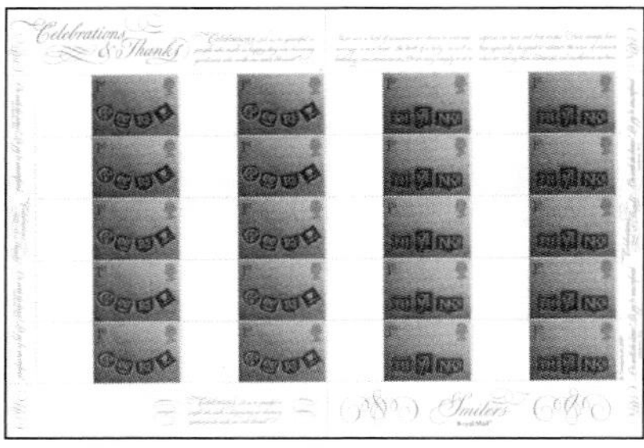

CS-004a—Celebrations and Thanks

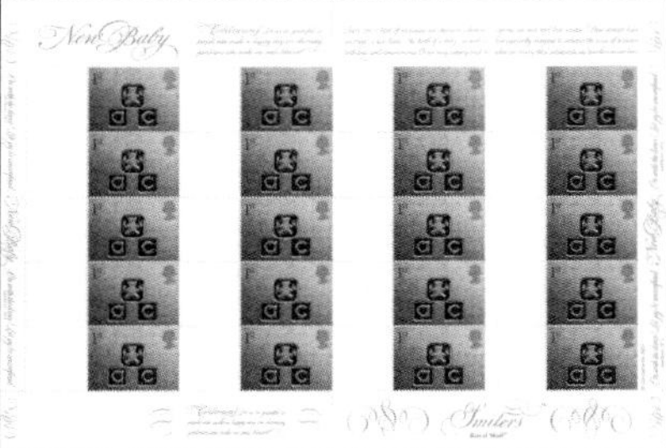

CS-004b—New Baby

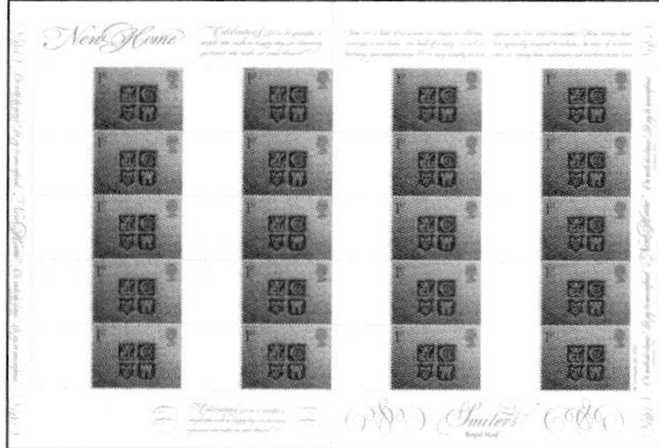

CS-004c

CS-004d

Customised

have the Queen's head and border inscriptions printed in dull light grey whereas the initial printing was much closer to the silver of the Generic issue.

Publicity material: Featured in Stamp Preview No. 70 – June 2001 (see page C-8, Appendix C). The *Celebrations and Thanks* sheet is also included in V1 and V2 of the Smilers brochures. See also pages C-14 and C-15, Appendix C.

First Day Covers: At least three first-day cover dealers (B. Alan Stamps, Cotswold Covers and 4d Post) serviced FDC's featuring customised stamps/photo tabs from this issue.

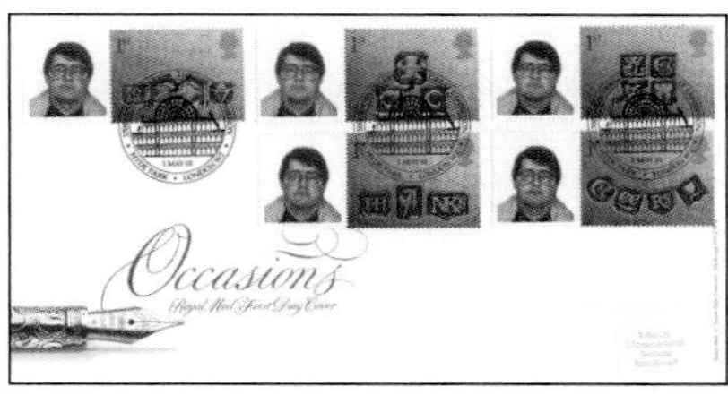

B. Alan Stamps

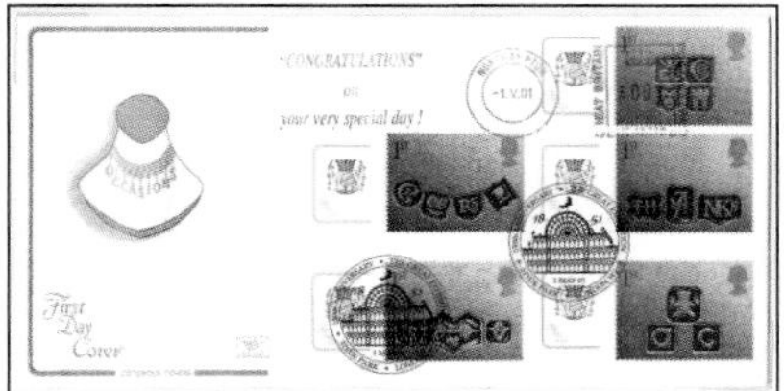

Cotswold Covers

4d Post

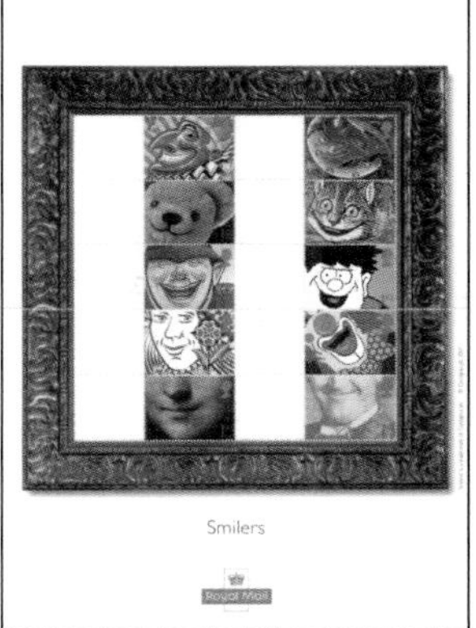

CS-005a

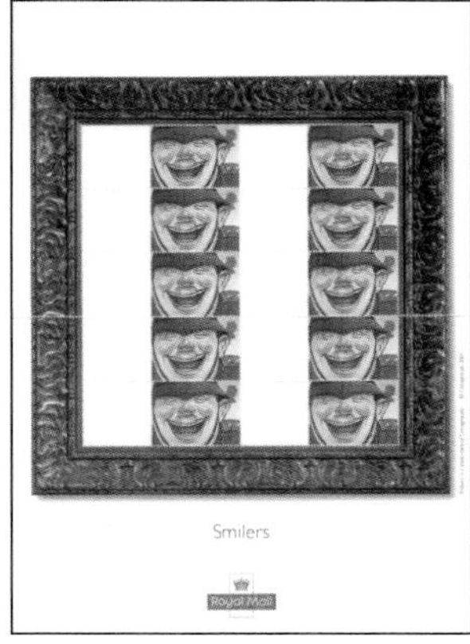

CS-005b

CS-005c

Customised

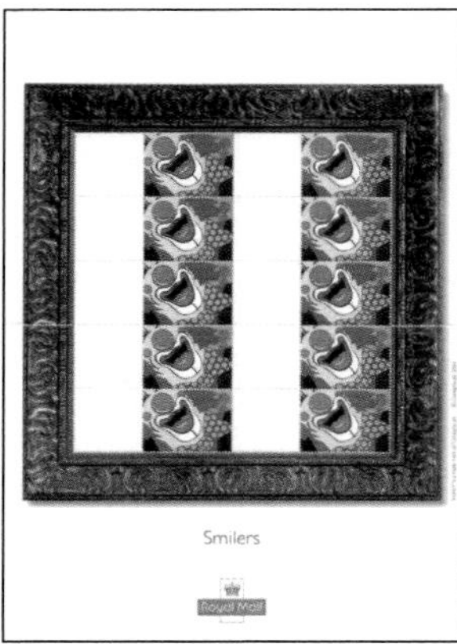

CS-005d

CS-005e

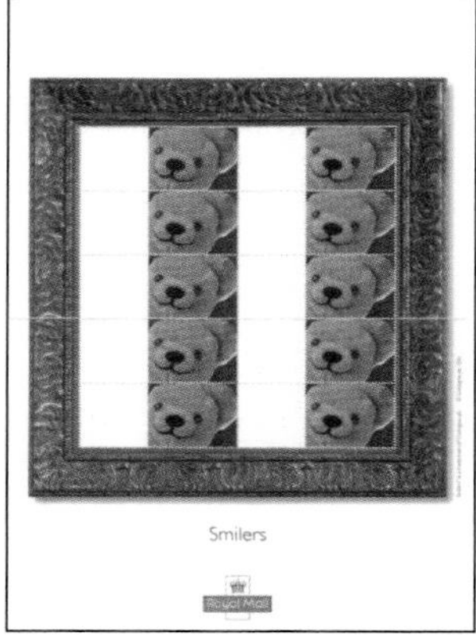

CS-005f

Customised

Greetings - Smiles

2001 (3 Jul), Litho by Questa, Perf 14½ x 14 ,
Initial selling price: £7.50

CS-005a .... £ 500.00

CS-005b .... £ 250.00

CS-005c .... £ 250.00

CS-005d .... £ 250.00

CS-005e .... £ 250.00

CS-005f .... £ 250.00

Issue Notes: Six sheets of 10 x 1st class Greetings (Smiles) stamps. One sheet contained all 10 Smiles Stamps whilst the other five contained an individual Smiles stamp from the set. All had identical border designs. The "Smiles" Greeting stamps first appeared as a set of ten 20p stamps on 2nd February 1990 in booklet format printed in Gravure by Harrison and Sons. A customised sheet (CS-001) featuring all ten 1st class stamps with generic photo tabs set in a guilt frame on a plain white background was issued on 22nd May 2000 for the London International Stamp Show held at Earls Court. These were © Post Office whilst the re-issued customised sheets in July 2001 were © Consignia plc. Due to the similarity in design these six customised sheets (CS-005a to f) seem to have been missed by most collectors and are therefore some of the rarest of the early customised sheets.

The five single-design customised sheets featured ten each of Policeman, Mona Lisa, Clown, Dennis and Teddy. It is unclear why these particular stamps were chosen over some of the others (e.g., Cheshire Cat or Man in the Moon) – possibly a trial marketing exercise by Consignia. An 'instant Smilers' vending trial based on photo-booths operating at six philatelic bureaux ran for three months from late October 2001 and utilised the 'mixed' version above (with CS-005a) – sales were described as 'negligible'. The Dennis & Teddy sheets appear to have been available until release of the 'Knock! Knock!' sheet in October 2002, judging from publicity brochures; the others were withdrawn earlier (probably in December 2001 for Policeman, Mona Lisa & Clown, and the end of January 2002 for the 'mixed' sheet). The sheets cost £7.50 each, bringing the cost of a set to £45 – all are rare, and commercially used customised singles are scarcer than the SS2000 equivalents.

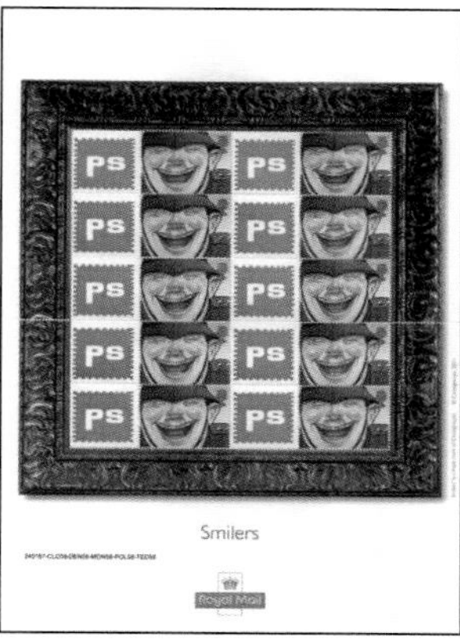

Portsmouth Stamp Shop Logo

Most of the sheets on the market bear a simulated 'stamp' in the photo tabs, printed in blue & containing the letters 'PS'. The initials stand for 'Portsmouth Stamps', who ordered them for their regular new issue customers. Some customers collected used stamps so a number of these sheets are known cancelled bearing the 'Albert Road, Southsea, Hants' postmark. Judging from the customer codes on these, fifty-eight of each of the single-issue sheets were ordered, but none of the mixed sheet.

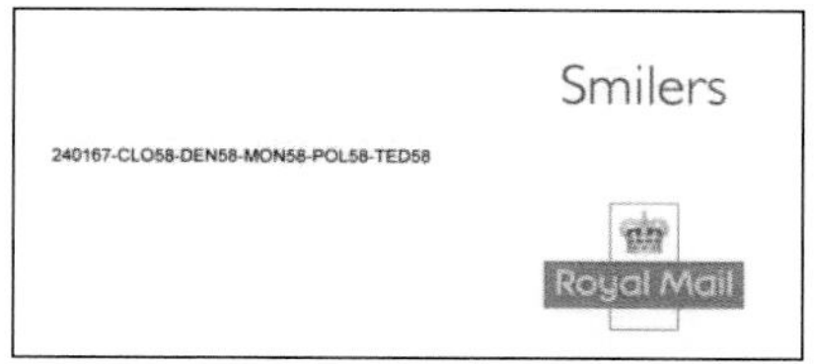

Rushstamps were selling used sets (five sheets) of these for £450 in 2004, an unused set reportedly sold for £1000 before this date.

Customers Codes – all of the form:

6581150-CLOX-DENX-MIXX-MONX-POLX-TEDX,

where X is the number of sheets printed. The 'instant Smilers' codes are presumably different.

Known varieties: None

Publicity material: Featured in an *Instant Smilers* brochure. The five single-value sheets (but not the mixed sheet) are also mentioned in a brochure describing the Smiles and Christmas 2001 customised stamps, "SMILERS FIRST CLASS IDEA" RM Ref: 02AAE (see Appendix C).

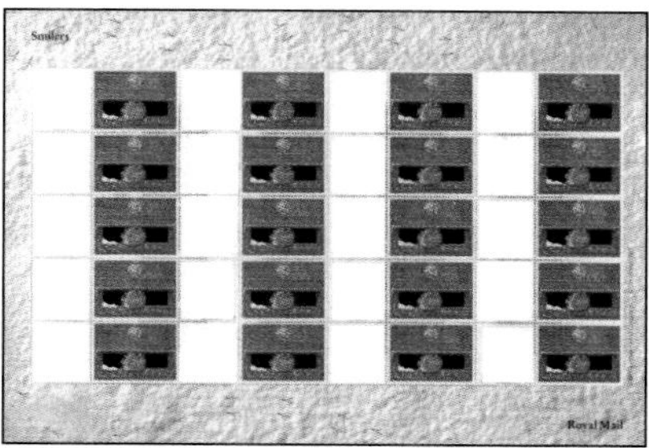

CS-006

CS-007

Christmas 2001

2001 (9 Oct), Photo by Questa, Perf 15 x 14,
Initial selling price: £8.75 (CS-006) £12.95 (CS-007)

CS-006 ....£ 250.00

CS-007 ....£ 250.00

Issue Notes: 20 x 19p Robin-in-Letterbox stamps plus personalised photo tabs set in a plain decorative border (CS-006) and 10 x 1st Santa and Cracker stamps plus personalised photo tabs set in a decorative Christmas cracker border design (CS-007). As with CS-005, Consignia showed little innovation with this issue – utilising the same designs as for the previous year. The two issues can be identified by differences in the sheet border inscriptions – in the 2001 issue the word *Smilers* has been added to the top left of both sheets, and the lower right inscription has been revised to © *Consignia plc.* The pair of Smilers sheets went off sale on 11th January 2002.

Commercially used singles with contemporary dates are as common as the 2000 predecessors, again showing a good non-philatelic demand for the service over the Christmas period. Intact sheets are rare – a pair sold on eBay for £260 in January 2006 (but less than one third the retail price of the Generic issue at the time). Codes – all of form 6668255-XRF2-XRS1.

As with the 2000 sheets, an "F" code designates First (Santa) and a "S" code Second (Robins). The Santa sheet was also available from October to December via the 'instant Smilers' vending trial noted under CS-005.

Known varieties: None

Publicity material – Featured on leaflets "SMILERS FOR EVERY OCASSION" (page C-5) and "GO CRACKERS WITH SMILERS™ FOR CHRIST-MAS" (see page C-9) no date code (c. September 2001).

Katie Price (Jordon)

Consignia participated in a number of promotional campaigns offering free sheets as prizes – a pair of 1st class sheets, issued in collaboration with the Daily Star newspaper and featuring a well-known celebrity (Jordon) sold for £535 in March 2006.

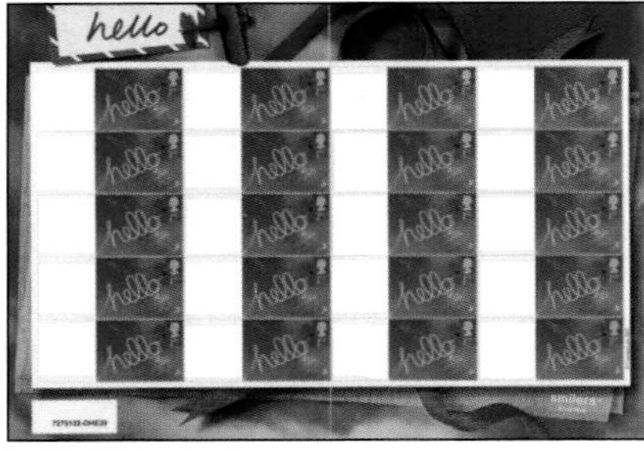

CS-008a - Hello

CS-008b - Moving Home

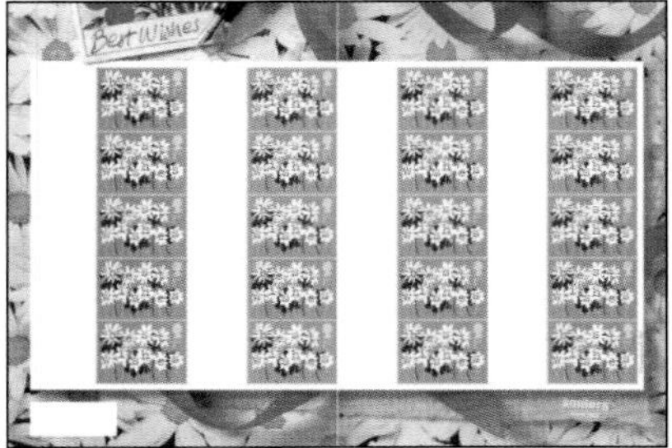

CS-008c - Best Wishes

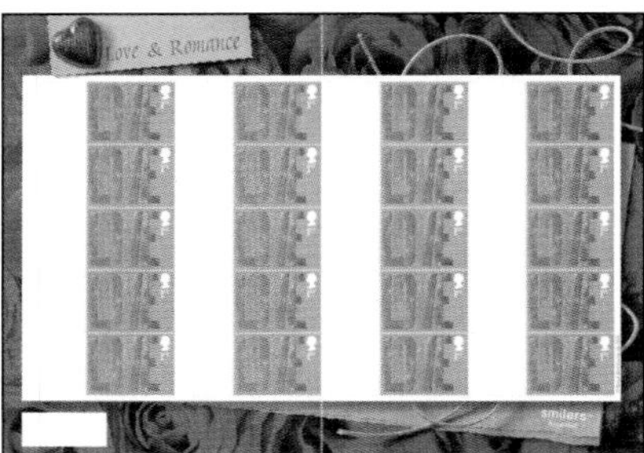

CS-008d - Love

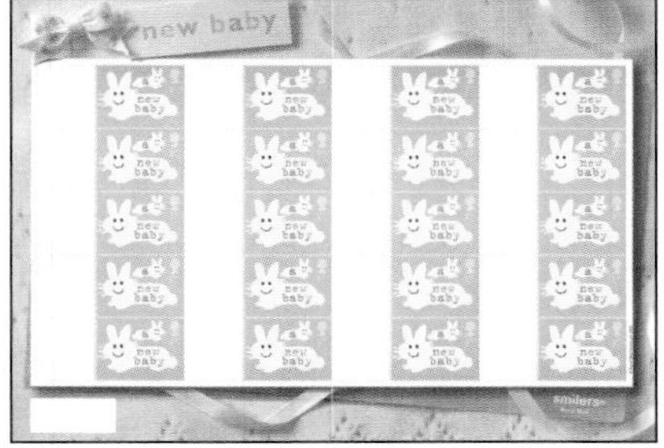

CS-008e - New Baby

Customised

Occasions 2002

2002 (23 Apr), Litho by Questa, De La Rue, Walsall or Cartor (see issue notes), Perf 14.5 x 14
Initial selling price: £12.95 (later £14.95)

CS-008a (Hello - Type Q) .... £ 125.00

CS-008a (Hello - Type D) .... £ 125.00

CS-008a (Hello - Type W) .... £ 125.00

CS-008a (Hello - Type C) .... £ 125.00

CS-008b (Moving Home - Type Q) .... £ 125.00

CS-008c (Best Wishes - Type Q) .... £ 125.00

CS-008c (Best Wishes - Type W) .... £ 125.00

CS-008c (Best Wishes - Type C) .... £ 125.00

CS-008d (Love - Type Q) .... £ 125.00

CS-008d (Love - Type D) .... £ 125.00

CS-008d (Love - Type W) .... £ 125.00

CS-008d (Love - Type C) .... £ 125.00

CS-008e (New Baby - Type Q) .... £ 125.00

CS-008e (New Baby - Type W) .... £ 125.00

CS-008e (New Baby - Type C) .... £ 125.00

Issue Notes: 20 x 1st class Occasions stamps in five different sheet designs (CS-008a to CS-008e) were made available from the same date as the Generic sheet (GS-009) by mail-order from Tallents House. For the first time, these sheets had a completely different border design to the Generic version (though Generic 'Hello' sheets were subsequently released in similar designs to commemorate the Hong Kong and Sydney stamp exhibitions held in 2004 and 2005). Five single-stamp sheet designs were available, each containing twenty stamps, priced at £12.95 per sheet . Subsequently the price increased to £14.95 per sheet or £13.95 for two or more sheets. The five sheets were *Hello*, *Moving Home*, *Best Wishes*, *Love*, *New Baby* and were designed as replacements for the similarly-themed GS-004 variants which had attracted unfavourable feedback from market research (too drab!).

Due to the popularity of these designs there was wide interest from the public and as a result a number of different printings were made:

Type Q- House of Questa

Type Q The original printing in Litho by House of Questa bearing © **Consignia plc 2002** in lower right hand margin of stamp sheet.

Type D - De La Rue

Type D The *Hello* and *Love* sheets were first reprinted in Litho by De La Rue bearing a revised imprint © **Royal Mail Group plc 2002** in lower right hand margin of stamp sheet. The Consignia plc brand had been changed to Royal Mail Group plc on 13th June 2002.

Type W

Type W All four sheets *Hello, Love, Best Wishes* and *New Baby* were re-printed again in 2004 by Walsall, all with the revised imprint **© Royal Mail Group plc 2002** except the *Best Wishes* sheet, which had an updated imprint © **Royal Mail Group plc 2003**. The *Best Wishes* reprint of 2004 is much closer to the original issue with the Queen's head a markedly greyer blue than either of the previous printings.

Type C

Type C Two sheets, *Love* and *Hello,* were re-printed again at some point in 2005 by Cartor : the latest versions still bear the © **Royal Mail Group plc 2002** imprint, but differ in shade and, more importantly, in the screening dot arrangement of the stamps. *Best Wishes* and *New Baby,* were again re-printed in early 2006 by Cartor and during this printing the © symbol on the Best Wishes sheet reverted to the **© Royal Mail Group plc 2002** and the ™ symbol adjacent to Smilers on both sheets was replaced with a ® symbol, creating two distinct new varieties. The blue of the Queens head in the Best Wishes sheet now a deeper shade of blue than seen in previous printings with the background also a deeper shade of blue.

Love & *Hello* were withdrawn at the end of March 2006 with *Best Wishes* and *New Baby* withdrawn by October 2006. *Moving Home* was finally withdrawn officially on 7 March 2007.

Codes: from June 2004 of type 20524SM1/Hello. The number is the customer reference (and maybe for Customised smilers only), the SM code is the Tallents sheet reference (listed under Chapter 5) – these are sometimes incorrect or left out altogether, and the last is the sheet title. Codes prior to early 2004 (not seen), but likely to be of format as the 2001 issues.

Known varieties: None, apart form those listed under printing varieties

Publicity material: V1/750k/MW/Sept02, S&C172DL. Featuring Occasions 2002. 'Choose from 9 available designs' – Occasions 2002 (x 5), Cheers & Thanks, Dennis, Teddy, World Cup. Also featured in V2/3.72m/MW/Sept02, S&C238DL and V3/1.6m/MW/Dec02, S&C252DL.

The "Hello" sheet was also featured in the MAGIC Presentation Pack insert card issued 15th March 2005, see page C-26, and features prominently on a number of the Truprint envelopes, see page C-47.

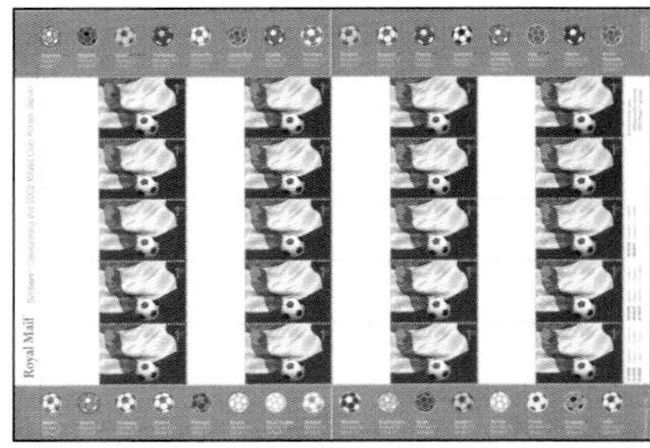

CS-009

World Cup 2002

2002 (21 May), Litho by Questa, Perf 14.5 x 14
Initial selling price: £12.95

CS-009 .... £ 500.00

Issue Notes: 20 x 1st World Cup football stamps (ex-mini sheet) plus personalised photo tabs, withdrawn 20th May 2003. The Generic sheet (GS-010) featured an unusual perforation format, containing four double -sized vertical photo tabs and twelve normal-sized ones. The perforation layout was revised in the Customised version to replace the 'double' sized vertical photo tabs with single size photo tabs. Probably one of the scarcest Customised Smilers sheets due to its relatively short life during a period when the Smilers brand was going through something of a low point.

It is also worth noting that the usual white box for the Customer Order Reference number is absent in this sheet design because a space had been left in the right hand border to accommodate the Customer Order Reference number.

Known varieties: None

Publicity material: Poorly advertised which may explain why it is extremely difficult to find in whole sheets. An insert card was included with the World Cup 2002 presentation pack and dated 05/02 (See page 4-59). Also mentioned in V1/750k/MW/Sept02, S&C172DL.

CS-010a

CS-010b

Knock, Knock

2002 (1 Oct), Litho by Questa, Perf 14.5 x 14
Initial selling price: £12.95

CS-010a .... £ 125.00

CS-010b .... £ 125.00

Issue Notes: Two customised sheet designs - 20 x 1st 'Teddy' stamps (SM2) + personalised photo tabs (CS-009) set against an image of a wooden brown door (knock, knock, who's there) and 20 x 1st 'Dennis the Menace' stamps (SM5) + personalised photo tabs (CS-010) set against an image of a red painted door complete with door-knocker. Both sheets have '© Consignia plc' imprints and look rather better than the 'hybrid' Generic version. The pair replaced the analogous 'Smiles' sheets of ten issued in 2001 and were presumably the most successful designs from the earlier series. Both were still on sale in late 2005 but were no longer available by March 2006. The 'Dennis' sheet features Dennis jumper printed in a shade of red (carmine) markedly different to that of the border (scarlet) or the Generic sheet (GS-011). Two printings of the 'Teddy' sheets are known. Originally printed by House of Questa, a reprint in 2005 was by Cartor.

Known varieties: None, apart form noted printings.

Publicity Material: Customised Teddy and Dennis Smilers mentioned in V1/750k/MW/Sept02, S&C172DL, V2/3.72m/MW/Sept02, S&C238DL and V3/1.6m/MW/Dec02, S&C252DL.

CS-011

Christmas 2002

2002 (1 Oct), Litho by Questa, Perf 14.5 x 14
Initial selling price: £12.95

CS-011 .... £ 125.00

Issue Notes: 20 x 1st 'Cracker and Santa' stamps (SM11) + personalised photo tabs (CS-011) set against a festive image of Christmas tree and trimmings. Similar to the Generic sheet except for the white box at lower left hand side. This Smilers sheet features the 1st 'Cracker and Santa' stamps (SM11) used for the Christmas Smilers of 2001 and 2002, but this time printed in sheets of twenty by litho rather than gravure. The phosphor bands are wider than those on stamps from 2001 and 2002, the perforation gauge is also different and the Queen's head is a darker shade of gold. The customised sheets remained available for 'seasonal' personalisation between October and December 2002 and again at the end of 2003 and 2004. In the intervening periods blank sheets were returned to the supplier. Used singles are common with 2002 postmarks, but Royal Mail did not publicise availability in the following two years and on phoning the Smilers 'helpline' in November 2004 it was confirmed that there was 'no demand for these'.

Known varieties: None

Publicity material: Featured in the Royal mail leaflet "Smilers™ make Christmas, or any occasion, special." and also V2/3.72m/MW/Sept02, S&C238DL.

CS-012

Flowers

2003 (21 Jan), Litho by Questa, Perf 14.5 x 14
Initial selling price: £12.95

CS-012 .... £ 75.00

Issue Notes: 20 x 1st 'Flower' Greetings stamps (SM4) + personalised photo tabs (CS-012) set against a decorative flower border. The stamp designs were first introduced in a 'Greetings' booklet released in 1997. Perhaps one of the most attractive sheets released to date, the customised sheet was withdrawn 31st March 2006. The sheet is identical to the Generic version (GS-013) apart from inclusion of the code box and deletion of the inscription in the lower left border '*The flower names...*' referring to the photo tabs in the Generic.

Known Varieties: The sheet was reprinted at some point between late 2004 and early 2005 by Cartor, The Cartor printing differs significantly to that available prior to June 2004. The 1st and 2nd printings of the 'Basingstoke' Customised Smilers (TS-04) are of the first type whilst the 3rd and 4th printings are of this second type, see also page 5-07. Some stamps show marked shade changes (notably the magnolia, third down on the left, which is much closer to the original Walsall Printing of 1997) and the print screen arrangement of the sheet as a whole is also different .

An easy point of distinction is the fourth stamp down at the left (Gentiana acaulis): in the 'Greetings' booklet of 1997 and the Customised reprint (Cartor) the lower left petal is separated from the background by a small white triangular (unscreened) area; in the Generic version and first Customised printing (House of Questa) this is screened in black.

Differences also exist between the second stamp down at the left and its greetings booklet equivalent. Apart from the absence of elliptical perforations, if one looks closely at the white area in the top left in the booklet version you will see four vertical coloured lines. These are absent from the Smilers sheet versions, in all printings.

Publicity material: Featured in V3/1.6m/MW/Dec02, S&C252DL. Featuring Flowers & Occasions 2003. 'Choose from 9 available designs' – Occasions 2003, Flowers, Occasions 2002 (x 5), Dennis, Teddy. The freepost envelopes for the 'Trueprint' photographic service featured the Gazania splendens design with the 'Hello' stamp from SM1 (code: S&C242DL),

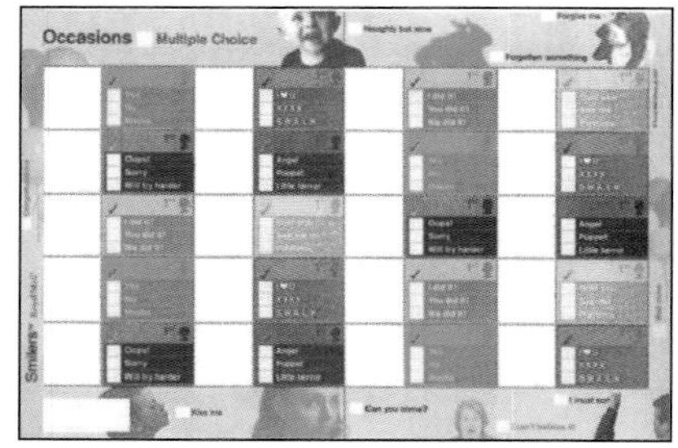

CS-013

Occasions - Multiple Choice

2003 (4 Feb), Litho by De La Rue, Perf 14.5 x 14

Initial selling price: £14.95

CS-013 .... £ 150.00

Issue Notes: 20 x 1st Multiple Choice Occasions stamps + personalised photo tabs class (CS-013). The individual stamps differ slightly in shade to the regular issue (markedly so in the case of the reddish purple variety which is more purple in the sheet version). The sheet was withdrawn from sale in late December 2004 when the blank sheets started spoiling during the printing process, The border is virtually identical to Generic sheet (GS-014), except for the boys head at lower left and 'kiss me', these have moved c. 1 cm to the right to accommodate the customer code box. The customised sheets show very slight shade differences to the Generic sheets.

Publicity material: included with the Flowers 2003 brochure V3/1.6m/MW/Dec02, S&C252DL. This shows a Customised version of GS-014a, rather than CS-013.

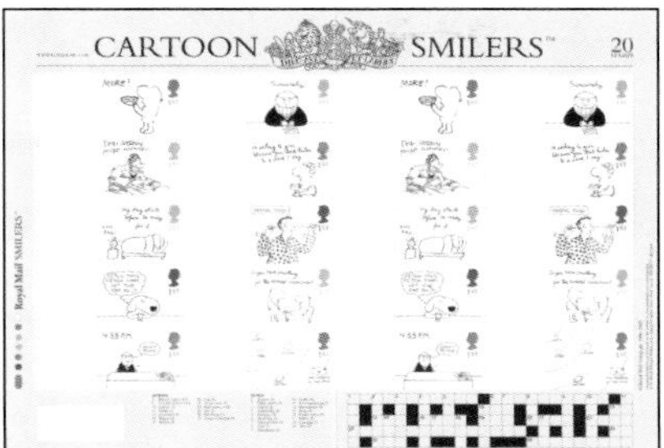

CS-014

Cartoons/Crosswords

2003 (29 Jul), Litho by De La Rue, Perf 14.5 x 14
Initial selling price: £14.95

CS-014 .... £ 125.00

Issue Notes: 20 x 1st Cartoons Greetings stamps (SM12) + personalised photo tabs. The customised sheets were withdrawn/exhausted by late 2005. The lower sheet border is completely different to the Generic sheet (GS-015), featuring the code box, a large crossword and clues.

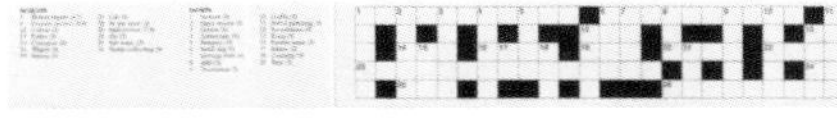

Known Varieties: None

Publicity material: Featured in V4/605k/SE/Jun03, S&C324DL.

CS-015

Winter Robins

2003 (30 Sep), Litho by De La Rue, simulated die-cut perfs. 14.5
Initial selling price: £12.95

CS-015 .... £ 125.00

Issue Notes: 20 x 1st Winter Robins stamps (SM13) + personalised photo tabs. The first personalised sheet to be printed on self-adhesive paper and in a new format. The sheet was withdrawn in December 2004. The sheet border is identical to the Generic sheet except for the omission of the scarf at the bottom left where the code box appears. Commercially used singles are plentiful but fragile - the stamp & photo tab are only weakly 'tied' together.

Known Varieties: None

Publicity material: – Featured on the front and internally of V5/1137k/SE/Sep03, S&C347DL

CS-016

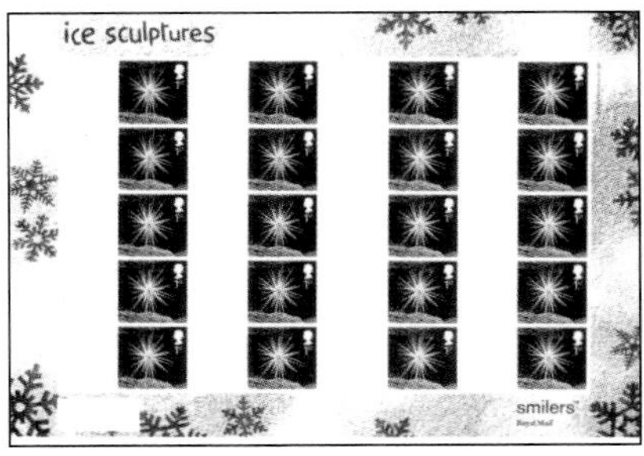

CS-017

Ice Sculptures - Christmas Issue 2003

2003 (4 Nov), Litho by De La Rue, simulated die-cut perfs. 14.5
Initial selling price: £9.95 (CS-016) £14.95 (CS-017)

CS-016.. £ 125.00

CS-017.. £ 125.00

Issue Notes: 20 x 2nd Ice Sculptures (SM14) + personalised photo tabs set against a background of ice crystals (CS-016) and 20 x 1st Ice Sculptures (SM15) + personalised photo tabs set against a background of ice crystals (CS-017) utilising the Ice Sculptures designs from the Christmas 2003 stamp set but printed in litho not gravure. The pair of Customised Smilers sheets were available from 4th November 2003 and withdrawn on 3rd November 2004. The first class sheet (CS-017) was available continuously over this period, but the second class sheet (CS-016) was 'seasonal', being withdrawn at the end of December 2003 and then re-appearing (briefly) in September 2004. Both sheets are identical to the Generic versions apart from inclusion of the code box except that the 2nd class sheet (CS-016) appears to be a more deeper shade of blue than the Generic sheet (GS-017). Both values have been seen commercially used, but they seem less plentiful than those from those from CS-015.

Known Varieties. There is reported to be a wide spectrum of shades on the second class sheet (GS-017) from violet-blue to Prussian blue, more obvious on the Customised versions of this sheet.

Publicity material: Featured on the front and internally of V5/1137k/SE/Sep03, S&C347DL.

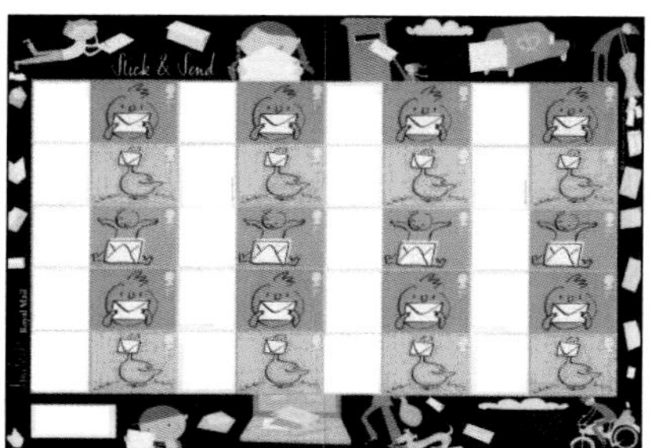

CS-018a

CS-018b

Entertaining Envelopes - Occasions

2004 (3 Feb), Litho by Walsall, Perf 14½ x 14
Initial selling price: £12.95

CS-018a (Home & Away) .... £ 125.00

CS-018b (Stick & Send) .... £ 125.00

Issue Notes: 20 x 1st class Entertaining Envelopes stamps (SM17 - designs vary depending on sheet) + personalised photo tabs set against a black background with various colourful images. Withdrawn 7th March 2007. Home & Away (CS-018a), comprises twelve of the 'plane' design and eight of the 'postman' design, and Stick & Send (CS-018b), comprises eight 'face', eight 'duck' and four 'baby' stamps, respectively. The first sheet (CS-018a) has a border similar to the Generic sheet, with slight alterations to the position and size of some of the images, while in the second sheet (CS-018b) the figure next to the code box has acquired a hat and shed about 40 years! The sheets are perforated vertically through the middle, unlike the Generic sheet.

Known Varieties: None

Publicity material: Featured in Royal Mail Smilers publicity leaflet V5/950k/SE/Jan04, S&C357DL. The arrangement of the stamps in the partial illustration of the Stick & Send sheet (CS-018b) is different to that actually issued.

CS-019

Royal Horticultural Society

2004 (25 May), Litho by Walsall, Perf 14½
Initial selling price: £12.95

CS-019 .... £ 125.00

Issue Notes: 20 x 1st Dahlias stamps (SM18) + personalised photo tabs, withdrawn around May 2005. There are no discernable difference between the customised sheet (CS-019) and the generic sheet (GS-021) apart from the inclusion of a white oblong code box in the bottom left hand corner.

Known Varieties: None

Publicity material: No specific release, details included in V6/950/TL/Jun04, RMMKG003DL (promoting the next generic issue, (GS-022). The 'Trueprint' freepost photographic service featured this design with the 'Hello' stamp from CS-008a (code: S&C373DL).

CS-020

Rule Britannia

2004 (27 Jul), Litho by Walsall, Perf 14½
Initial selling price: £14.95

CS-020 .... £ 75.00

Issue Notes: 20 x 1st "Union Flag" stamps (SM19) + personalised photo tabs, the stamps first appeared in 2001 as part of a British flags mini-sheet. Customised sheet withdrawn late 2005, presumably when stocks were exhausted. The border artwork for this sheet depicts a Union Flag with what look like on first inspection prominent scratches all round, however these are believed to denote stitching although it is not clearly shown. No visible difference in boarder design with the generic sheet (GS-022), apart from the inclusion of the oblong white code box.

Known Varieties. None

Publicity material: Featured in Royal Mail Smilers publicity leaflet V6/950/TL/Jun04, RMMKG003DL

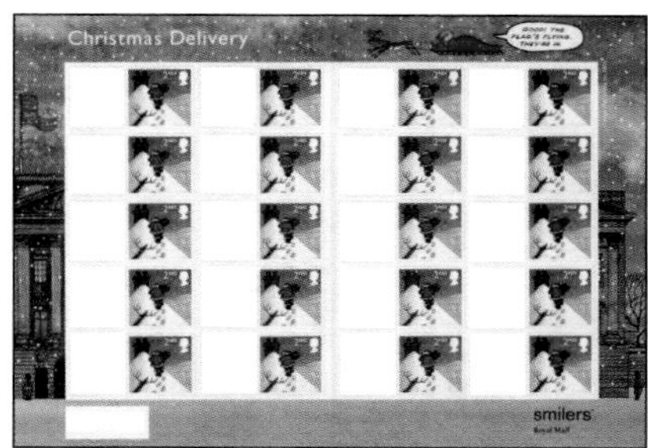

CS-021a

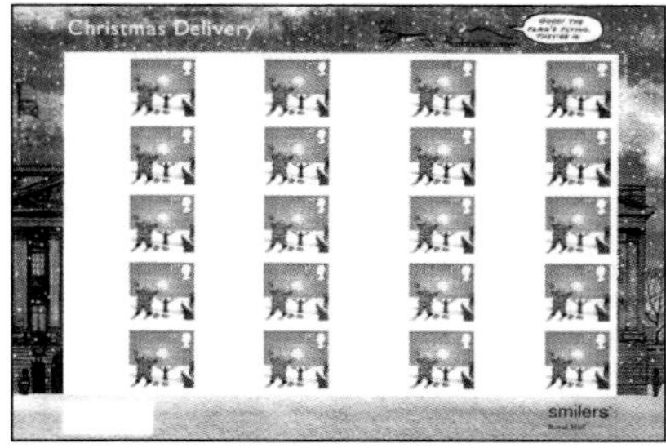

CS-021a

Christmas 2004

2004 (27 Jul), Litho by Walsall, simulated die-cut perfs. 14½ x 14. Initial selling price: £14.95

CS-021a .... £ 125.00

CS-021b .... £ 125.00

Issue Notes: 20 x 2nd "Santa on roof top" (SM21) + personalised photo tabs (CS-021a) and 20 x 1st "Santa (SM22) at Sunrise" (CS-021b) + personalised photo tabs, both with identical border designs to the Generic sheet issue (GS-023) apart from the inclusion of an oblong white box at bottom left for printing the Royal Mail order reference, to be quoted by the customer in the event of re-printing.

Known Varieties: One customer received a pair of unprinted sheets (the photo tabs and code box are blank) in error – the pair, which are slightly damaged (they bear tooth marks after being appropriated by the family dog), sold for £450 in mid 2005.

Publicity material: The sheets featured in 945/TL/September04, RMMKG020DL and Royal Mail preview Number 137 (November 2005). The brochure has a partial illustration of CS-021a and CS-021b.

CS-022

Farm Animals

2005 (11 Jan), Litho by Walsall, perfs. 14½ x 14.
Initial selling price: £14.95

CS-022 .... £ 125.00

Issue Notes: 20 x 1st farm animal stamps (SM22) + personalised photo tabs set in background farm-yard scene. No discernable difference with the Generic sheet, apart from the addition of a white oblong box at bottom left.

Known Varieties. None

Publicity material: Royal Mail Smilers publicity leaflet 560/PJM/June05, RMMKH001DL mentions the Farm Animals stamp but no illustration of either the generic or customised sheet.

CS-022

Magic! - The Magic Circle Centenary

2005 (15 Mar), Litho by Walsall, perfs. 14½ x 14.
Initial selling price: £14.95

CS-023 .... £ 125.00

Issue Notes: 20 x 1st spinning coin stamps (SM23) + personalised photo tabs set against a starry night sky background with border lettering identical to the generic sheet design except for the inclusion of order code box in the lower left hand border. The sheet design is somewhat spoilt by the inclusion of this white box and in the opinion of the author it would have been a relatively simply task to adjust the lettering of the word ABRACADABRA to fit the available space.

Known Varieties: Towards the end of 2005 the process of printing the order reference number in the white oblong box was dropped by the Royal Mail (see also issue notes for GS-029) and therefore this sheet exists with and without the customer order reference number printed in the white box, depending when the sheet was ordered. The process of including the customer order reference was again re-introduced by the Royal Mail in October 2006 and it follows that any Customised Smilers sheets available during the intervening period may exist with and without the customer order reference number included.

Publicity material: Featured in Royal Mail Smilers publicity leaflet 560/PJM/June05, RMMKH001DL

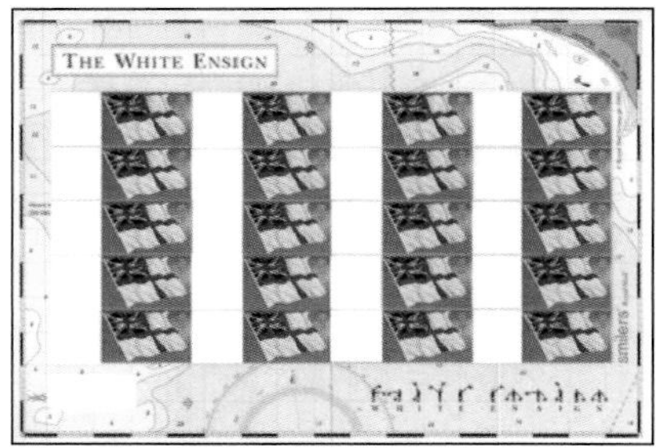

CS-024

The White Ensign

2005 (21 Jun), Litho by Cartor, perfs. 14½
Initial selling price: £14.95

CS-024 .... £ 50.00

CS-024a 2nd Printing .... £ 75.00

Issue Notes: 20 x 1st "White Ensign" stamps (SM24) + personalised photo tabs (CS-024) with navigational chart background. Withdrawn 7th March 2007. No significant differences exists between GS-027 and CS-024 apart from of the inclusion of the white customer order code box at bottom left.

Known Varieties: As with the Generic sheet, at least two different printings of the customised sheet exist (both by Cartor) and these are relatively easy to spot. The difference between the two printings can easily be identified by comparing the green colour in the top right hand corner.

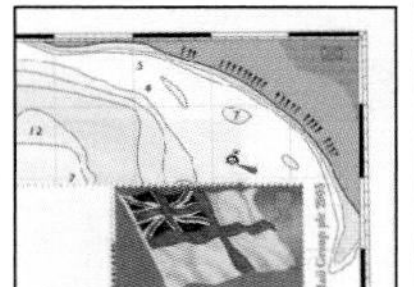
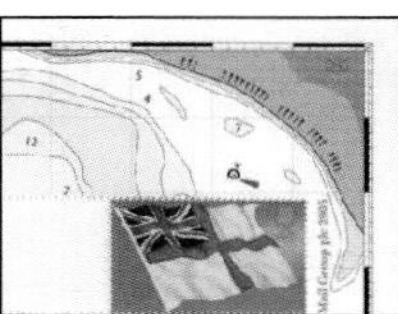

Original (L) and re-print (R)

The re-print (CS-024a) is a brighter, more yellow green than the original printing. There are also notably differences in the reds on the flags.

Publicity material: Featured in Royal Mail Smilers publicity leaflet 560/PJM/June05, RMMKH001DL

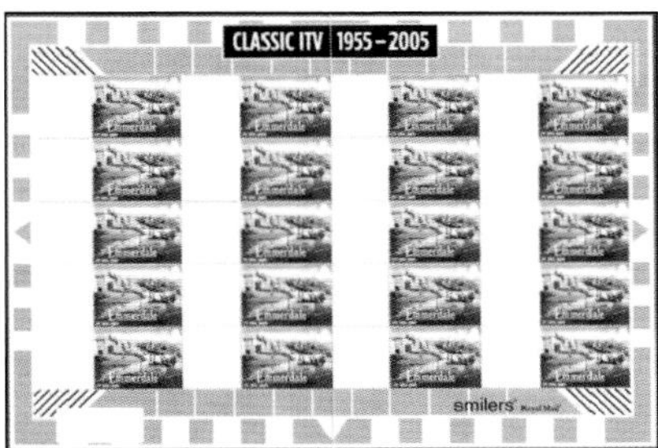

CS-025

Classic ITV

2005 (15 Sep), Litho by Cartor, perfs. 14½ x 14
Initial selling price: £14.95

CS-025 .... £ 125.00

Issue Notes: 20 x 1st "Emmerdale" stamps from the classic ITV issue (SM25) + personalised photo tabs (CS-024) on a background depicting a 50's style station identification screen. The sheet was withdrawn some time during the first half of 2006 (exact date unknown) due to production problems of the customised sheets. It is understood that many of the Customised Smilers sheets jammed during the Royal Mail printing process. The customised sheet was on sale at the Royal Mail Smilers booth at STAMPEX in February 2006. Due to the noted production problems relating to the Generic sheet (see page 2-13) and the last minute Royal Mail reprinting of the generic sheet, this is the first instance of a Customised sheet being printed by a different printer to that responsible for the Generic sheet. The actual stamps are very similar in comparison, although they differ in the screen pattern under magnification and the phosphor bands are more clearly defined on the Customised Smilers sheets.

Known Varieties : None known on Customised version

Publicity material: Stamp featured in 924/PM/Nov05, RMMH053. Cartor generic sheet featured in *Stamp Preview* (page 4-72).

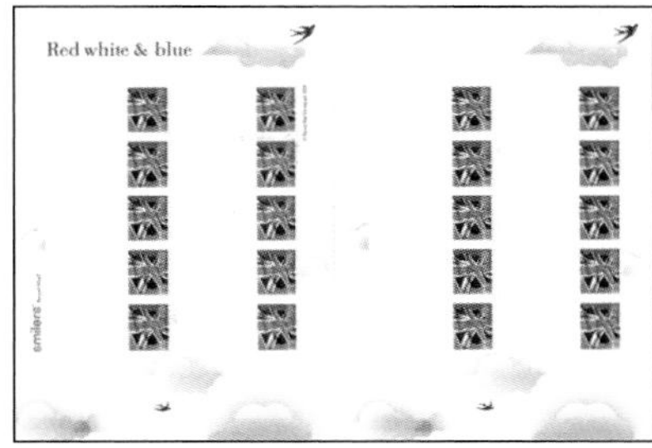

CS-026a

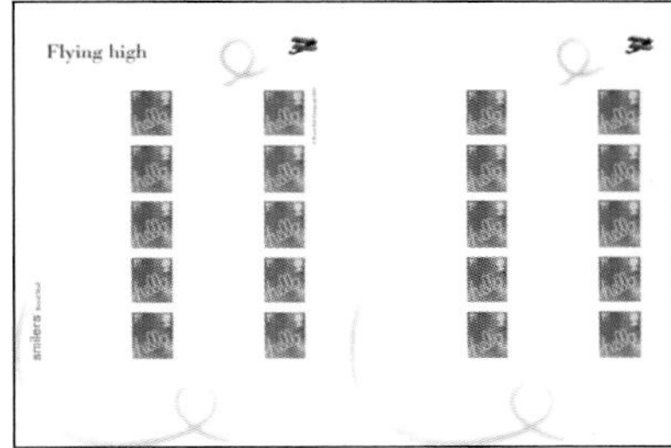

CS-026b

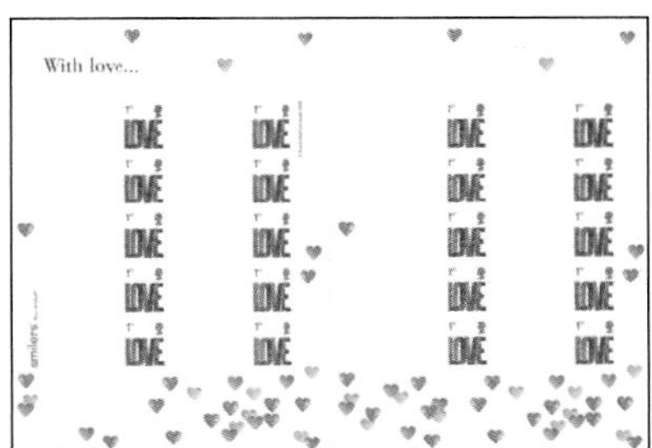

CS-026c

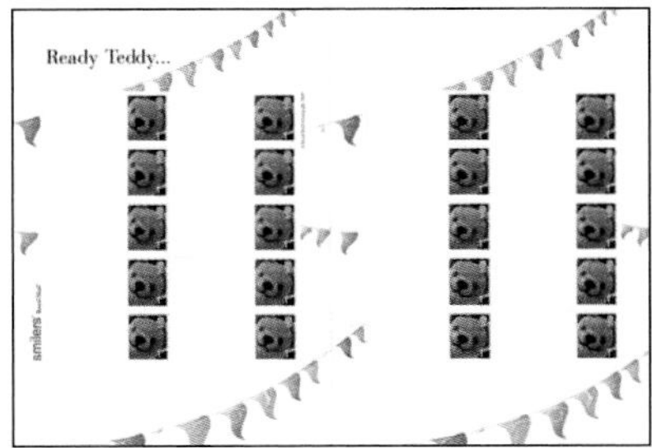

CS-026d

Customised

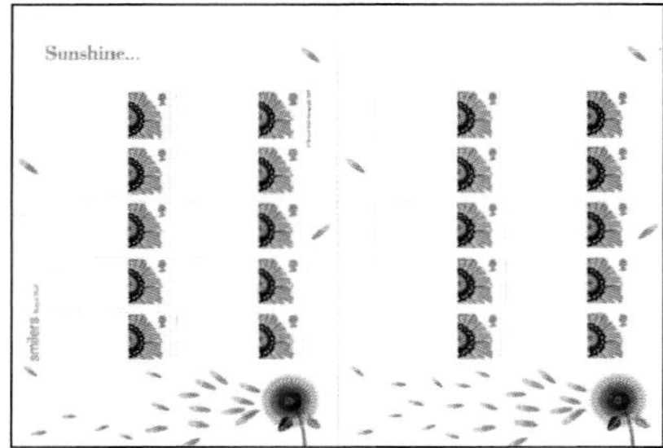

CS-026e

CS-026f

Occasions (2005)

2005 (4 Oct), Litho by Cartor, simulated die-cut perfs. 15 x 14. Initial selling price: £14.95

CS-026a - © Royal Mail Group plc............... £ 30.00

CS-026a/a - © *Royal Mail Group Ltd (09/08).* £ 30.00

CS-026b - © Royal Mail Group plc............... £ 30.00

CS-026b/a - © *Royal Mail Group Ltd (05/09).* £ 30.00

CS-026c - © Royal Mail Group plc.............. £ 30.00

CS-026c/a - © *Royal Mail Group Ltd (12/09)..* £ 30.00

CS-026d .... £ 30.00

CS-026e .... £ 30.00

CS-026f - © Royal Mail Group plc................ £ 30.00

CS-026f/a - © *Royal Mail Group Ltd (12/07).* £ 30.00

Issue Notes: 20 x 1st definitive-sized, self-adhesive, stamps of differing designs (DS01 to DS06) adapted from previous Royal Mail occasion stamp designs to fit the re-sized stamps. By reducing the stamp sizes it was possible to create larger label designs more aligned to a normal photographic image and this is thought to be the reason for re-issuing these stamps in the smaller definitive size format. The smaller-sized stamps allowed for a larger Customised image, in response to consumer feedback surveys, and Royal Mail now seem to have made the move to this format for most of its Customised Smilers sheet formats. Soon after the release of this issue the internet Smilers 'online' ordering process was restricted to this series and the all other pre-existing gummed formats could only be obtained by mail-order.

Issued in six interesting and different sheet designs (CS-026a to CS-026f) the sheets were issued on 4th October 2005, just in time for Christmas and some nine months before the Generic version was issued. At the time they were the only source of Litho printed stamps and this caused something of a stir amongst the collecting community. The sheets, printed by Cartor, were recognisably different from the booklet stamps issued on the same day (printed by Walsall in gravure), and this led to much criticism – collectors facing an outlay of £89.70 to obtain the set.

The six customised, self-adhesive sheets released were as follows:

Red white & blue featuring 20 x 1st class UNION FLAG (DS01) set in a border design comprising larks and clouds(CS-026a), and

With Love featuring 20 x 1st class LOVE (DS02) set in a border design comprising hearts (CS-026b) , and

Flying high featuring 20 x 1st class HELLO (DS03) set in a border design comprising clouds and bi-planes (CS-026c), and

Ready teddy featuring 20 x 1st class TEDDY (DS04) set in a border design comprising bunting (CS-026d), and

Sunshine featuring 20 x 1st class SUNFLOWER (DS05) set in a border design comprising flowers and petals (CS-026e), and

In the post featuring 20 x 1st class ROBIN IN PILLERBOX (DS06) set in a border design comprising pillar-boxes and letters (CS-026f).

All six sheets have been used extensively to publicise various national or international philatelic exhibitions and other events, since small orders (less than 100 sheets) can be placed, they offer a cheap alternative to the Business Customised sheets covered in Chapter 4. See also Chapter 5 for a listing of the commercially available Themed Customised Smilers sheets using these designs.

From early 2008 the sheets were available at a reduced retail price of £13.50 per sheet or £12.50 for two or more sheets. It was also possible to order a half sheet of 10 stamps + labels at a cost of £7.50 per sheet of 10 stamps. On request, Royal Mail at Tallants House would produce an un-separated sheet of 20 stamps with 2 panes of 10 stamps + labels with different images on each pane.

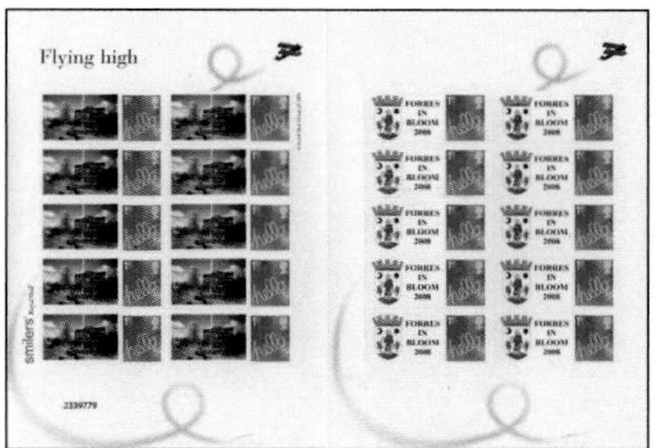

Example of two different images on one sheet

Known Varieties: Two sheets to date have been reprinted with the change from © Royal Mail Group plc to © Royal Mail Group Ltd. Other than this, none known.

Publicity material: Smilers Leaflet 924/PM/Nov05, RMMH053 introduced the new definitive-size format stamps DS1-DS6, Three of the 6 sheets are shown. Five of the definitive sized stamps also appeared in leaflets 924/PM/Nov05, RMMH053

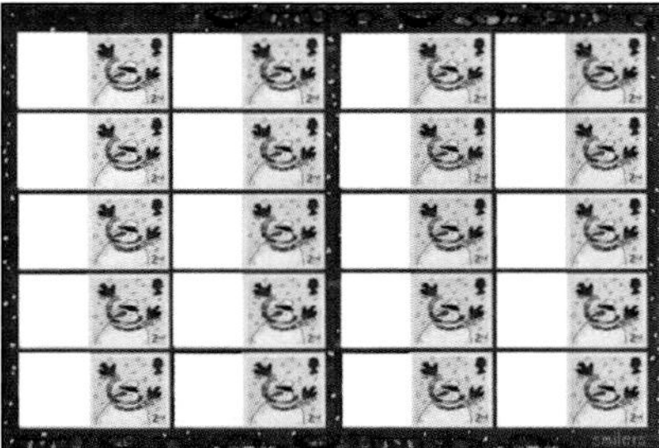

CS-027a

CS-027b

Christmas Robins - Christmas Issue

2005 (1 Nov), Litho by Cartor, simulated die-cut perfs. 14½ . Initial selling price: £14.95

CS-027a .... £ 125.00

CS-027b .... £ 125.00

Issue Notes: 20 x 2nd Winter Robins stamps (SM26) + personalised labels (CS-027a) and 20 x 1st Winter Robins stamps (SM27) + personalised labels (CS-027b) on dark blue background decorated with winter images (scarves, crackers, soup bowls etc.), withdrawn November 2006. The borders are identical to the generic sheet, and for the first time the code box at bottom left has been omitted. Royal Mail ceased using the code box to print the Customer Order Reference Number some time during 2005 and through this issue seem to have officially acknowledged that this was no longer a processing requirement. This continued to be the practice throughout the better part of 2006 although subsequent sheets all contain a white code box. In October 2006 the printing of the Customer Order Reference Number was re-introduced by Royal Mail it being no longer optional. That said, the author has seen the Christmas 2006 Customised Smilers sheets (issued in November 2006) with and without the customer order reference number printed in the white code box. The official line is that the customer order reference number is not optional and will be printed, the practice is (still) somewhat different.

Known Varieties: None

Publicity material: 924/PM/Nov05, RMMH053 introduces the new definitive-size formatted stamps, but also shows eleven 'conventional' ones including SM26 and SM27. Three of the new sheets are illustrated and the Occasions 2002 'New Baby'!

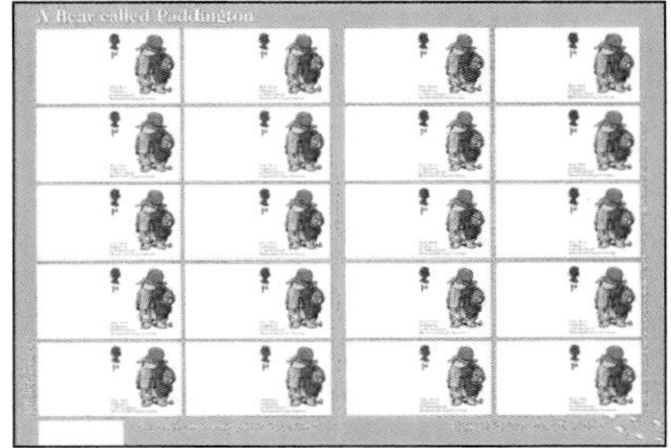

CS-028

Paddington Bear

2006 (10 Jan), Litho by Cartor, simulated die-cut perfs. 14½ . Initial selling price: £14.95

CS-028 .... £ 100.00

Customised

Issue Notes: 20 x 1st Paddington Bear stamps (SM29) + personalised labels set on dull yellow background. The borders are identical to that of the Generic sheet, except for the inclusion of a white box in the lower left-hand border. The stamps have a micrographed date '2006' in the value tablet of each stamp.

Known Varieties: None

Publicity material: 62/PM/Feb06 and 150/PM/May06. Paddington Bear Smilers stamp and label featured on front of leaflet and inside a sheet of Customised Paddington Bear is illustrated. Leaflet 62/PM/Feb06 also features 5 of the 6 definitive size Smilers stamps (the Robin is omitted in error). This explains why the leaflet was re-printed in May 06 with this omission corrected. Apparently the people responsible for the publicity leaflet removed the Robin in pillar box as it was thought this was only seasonally available!

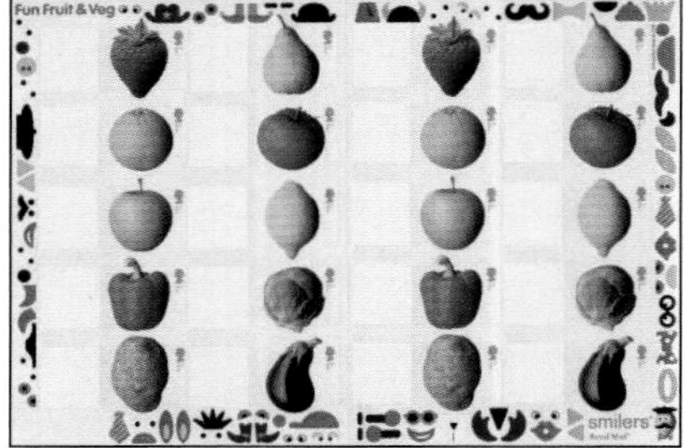

CS-029

Fun Fruit and Veg

2006 (7 Mar), Litho by Cartor, simulated die-cut perfs. 14½ . Initial selling price: £14.95

CS-029 .... £ 100.00

Issue Notes: 20 x 1st class Fun Fruit and Veg design stamps (SM30) + personalised labels set on background of face cut-outs which could be used with the stamps to further customise their appearance. . The borders are identical to that of the Generic sheet, except for the removal of the border design in the bottom left corner to provide a space for the customer order number—which was subsequently not applied to these sheets!!

Known Varieties: None

Publicity material: A Fun Fruit & Veg Smilers stamp is illustrated in both 62/PM/Feb06, 150/PM/May06 although there is no illustration of a full of partial Smilers sheet.

CS-030a

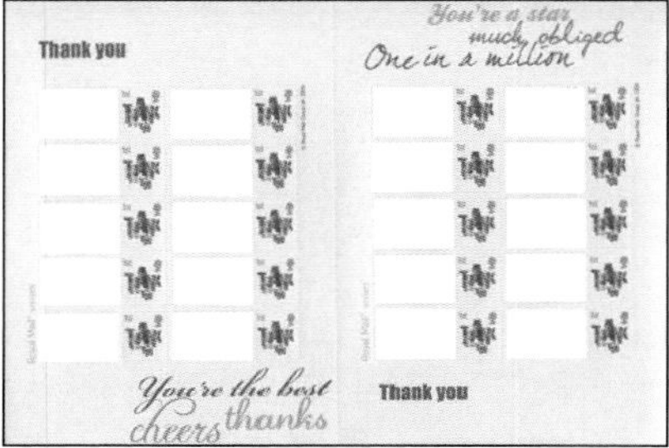

CS-030b

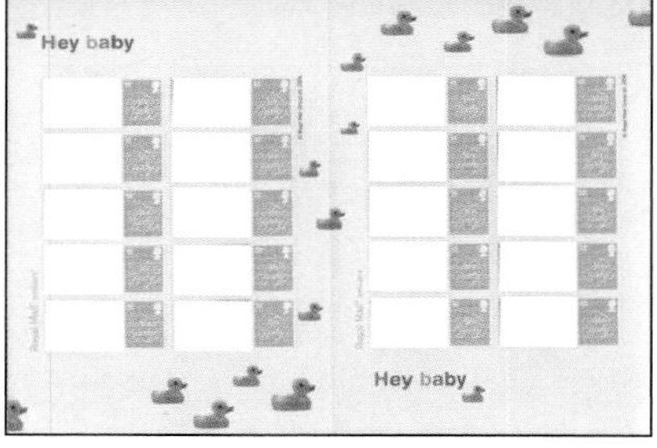

CS-030c

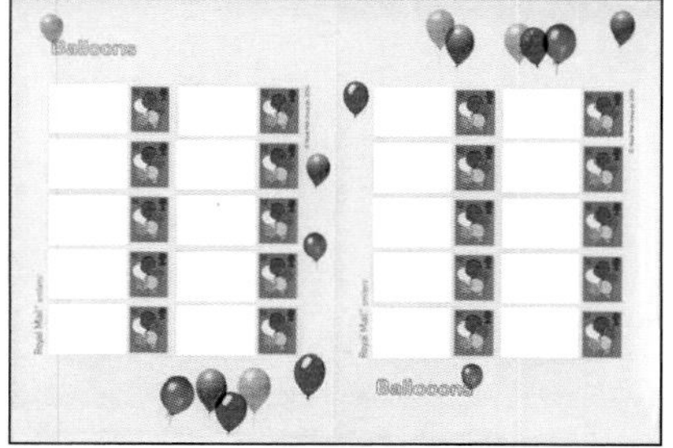

CS-030d

CS-030d - *"Ballooons"* instead of Balloons

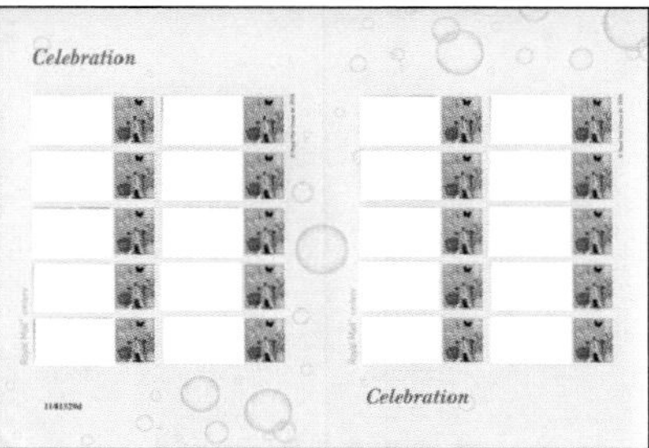

CS-030e

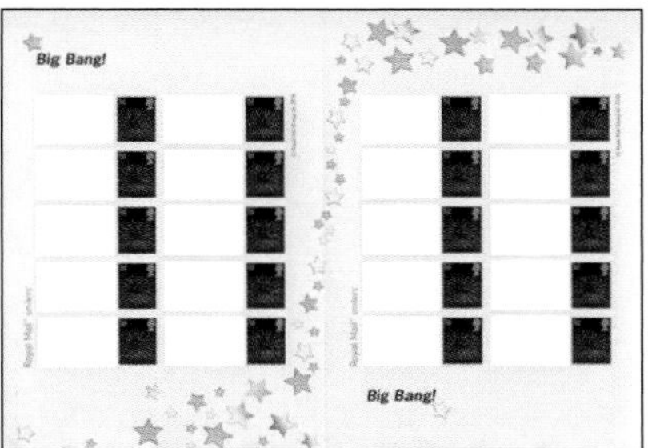

CS-030f

Extra Special Moments

2006 (17 Oct), Litho by Cartor, simulated die-cut perfs. 14½ . Initial selling price: £14.95

CS-030a	£ 30.00
CS-030b	£ 30.00
CS-030c	£ 30.00
CS-030d	£ 30.00
CS-030e	£ 30.00
CS-030f	£ 30.00

Issue Notes: 20 x 1st class definitive sized Smilers stamps (DS07 - DS12)) with corresponding border art and theme. This issue may be considered as the 2006 Occasions set with more than a passing resemblance to Customised Smilers sheets CS-026a to CS -026f, the new designs have one notable exception to their predecessors. Royal Mail appear to have "filled-in" most of the previously non-printed areas, presumably in an effort to thwart the over-printer's efforts in adding to the sheet design border detail.

CS30d has the word *balloons* misspelled in the right-hand panel.

Issued in six interesting and different sheet designs (CS-030a to CS-030f) as follows:

Best Wishes comprising 20 x 1st class BEST WISHES (DS07) set in a border design featuring butterflies (CS-030a), and

Thank You comprising 20 x 1st class THANK YOU (DS08) set in a border design featuring words of friendship and thanks (CS-030b) , and

Hey Baby featuring 20 x 1st class NEW BABY (DS09) set in a border design comprising rubber ducks (CS-030c), and

Balloons featuring 20 x 1st class BALLOONS (DS10) set in a border design comprising Balloons - note misspelling of *Ballooons* in lower left hand pane. (CS-030d), and

Celebration featuring 20 x 1st class CHAMPAGNE/ FLOWERS (DS11) set in a border design comprising Champagne bubbles (CS-030e), and

Big Bang featuring 20 x 1st class FIREWORKS (DS12) set in a border design exploding stars (CS-030f).

The sheets have been used extensively to publicise various national or international philatelic exhibitions and other events, since small orders (less than 100 sheets) can be placed, they offer a cheap alternative to the Business Customised sheets covered in Chapter 4. See also Chapter 5 for a listing of the commercially available Themed Customised Smilers sheets using these designs.

From early 2008 the sheets were available at a reduced retail price of £13.50 per sheet or £12.50 for two or more sheets. It was also possible to order a half sheet of 10 stamps + labels at a cost of £7.50 per sheet of 10 stamps. On request, Royal Mail at Tallants House would produce a non-separated sheet of 20 stamps with 2 panes of 10 stamps + labels with different images on each pane.

Known Varieties: None

Publicity material: 150/PM/ Sept06, RMJ046DL introduced the new definitive-size format stamps DS07-DS12, The new smilers stamps were also featured in Royal Mail Stamp Preview No. 153 (October 2006).

CS-031a

CS-031b

Christmas (2006)

2006 (7 Nov), Litho by Cartor, printed on self adhesive paper with simulated die-cut perfs 15 x 14. Initial selling price: 2nd Class - £9.95, 1st Class - £14.95

£14.95

CS-031a .... £ 30.00

CS-031b .... £ 30.00

Issue Notes: 20 x 2nd class (DS13) and 20 x 1st class (DS14). The borders are identical to that in the Generic, except for the inclusion of a white code box at bottom left.

Known Varieties: The sheets were reprinted in 2009 and the re-prints can be easily distinguished from the original printings, refer CS-041a and CS-041b, page 3-28.

Publicity material: A sheet of CS-031b is shown in Royal Mail smilers publicity leaflet 150/PM/Sept06, RMJ046DL.

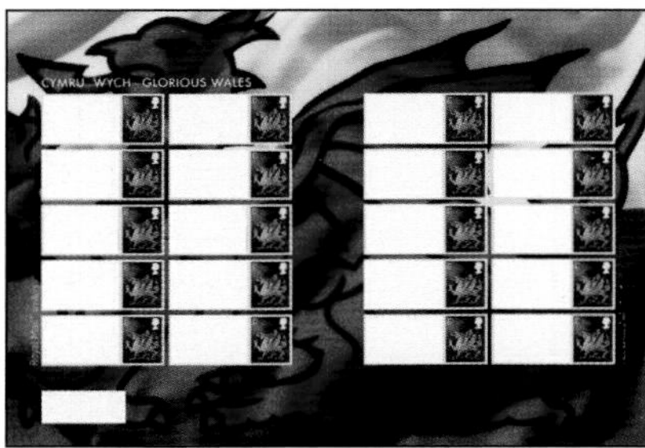

CS-032

Glorious Wales

2007 (1 Mar), Litho by Cartor, printed on self adhesive paper with simulated die-cut perfs 15 x 14. Initial selling price: £14.95

CS-032 .... £ 30.00

Issue Notes: 20 x 1st class Welsh definitive smilers stamp (DS15) set against a background of the Welsh flag, the background is identical to the Generic sheet, except for the inclusion of a white code box. This is first sheet in a series of four themed customised Smilers sheets to be issued by Royal Mail, with England, Scotland, and Northern Ireland yet to be released.

From early 2008 the sheets were available at a reduced retail price of £13.50 per sheet or £12.50 for two or more sheets. It was also possible to order a half sheet of 10 stamps + labels at a cost of £7.50 per sheet of 10 stamps. On request, Royal Mail at Tallants House would produce an non-separated sheet of 20 stamps with 2 panes of 10 stamps + labels with different images on each pane.

Known Varieties: None

Publicity material: None seen

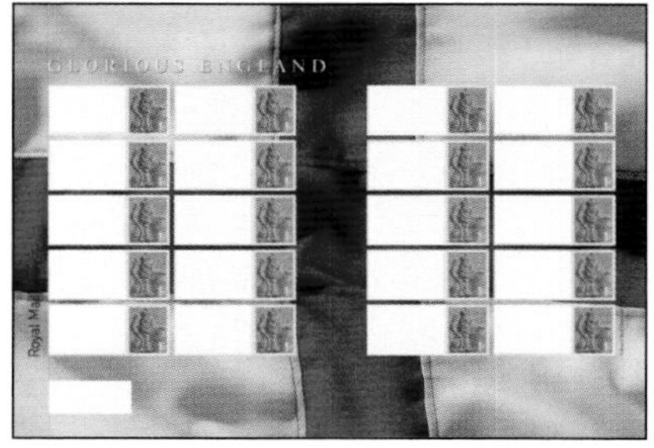

CS-033

Glorious England

2007 (23 Apr), Litho by Cartor, printed on self adhesive paper with simulated die-cut perfs 15 x 14. Initial selling price: £14.95

CS-033 .... £ 30.00

Issue Notes: 20 x 1st class English definitive smilers stamp (DS16) set against a background of the St. George Cross national flag of England, the background is identical to the Generic sheet, except for the inclusion of a white code box. This is second sheet in a series of four themed customised Smilers sheets to be issued by Royal Mail, with Scotland, and Northern Ireland yet to be released.

Known Varieties: None

Publicity material: None seen

From early 2008 the sheets were available at a reduced retail price of £13.50 per sheet or £12.50 for two or more sheets. It was also possible to order a half sheet of 10 stamps + labels at a cost of £7.50 per sheet of 10 stamps. On request, Royal Mail at Tallants House would produce a non-separated sheet of 20 stamps with 2 panes of 10 stamps + labels with different images on each pane.

CS-034

Harry Potter

2007 (17 Jul), Litho by Cartor, printed on self adhesive paper with simulated die-cut perfs 15 x 14
Initial selling price: £14.95

CS-034 .... £ 30.00

Issue Notes: 4 x 5 x 1st class Harry Potter definitive smilers stamp - there were five different designs (DS17) set against a background of a spell book and wand, the background is identical to the Generic sheet, except for the inclusion of a white code box and modified label in bottom right.

Known Varieties: RMJ101DL (May 2007)

Publicity material: None seen

From early 2008 the sheets were available at a reduced retail price of £13.50 per sheet or £12.50 for two or more sheets. It was also possible to order a half sheet of 10 stamps + labels at a cost of £7.50 per sheet of 10 stamps. On request, Royal Mail at Tallants House would produce a non-separated sheet of 20 stamps with 2 panes of 10 stamps + labels with different images on each pane.

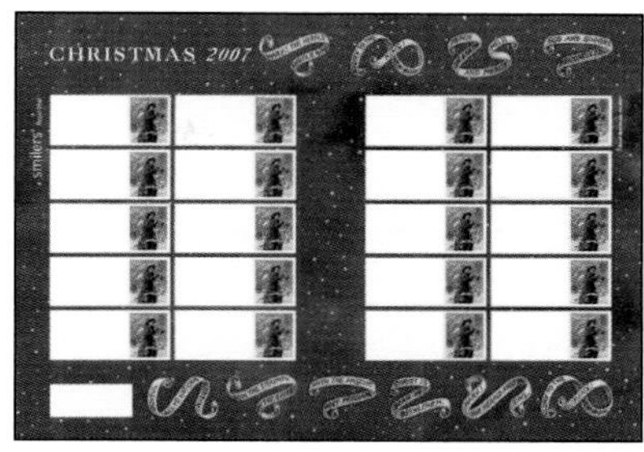

CS-035a

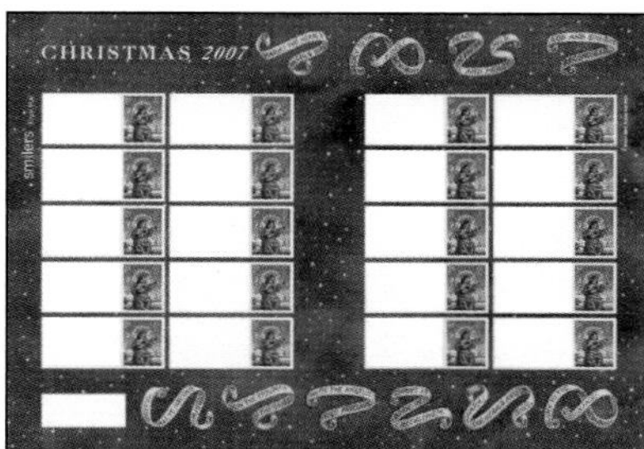

CS-035b

CS-035c

Christmas (2007)

2007 (6 Nov), Litho by Cartor, printed on self adhesive paper with simulated die-cut perfs 15 x 14
Initial selling price: 2nd class - £9.95, 1st class - £14.95, Overseas (76p) x 10 - £12.50

CS-035a .... £ 25.00

CS-035b .... £ 30.00

CS-035c 10 x 76p .... £ 25.00

CS-035c 20 x 76p (Illustrated) .... £ 50.00

Issue Notes: 20 x 2nd class (DS18) and 20 x 1st class (DS19) 10 x 76p (DS20) . The borders are significantly different to that of the Generic Christmas Smilers sheet (GS-044) which featured Angles with a background scene of a carols being sung in a village centre. The personalised sheets are on a relatively plain border with some elements of the generic sheet design transferred to the personalised sheets. The 76p stamps were supplied in sheets of 10 stamps/ labels but were also available upon special request in double sheets of 20 (i.e. two joined sheets of 10) and this explains the double white customer order box which appears on these sheets. The sheets were withdrawn in January 2008 but reappeared again in the run-up to Christmas 2008 and were made available alongside the 2006 and 2008 Christmas Smilers sheets. There are apparently no differences in the sheets issued in 2008 from those issued in 2007.

Known Varieties: None

Publicity material: RMJ117DL Oct 2007

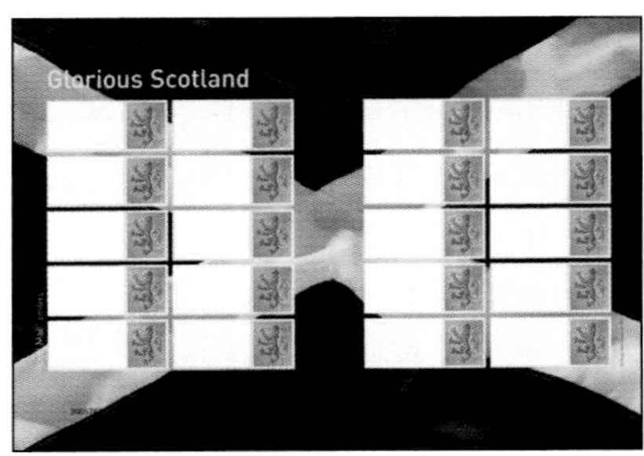

CS-036

Glorious Scotland

2007 (30 Nov), Litho by Cartor, printed on self adhesive paper with simulated die-cut perfs 15 x 14. Initial selling price: £14.95

CS-036 .... £ 30.00

Issue Notes: 20 x 1st class Scottish definitive smilers stamp (DS21) set against a background of the St. Andrew's Cross national flag of Scotland, the background is identical to the Generic sheet. In an unusual move by Royal Mail the normal white box in the lower left hand corner of the sheet was omitted in this design, the first time since the Christmas 2005 sheet. This is the third sheet in a planned series of four customised Smilers sheets featuring flags of the UK countries to be issued by Royal Mail, with Northern Ireland yet to be released.

Known Varieties: None

Publicity material: None seen

From early 2008 the sheets were available at a reduced retail price of £13.50 per sheet or £12.50 for two or more sheets. It was also possible to order a half sheet of 10 stamps + labels at a cost of £7.50 per sheet of 10 stamps. On request, Royal Mail at Tallants House would produce a non-separated sheet of 20 stamps with 2 panes of 10 stamps + labels with different images on each pane, see Appendix B - 3.

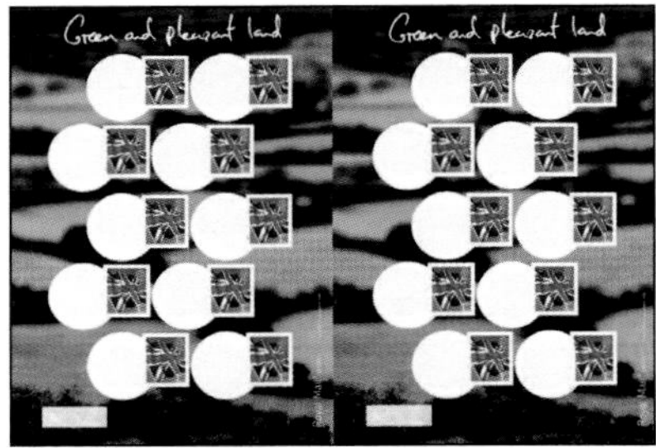

CS-037a

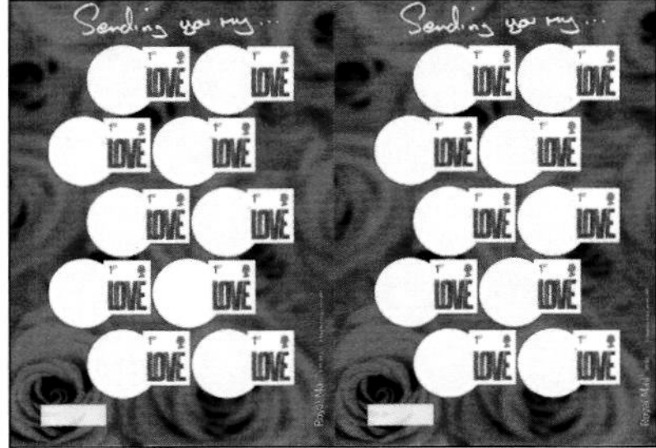

CS-037b

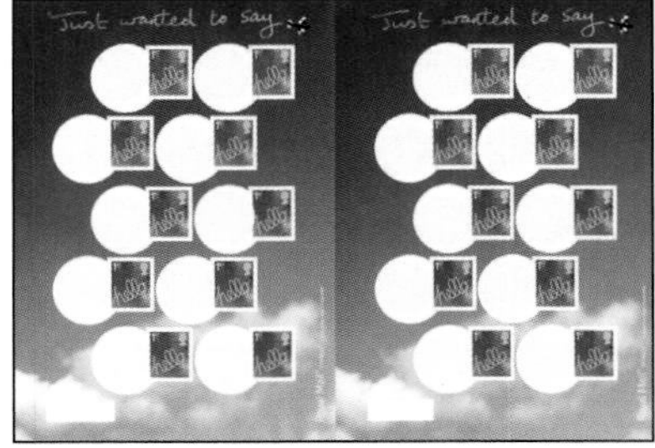

CS-037c

Customised

Greetings Smilers - "Circular" Labels

2008 (15 Jan), Litho by Cartor, printed on self adhesive paper with simulated die-cut perfs 15 x 14 with elliptical perfs. Initial selling price: £13.50 for sheet of 20 of £7.50 for sheet of 10

CS-037a - 20 x 1st Circular Labels .... £ 30.00

CS-037b - 20 x 1st Circular Labels .... £ 30.00

CS-037c - 20 x 1st Circular Labels .... £ 30.00

Issue Notes: 20 (or 10) x 1st class definitive-sized, self-adhesive, stamps of differing designs (DS01, DS02 and DS03), issued in three different colourful sheet designs (CS-037a to CS-037c).

The three customised, self-adhesive sheets released were as follows:

Green and pleasant land featuring 20 x 1st class UNION FLAG (DS01) set in a background of green fields, pastures and hedgerows. (CS-037a), and

Sending you my Love featuring 20 x 1st class LOVE (DS02) set in a border design of red roses (CS-037b) , and

Just wanted to say featuring 20 x 1st class HELLO (DS03) set in a border design comprising blue sky and clouds (CS-037c).

The sheet designs owe much to their earlier rectangular label counterparts issued in 2005 and were provided as an alternative to the rectangular labels, representing the three most popular stamp/sheet design combinations. It is likely they were influenced by the Smilers for Kids sheets which were to appear later that year as the sheet formats are identical.

In a break with the past the sheets were made available by Royal Mail at the reduced retail price of £13.50 per sheet of 20 stamps/labels or £12.50 for two or more sheets. They were also available in half sheets of 10 stamps/labels at the reduced price of £7.50 per sheet of 10 stamps. On request, Royal Mail at Tallants House would produce a non-separated sheet of 20 stamps with 2 panes of 10 stamps + labels with different images on each pane, priced £15.00.

This was the first time that these stamps had been made available by Royal Mail with elliptical perforations in sheet format.

Known Varieties: None

Publicity material: The "HELLO" stamp and circular label was featured in a RM Smilers-by-post publicity leaflet - RMP005 DL 08 (JLN)

CS-038

Glorious Northern Ireland

2007 (11 Mar), Litho by Cartor, printed on self adhesive paper with simulated die-cut perfs 15 x 14. Initial selling price: £13.50 for one sheet or £12.50 for two or more sheets.

CS-038 .... £ 30.00

Issue Notes: 20 x 1st class Northern Ireland definitive smilers stamp (DS22) set against a background image of the Devil's Causeway. In what looks to be an oversight on the part of Royal Mail, the series of Smilers sheets displaying the national flags of the UK was adapted for Northern Ireland to show the devil's causeway instead of the Ulster Banner, the national flag of Northern Ireland between 1953 and 1973 when it ceased to have official government sanction following the dissolution of the Parliament of Northern Ireland by the British government under the Northern Ireland Constitution Act 1973. The Northern Ireland Flag (Ulster Banner) is still used for some sporting events but is not officially sanctioned.

The white box omitted in the design of the Glorious Scotland sheet was reinstated for this issue.

The sheets were also available in half sheets of 10 stamps + labels at a cost of £7.50 per sheet of 10 stamps. On request, Royal Mail at Tallants House would produce a non-separated sheet of 20 stamps with 2 panes of 10 stamps + labels with different images on each pane, priced £15.00

See also sheets: CS-032, CS-033 and CS-036

Known Varieties: None

Publicity material: The Northern Ireland stamp was mentioned in a RM Smilers-by-post publicity leaflet - RMP005 DL 08 (JLN)

New Smilers Codes: *From October 2008 Royal Mail introduced a new "Smilers" code system, see Appendix B - 3. From hereon the new codes are used to refer to the stamp/sheet layout and formatting.*

CS-039a

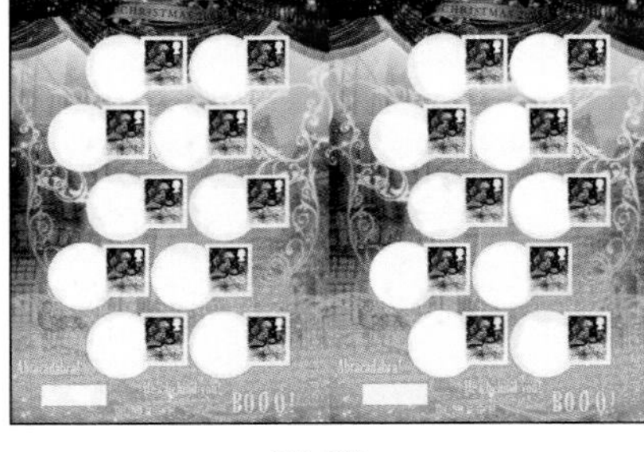

CS-039e

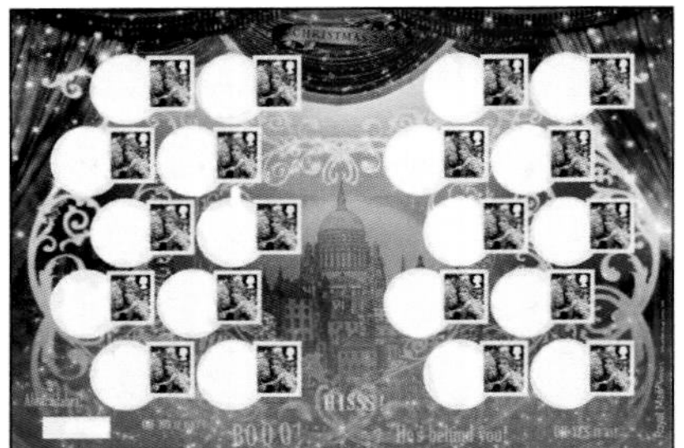

CS-039b

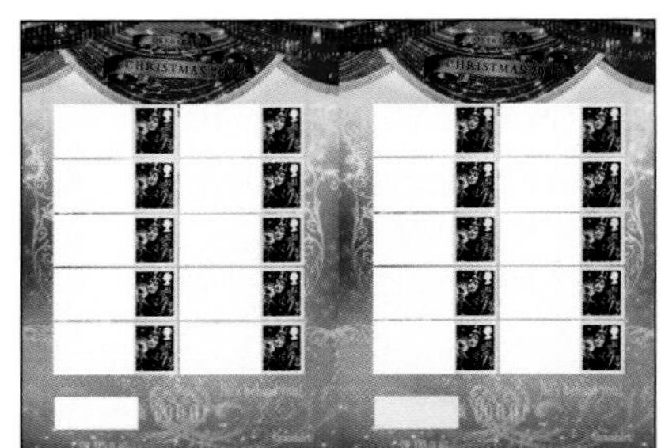

CS-039f

CS-039c

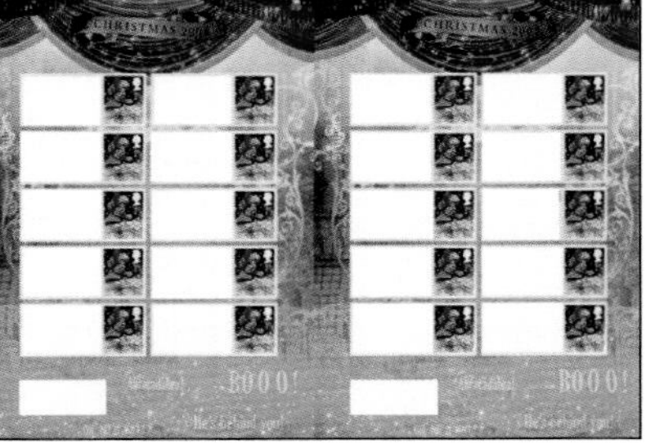

CS-039d

Christmas (2008)

2008 (4 Nov), Litho by Cartor, printed on self adhesive paper with simulated die-cut perfs 15 x 14
Initial selling price: 2nd Class - £8.50 for one sheet or £8.00 for two or more sheets; 1st Class - £13.50 for one sheet or £12.50 for two or more sheets; 81p x 10 - £13.50 for one sheet or £12.50 for two or more sheets.

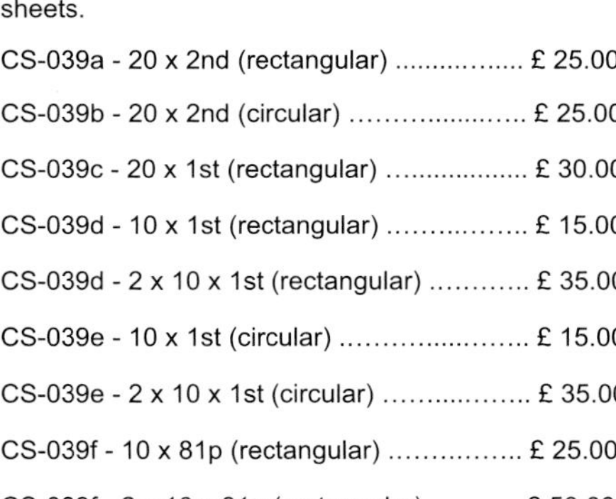

CS-039a - 20 x 2nd (rectangular) .... £ 25.00

CS-039b - 20 x 2nd (circular) .... £ 25.00

CS-039c - 20 x 1st (rectangular) .... £ 30.00

CS-039d - 10 x 1st (rectangular) .... £ 15.00

CS-039d - 2 x 10 x 1st (rectangular) .... £ 35.00

CS-039e - 10 x 1st (circular) .... £ 15.00

CS-039e - 2 x 10 x 1st (circular) .... £ 35.00

CS-039f - 10 x 81p (rectangular) .... £ 25.00

CS-039f - 2 x 10 x 81p (rectangular) .... £ 50.00

Issue Notes: 20 x 2nd class (Rectangular) RM Code SM45; 20 x 2nd class (Circular) RM Code SM46; 20 x 1st class (Rectangular) RM Code SM41; 20 x 1st class (Circular) RM Code SM42; 10 x 1st class

(Rectangular) RM Code SM43; 10 x 1st class (Circular) RM Code SM44; 10 x 76p) RM Code SM47.

The border designs of the customised sheets compliment the design of the generic pantomime smilers sheet and the sheet colours match those of the associated stamp designs. Three sheets (CS-039d, CS-039e and CS-039f) could be supplied as sheets of 10 stamps/labels and for this reason, the sheets of 20 had two white (customer) order reference boxes. The sheets were withdrawn in January 2009.

Whilst sheets CS-039d, CS-039e and CS-039f were intended to be supplied as either sheets of 10 or sheets of 20 with two images (one per pane) they were also available on request from Royal Mail at Tallants House in non-separated sheets of 20 stamps with 2 panes of 10 stamps using a single image at the same price as for sheets of 20. If dual images were used then they were supplied in un-separated sheets of 20 at twice the price of sheets of 10 stamps/images i.e. £15.00 (2 x 10 x 1st) or £25.00 (2 x 10 x 81p)

Known Varieties: None

Publicity material: RM publicity leaflet RM116-09 (JAB)

CS-040a

CS-040b

CS-040c

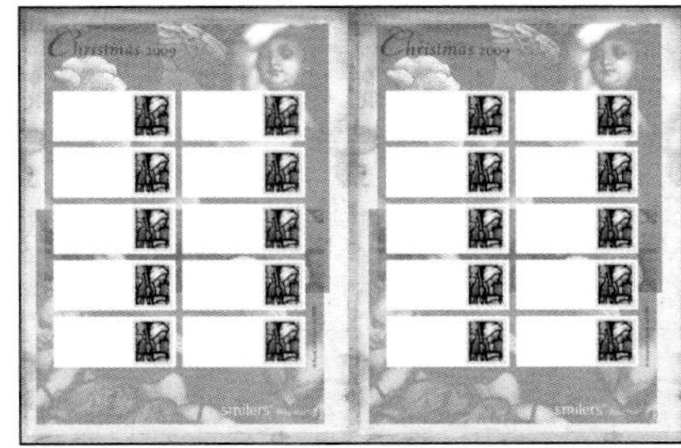

CS-040d

Christmas 2009

2009 (3 Nov), Litho by Cartor, printed on self adhesive paper with simulated die-cut perfs 15 x 14
Initial selling price: 2nd Class - £8.50 for one sheet or £8.00 for two or more sheets; 1st Class - £13.50 for one sheet or £12.50 for two or more sheets; 56p x 10 - £9.50 for one sheet or £8.50 for two or more sheets. 90p x 10 - £13.50 for one sheet or £12.50 for two or more sheets.

CS-040a - 20 x 2nd .... £ 25.00

CS-040b - 10 x 1st .... £ 15.00

CS-040b - 2 x 10 x 1st .... £ 30.00

CS-040c - 10 x 56p .... £ 15.00

CS-040c - 2 x 10 x 56p .... £ 35.00

CS-040d - 10 x 90p .... £ 25.00

CS-040d - 2 x 10 x 90p .... £ 50.00

Issue Notes: 20 x 1st class RM Code SM54; 10 x 1st class RM Code SM55; 20 x 2nd class RM Code SM56; 10 x 56p class RM Code SM57; 10 x 90p RM Code SM58. The subtle border designs of the customised sheets compliment the religious themes of the stamps and generic sheet design. Three sheets (CS-040b, CS-040c and CS-040d) could be ordered/

Customised

supplied as sheets of 10 stamps/labels. They could also be ordered/supplied as sheets of 20 with two images (one per pane). Additionally, upon special request to Royal Mail at Tallants House, they were available also in non-separated sheets of 20 stamps with 2 panes of 10 stamps using a single image, supplied at the same price as for sheets of 20. If dual images were used then they were supplied in un-separated sheets of 20 at twice the price of sheets of 10 stamps/images i.e. £15.00 (2 x 10 x 1st), £19.00 (2 x 10 x 56p) or £27.00 (2 x 10 x 90p). The sheets were withdrawn in January 2010.

Known Varieties: None

Publicity material: RMX20-10 JAB (Oct 09)

CS-041a

CS-041b

Christmas 2009 (Secular)

2009 (3 Nov), Litho by Cartor, printed on self adhesive paper with simulated die-cut perfs 15 x 14
Initial selling price: 2nd Class - £8.50 for one sheet or £8.00 for two or more sheets; 1st Class - £13.50 for one sheet or £12.50 for two or more sheets.

CS-041a - 20 x 2nd .... £ 25.00

CS-041b - 10 x 1st .... £ 15.00

CS-041b - 2 x 10 x 1st .... £ 30.00

Issue Notes: 20 x 1st class RM Code SM51; 10 x 1st class RM Code SM52; 20 x 2nd class RM Code SM53. The 2006 Christmas sheets were re-issued in 2009 to provide an alternative (secular) choice for Royal Mail customers. The 2006 sheets were also available in 2007 and 2008 in their original formats, but the sheets issued in 2009 were re-printed and differed from the original 2006 issue in four subtle areas.

A) The sheets are renamed “Christmas” instead of “Christmas 2006”,

B) The White box in the lower left hand corner has been omitted ,

C) The perforations now contain two elliptical perforations one either side, and

D) The © statement has been changed from © Royal Mail Group plc, to © Royal Mail Group Ltd.

Known Varieties: None

Publicity material: RMX20-10 JAB (Oct 09)

CS-042a

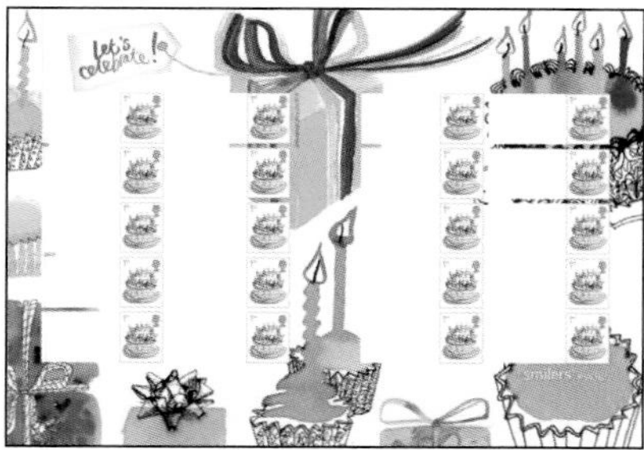

CS-042b

CS-042c

CS-042c

Customised

For All Occasions

2010 (27 Jan), Litho by Cartor, printed on self adhesive paper with simulated die-cut perfs 15 x 14
Initial selling price: 1st Class - £13.50 for one sheet or £12.50 for two or more sheets; European Letter Rate 20g (56p) x 20 - £19.00 for one sheet or £17.00 for two or more sheets. Worldwide Letter Rate 20g (90p) x 20 - £27.00 for one sheet or £25.00 for two or more sheets.

CS-042a .... £ 30.00

CS-042b .... £ 30.00

CS-042c .... £ 35.00

CS-042d .... £ 50.00

Issue Notes: 20 x 1st class "Presents" RM Code SM59; 20 x 1st class "Birthday Cake" RM Code SM60; 20 x Europe Letter Rate (20g) RM Code SM61; 20 x Worldwide Letter Rate (20g) RM Code SM62. The border designs of the customised sheets compliment the theme of each sheet and supplement the existing smilers stamps (see Appendix C).

Publicity material: Featured in RMSMIL01-0JBB (Jan 2010)

Chapter 4 - Business Customised Sheets

Business Customised Sheets

Business Customised Sheets are similar to the Generic stamp sheets, in that they comprise stamps and labels set in a decorative broader and contain the same Royal Mail stamps, but the borders and labels are designed by commercial organisations to promote a theme or commercial message. Generally these sheets are produced in much smaller quantities than the Generic stamp sheets and are sold to the sheet producer by Royal Mail at a premium over face value of the stamps in the sheet, depending upon the quantity of sheets ordered.

When first introduced, Royal Mail's production costs ranged from £3.70 a sheet of 10 x 1st class, i.e. £1 above face value for orders greater than 6000 sheets, to £9.00 a sheet of 10 x 1st class for orders of between 500-999 sheets, 500 sheets being (the then) minimum order. Additional options associated with the printing process, e.g. additional colours, unique sheet numbering etc., were also available at additional cost.

With the introduction of self-adhesive Smilers sheets in 2006, a two-tier pricing structure has existed, introduced in 2007, for both gummed and self-adhesive sheets. From 2007 Royal Mail relaxed the minimum print-run of these sheets from 500 to 100. Prices for gummed sheets range between £17.50 a sheet for the minimum order of 100 sheets to £4.25 a sheet for 6000 or more sheets. For self-adhesive sheets the price starts at £24.50 a sheet for orders in the range 100-199 and decrease to £4.50 a sheet for orders of 6000 sheets or more.

Sheet BC-099 is perhaps the first example of a low-print run business sheets ordered by a customer who only required 100 sheets to be printed.

The First Business Customised Sheet - Eagle Coaches

BC-001

Eagle Coaches 75th Anniversary

2001 (?? Dec), Photo by Questa, Perf 14½ x 14,

Initial selling price: Not sold to public

BC-001 .... £ 1750.00

Produced by: Royal Mail **Qty:** unknown

Issue Notes: 10 x 1st class *Cartoons* stamps plus photo labels set in a decorative border celebrating the 75th Anniversary of Bristol Coaches. Believed to be the first example of a Business Customised stamp sheet. Produced with the help of Royal Mail who are thought to have targeted an unknown number of small businesses in an effort to promote the Business Customised sheet concept. It seems that the majority of sheets were broken up and used on promotional postage. A few (c. 5-10) pairs of these sheets (see BC-002) are thought to have survived. They are keenly fought over when the do come up for sale/ auction with the last pair sold realising a whopping £3,500 a pair.

BC-002

Eagle Coaches 75th Anniversary

2001 (?? Dec), Photo by Questa, Perf 14½ x 14,

Initial selling price: Not sold to public

BC-002 .... £ 1750.00

Produced by: Royal Mail **Qty:** unknown

Issue Notes: 10 x 1st class *Occasions Hallmarks "Cheers"* stamps plus photo labels set in a decorative border celebrating the 75th Anniversary of Bristol Coaches. See BC-002 for further details.

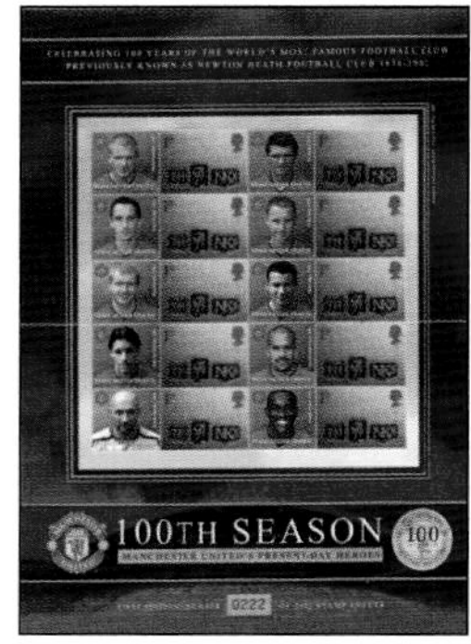

BC-003

Man United—100th Season

2002 (19 Feb), Litho by Questa, Perf 14½ x 14,

Initial selling price: £21.95

BC-003 .... £ 65.00

Produced by: Benham Covers **Qty:** 2002

Issue Notes: 10 x 1st class *Occasions Hallmarks "Thanks"* stamps plus labels marking Manchester United's 100th season. Generally recognised as the first Business Customised sheet. Many sheets were broken up and used on commercial covers, most dated 6th March 2002. Becoming difficult to find.

BC-004

Man United - Heroes 2002/2003

2002 (19 Feb), Litho by Questa, Perf 14½ x 14,

Initial selling price: £21.95.

BC-004 .... £ 30.00

Produced by: Benham Covers **Qty:** 5000

Issue Notes: 10 x 1st class *Occasions Hallmarks* stamps plus photo labels featuring Man Utd's 2002/2003 first team squad. Some sheets were broken up and used on philatelic covers.

BC-006

Liverpool - Heroes 2002/2003

2002 (19 Feb), Litho by Questa, Perf 14½ x 14,

Initial selling price: £21.95.

BC-006 .... £ 30.00

Produced by: Benham Covers **Qty:** 5000

Issue Notes: 10 x 1st class *Occasions Hallmarks "Thanks"* stamps plus photo labels featuring Liverpool's 2002/2003 season first team squad. Many sheets were broken up and used on philatelic covers.

BC-005

Arsenal - Heroes 2002/2003

2002 (19 Feb), Litho by Questa, Perf 14½ x 14,

Initial selling price: £21.95.

BC-005 .... £ 30.00

Produced by: Benham Covers **Qty:** 2002

Issue Notes: 10 x 1st class *Occasions Hallmarks "Thanks"* stamps plus photo labels featuring Arsenal's 2002/2003 first team squad. Many sheets were broken up and used on philatelic covers.

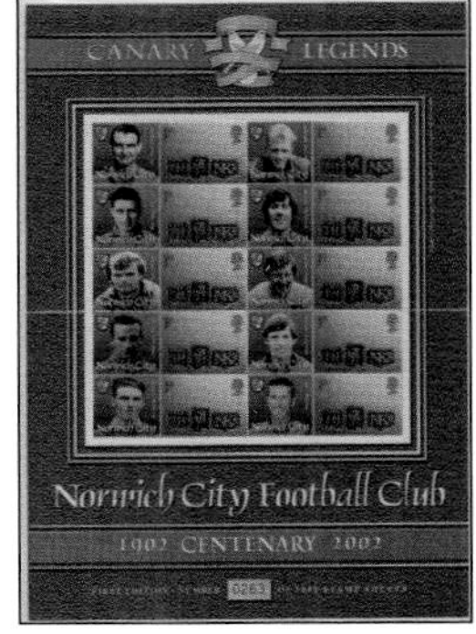

BC-007

Norwich City—100th Anniversary

2002 (19 Feb), Litho by Questa, Perf 14½ x 14,

Initial selling price: £21.95.

BC-007 .... £ 30.00

Produced by: Benham Covers **Qty:** 2002

Issue Notes: 10 x 1st class *Occasions Hallmarks "Thanks"* stamps plus photo labels featuring Norwich City players past and present and commemorating the centenary of Norwich Football Club.

BC-008

Rangers Hall of Fame

2002 (19 Feb), Litho by Questa, Perf 14½ x 14,

Initial selling price: £21.95.

BC-008 .... £ 30.00

Produced by: Benham Covers **Qty:** 1000

Issue Notes: 10 x 1st class *Occasions Hallmarks "Thanks"* stamps plus photo labels featuring Rangers players past and present.

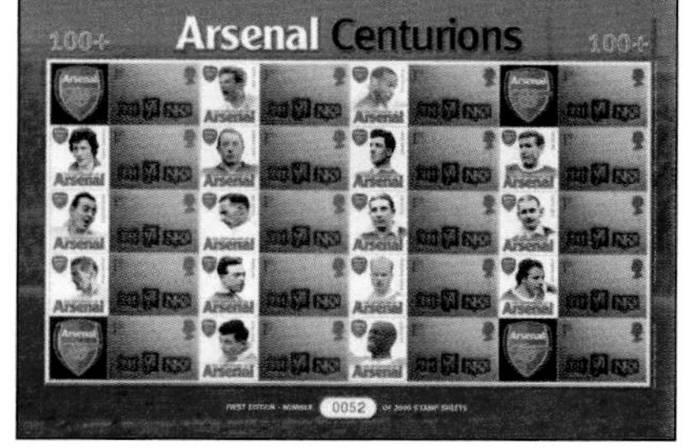

BC-009

Arsenal Centurions

2002 (19 Feb), Litho by De La Rue, Perf 14½ x 14,

Initial selling price: £22.95.

BC-009 .... £ 30.00

Produced by: Benham Covers **Qty:** 2000

Issue Notes: 20 x 1st class *Occasions Hallmarks "Thanks"* stamps plus photo labels featuring Arsenal players past and present. The First horizontal-format business sheet (20 x 1st) produced. It was marketed directly by Benham and sold indirectly through a number of other retail outlets (Rushstamps, Mark Sargent). It retailed at similar pricing to the previous 10 x 1st class sheets despite its higher production costs.

BC-010

Stampex - Spring 2003

2003 (26 Feb), Litho by Questa (DLR), Perf 14½ x 14,

Initial selling price: £21.95.

BC-010 .... £ 15.00

Produced by: PTS **Qty:** 3100

Issue Notes: 10 x 1st class *Occasions "Hello"* stamps plus labels. Issued to celebrate the 50th Anniversary of the STAMPEX event held by the Philatelic Traders Society, a specially commissioned Business Customised Sheet was sold to the public at the show. A total of 3100 sheets were printed but the first 7500 visitors to the show each received a STAMPEX programme which contained a single stamp from this sheet free of charge, additional singles were available at £1. It is understood after breaking up these sheets some 2250 whole sheets remained for sale.

BC-011

Stampex - Autumn 2003

2003 (17 Sep), Litho by Walsall, Perf 14½ x 14,

Initial selling price: £9.00.

BC-011 .... £ 25.00

Produced by: PTS **Qty:** 3500

Issue Notes: 10 x 1st class *Occasions "Teddy Bear"* stamps plus labels. The 2003 Autumn Stampex sheet celebrated the 50th Anniversary of STAMPEX . Visitors to the event could purchase a complete stamp sheet at the reception desk and the first 7500 visitors to the show each received a single stamp with the free STAMPEX programme, additional singles were available at £1. It is understood after breaking up these sheets all 2912 remaining sheets were sold on the first day of the show.

BC-012

Rushstamps 45th Anniversary (1)

2003 (Sep), Litho by Walsall, Perf 14½ x 14,

Initial selling price: £8.50.

BC-012 .... £ 20.00

Produced by: Rushstamps **Qty:** 1500

Issue Notes: 10 x 1st class *Occasions "Flowers"* stamps plus labels. Many of these sheets were broken up and used in mail shots to existing customers. In the stamps at left (Gentiana acaulis) the lower left petal is separated from the background by a small white triangular (unscreened) area; in the Generic version and first Customised printing this is screened in black. See page 3-12 for further details of this smilers variety.

BC-013

Spurs Hall of Fame

2003 (3 Oct), Litho by De La Rue, Perf 14½ x 14,

Initial selling price: £21.95.

BC-013 .... £ 30.00

Produced by: Benham/Victory Cards **Qty:** 2000

Issue Notes: 10 x 1st class *Occasions Hallmarks "Thanks"* stamps plus labels featuring Spurs players past and present.

BC-014

Man City - Maine Road Greats

2003 (3 Oct), Litho by De La Rue, Perf 14½ x 14,

Initial selling price: £21.95.

BC-014 .... £ 30.00

Produced by: Benham/Victory Cards **Qty:** 2003

Issue Notes: 10 x 1st class *Occasions Hallmarks "Thanks"* stamps plus labels featuring Man City players past and present.

Business

BC-015

England Rugby Heroes 2003

2003 (10 Oct), Litho by Walsall, Perf 14½ x 14,

Initial selling price: £29.95.

BC-015 .... £ 50.00

Produced by: Benham Covers **Qty:** 2003

Issue Notes: 10 x 1st class *Occasions Hallmarks "Thanks"* stamps plus labels celebrating England's participation in the Rugby World Championship. At least 250 whole sheets were used for First Day Covers prepared by Benham Covers.

BC-016

Rugby World Champions 2003

2003 (8 Dec), Litho by Walsall, Perf 14½ x 14,

Initial selling price: £39.95.

BC-016 .... £ 70.00

Produced by: Benham Covers **Qty:** 2003

Issue Notes: 10 x 1st class *Occasions Hallmarks "Thanks"* stamps plus labels celebrating England's victory at the Rugby World Championship. Similar to BC-014 but with additional detail in all four corners. At least 350 whole sheets were used for First Day Covers prepared by Benham Covers.

BC-017

Rushstamps 45th Anniversary (2)

2003 (Dec), Litho by Walsall, Perf 14½ x 14,

Initial selling price: £8.50.

BC-017 .... £ 20.00

Produced by: Rushstamps **Qty:** 1000

Issue Notes: 10 x 1st class *Occasions Hallmarks "Cheers" and "Thanks"* stamps plus labels. Second issue celebrating Rushstamps 45th anniversary.

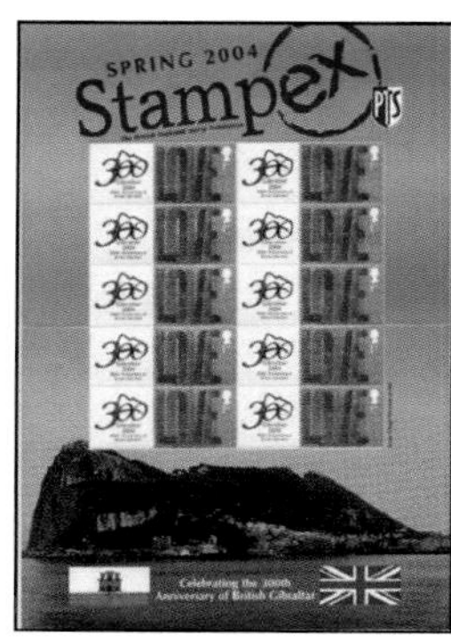

BC-018

Stampex - Spring 2004

2004 (25 Feb), Litho by Walsall, Perf 14½ x 14,

Initial selling price: £9.00

BC-018 .... £ 15.00

Produced by: PTS **Qty:** 3500

Issue Notes: 10 x 1st class *Occasions "Love"* stamps plus labels. The sheet celebrated the 300th Anniversary of British Gibraltar. Visitors to the event could purchase a complete sheet at the reception desk and the first 7500 visitors to the show each received a single stamp with the free official programme, additional singles were available at £1. It is understood after breaking up these sheets 2791 whole sheets remained.

BC-019

Collect British Stamps (1)

2004 (Mar), Litho by Walsall, Perf 14½ x 14,

Initial selling price: £9.00

BC-019 .... £ 15.00

Produced by: Rushstamps **Qty:** 1500

Issue Notes: 10 x 1st class *Occasions "Entertaining Envelopes"* stamps plus labels. The first sheet in a series of three sheets produced by stamp dealers Rushstamps.

BC-020

Collect British Stamps (2)

2004 (Mar), Litho by Walsall, Perf 14½ x 14,

Initial selling price: £9.00

BC-020 .... £ 15.00

Produced by: Rushstamps **Qty:** 1500

Issue Notes: 10 x 1st class *Occasions "Entertaining Envelopes"* stamps plus labels. The second sheet in a series of three sheets produced by stamp dealers Rushstamps.

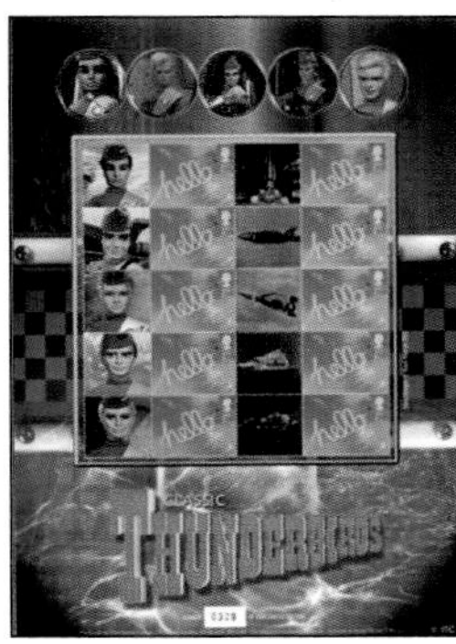

BC-021

Thunderbirds

2004 (Apr), Litho by Walsall, Perf 14½ x 14,

Initial selling price: £14.95

BC-021 .... £ 25.00

Produced by: The Stamp Centre **Qty:** 2500

Issue Notes: 10 x 1st class *Occasions "Hello"* stamps plus labels. The first sheet from Steven Scott/The Stamp Centres in what was to become a long line of TV/Sci-Fi based Business Customised Sheets. Primarily produced to service their range of sci-fi covers, The Stamp Centre soon realised that the sheets were as popular as their covers.

BC-022

England Rugby - Heroes of the Final (1)

2004 (1 Jun), Litho by Walsall, Perf 14½ x 14,

Initial selling price: £14.95

BC-022 .... £ 25.00

Produced by: Benham/Victory Cards **Qty:** 2003

Issue Notes: 10 x 1st class *Occasions Hallmarks "Cheers"* stamps plus photo labels. Benham's second business sheet series commemorating England's Rugby World Cup triumph.

BC-023

England Rugby - Heroes of the Final (2)

2004 (1 Jun), Litho by Walsall, Perf 14½ x 14,

Initial selling price: £14.95

BC-023 .... £ 25.00

Produced by: Benham/Victory Cards **Qty:** 2003

Issue Notes: 10 x 1st class *Occasions Hallmarks "Cheers"* stamps plus photo labels. Benham's second business sheet series commemorating England's Rugby World Cup triumph.

BC-024

60th Anniversary of D-Day Landings

2004 (6 Jun), Litho by Cartor, Perf 14½ x 14,

Initial selling price: £17.95

BC-024 .... £ 125.00

Produced by: Westminster Collection **Qty:** Unknown

Issue Notes: 10 x 1st class Flags "Union Flag" stamps plus photo labels. The stamps/labels were service a range of smilers covers on the 60th Anniversary of the D-Day landings. Twenty-four covers were produced, some of which featured this stamp/label combination. Other covers showed different label designs (e..g. Tank) which may indicate other sheets with different label designs were produced.

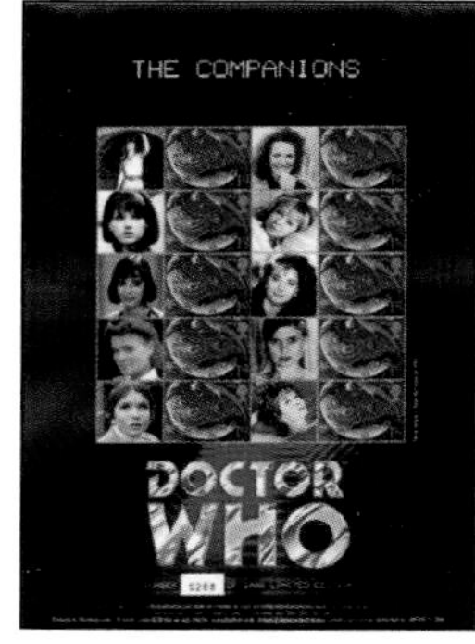

BC-025

Dr. Who - The Companions

2004 (1 Jul), Litho by Walsall, Perf 14½ x 14,

Initial selling price: £ 24.95

BC-025 .... £ 30.00

Produced by: The Stamp Centre **Qty:** 1000

Issue Notes: 10 x 1st class *Smiles "Moon"* stamps plus labels. The first in a series of science fiction Customised stamp sheets produced by The Stamp Centre, to service cover collectibles by Steven Scott Covers. These sheets were produced in batches of 500 and it is by no means certain that 1000 sheets were produced. The majority of sheets were broken up to service collections of themed covers to which the public could subscribe.

BC-026

Dr. Who - The Companions 2

2004 (1 Jul), Litho by Walsall, Perf 14½ x 14,

Initial selling price: £ 24.95

BC-026 .... £ 30.00

Produced by: The Stamp Centre **Qty:** 1000

Issue Notes: 10 x 1st class *Smiles "Moon"* stamps plus labels. The first in a series of science fiction Customised stamp sheets produced by The Stamp Centre, to service cover collectibles by Steven Scott Covers. These sheets were produced in batches of 500 and it is by no means certain that 1000 sheets were produced. The majority of sheets were broken up to service collections of themed covers to which the public could subscribe.

BC-027

Dr. Who - The Daleks

2004 (1 Jul), Litho by Walsall, Perf 14½ x 14,

Initial selling price: £ 24.95

BC-027 .... £ 30.00

Produced by: The Stamp Centre **Qty:** 2000

Issue Notes: 10 x 1st class *Smiles "Moon"* stamps plus labels. The third business sheet in the Dr. Who series and the second to feature the orange coloured value tablet (1st) variety (see BC-026). Sheet indicates 1000 were printed but we understand 2000 of this sheet were printed. Some of the Business Customised sheets are printed in batches of 500 and depending on demand further re-prints are ordered as required so it is by no means certain that the stated number of sheets exist.

BC-028

Dr. Who - The 4th Doctor

2004 (1 Jul), Litho by Walsall, Perf 14½ x 14,

Initial selling price: £ 24.95

BC-028 .... £ 40.00

Produced by: The Stamp Centre **Qty:** 1000

Issue Notes: 10 x 1st class *Smiles "Moon"* stamps plus labels. The fourth in the Dr. Who series and the third to feature the orange coloured value tablet (1st) variety (see BC-026).

BC-029

Collect British Stamps (3)

2004 (Aug), Litho by Walsall, Perf 14½ x 14,

Initial selling price: £ 14.95

BC-029 .... £ 17.50

Produced by: Rushstamps **Qty:** 1000

Issue Notes: 10 x 1st class *Smiles.* This is the final sheet in a series of three Business Customised stamp sheets produced by Rushstamps (see BC-019 and BC-020.

BC-030

Spiderman

2004 (15 Aug), Litho by Walsall, Perf 14½ x 14,

Initial selling price: £ 17.95

BC-030 .... £ 17.95

Produced by: Benham **Qty:** 2500

Issue Notes: 10 x 1st class *Occasions Hallmarks "Cheers"* stamps plus labels. Sheet still available from producers at guide price.

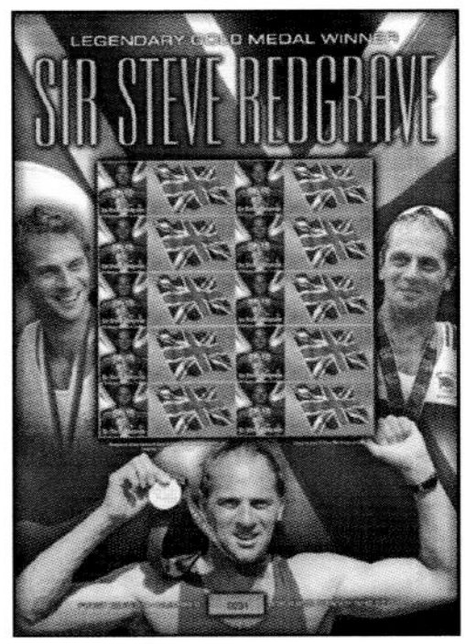

BC-031

Sir Steve Redgrave

2004 (29 Aug), Litho by Walsall, Perf 14½ x 14,

Initial selling price: £ 17.95

BC-031 .... £ 17.95

Produced by: Benham Covers **Qty:** 4950

Issue Notes: 10 x 1st class *Flags "Union Flag"* stamps plus labels. Sheet still available from producers at guide price.

BC-032

Gold Medal Winners

2004 (29 Aug), Litho by Walsall, Perf 14½ x 14,

Initial selling price: £ 17.95

BC-032 .... £ 17.95

Produced by: Benham Covers **Qty:** 4950

Issue Notes: 10 x 1st class *Flags "Union Flag"* stamps plus labels. Sheet still available from producers at guide price.

BC-033

X-Men United

2004 (1 Sep), Litho by Walsall, Perf 14½ x 14,

Initial selling price: £ 17.95

BC-033 .... £ 21.95

Produced by: Benham Covers **Qty:** 2500

Issue Notes: 10 x 1st class *Occasions Hallmarks "Welcome" (7) and "Thanks" (3)* stamps plus labels. Sheet still available from producers at guide price.

BC-034

Elvis Movies (1956-1961)

2004 (1 Sep), Litho by Walsall, Perf 14½ x 14,

Initial selling price: £ 17.95

BC-034 .... £ 17.95

Produced by: Benham Covers **Qty:** 2500

Issue Notes: 10 x 1st class *Occasions "Love"* stamps plus labels. Part of a set of four sheets issued by the producer as part of an Elvis Movies collection. Although noted as 2500 sheets printed, as many as half were broken up to service a collection of 32 covers "Elvis Movie Collection". Each cover bore a single stamp and label depicting one of 32 movies featured on the four stamp sheets produced and each cover bore a special "Rock and Roll" hand-stamp. As a result, it is estimated that less than 1250 whole sheets exist. Sheet still available from producers at Guide price.

BC-035

Elvis Movies (1962-1964)

2004 (1 Sep), Litho by Walsall, Perf 14½ x 14,

Initial selling price: £ 17.95

BC-035 .... £ 17.95

Produced by: Benham Covers **Qty:** 2500

Issue Notes: 10 x 1st class *Occasions "Love"* stamps plus labels. Sheet still available from producers at guide price. See BC-034 for additional notes.

BC-036

Elvis Movies (1965-1967)

2004 (1 Sep), Litho by Walsall, Perf 14½ x 14,

Initial selling price: £ 17.95

BC-036 .... £ 17.95

Produced by: Benham Covers **Qty:** 2500

Issue Notes: 10 x 1st class *Occasions "Love"* stamps plus labels. Sheet still available from producers at guide price. See BC-034 for additional notes.

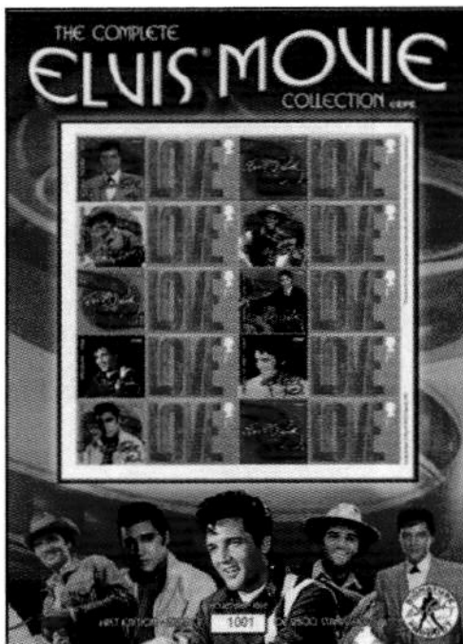

BC-037

Elvis Movies (1967-1969)

2004 (1 Sep), Litho by Walsall, Perf 14½ x 14,

Initial selling price: £ 17.95

BC-037 .... £ 17.95

Produced by: Benham Covers **Qty:** 2500

Issue Notes: 10 x 1st class *Occasions "Love"* stamps plus labels. Sheet still available from producers at guide price. See BC-034 for additional notes.

BC-038

Jordan F1

2004 (12 Sep), Litho by Walsall, Perf 14½ x 14,

Initial selling price: £ 17.95

BC-038 .... £ 17.95

Produced by: Benham Covers **Qty:** 950

Issue Notes: 10 x 1st class *Occasions Hallmarks "Cheers"* stamps plus labels. Sheet still available from producers at guide price.

BC-039

STAMPEX - Autumn 2004

2004 (15 Sep), Litho by Walsall, Perf 14½ x 14,

Initial selling price: £ 9.00

BC-039 .... £ 12.50

Produced by: PTS **Qty:** 3000

Issue Notes: 10 x 1st class *Flags "Union Flag"* stamps plus labels. A fourth business stamp sheet released by the Philatelic Traders Society to coincide with the Autumn STAMPEX event held in London celebrated the British Philatelic Competitions. Visitors to the event could purchase a complete stamp sheet at the reception desk and each visitor to the show received a single stamp with the free official programme, additional singles were available at £1. It is understood after breaking up these sheets 1825 whole sheets remained.

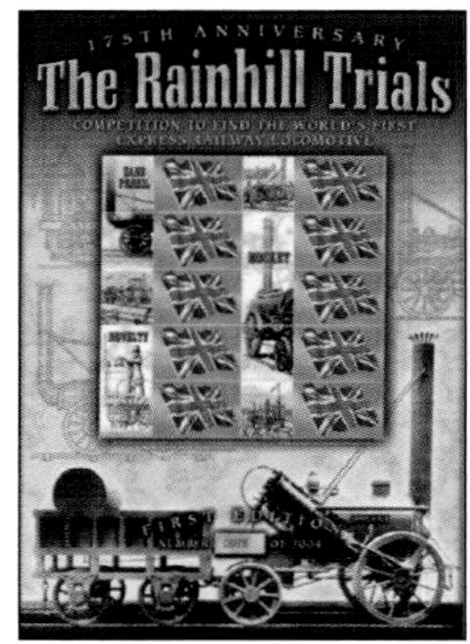

BC-040

17th Anniversary of The Rainhill Trials

2004 (6 Oct), Litho by Walsall, Perf 14½ x 14,

Initial selling price: £ 17.95

BC-040 .... £ 25.00

Produced by: Benham Covers **Qty:** 2004

Issue Notes: 10 x 1st class *Flags "Union Flag"* stamps plus labels. Also available from Benham was a set of commemorative covers bearing a single stamp/label from this sheet with special hand-stamp.

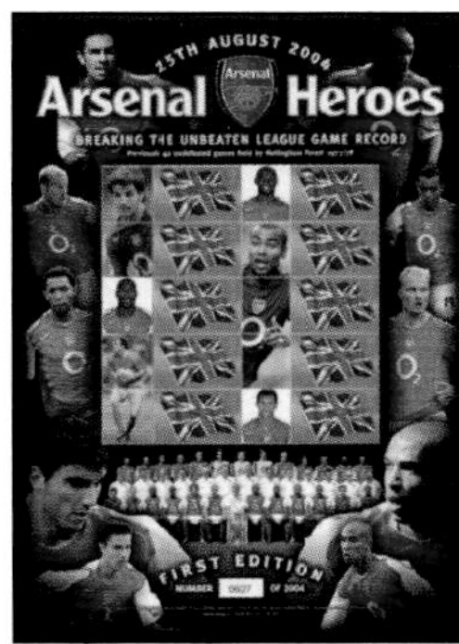

BC-041

Arsenal Heroes 04/05 Squad

2004 (14 Oct), Litho by Walsall, Perf 14½ x 14,

Initial selling price: £ 17.95

BC-041 .... £ 21.95

Produced by: Victory Cards/Benham **Qty:** 2004

Issue Notes: 10 x 1st class *Flags "Union Flag"* stamps plus labels.

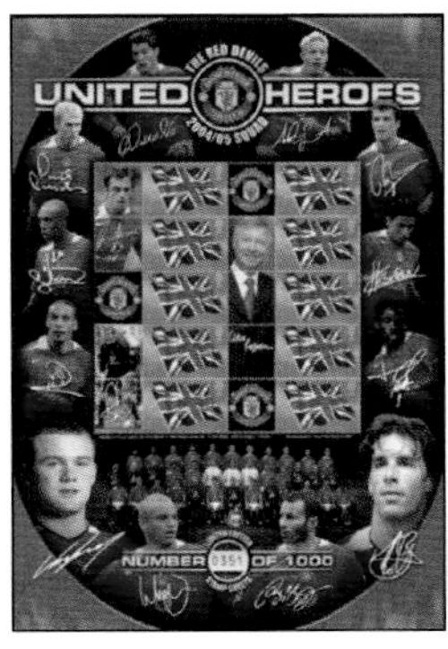

BC-042

Man United Heroes - 04/05 Squad

2004 (6 Dec), Litho by Walsall, Perf 14½ x 14,

Initial selling price: £ 17.95

BC-042 .... £ 17.95

Produced by: Victory Cards/Benham **Qty:** 1000

Issue Notes: 10 x 1st class *Flags "Union Flag"* stamps plus labels. Sheet still available from producers at guide price.

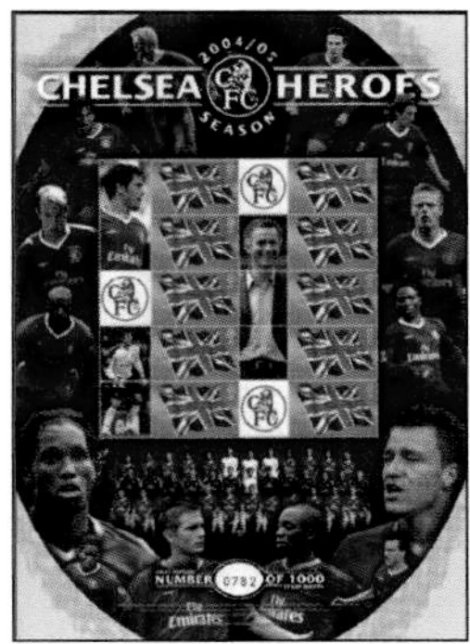

BC-043

Chelsea Heroes 04/05 Squad

2004 (13 Dec), Litho by Walsall, Perf 14½ x 14,

Initial selling price: £ 17.95

BC-043 .... £ 21.95

Produced by: Victory Cards/Benham **Qty:** 1000

Issue Notes: 10 x 1st class *Flags "Union Flag"* stamps plus labels.

BC-044

Dr Who—Katy Manning

2004 (Dec), Litho by Walsall, Perf 14½ x 14,

Initial selling price: £ 14.95

BC-044 .... £ 25.00

Produced by: The Stamp Centre **Qty:** 1000

Issue Notes: 10 x 1st class *Smiles "Moon"* stamps plus labels. The fifth sheet in the Dr. Who series.

Business

BC-045

Dr Who - The Sixth Doctor

2004 (Dec), Litho by Cartor, Perf 14½ x 14,

Initial selling price: £ 14.95

BC-045 .... £ 25.00

Produced by: The Stamp Centre **Qty:** 1000

Issue Notes: 10 x 1st class *Smiles "Moon"* stamps plus labels. The sixth sheet in the Dr. Who series.

BC-046

Dr Who - The Seventh Doctor

2004 (Dec), Litho by Cartor, Perf 14½ x 14,

Initial selling price: £ 14.95

BC-046 .... £ 25.00

Produced by: The Stamp Centre **Qty:** 1000

Issue Notes: 10 x 1st class *Smiles "Moon"* stamps plus labels. The seventh sheet in the Dr. Who series.

BC-047

Red Dwarf

2004 (Dec), Litho by Cartor, Perf 14½ x 14,

Initial selling price: £ 14.95

BC-047 .... £ 25.00

Produced by: The Stamp Centre **Qty:** 1000

Issue Notes: 10 x 1st class *Smiles "Moon"* stamps plus labels.

BC-048

Bicentenary of the Battle of Trafalgar

2005 (4 Feb), Litho by Cartor, Perf 14½ x 14,

Initial selling price: £ 14.95

BC-048 .... £ 25.00

Produced by: Benham Covers **Qty:** 1805

Issue Notes: 10 x 1st class Flags "Union Flag" stamps plus labels. As many as one third of all sheets may have been broken up to service a series of Nelson inspired covers (at least 3 different covers exist bearing this combination) of which 2000 covers of each design were produced.

BC-049

STAMPEX—Spring 2005

2005 (23 Feb), Litho by Cartor, Perf 14½ x 14,

Initial selling price: £ 9.00

BC-049 .... £ 15.00

Produced by: PTS **Qty:** 3000 (est.)

Issue Notes: 10 x 1st class Occasions *"Hello"* stamps plus labels. A fifth commemorative stamp sheet released by the Philatelic Traders Society to coincide with the Spring STAMPEX event held in London which celebrated the 100th Anniversary of Rotary International. Visitors to the event could purchase a complete stamp sheet at the reception desk and each visitor to the show received a single stamp with the free official programme, additional singles were available at £1. It is understood after breaking up these sheets 2250 whole sheets remained.

BC-050

British Steam Locomotion (1822-1866)

2005 (18 Mar), Litho by Cartor, Perf 14½ x 14,

Initial selling price: £ 24.95

BC-050 .... £ 25.00

Produced by: Benham Covers **Qty:** 1000

Issue Notes: 10 x 1st class Flags "Union Flag" stamps plus labels. Although noted as 1000 sheets printed, as many as half were broken up to service a collection of 50 covers "British Steam Locomotion". Each cover bore a single stamp and label from one of the four stamp sheets and each cover was limited to a production of 500. It is estimated therefore that less than 500 whole sheets exist.

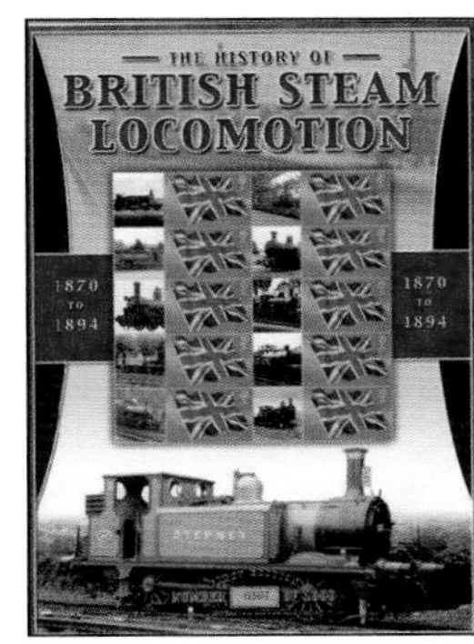

BC-051

British Steam Locomotion (1870-1894)

2005 (18 Mar), Litho by Cartor, Perf 14½ x 14,

Initial selling price: £ 24.95

BC-051 .... £ 25.00

Produced by: Benham Covers **Qty:** 1000

Issue Notes: 10 x 1st class Flags "Union Flag" stamps plus labels. See BC-050 for additional notes.

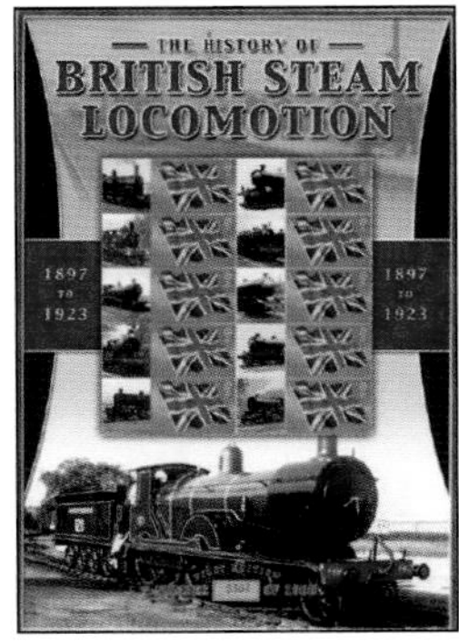

BC-052

British Steam Locomotion (1897-1923)

2005 (18 Mar), Litho by Cartor, Perf 14½ x 14,

Initial selling price: £ 24.95

Business

BC-052 .... £ 25.00

Produced by: Benham Covers **Qty:** 1000

Issue Notes: 10 x 1st class Flags "Union Flag" stamps plus labels. See BC-050 for additional notes.

BC-053

British Steam Locomotion (1923-1928)

2005 (18 Mar), Litho by Cartor, Perf 14½ x 14,

Initial selling price: £ 24.95

BC-053 .... £ 25.00

Produced by: Benham Covers **Qty:** 1000

Issue Notes: 10 x 1st class Flags "Union Flag" stamps plus labels. See BC-050 for additional notes.

BC-054

British Steam Locomotion (1938-1960)

2005 (18 Mar), Litho by Cartor, Perf 14½ x 14,

Initial selling price: £ 24.95

BC-054 .... £ 25.00

Produced by: Benham Covers **Qty:** 1000

Issue Notes: 10 x 1st class Flags "Union Flag" stamps plus labels. See BC-050 for additional notes.

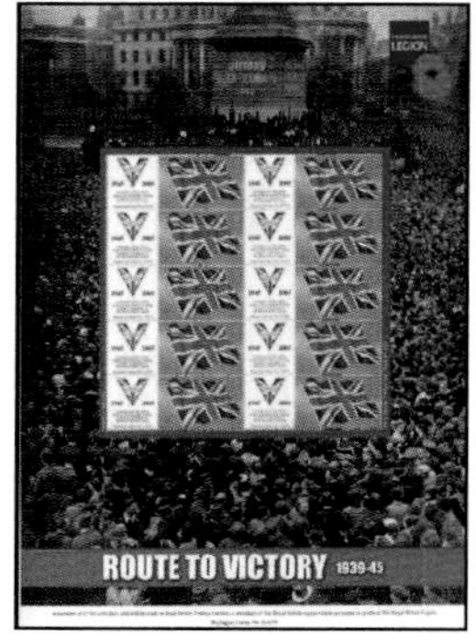

BC-055

Route to Victory

2005 (7 Apr), Litho by Cartor, Perf 14½ x 14,

Initial selling price: £ 24.95

BC-055 .... £ 25.00

Produced by: Westminster **Qty:** Unknown

Issue Notes: 10 x 1st class Flags "Union Flag" stamps plus labels. The first Business Customised Stamp sheet to be issued by the Westminster Collection, part of the Harry Allan Group of companies specialising in collectibles. This charity inspired sheet was produced to service a range of covers commemorating the 60th anniversary of the end of World War II. The covers appeared monthly from mid-2005. This particular sheet has the distinction of being the first Business Customised stamp sheet to be sold at face value plus a donation of £1 to the British Legion. See page 1-9 for further information on an earlier (2003) charity sheet - Cancer Research.

BC-056

Red Arrows

2005 (May), Litho by Cartor, Perf 14½ x 14,

Initial selling price: £ 24.95

BC-056 .... £ 350.00

Produced by: Westminster **Qty:** 1000

Issue Notes: 10 x 1st class Flags "Union Flag" stamps plus labels. Primarily produced to service 9500 covers issued by Mercury Covers/The Westminster Collection. Likely print run was 1000 sheets of which 950 were broken up for covers. As a result a rare business sheet and difficult to find. Most sheets were sold framed and an element of those framed were damaged during the framing process. A rare sheet in any condition.

BC-057

Dr. Who - U.N.I.T.

2005 (May), Litho by Cartor, Perf 14½ x 14,

Initial selling price: £ 14.95

BC-057 .... £ 25.00

Produced by: The Stamp Centre **Qty:** 1000

Issue Notes: 10 x 1st class Smiles *"Moon"* stamps plus labels. The eighth sheet in the Dr. Who series.

BC-058

Dr. Who - The New Doctor

2005 (May), Litho by Cartor, Perf 14½ x 14,

Initial selling price: £ 14.95

BC-058 .... £ 25.00

Produced by: The Stamp Centre **Qty:** 1500

Issue Notes: 10 x 1st class Occasions *"Hello"* stamps plus labels. The ninth sheet in the Dr. Who series.

BC-059

Admiral Lord Nelson

2005 (Jul), Litho by Cartor, Perf 14½ x 14,

Initial selling price: £ 17.95

BC-059 .... £ 40.00

Produced by: AG Bradbury **Qty:** 1805

Issue Notes: 10 x 1st class Flags *"White Ensign"* stamps plus labels. This is the first Business customised stamp sheet from AG Bradbury who has previously supplied collectible first day covers. It appears this may not be the last as the sheet is sub-titled *No. 1 in the History of Britain Series.* It is believed that the majority of sheets were broken up to service a number of different covers to celebrate the bicentenary of the Battle of Waterloo and other related anniversaries. It is estimated that less than 250 whole sheets exist.

BC-060

Dr. Who - The Monsters

2005 (Jul), Litho by Cartor, Perf 14½ x 14,

Initial selling price: £ 24.95

BC-060 .... £ 30.00

Produced by: The Stamp Centre **Qty:** 1500

Issue Notes: 10 x 1st class Occasion *"Hello"* stamps plus labels. The tenth sheet in the Dr. Who series.

BC-061

Dr. Who - The 5th Doctor

2005 (Jul), Litho by Cartor, Perf 14½ x 14,

Initial selling price: £ 24.95

BC-061 .... £ 30.00

Produced by: Westminster **Qty:** 1000

Issue Notes: 10 x 1st class Smiles *"Moon"* stamps plus labels. The eleventh sheet in the Dr. Who series.

BC-062

Hammer Films: Frankenstein

2005 (May), Litho by Cartor, Perf 14½ x 14,

Initial selling price: £ 24.95

BC-062 .... £ 30.00

BC-062a Unnumbered ....£ 60.00

Produced by: The Stamp Centre **Qty:** 1000

Issue Notes: 10 x 1st class Smiles *"Moon"* stamps plus labels. BC-62a were sheets intended to be used on souvenir covers. A small number of unnumbered sheets were sold by the Stamp Centre.

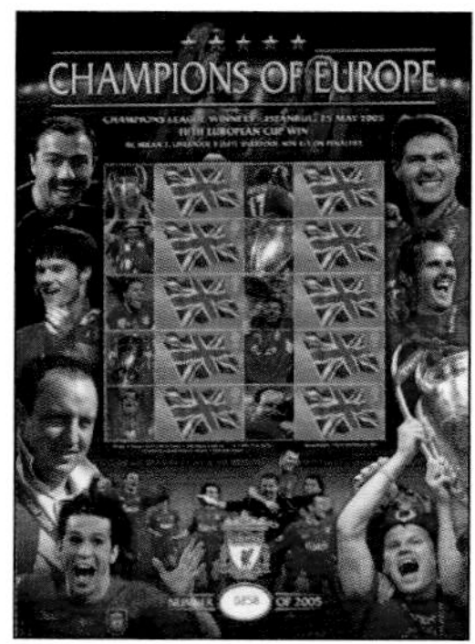

BC-063

Liverpool - Champions of Europe

2005 (1 Aug), Litho by Cartor, Perf 14½ x 14,

Initial selling price: £ 21.95

BC-063 .... £ 25.00

Produced by: Victory Cards/Benham **Qty:** 2005

Issue Notes: 10 x 1st class *Flags "Union Flag"* stamps plus labels.

BC-064

Chelsea - Carling Cup Winners

2005 (1 Aug), Litho by Cartor, Perf 14½ x 14,

Initial selling price: £ 21.95

BC-064 .... £ 25.00

Produced by: Victory Cards/Benham **Qty:** 1000

Issue Notes: 10 x 1st class *Flags "Union Flag"* stamps plus labels. Sheet still available from producers at guide price. Benham Covers also produced 50 whole-sheet First Day Cards for this issue.

BC-065

Carl Fogarty

2005 (1 Aug), Litho by Cartor, Perf 14½ x 14,

Initial selling price: £ 24.95

BC-065 .... £ 30.00

Produced by: The Stamp Centre **Qty:** 1000

Issue Notes: 10 x 1st class *Flags "Union Flag"* stamps plus labels. In an apparent departure from its usual fare of science-fiction related Business Customised stamp sheets The Stamp Centre sponsored this Customised sheet commemorating the 7th World Championship title won by Carl Fogarty in the F1 super-bikes category.

BC-066

Captain Scarlet

2005 (1 Aug), Litho by Cartor, Perf 14½ x 14,

Initial selling price: £ 24.95

BC-066 .... £ 30.00

Produced by: The Stamp Centre **Qty:** 1000

Issue Notes: 10 x 1st class Smiles *"Moon"* stamps plus labels. The Stamp Centre continued its series of science-fiction related Business Customised stamp sheets with an offering featuring Captain Scarlet, under licence from ITC, again featuring the colourful artwork of artist, Ian F. Burgess. The Smilers stamp featured on this sheet is much more true to the original 1991 gravure printing method by Harrison and Sons. The Queen's head and value tablet are both in gold .

BC-067

Farewell Concorde

2005 (1 Sep), Litho by Cartor, Perf 14½ x 14,

Initial selling price: £ 21.95

BC-067 .... £ 75.00

Produced by: Benham **Qty:** 1000

Issue Notes: 10 x 1st class *Flags "Union Flag"* stamps plus labels. The first in a number of Business Customised stamp sheets to celebrate the demise of Concorde. See also BC-078 which is, perhaps, the rarest of the crop. Benham Covers also produced 50 whole-sheet First Day Cards for this issue.

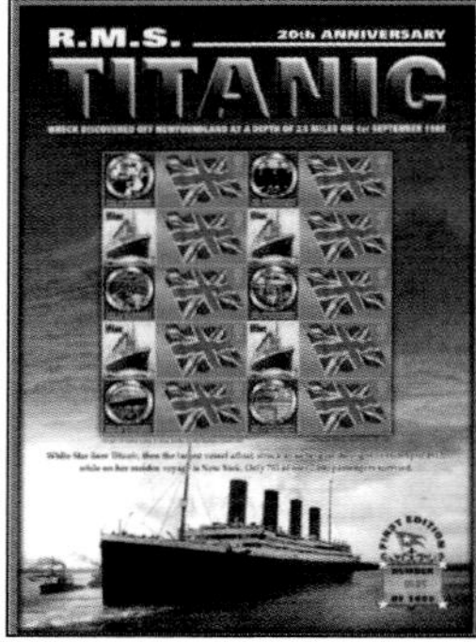

BC-068

RMS Titanic (1)

2005 (1 Sep), Litho by Cartor, Perf 14½ x 14,

Initial selling price: £ 21.95

BC-068 .... £ 25.00

Produced by: Benham Covers **Qty:** 1000

Issue Notes: 10 x 1st class *Flags "Union Flag"* stamps plus labels. Sheet still available from producers at guide price. Benham Covers also produced 50 whole-sheet First Day Cards for this issue plus a set of 10 commemorative covers with each cover bearing a different stamp/label combination.

BC-069

RMS Titanic (2)

2005 (1 Sep), Litho by Cartor, Perf 14½ x 14,

Initial selling price: £ 21.95

BC-069 .... £ 25.00

Produced by: Benham Covers **Qty:** 1000

Issue Notes: 10 x 1st class *Flags "White Ensign"* stamps plus labels. Sheet still available from producers at guide price. See additional notes under BC-068.

BC-070

STAMPEX - Autumn 2005

2005 (14 Sep), Litho by Cartor, Perf 14½ x 14,

Initial selling price: £ 10.00

BC-070 .... £ 15.00

Produced by: PTS **Qty:** 3000

Issue Notes: 10 x 1st class *Flags "White Ensign Flag"* stamps plus labels. A sixth commemorative stamp sheet released by the Philatelic Traders Society to coincide with the Autumn STAMPEX event held in London celebrated the 200th Anniversary of the death of Lord Nelson. Visitors to the event could purchase a complete stamp sheet at the reception desk. Unlike earlier events, singles were not given away free but sold at £1 each. It is understood after breaking up these sheets 2669 whole sheets were available for sale.

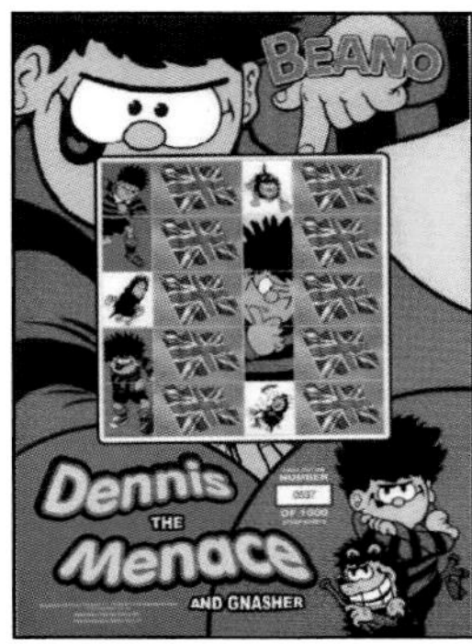

BC-071

Beano (Dennis the Menace)

2005 (16 Sep), Litho by Cartor, Perf 14½ x 14,

Initial selling price: £ 21.95

BC-071 .... £ 25.00

Produced by: Benham Covers **Qty:** 1000

Issue Notes: 10 x 1st class *Flags "Union Flag"* stamps plus labels. Produced by cover specialist Benham who subsequently produced a set of six covers (quantity unknown) in September 2005 which between them featured all 10 stamps and labels from this sheet. Issued on 16th September 2005 on the occasion of the 66th Anniversary of the first Beano Book, 16th September 1939. Sheet still available from producers at guide price.

BC-072

Dandy

2005 (16 Sep), Litho by Cartor, Perf 14½ x 14,

Initial selling price: £ 21.95

BC-072 .... £ 25.00

Produced by: Benham Covers **Qty:** 1000

Issue Notes: 10 x 1st class *Flags "Union Flag"* stamps plus labels. Produced by cover specialist Benham who subsequently produced a set of six covers (quantity unknown) in September 2005 which between them featured all 10 stamps and labels from this sheet. Issued on 16th September 2005 on the occasion of the 67th Anniversary of the first Dandy Annual, 16th September 1938. Sheet still available from producers at guide price.

BC-073

Beano (The Bash Street Kids)

2005 (16 Sep), Litho by Cartor, Perf 14½ x 14,

Initial selling price: £ 21.95

BC-073 .... £ 21.95

Produced by: Benham Covers **Qty:** 1000

Issue Notes: 10 x 1st class *Flags "Union Flag"* stamps plus labels. Produced by cover specialist Benham who subsequently produced a set of six covers (quantity unknown) in September 2005 which between them featured all 10 stamps and labels from this sheet. Issued on 16th September 2005 on the occasion of the 66th Anniversary of the first Beano Book, 16th September 1939. Sheet still available from producers at guide price.

BC-074

Cats

2005 (4 Oct), Litho by Cartor, Perf 14½ x 14,

Initial selling price: £ 21.95

BC-074 .... £ 21.95

Produced by: Benham Covers **Qty:** 1000

Issue Notes: 10 x 1st class *Flags "Union Flag"* stamps plus labels. Sheet still available from producers at guide price.

BC-075

Teddy Bears

2005 (4 Oct), Litho by Cartor, Perf 14½ x 14,

Initial selling price: £ 21.95

BC-075 .... £ 21.95

Produced by: Benham Covers **Qty:** 1000

Issue Notes: 10 x 1st class *Smiles "Teddy"* stamps plus labels. Sheet still available from producers at guide price.

BC-076

The Gunpowder Plot

2005 (4 Oct), Litho by Cartor, Perf 14½ x 14,

Initial selling price: £ 24.95

BC-076 .... £ 30.00

Produced by: AG Bradbury **Qty:** 1605

Issue Notes: 10 x 1st class Flags *"Union Flag"* stamps plus labels. No. 2 in a series produced by cover specialist AG Bradbury featuring various aspects of the History of Britain. These stamps and labels featured on a series of covers produced by A.G. Bradbury.

BC-077

The Year of the Three Kings

2005 (15 Dec), Litho by Cartor, Perf 14½ x 14,

Initial selling price: £ 24.95

BC-077 .... £ 30.00

Produced by: AG Bradbury **Qty:** 1000

Issue Notes: 10 x 1st class Flags *"Union Flag"* stamps plus labels. No. 3 in a series produced by cover specialist A.G. Bradbury. Although noted as

1936 sheets printed, it is understood that only 1000 sheets were actually printed. The majority of which were broken up to service a number of different covers to celebrate the Year of the Three Kings. It is estimated that less than 500 whole sheets exist.

BC-078

Concorde 30th Anniversary - First Flight (Type 1)

2006 (21 Jan), Litho by Cartor, printed on self adhesive paper with die-cut perfs 15 x 14.
Initial selling price: £ 24.95

BC-078 .... £ 150.00

BC-078a 2 x 9.5 mm Phosphor Bands £2,000.00

Produced by: Buckingham Covers **Qty:** 1000

Issue Notes: 10 x 1st class DS *"Union Flag"* stamps plus labels. The first self adhesive Business Customised sheet, published by Buckingham covers. Although the sheet indicates 1976 sheets were printed it is understood from Buckingham Covers that only 1000 sheets were printed, many of these being broken up for special covers issued by Buckingham Covers. There was a delay in issuing these sheets as a result of Royal Mail requiring these sheet to be reprinted. See Known Varieties for further information.

Known Varieties: 3 sheets of this sheet exist with 2 x 9.5 mm Phosphor bands applied in error by printers instead of 2 x 6.5 mm bands. This error was apparently the fault of the printers and here is the story as told by Tony Buckingham.

"The sheets were printed in France by Cartor. They were delivered to us by courier and were immediately dispatched to our home-workers so that they could start affixing the stamps to covers. Later that day, we had a phone call from Royal Mail. They said that there had been an error on the sheets and that they all had to be returned. We explained that many of them had already been broken up and the stamps affixed to covers. We were allowed to keep the covers but all complete sheets were returned. It was later when a home-worker returned her work that we discovered 3 complete error sheets had been overlooked."

These error sheets are the only known source of the self-adhesive definitive-sized Union Flag stamp with 2 x 9.5mm phosphor bands. Some are also known to exist on Tony Buckingham covers which are changing hands for c. £100 each in 2009.

BC-079

STAMPEX - Spring 2006

2006 (22 Feb), Litho by Cartor, Perf 14½ x 14, Initial selling price: £ 10.00

BC-079 .... £ 15.00

Produced by: PTS **Qty:** 3000

Issue Notes: 10 x 1st class Hallmarks *"Cheers"* stamps plus labels. A seventh commemorative stamp sheet released by the Philatelic Traders Society to coincide with the Spring STAMPEX event held in London celebrated the 200th Anniversary of the birth of Brunel. Visitors to the show could purchase a complete stamp sheet at the reception desk. Singles were also on sale at £1 each.

BC-080

The Victoria Cross

2006 (1 Apr), Litho by Cartor, Perf 14½ x 14, Initial selling price: £ 24.95

BC-080 .... £ 50.00

Produced by: AG Bradbury **Qty:** 500

Issue Notes: 10 x 1st class Flags *"Union Flag"* stamps plus labels. No. 4 in a series produced by cover specialist A.G. Bradbury featuring various aspects of the History of Britain. These stamps/labels also featured on a series of covers produced by A.G. Bradbury.

BC-081

80th Birthday - HM Queen Elizabeth II (1)

2006 (21 Apr), Litho by Cartor, Perf 14½ x 14, Initial selling price: £ 24.95

BC-081 .... £ 30.00

Produced by: Benham Covers **Qty:** 1000

Issue Notes: 10 x 1st class Flags *"Union Flag"* stamps plus labels.

BC-082

Concorde: 30th Anniversary - London to Washington Flight

2006 (12 May), Litho by Cartor, printed on self adhesive paper with die-cut perfs 15 x 14.
Initial selling price: £ 24.95

BC-082 .... £ 35.00

Produced by: Benham Covers **Qty:** 1000

Issue Notes: 10 x 1st class DS *"Union Flag"* stamps plus labels.

BC-083

Isambard Kingdom Brunel

2006 (15 May), Litho by Cartor, printed on self adhesive paper with die-cut perfs 15 x 14.
Initial selling price: £ 29.95

BC-083 .... £ 75.00

Produced by: AG Bradbury **Qty:** 500

Issue Notes: 10 x 1st class DS *"Union Flag"* stamps plus labels. No. 5 in a series produced by cover specialist A.G. Bradbury featuring various aspects of the History of Britain. These stamps and labels featured

Business

on a series of covers produced by A.G. Bradbury.

BC-084

Concorde: 30th Anniversary - First Flight (Type 2)

2006 (24 May), Litho by Cartor, printed on self adhesive paper with die-cut perfs 15 x 14.
Initial selling price: £ 19.95

BC-084 .... £ 35.00

Produced by: Buckingham Covers **Qty:** 1976

Issue Notes: 10 x 1st class DS *"Union Flag"* stamps plus labels.

BC-085

80th Birthday - HM Queen Elizabeth II (2)

2006 (Jun), Litho by Cartor, Perf 14½ x 14, Initial selling price: £ 21.95

BC-085 .... £ 1,000.00

Produced by: Westminster **Qty:** See Notes

Issue Notes: 20 x 1st class Flags *"Union Flag"* stamps plus labels. Primarily produced to service a stamp/coin cover, of which 9500 were produced. It seems Westminster did not plan to release this sheet which may explain its rather featureless design. They however did sell the balance of their stock (est. 20 sheets) which would indicate a print run of c. 1000 sheets. This sheet is often missing from most collections and is much sought after when offered for sale. A sheet sold on eBay in 2009 for c. £850!

BC-086

England Winners 1966

2006 (6 Jun), Litho by Cartor, Perf 14½, Initial selling price: £ 4.20

BC-086 .... £ 15.00

Produced by: Westminster **Qty:** 6000

Issue Notes: 10 x 1st class Flags *"Union Flag"* stamps plus labels. An interesting and popular charity sheet produced in aid of the Bobby Moore fund for Cancer. Produced at face value plus £1, which was donated to the charity by the cover producer. See page 1-9 for further information on an earlier (2003) charity sheet - Cancer Research.

BC-087

Bristol NW Scout District 1974-2006

2006 (6 Jun), Litho by Cartor, printed on self adhesive paper with die-cut perfs 15 x 14.
Initial selling price: £ 8.00

BC-087 .... £ 250.00

BC-087a Set of 10 Presentation Cards ..... £ 250.00

BC-087b Centenary of Scouting o/p.......... £ 500.00

Produced by: Bristol NW Scout Group **Qty:** 1000

Issue Notes: 10 x 1st class DS *"Union Flag"* stamps plus labels. The sheet was issued on the demise of the Bristol NW Scout District. Sheets were sold to scouts in the Bristol area (maximum 3 sheets per household) and the remainder sold to the philatelic market by individuals with access to the sheets. A rare sheet due to its non-philatelic distribution.

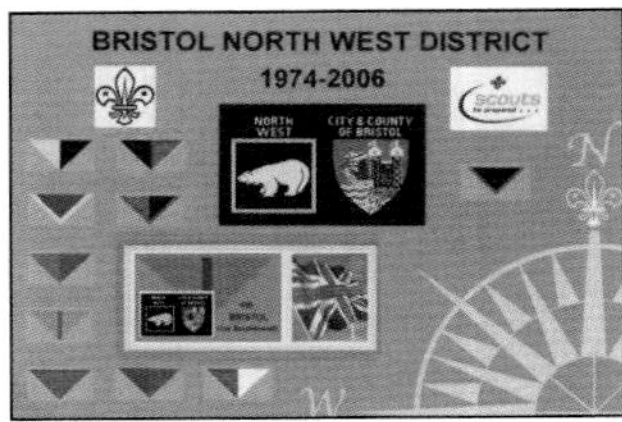

BC-087a

Presentation cards (10 different) were also produced and distributed, one to each of the 850+ scouts that formed the defunct Bristol NW Scouts.

BC-087b

In 2007 the owners of the remaining stock of Bristol sheets sought permission from Royal Mail to over-print the remaining stock of sheets with suitable lettering to commemorate the 100th Anniversary of the Scouting movement which was celebrated in 2007. This they duly received and c. 100 sheets were over-printed with gold-leaf lettering on the sheet and on each label adjoining each of the 10 stamps. The sheets were sold as a numbered limited edition to members of the scouting movement in Bristol on the undertaking that they would not be sold for profit for at least 5-years after the purchase date.

BC-088

Dr Who—The Tenth Doctor

2006 (12 Jul), Litho by Cartor, Perf 14½ x 14, Initial selling price: £ 24.95

BC-088 .... £ 30.00

BC-088a Unnumbered .... £ 30.00

Produced by: The Stamp Centre **Qty:** 1000

Issue Notes: 10 x 1st class Occasions *"Hello"* stamps plus labels. The twelfth sheet in the Dr. Who series. BC-88a were sheets intended to be used on souvenir covers. A small number of unnumbered sheets were sold by the Stamp Centre.

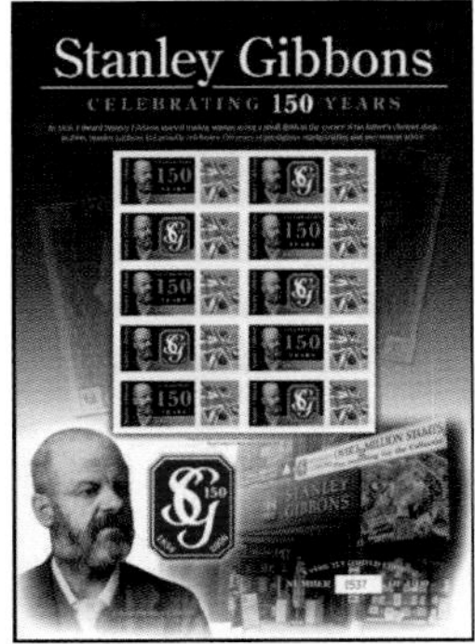

BC-089

Stanley Gibbons 150th Anniversary

2006 (20 Jul), Litho by Cartor, printed on self adhesive paper with die-cut perfs 15 x 14.
Initial selling price: £ 24.95

BC-089 .... £ 30.00

Produced by: Benham Covers **Qty:** 1000

Issue Notes: 10 x 1st class DS *"Union Flag"* stamps plus labels. Issued to commemorate the 150th Anni-

Business

versary of perhaps the world's most famous stamp dealer, Stanley Gibbons. Benham and Gibbons appear to have joined forces to produce this sheet.

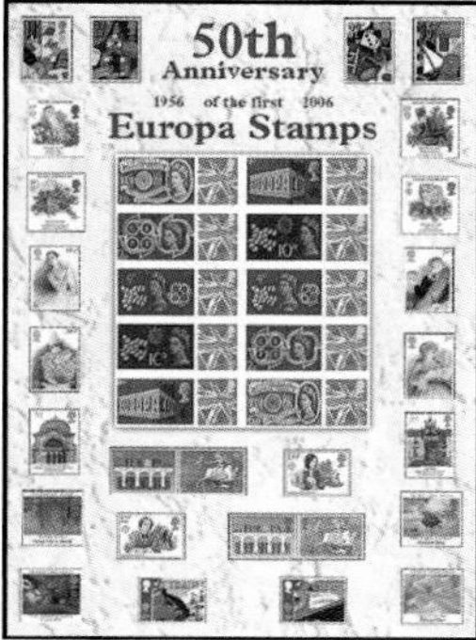

BC-090

50th Anniversary of the Europa Stamps

2006 (1 Sep), Litho by Cartor, printed on self adhesive paper with die-cut perfs 15 x 14.
Initial selling price: £ 12.50

BC-090 .... £ 15.00

Produced by: Rushstamps **Qty:** 1000

Issue Notes: 10 x 1st class DS *"Union Flag"* stamps plus labels. One of three sheets produced by Rushstamps to commemorate the 50th Anniversary of Europa Stamps, see also BC-091 ands BC-094

BC-091

Europa (plus Belgica Logo)

2006 (1 Sep), Litho by Cartor, printed on self adhesive paper with die-cut perfs 15 x 14.
Initial selling price: £ 12.50

BC-091 .... £ 15.00

Produced by: Rushstamps **Qty:** 1000

Issue Notes: 10 x 1st class DS *"Union Flag"* stamps plus labels. One of three sheets produced by Rushstamps to commemorate the 50th Anniversary of Europa Stamps.

BC-092

Golden Arrow & Fleche D'Or (1)

2006 (13 Sep), Litho by Cartor, printed on self adhesive paper with die-cut perfs 15 x 14.
Initial selling price: £ 24.95

BC-092 .... £ 30.00

Produced by: Benham Covers **Qty:** 1000

Issue Notes: 10 x 1st class DS *"Union Flag"* stamps plus labels.

BC-093

Golden Arrow & Fleche D'Or (2)

2006 (13 Sep), Litho by Cartor, printed on self adhesive paper with die-cut perfs 15 x 14.
Initial selling price: £ 24.95

BC-093 .... £ 30.00

Produced by: Benham Covers **Qty:** 1000

Issue Notes: 10 x 1st class DS *"Union Flag"* stamps

plus labels.

BC-094

Europa (plus STAMPEX Logo)

2006 (20 Sep), Litho by Cartor, printed on self adhesive paper with die-cut perfs 15 x 14.
Initial selling price: £ 18.50

BC-094 .... £ 25.00

Produced by: Benham Covers **Qty:** 500

Issue Notes: 10 x 1st class DS *"Union Flag"* stamps plus labels. One of three sheets produced by Rushstamps to commemorate the 50th Anniversary of Europa Stamps.

BC-095

STAMPEX - Autumn 2006

2006 (20 Sep), Litho by Cartor, Perf 14½ x 14, Initial selling price: £ 10.00

BC-095 .... £ 15.00

Produced by: PTS **Qty:** 3000

Issue Notes: 10 x 1st class Hallmarks *"Cheers"* stamps plus labels. The eighth commemorative stamp sheet released by the Philatelic Traders Society to coincide with the Autumn STAMPEX event held in London celebrated the 150th Anniversary of the Victoria Cross. Visitors to the show could purchase a complete stamp sheet at the reception desk. Singles were also on sale at £1 each.

BC-096

First Class - Grande Punto

2006 (21 Sep), Litho by Cartor, Perf 14½ x 14, Initial selling price: £ 11.50

BC-096 .... £ 15.00

BC-096a FIA European Champions o/p ...... £ 50.00

Produced by: FIAT Auto UK **Qty:** 6000

Issue Notes: 20 x 1st class Occasions *"Hello"* stamps plus labels. The first *truly* Business Customised Sheet - not inspired by the philatelic trade or Royal Mail. To celebrate their success at the FIA European Rally Championships and to promote sales of their successful Grande Punto Model, FIAT UK commissioned 6000 sheets of this attractive Business Customised Sheet and made them available to their network of dealers through their UK parts distribution under part number 46002995. Despite FIAT's intentions, the sheet was advertised on eBay by FIAT UK and proved popular with collectors, many found their way on to the philatelic market. A small quantity (c. 100) were overprinted *FIA European Champions 2006.*

BC-097

The Snowman

2006 (30 Oct), Litho by Cartor, printed on self adhesive paper with die-cut perfs 15 x 14.
Initial selling price: £ 19.95

BC-097 .... £ 35.00

Produced by: Buckingham Covers **Qty:** 1000

Issue Notes: 10 x 1st class DS *"Robin in Letter-Box"* stamps plus labels. A Charity inspired Business Customised Stamp sheet issued on the occasion of the 20th Anniversary of ChildLine helpline. A proportion of the proceeds of this sheet were donated to ChildLine. This is the third charity Customised stamp sheet to be produced behind, Route to Victory (BC-055) and the Bobby Moore (BC-086) sheets, ignoring the Cancer Research stamp sheet which was only available in presentation packs.

BC-098

70th Anniv. of Coronation of George VI

2007 (1 Jan), Litho by Cartor, printed on self adhesive paper with die-cut perfs 15 x 14.
Initial selling price: £ 29.75

BC-098 .... £ 75.00

Produced by: AG Bradbury **Qty:** 500

Issue Notes: 10 x 1st class DS *"Union Flag"* stamps plus labels. No. 6 in a series produced by cover specialist A.G. Bradbury featuring various aspects of the History of Britain. These stamps and labels feature on a series of covers produced by A.G. Bradbury.

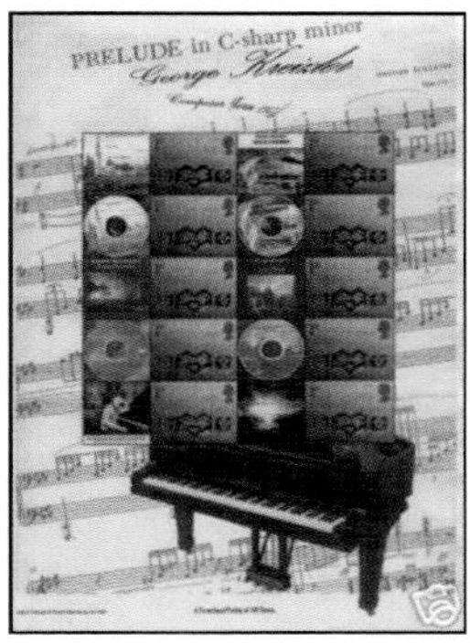

BC-099

George Kreizler Promotion

2007 (2 Jan), Litho by Cartor, Perf 14½ x 14, Initial selling price: £ 125.00

BC-099 .... £ 250.00

BC-099a Overprinted .... £ 250.00

Produced by: George Kreizler **Qty:** 100

Issue Notes: 10 x 1st class Hallmarks *"LOVE"* stamps plus labels. This sheet was produced in a limited edition of 100 by music composer George Kreizler as a way of promoting his music and CD sales. Most sheets are reported to have been broken up for promotional purposes. From January 2007 around 10-15 were offered on eBay at the rather eye-popping price of £125 each. Some are known to be signed by the composer. The apparent print run of 100 sheets is itself unusual as prior to this issue Royal Mail's minimum print order was 500 sheets. Additionally, the sheet boasts other interesting features; the first Customised sheet to have used exclusively the Hallmarks "LOVE" stamps and one of only four Business Customised sheets to be produced without the ubiquitous sheet serial number.

BC-099a

Almost a year after the sheets came on to the market (a few further sheets appeared subsequently) an additional number of sheets were offered on eBay with the following commentary.

"2007 The Kreizler Music Sheet - 60th Birthday Anniversary. The Music Sheet was overprinted for the composer's birthday anniversary (top left label and bottom left of sheet). Sheets were lost and thought to have been destroyed but were recently discovered intact. The composer will provide a signed Certificate of Authenticity confirming that he had these sheets privately overprinted. He is also willing to sign or personalise this sheet at no extra cost. Only 15 sheets were overprinted and numbered 1-15 ."

BC-100

Terence Cuneo

2007 (8 Jan), Litho by Cartor, printed on self adhesive paper with die-cut perfs 15 x 14.
Initial selling price: £ 19.95

BC-100 .... £ 75.00

Produced by: Buckingham Covers **Qty:** 1000

Issue Notes: 10 x 1st class DS *"Big Bang"* stamps plus labels. Produced by cover specialist Buckingham Covers featuring the Railway Art of well-known artist Terrence Cuneo. These stamps and labels featured on a series of covers produced by Buckingham Covers and consequently a number (unknown) of these sheets were broken up to service these covers.

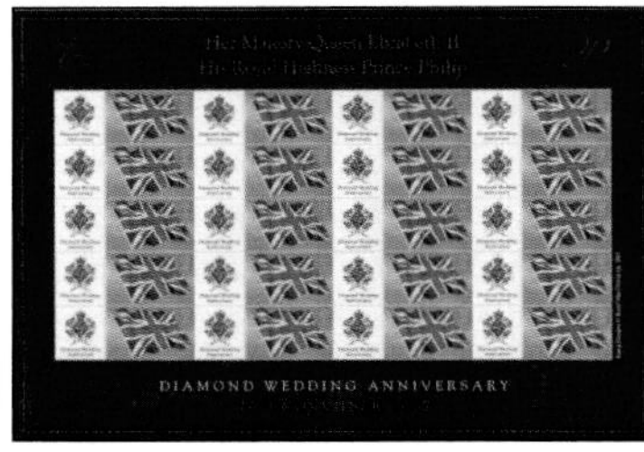

BC-101

HM Queen Elizabeth 2 - Diamond Wedding

2007 (15 Jan), Litho by Cartor, Perf 14½ x 14, Initial selling price: £ 19.95

BC-101 .... £ 35.00

Produced by: Westminster **Qty:** See Notes

Issue Notes: 10 x 1st class Flags *"Union Flag"* stamps plus labels. Produced to service a commemorative stamp/coin cover, of which 9500 were produced by The Westminster Collection, a number of whole sheets were sold directly to Smilers sheet collectors but the exact number of whole sheets in circulation is unknown.

BC-102

Spirit of the 60's

2007 (25 Feb), Litho by Cartor, Perf 14½ x 14, Initial selling price: £ 9.99

BC-102 .... £ 30.00

Produced by: Westminster **Qty:** See notes

Issue Notes: 10 x 1st class Occasions *"Love"* stamps plus labels. Westminster also produced a cover collection featuring these stamp/label combinations so an unknown quantity of sheets are believed to have been broken up to service these covers. It is estimated that c. 1000 sheets were originally produced and perhaps c. 800 sheet remain intact.

BC-103

STAMPEX - Spring 2007

2007 (28 Feb), Litho by Cartor, Perf 14½ x 14, Initial selling price: £ 10.00

BC-103 .... £ 15.00

Produced by: PTS **Qty:** c. 3000 (See notes)

Issue Notes: 10 x 1st class Hallmarks *"Thanks"* stamps plus labels. The ninth in an on-going series of commemorative stamp sheets released by the Philatelic Traders Society to coincide with the Spring STAMPEX event held in London celebrated innovators and inventors and was released to coincide with a similarly themed Royal Mail stamp issue. Visitors to the show could purchase a complete stamp sheet at the reception desk. Singles were also on sale at £1 each.

BC-104

The Falklands War

2007 (01 Mar), Litho by Cartor, Perf 14½ x 14, Initial selling price: £ 29.95

BC-104 .... £ 75.00

Produced by: AG Bradbury **Qty:** 500

Issue Notes: 10 x 1st class Flags *"White Ensign"* stamps plus labels. No. 8 in a series produced by cover specialist A.G. Bradbury featuring various aspects of the History of Britain. These stamps and labels featured on a cover produced by A.G. Bradbury.

BC-105

Sinking of the Titanic—95th Anniversary

2007 (20 Apr), Litho by Cartor, printed on self adhesive paper with die-cut perfs 15 x 14.
Initial selling price: £ 29.95

BC-105 .... £ 125.00

Produced by: AG Bradbury/Titanic Heritage Trust
Qty: 400

Issue Notes: 10 x 1st class DS *"Union Flag"* stamps plus labels. History of Britain Sheet No. 7. This sheet was produced by AG Bradbury with the help and support of the Titanic Heritage Trust which an international charitable trust set up to protect the history and name of RMS Titanic and those connected to it. This stamp sheet represents the first of a collection of 6 Titanic sheets to be issued between 2007 and 2012.

BC-106

Battle of Britain Memorial Flight

2007 (5 May), Litho by Cartor, printed on self adhesive paper with die-cut perfs 15 x 14.
Initial selling price: £ 40.00

BC-106 .... £ 100.00

BC-106a Unnumbered .... £ 150.00

Produced by: Bletchley Park Post Office/AG Bradbury **Qty:** 500

Issue Notes: 10 x 1st class DS *"Union Flag"* stamps plus labels. The sheet was a co-production between the Bletchley Park Post Office and AG Bradbury. Sheets 1-250 were sold by Bletchley Park Post Office and the remainder sold by AG Bradbury. An additional quantity of these sheets (unknown) were broken up and used for a series of souvenir covers produced by Bletchley Park Post Office. A few of these (unnumbered) sheets were sold to the philatelic community.

BC-107

25th Anniv. of the Falklands Conflict

2007 (14 Jun), Litho by Cartor, perf. 14½
Initial selling price: £ 19.95

BC-107 .... £ 65.00

Produced by: Buckingham Covers **Qty:** 1000

Issue Notes: 10 x 1st class Poppy (2006) stamps plus labels. This sheet was produced in association with the Falklands Memorial Chapel Fund and a proportion of the profits from this sheet were donated to the fund. The sheet was also available signed by Admiral Sir John Woodward, Task Force Commander.

BC-108

175th Anniv. of the Birth of Lewis Carroll

2007 (18 Jul), Litho by Cartor, perf. 14½
Initial selling price: £ 40.00

BC-108 .... £ 75.00

Produced by: AG Bradbury **Qty:** 400

Issue Notes: 10 x 1st class DS "*Flowers*" stamps plus labels. Featuring the illustrations of John Tenniel this sheet is the first self-adhesive Business Customised sheet to feature the Litho printed definitive sized

Business

Flower stamps. Sheet No. 9 in AG Bradbury's *History of Britain* series of stamp sheets.

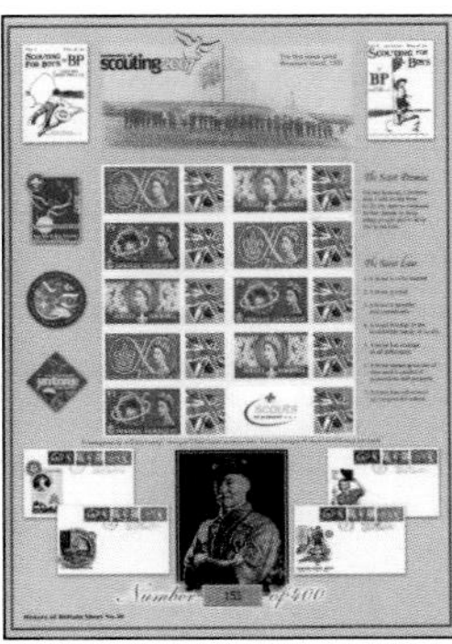

BC-109

Centenary of Scouting

2007 (21 Jul), Litho by Cartor, printed on self adhesive paper with die-cut perfs 15 x 14.
Initial selling price: £ 40.00

BC-109 .... £ 75.00

Produced by: AG Bradbury **Qty:** 400

Issue Notes: 10 x 1st class DS "*Union Flag*" stamps plus labels. Issued to commemorate the Centenary of Scouting and featuring the latest Scouting badges with images of the Jubilee Jamboree stamps issued by the Post Office in 1957. The sheet carried a donation to the Scout Association and was produced with their co-operation. History of Britain Sheet No. 10.

BC-110

Battle of Britain Memorial Flight

2007 (25 Jul), Litho by Cartor, printed on self adhesive paper with die-cut perfs 15 x 14.
Initial selling price: £ 20.00

BC-110 .... £ 250.00

Produced by: Westminster **Qty:** 100

Issue Notes: 10 x 1st class DS "*Union Flag*" stamps plus labels. A limited edition Business sheet produced by The Westminster Collection, originally produced to service a collection of covers bearing these stamps/labels. A small number (c. 100) sheets sold under stock code: 185/4134 but disappeared very quickly from sale.

BC-111

60th Anniversary of the Nationalisation of the Big Four - Great Western Railway

2007 (6 Aug), Litho by Cartor, printed on self adhesive paper with die-cut perfs 15 x 14.
Initial selling price: £ 22.50

BC-111 .... £ 25.00

Produced by: Benham Covers **Qty:** 947

Issue Notes: 10 x 1st class DS "*Union Flag*" stamps plus labels. Issued to mark the 60th anniversary of the nationalisation of the Big Four Railways in Great Britain, a set of four sheets were produced primarily to service a collection of commemorative covers sold separately by Benham. Approximately half of the 947 sheets are thought to be intact as whole sheets. This is the first of four sheets and features Great Western Railway. Benham Stock Code: GSP513 (4 sheets).

BC-112

60th Anniversary of the Nationalisation of the Big Four - London Midland & Scottish Railway

2007 (6 Aug), Litho by Cartor, printed on self adhesive paper with die-cut perfs 15 x 14.
Initial selling price: £ 22.50

BC-112 .... £ 25.00

Produced by: Benham Covers **Qty:** 947

Issue Notes: 10 x 1st class DS "*Union Flag*" stamps plus labels. This is the second of four sheets and features London Midland & Scottish Railway. Benham Stock Code: GSP513 (4 sheets). See BC-111 for additional issue notes.

BC-113

60th Anniversary of the Nationalisation of the Big Four - London & North-Eastern Railway

2007 (6 Aug), Litho by Cartor, printed on self adhesive paper with die-cut perfs 15 x 14.
Initial selling price: £ 22.50

BC-113 .... £ 25.00

Produced by: Benham Covers **Qty:** 947

Issue Notes: 10 x 1st class DS "*Union Flag*" stamps plus labels. This is the third of four sheets and features London & North Eastern Railway. Benham Stock Code: GSP513 (4 sheets). See BC-111 for additional issue notes.

BC-114

60th Anniversary of the Nationalisation of the Big Four - Southern Railway

2007 (6 Aug), Litho by Cartor, printed on self adhesive paper with die-cut perfs 15 x 14.
Initial selling price: £ 22.50

BC-114 .... £ 25.00

Produced by: Benham Covers **Qty:** 947

Issue Notes: 10 x 1st class DS "*Union Flag*" stamps plus labels. The final sheet of four sheets and features the Southern Railway. Benham Stock Code: GSP513 (4 sheets). See BC-111 for additional issue notes.

BC-115

Working Horses

2007 (15 Sep), Litho by Cartor, printed on self adhesive paper with die-cut perfs 15 x 14.
Initial selling price: £ 27.50

BC-115 .... £ 75.00

Produced by: AG Bradbury **Qty:** 1000

Issue Notes: 10 x 1st class DS "*Flower*" stamps plus labels. No. 11 in AG Bradbury's *History of Britain* series. The labels feature the paintings of Malcolm Greensmith and depict working horses in Britain.

BC-116

STAMPEX - Autumn 2007

2007 (19 Sep), Litho by Cartor, printed Perf 14½ x 14. Initial selling price: £ 10.00

BC-116 .... £ 15.00

Produced by: PTS **Qty:** c. 3000

Issue Notes: 10 x 1st class Flags "Union Flag" stamps plus labels. Issued to coincide with the Autumn Stampex event, organised by the Philatelic Traders' Society, and held at the Business Design Centre, Islington, from 19th to the 22nd September 2007. The sheet design complements the Royal Mail "Birds" issue issued earlier in the month. The sheet features ten different British garden birds.

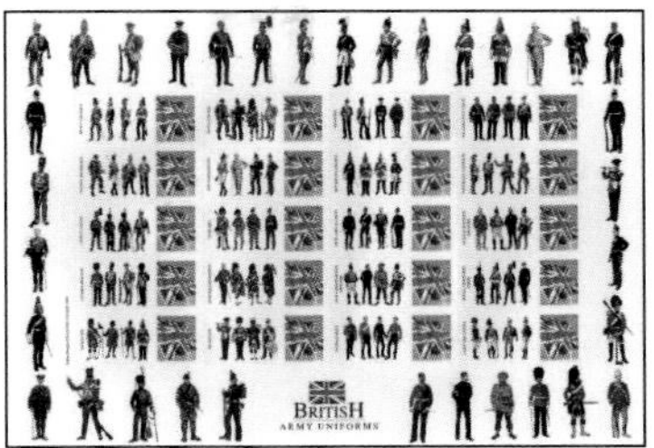

BC-117

British Army Uniforms

2007 (20 Sep), Litho by Cartor, printed on self adhesive paper with die-cut perfs 15 x 14. BC117a - as BC-117 but with elliptical die cut perfs.
Initial selling price: £ 27.50

BC-117 .... £ 50.00

BC-117a Royal Mail Group Ltd. .... £ 25.00

Produced by: Westminster **Qty:** 2500 (See Notes)

Issue Notes: 20 x 1st class DS "Union Fag" stamps plus labels. The sheet producers in early publicity for this sheet indicated that 14,950 sheets had been printed. My estimate is less than 2500 of each BC-117 and BC-117a (see Known Varieties).

Known Varieties: Sheet BC-117 was produced by collectibles specialist Westminster Collection as a promotional item for a collection of stamps and covers featuring the History of British Army Uniforms. By Jan 2008 Westminster would appear to have exhausted stocks of the original printing and advanced sold an A4 variant of this sheet at £9.99 each.

Publicity image of un-issued A4 variant

Business

Westminster seem to have had a last-minute change of heart. What eventually was issued around April 2008 was a stamp sheet identical to BC-117 in all respects (20 x 1st, horizontal format etc.) except for two significant differences.

a. The Royal Mail copyright strap-line now refers to **Royal Mail Group Ltd** instead of the former **Royal Mail Group plc**, and

b. the stamp perforations on this re-issued sheet now included elliptical perfs.

As a result of the re-print we have revised the estimate of the total number of sheets produced to an estimated figure which I think more accurately reflects the number of sheets printed.

BC-118

40th Anniversary of QE2

2007 (30 Sep), Litho by Cartor, printed on self adhesive paper with die-cut perfs 15 x 14.
Initial selling price: £ 22.95

BC-118 .... £ 30.00

Produced by: Buckingham Covers **Qty:** 1000

Issue Notes: 10 x 1st class DS "Big Bang" stamps plus labels. Although indicated to be a printing of 1967 sheets 1000 sheets were actually printed, 1967 being a reference to the 40th Anniversary base-year. In reality something less than 1000 sheets exist as a quantity were broken up for commemorative covers.

The sheet is also separately available signed by the Captain of the QE2. It is also available bearing a blue hand-stamp/cachet "Carried Aboard QE2".

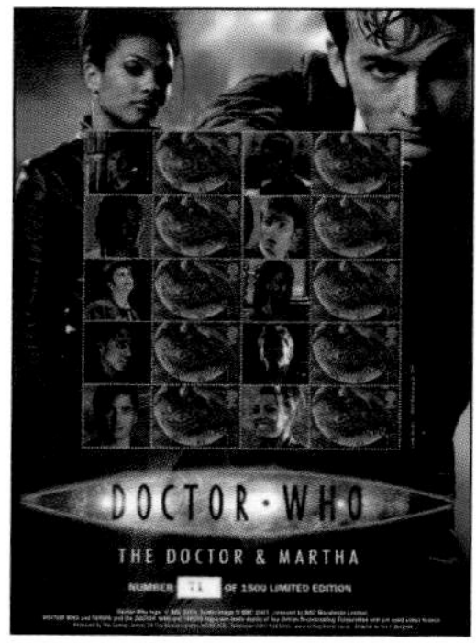

BC-119

Dr. Who - The Doctor and Martha

2007 (4 Oct), Litho by Cartor, Perf 14½ x 14.
Initial selling price: £ 24.95

BC-119 .... £ 25.00

BC-119a Unnumbered .... £ 50.00

Produced by: The Stamp Centre **Qty:** 1500

Issue Notes: 10 x 1st class Smilers "Moon" stamps plus labels. The twelfth in a series of sheets featuring Dr. Who. BC-119a are unnumbered sheets which were sheets from an additional batch intended for use on Dr. Who souvenir covers sold by The Stamp Centre.

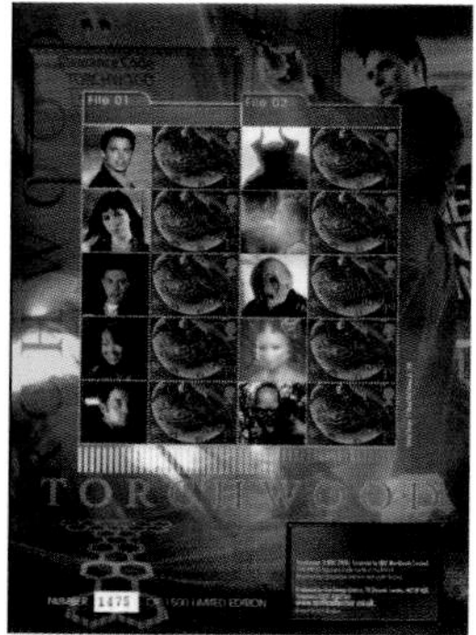

BC-120

Torchwood

2007 (4 Oct), Litho by Cartor, Perf 14½ x 14.
Initial selling price: £ 24.95

BC-120 .... £ 25.00

BC-120a Unnumbered .... £ 50.00

Produced by: The Stamp Centre **Qty:** 1500

Issue Notes: 10 x 1st class Smilers "Moon" stamps plus labels. Featuring the popular Dr. Who spin-off programme Torchwood character Jack Harkness. BC-120a are unnumbered sheets which were sheets from an additional batch intended for use on Torchwood souvenir covers sold by The Stamp Centre.

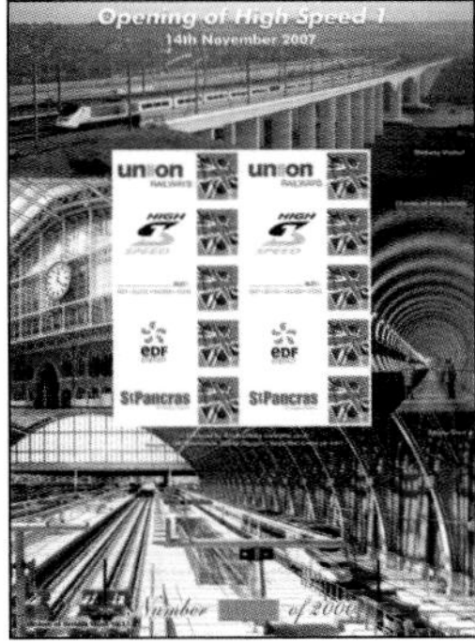

BC-121

Opening of High Speed 1

2007 (20 Oct), Litho by Cartor, printed on self adhesive paper with die-cut perfs 15 x 14.
Initial selling price: £ 29.95

BC-121 .... £ 30.00

Produced by: AG Bradbury **Qty:** 2000

Issue Notes: 10 x 1st class DS *"Union Flag"* stamps plus labels. Sheet No. 13 in the Bradbury *"History of Britain"* series. The sheets features the opening of the High Speed One (HS1) track from St. Pancras Station to Dover and the label designs feature companies or organisations connected with that event.

BC-122

Concorde - 30th Anniv. of First Flights

2007 (26 Oct), Litho by Cartor, printed on self adhesive paper with die-cut perfs 15 x 14.
Initial selling price: £ 29.95

BC-122 .... £ 30.00

Produced by: Buckingham Covers **Qty:** 1000

Issue Notes: 10 x 1st class DS *"Union Flag"* stamps plus labels. The third in a series of Concorde related sheets from Buckingham Covers. A limited edition of 1000 although 1977 printed on sheet. In reality something less than 1000 sheets exist as a quantity are known to have been broken up for commemorative covers.

BC-123

Concorde 001

2007 (27 Oct), Litho by Cartor, printed on self adhesive paper with die-cut perfs 15 x 14.
Initial selling price: £ 19.99

BC-123 .... £ 35.00

Produced by: Westminster **Qty:** est. 1000

Issue Notes: 10 x 1st class DS *"Union Flag"* stamps plus labels. Produced by the Westminster Collection to commemorate the production of the first Concorde (001) in Toulouse, France in 1967.

BC-124

The Great War (1914-18)

2007 (8 Nov), Litho by Cartor, printed on self adhesive paper with die-cut perfs 15 x 14.
Initial selling price: £ 29.95

BC-124.. £ 100.00

Produced by: AG Bradbury **Qty:** 1000

Issue Notes: 10 x 1st class Poppy (2007) stamps plus labels. Sheet No. 12 from A.G. Bradbury's *History of Britain* series. This sheet is the first Business Customised sheet to feature the 2007 Poppy stamp. A number of sheets were broken up to service First Day covers.

BC-125

Eurostar

2007 (14 Nov), Litho by Cartor, printed on self adhesive paper with die-cut perfs 15 x 14.
Initial selling price: £ 29.95

BC-125.. £ 75.00

Produced by: Buckingham Covers **Qty:** 1000

Issue Notes: 10 x 1st class DS "Big Bang" stamps plus labels. This sheet was issued in co-operation with Eurostar and incorporates the new Eurostar logo. The labels depict various Eurostar trains and destinations. It was released to coincide with the opening of the new Eurostar terminal in London at St. Pancras Station and the opening of the new High Speed track between London and Dover.

BC-126

85th Anniversary of the Big Four

2008 (5 Jan), Litho by Cartor, printed on self adhesive paper with die-cut perfs 15 x 14.
Initial selling price: £ 29.95

BC-126.. £ 45.00

Produced by: Buckingham Covers **Qty:** 1000

Issue Notes: 10 x 1st class DS "Big Bang" stamps plus labels. A rather strange anniversary but a sheet to appeal to the railway thematic collectors, the 85th Anniversary of the nationalisation of the Big Four Railway companies in 1923. Apparently only 1000 sheets were printed although 1923 are indicated on sheet. In reality something less than 1000 sheets exist as a quantity are known to have been broken up to service commemorative covers.

BC-127

Maiden Voyage of Queen Victoria

2008 (6 Jan), Litho by Cartor, printed on self adhesive paper with die-cut perfs 15 x 14.
Initial selling price: £ 29.95

BC-127.. £ 30.00

Produced by: Buckingham Covers **Qty:** 1000

Issue Notes: 10 x 1st class DS "Big Bang" stamps plus labels. Apparently only 1000 sheets were printed although 2007 are indicated on sheet, of which some are known to have been broken-up to service covers.

BC-128

History of the RAF

2008 (6 Jan), Litho by Cartor, printed on self adhesive paper with die-cut perfs 15 x 14.
Initial selling price: £ 19.99

BC-128.. £ 20.00

Produced by: Westminster Collection **Qty:** 1000

Issue Notes: 10 x 1st class DS "Union Flag" stamps plus labels. Issued to commemorate the 90th Anniversary of the RAF, this sheet is unnumbered and it is estimated that c. 1000 sheets were printed.

BC-129

Honouring the Spitfire

2008 (6 Jan), Litho by Cartor, printed on self adhesive paper with die-cut perfs 15 x 14.
Initial selling price: £ 19.99

BC-129.. £ 40.00

Produced by: Westminster Collection **Qty:** 1000

Issue Notes: 10 x 1st class DS "Union Flag" stamps plus labels. Issued to commemorate the 90th Anniversary of the RAF, this sheet is unnumbered and it is estimated that c. 1000 sheets were printed.

BC-130

St. Valentines Day

2008 (15 Jan), Litho by Cartor, printed on self adhesive paper with die-cut perfs 15 x 14.
Initial selling price: £ 29.95

BC-130.. £ 35.00

Produced by: AG Bradbury **Qty:** 500

Issue Notes: 10 x 1st class DS "Love" stamps plus labels. This is sheet is No. 14 in the Bradbury series *History of Britain*. It is also the first Business Sheet to feature the LOVE self-adhesive stamp.

BC-131

Kings & Queens of England (1066-1399)

2008 (1 Feb), Litho by Cartor, printed on self adhesive paper with die-cut perfs 15 x 14.
Initial selling price: £ 29.95

BC-131... £ 40.00

Produced by: AG Bradbury **Qty:** 1500

Issue Notes: 10 x 1st class DS "England" stamps plus labels. One of a pair of Sheets featuring the first use of the Litho printed Definitive Sized England stamps. This is sheet No. 15 in the Bradbury *History of Britain* series.

BC-132

Kings & Queens of England (1399-1485)

2008 (1 Feb), Litho by Cartor, printed on self adhesive paper with die-cut perfs 15 x 14.
Initial selling price: £ 29.95

BC-132... £ 40.00

Produced by: AG Bradbury **Qty:** 1500

Issue Notes: 10 x 1st class DS "England" stamps plus labels. One of a pair of Sheets featuring the first use of the Litho printed Definitive Sized England stamps. This is sheet No. 16 in the Bradbury *History of Britain* series.

BC-133

STAMPEX - Spring 2008

2008 (27 Feb), Litho by Cartor, printed Perf 14½ x 14. Initial selling price: £ 10.00

BC-133 .... £ 15.00

Produced by: PTS **Qty:** c. 3000

Issue Notes: 10 x 1st class Hallmarks "Cheers" stamps plus labels. Issued to coincide with the Spring Stampex event, organised by the Philatelic Traders' Society, and held at the Business Design Centre, London, in February 2008. The labels feature different modes of transport between 1908 and 2008.

BC-134

450th Anniversary Of the Accession Of Queen Elizabeth 1 (1558-1603)

2008 (13 Mar), Litho by Cartor, printed on self adhesive paper with die-cut perfs 15 x 14.
Initial selling price: £ 19.95

BC-134... £ 25.00

Produced by: Westminster Collection **Qty:** c. 1000

Issue Notes: 10 x 1st class DS "England" stamps

plus labels. From an unnumbered printing thought to be c. 1000. The sheet was offered as a promotional item as part of a collection of stamps and covers offered by the Westminster Collection.

BC-135

Royal National Lifeboat Institution

2008 (13 Mar), Litho by Cartor, printed on self adhesive paper with elliptical die-cut perfs 15 x 14.
Initial selling price: £ 22.95

BC-135.. £ 25.00

Produced by: Buckingham Covers **Qty:** c. 1908

Issue Notes: 10 x 1st class DS "England" stamps plus labels. Issued to coincide with Royal Mail's RNLI stamp issue. Four pounds from each sale was donated to the RNLI charities. This sheet has the distinction of being the first Business sheet to feature elliptical die-cut perfs. All self-adhesive Business sheets printed after March 2008 feature this type of perforation.

BC-136

The First Flight A380 flight from the UK

2008 (18 Mar), Litho by Cartor, printed on self adhesive paper with elliptical die-cut perfs 15 x 14.
Initial selling price: £ 22.95

BC-136..£ 30.00

Produced by: Buckingham Covers **Qty:** 2007

Issue Notes: 10 x 1st class DS "England" stamps plus labels. Issued to coincide with the maiden flight of Singapore Airline's Airbus A380 from Singapore to London. The sheet had been delayed by c. 18 months whilst technical problems with the plane were resolved. During this time the proposed sheet design underwent a radical design change. The following image is an earlier publicity image for this sheet.

Early publicity image for BC-136

BC-137

Wintons Fishery - 20th Anniversary

2008 (1 Apr), Litho by Cartor, printed on self adhesive paper with elliptical die-cut perfs 15 x 14.
Initial selling price: £ 100

BC-137..£ 200.00

Produced by: Wintons Fishery **Qty:** 100

Issue Notes: 10 x 1st class DS "Union Flag" stamps plus labels. Designed by Ridgewood Designs on behalf of Wintons Fishery to commemorate their 20th Anniversary. Low print run produced primarily as a promotional aid. Many sheets broken up for mail shots or used as corporate give-away's. Fewer than 50 sheets estimated to exist. A difficult sheet to find.

BC-138

British Butterflies

2008 (1 Apr), Litho by Cartor, printed on self adhesive paper with elliptical die-cut perfs 15 x 14.
Initial selling price: £ 24.95

BC-138 .... £ 100.00

Produced by: AG Bradbury **Qty:** 1500

Issue Notes: 10 x 1st class DS "Flower" stamps plus labels. Issued to coincide with Royal Mail's Butterflies issue - this sheet intriguingly sub-titled *History of Britain* Sheet No. 18.

BC-139

90th Anniversary of the RAF

2008 (1 Apr), Litho by Cartor, printed on self adhesive paper with elliptical die-cut perfs 15 x 14.
Initial selling price: £ 29.95

BC-139 ....£ 35.00

Produced by: Buckingham Covers **Qty:** 1918

Issue Notes: 10 x 1st class DS "Union Flag" stamps plus labels. This sheet features 11 different paintings of historic RAF aircraft by the great war artist, Frank Wootton. The copyright fees for these were donated to the Battle of Britain Memorial Trust by his widow, Mrs Ginny Wooton. A proportion of the sales of this sheet were donated to the charity.

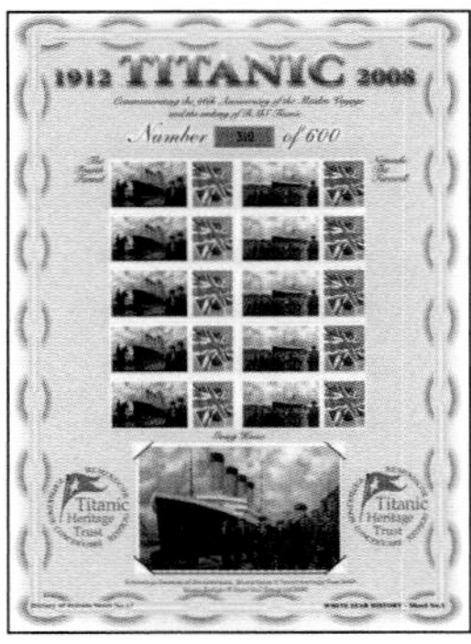

BC-140

96th Anniversary of Sinking of the Titanic

2008 (15 Apr), Litho by Cartor, printed on self adhesive paper with elliptical die-cut perfs 15 x 14.
Initial selling price: £ 30.00

BC-140 ....£ 100.00

Produced by: AG Bradbury **Qty:** 600

Issue Notes: 10 x 1st class DS "Union Flag" stamps plus labels. This stamp sheet has been designed by Adrian Bradbury in co-operation with The Titanic Heritage Trust, and is the 2nd in a collection of 6 Titanic sheets to be issued between 2007 and 2012, the centenary of the sinking of this great liner. AG Bradbury's *History of Britain* Sheet No. 17.

BC-141

The Third Doctor - Jon Pertwee

2008 (15 Apr), Litho by Cartor, printed Perf 14½ x 14.
Initial selling price: £ 24.95

BC-141 ....£ 30.00

BC-141a Unnumbered ....£ 60.00

Produced by: The Stamp Centre **Qty:** 1000

Issue Notes: 10 x 1st class Smiles "Moon" stamps plus labels. BC-141a are unnumbered sheets which were sheets from an additional batch intended for use on Dr. Who souvenir covers sold by The Stamp Centre.

BC-142

50 Years of "Carry On"

2008 (9 May), Litho by Cartor, printed on self adhesive paper with elliptical die-cut perfs 15 x 14.
Initial selling price: £ 30.00

BC-142 ....£ 40.00

Produced by: AG Bradbury **Qty:** 1500

Issue Notes: 10 x 1st class DS "Union Flag" stamps plus labels. An eye-catching sheet featuring early Carry On film posters. This is sheet No. 19 in Bradbury's *History of Britain* series.

BC-143

History of the Monarchy

2008 (20 May), Litho by Cartor, printed on self adhesive paper with elliptical die-cut perfs 15 x 14.
Initial selling price: £ 19.95

BC-143 ....£ 25.00

Produced by: Westminster Collection **Qty:** 9500

Issue Notes: 10 x 1st class DS "England" stamps plus labels. A celebration of the 40 Kings and Queens of England who have reigned since 1066. Each of the 10 labels features four monarchs whilst the border area illustrates the monarchy through the ages. Given the unified crowns of Scotland and England since the accession of King James 1 of England, the choice of the English definitive-sized smilers stamp is a strange, if not emotive, one. The sheet was initially offered at an introductory price of £9.95 as part of a promotion in connection with a collection of 40 souvenir covers bearing these stamps/labels offered by Westminster.

BC-144

The Dambusters

2008 (20 May), Litho by Cartor, printed on self adhesive paper with elliptical die-cut perfs 15 x 14.
Initial selling price: £ 19.95

BC-144 ....£ 25.00

Produced by: Westminster Collection **Qty:** 14,950

Issue Notes: 10 x 1st class DS "Union Flag" stamps plus labels. Celebrate the 65th anniversary of the Dambusters raid on the dams in Germany's Ruhr valleys, the sheet illustrates the night scene of an Avro Lancaster in flight with the broken dam in the backdrop. As with BC-143, the sheet was initially offered at an introductory price of £9.95 as part of a promotion in connection with a collection of souvenir covers bearing these stamps/labels marketed by Westminster Collection.

BC-145

The Mallard

2008 (2 Jun), Litho by Cartor, printed on self adhesive paper with elliptical die-cut perfs 15 x 14.
Initial selling price: £ 24.95

BC-145 ....£ 25.00

Produced by: Benham Covers **Qty:** 750

Issue Notes: 10 x 1st class DS "Union Flag" stamps plus labels. Issued on the occasion of the 70th anniversary of the LNER steam locomotive 'Mallard' setting the still unbroken world steam speed record of 126 mph on 3rd July 1938.

BC-146

90th Anniversary of the RAF - The Red Arrows

2008 (4 Jun), Litho by Cartor, printed on self adhesive paper with elliptical die-cut perfs 15 x 14.
Initial selling price: £ 29.95

BC-146 ....£ 30.00

Produced by: AG Bradbury **Qty:** 1500

Issue Notes: 10 x 1st class DS "Union Flag" stamps plus labels. Marking both the centenary of the first ever public Air Display at Farnborough and the 90th anniversary of the RAF, this sheet features the paintings of Mark Postlethwaite (Guild of Aviation Artists) with the Red Arrows flying over Fowey (top image) and Silverstone (bottom image). The ten stamp labels feature ten of Mark's paintings depicting famous RAF planes from 1918 through to the Harrier still in use in 2008. This is sheet No. 20 in Bradbury's *History of Britain* series.

BC-147

Captain Jack Hawkness

2008 (16 Jun), Litho by Cartor, printed Perf 14½ x 14.
Initial selling price: £ 24.95

BC-147 ....£ 25.00

BC-147a Unnumbered ....£ 50.00

Produced by: The Stamp Centre **Qty:** 1500

Issue Notes: 10 x 1st class Occasions "Hello" stamps plus labels. Featuring Captain Jack Harkness as played by actor John Barrowman in the Dr. Who spin-off show, Torchwood. BC-147a are unnumbered sheets which were sheets from an additional batch intended for use on Torchwood souvenir covers sold by The Stamp Centre.

BC-148

Chitty, Chitty Bang Bang

2008 (19 Jun), Litho by Cartor, printed on self adhesive paper with elliptical die-cut perfs 15 x 14.
Initial selling price: £ 40.00

BC-148 ....£ 50.00

Produced by: Bletchley Park Post Office **Qty:** 200

Issue Notes: 10 x 1st class DS "Hello" stamps plus labels. The car from Chitty, Chitty Bang Bang featured at a special event weekend held at the park. A number of collectible Smilers covers were also produced using a circular smilers format because the BCS sheets were not available in time.

BC-149

The Jubilee Issue of Queen Victoria

2008 (19 Jun), Litho by Cartor, printed Perf 14½ x 14.
Initial selling price: £ 19.95

BC-149 ....£ 25.00

Produced by: Westminster Collection **Qty:** 19,500

Issue Notes: 10 x 1st class Occasions "Union Flag" stamps plus labels. As with BC-143, the sheet was initially offered at an introductory price of £9.95 as part of a promotion in connection with a collection of souvenir covers bearing these stamps/labels marketed by Westminster Collection.

BC-150

50th Anniversary of Paddington Bear

2008 (19 Jun), Litho by Cartor, printed on self adhesive paper with elliptical die-cut perfs 15 x 14.
Initial selling price: £ 24.95

BC-150 ....£ 35.00

Produced by: Buckingham Covers **Qty:** 1000

Issue Notes: 10 x 1st class DS "Union Flag" stamps plus labels. The sheet was also available signed by Paddington Bear creator, Michael Bond (est. £60)

BC-151

Dambusters

2008 (25 Jun), Litho by Cartor, printed on self adhesive paper with elliptical die-cut perfs 15 x 14.
Initial selling price: £ 26.95

BC-151 ....£ 100.00

Produced by: Buckingham Covers **Qty:** 617

Issue Notes: 10 x 1st class DS "Union Flag" stamps plus labels. This sheet was from a relatively small print run and was the first in Buckingham's so-called Platinum Editions.

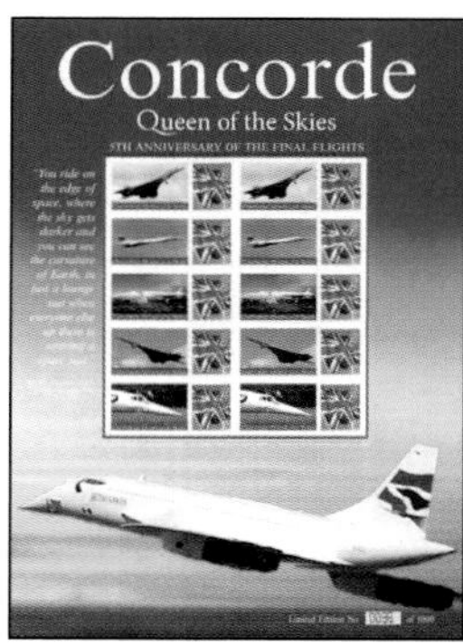

BC-152

Concorde - Queen of the Skies

2008 (25 Jun), Litho by Cartor, printed on self adhesive paper with elliptical die-cut perfs 15 x 14.
Initial selling price: £ 26.95

BC-152 ....£ 65.00

Produced by: Buckingham Covers **Qty:** 1000

Issue Notes: 10 x 1st class DS "Union Flag" stamps plus labels. Popular with Concorde and Thematic collectors alike and despite the large print run, the sheet quickly sold out from supplier.

BC-153

Honouring the Few

2008 (1 Jul), Litho by Cartor, printed on self adhesive paper with elliptical die-cut perfs 15 x 14.
Initial selling price: £ 19.95

BC-153 ....£ 30.00

Produced by: Westminster Collection **Qty:** 1000 est.

Issue Notes: 10 x 1st class DS "Union Flag" stamps plus labels. Initially offered at an introductory price of £9.95 as part of a cover collection offer. 100 sheets were sold framed and signed by the pilots. Original price of the signed sheets was £125 (est. £250).

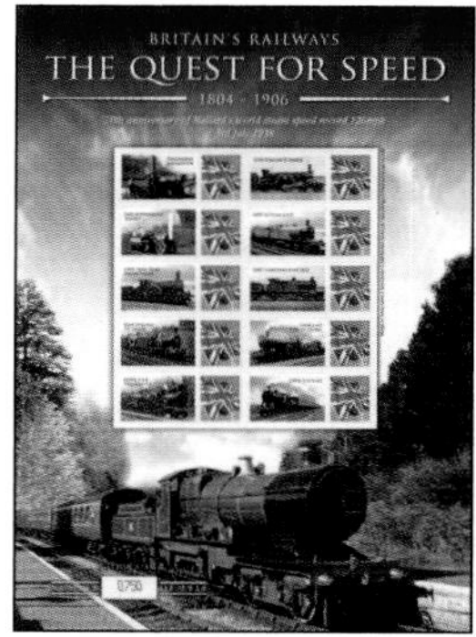

BC-154

The Quest for Speed (1)

2008 (9 Jul), Litho by Cartor, printed on self adhesive paper with elliptical die-cut perfs 15 x 14.
Initial selling price: £ 24.95

BC-154 ....£ 30.00

Produced by: Westminster Collection **Qty:** 1938

Issue Notes: 10 x 1st class DS "Union Flag" stamps plus labels. One of a pair of sheets released to commemorate the 70th anniversary of the record breaking Mallard speed trial of 1938. A collection of Smilers covers bearing these stamp/labels were also available from Benham.

BC-155

The Quest for Speed (2)

2008 (9 Jul), Litho by Cartor, printed on self adhesive paper with elliptical die-cut perfs 15 x 14.
Initial selling price: £ 24.95

BC-155 ....£ 30.00

Produced by: Westminster Collection **Qty:** 1938

Issue Notes: 10 x 1st class DS "Union Flag" stamps plus labels. See additional notes BC-154.

BC-156

90th Anniversary of the RAF (1918-1939)

2008 (10 Jul), Litho by Cartor, printed on self adhesive paper with elliptical die-cut perfs 15 x 14.
Initial selling price: £ 24.95

BC-156 ....£ 35.00

Produced by: Benham Covers **Qty:** 1918

Issue Notes: 10 x 1st class DS "Union Flag" stamps plus labels. One of a set of three sheets released to commemorate the 90th anniversary of the formation of the RAF in 1918. A collection of Smilers covers bearing these stamp/labels were also available from Benham.

BC-157

90th Anniversary of the RAF (1939-1945)

2008 (10 Jul), Litho by Cartor, printed on self adhesive paper with elliptical die-cut perfs 15 x 14.
Initial selling price: £ 24.95

BC-157 ....£ 35.00

Produced by: Benham Covers **Qty:** 1918

Issue Notes: 10 x 1st class DS "Union Flag" stamps plus labels. See additional notes BC-156.

BC-158

90th Anniversary of the RAF (Post War)

2008 (10 Jul), Litho by Cartor, printed on self adhesive paper with elliptical die-cut perfs 15 x 14.
Initial selling price: £ 24.95

BC-158 ....£ 35.00

Produced by: Benham Covers **Qty:** 1918

Issue Notes: 10 x 1st class DS "Union Flag" stamps plus labels. See additional notes BC-156.

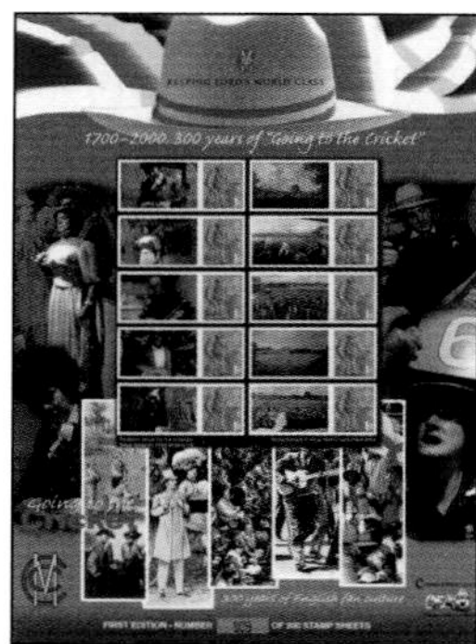

BC-159

Going to the Cricket

2008 (10 Jul), Litho by Cartor, printed on self adhesive paper with elliptical die-cut perfs 15 x 14.
Initial selling price: £ 40.00

BC-159 ....£ 125.00

Produced by: Bletchley Park Post Office **Qty:** 200

Issue Notes: 10 x 1st class DS "England" stamps plus labels. The first customised stamp sheet produced by BPPO for the MCC. It features the MCC "Going to the Cricket" exhibition at Lord's. The sheet covers 300 years of cricket history.

BC-160

New Forest Golf Club

2008 (28 Jul), Litho by Cartor, printed on self adhesive paper with elliptical die-cut perfs 15 x 14.
Initial selling price: £ 30.00

BC-160 ....£ 40.00

Produced by: Rushstamps **Qty:** 500

Issue Notes: 10 x 1st class DS "Union Flag" stamps plus labels. Designed by Ridgewood Publications for the New Forest Golf Club in celebration of their 120th Anniversary.

BC-161

Olympic Anniversaries

2008 (28 Jul), Litho by Cartor, printed on self adhesive paper with elliptical die-cut perfs 15 x 14.
Initial selling price: £ 30.00

BC-161 ....£ 45.00

Produced by: AG Bradbury **Qty:** 500

Issue Notes: 10 x 1st class DS "Union Flag" stamps plus labels. This sheet celebrates a double anniversary; the 100th anniversary of the 1908 Olympics and the 60th Anniversary of the 1948 Olympics, both held in London. This is sheet No. 26 in Bradbury's History of Britain series.

BC-162

The A1 Pacifics

2008 (30 Jul), Litho by Cartor, printed on self adhesive paper with elliptical die-cut perfs 15 x 14.
Initial selling price: £ 29.95

BC-162 ....£ 35.00

Produced by: Buckingham Covers **Qty:** 1965

Issue Notes: 10 x 1st class DS "Union Flag" stamps plus labels. The sheet celebrates Britain's first new steam train in over half a century. Inaugurated on 9 January 2008, the newly built A1 Pacific No 60163 Tornado class steam engine.

BC-163

St. Paul's Cathedral (1708-2008)

2008 (30 Jul), Litho by Cartor, printed on self adhesive paper with elliptical die-cut perfs 15 x 14.
Initial selling price: £ 30.00

BC-163 ....£ 35.00

Produced by: AG Bradbury **Qty:** 1000

Issue Notes: 10 x 1st class DS "Union Flag" stamps plus labels. Commemorating the 300th Anniversary of St. Paul's Cathedral this is sheet No. 27 in Bradbury's History of Britain Series.

BC-164

Freshwater Fish

2008 (31 Aug), Litho by Cartor, printed on self adhesive paper with elliptical die-cut perfs 15 x 14.
Initial selling price: £ 100.00

BC-164 ....£ 125.00

Produced by: Planet Prints **Qty:** 100

Issue Notes: 10 x 1st class DS "Union Flag" stamps plus labels. The limited availability of this sheet makes this a difficult sheet to find. It is understood a number of sheets were broken up for promotional purposes.

BC-165

65th Anniversary of the Dambusters

2008 (1 Sep), Litho by Cartor, printed on self adhesive paper with elliptical die-cut perfs 15 x 14.
Initial selling price: £ 30.00

BC-165 ....£ 35.00

Produced by: AG Bradbury **Qty:** 1200

Issue Notes: 10 x 1st class DS "Union Flag" stamps plus labels. This is Sheet No. 21 in Bradbury's History of Britain Stamp Sheet Series.

BC-166

50th Anniversary of Country Definitive's

2008 (1 Sep), Litho by Cartor, printed on self adhesive paper with elliptical die-cut perfs 15 x 14.
Initial selling price: £ 30.00

BC-166 ....£ 35.00

Produced by: AG Bradbury **Qty:** 1500

Issue Notes: 10 x 1st class DS "Union Flag" stamps plus labels. This is Sheet No. 22 in Bradbury's History of Britain Stamp Sheet Series.

BC-167

STAMPEX - Autumn 2008

2008 (17 Sep), Litho by Cartor, printed Perf 14½ x 14. Initial selling price: £ 10.00

BC-167 ....£ 15.00

Produced by: PTS **Qty:** Est. 2000

Issue Notes: 10 x 1st class Hallmarks "Thanks" stamps plus labels. Produced by the Philatelic Traders Society (PTS) on the occasion of the Autumn STAMPEX event held at The British Design Centre, Islington, London, 17th-20th September 2008.

BC-168

100th Anniversary of Votes for Women

2008 (18 Sep), Litho by Cartor, printed on self adhesive paper with elliptical die-cut perfs 15 x 14. Initial selling price: £ 30.00

BC-168 ....£ 35.00

Produced by: AG Bradbury **Qty:** 500

Issue Notes: 10 x 1st class DS "Union Flag" stamps plus labels. This is Sheet No. 23 in AG Bradbury's History of Britain Series.

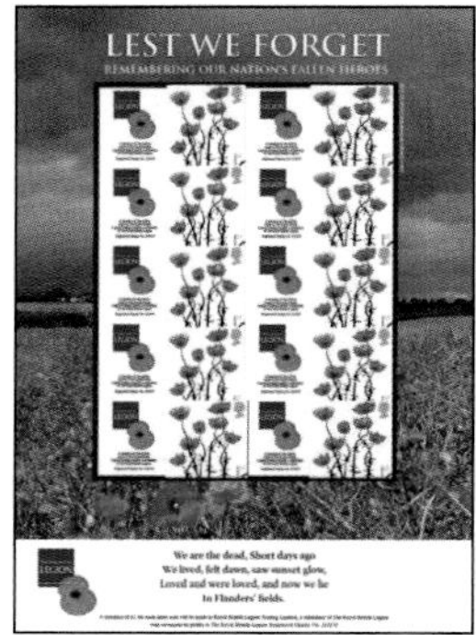

BC-169

Lest We Forget

2008 (23 Sep), Litho by Cartor, printed Perf 14½. Initial selling price: £ 4.95

BC-169 ....£ 10.00

Produced by: Westminster Collection **Qty:** 14,950

Issue Notes: 10 x 1st class Poppy (2006) stamps plus labels. Sold in aid of the British Legion at £1.50 over face value.

BC-170

Horatio Nelson (1758-1805)

2008 (30 Sep), Litho by Cartor, printed on self adhesive paper with elliptical die-cut perfs 15 x 14. Initial selling price: £ 24.95

BC-170 ....£ 30.00

Produced by: Buckingham Covers **Qty:** 1758

Issue Notes: 10 x 1st class DS "Union Flag" stamps

plus labels. Issued on the occasion of the 250th Anniversary of the birth of Lord Nelson.

BC-171

The Last Voyages of QE2

2008 (30 Sep), Litho by Cartor, printed on self adhesive paper with elliptical die-cut perfs 15 x 14.
Initial selling price: £ 26.95

BC-171 ....£ 35.00

Produced by: Buckingham Covers **Qty:** 2008

Issue Notes: 10 x 1st class DS "Union Flag" stamps plus labels. Commemorating the last voyages of the QE2 between September and November 2008 prior to being laid-up in Dubai.

BC-172

Best of British

2008 (1 Oct), Litho by Cartor, printed on self adhesive paper with elliptical die-cut perfs 15 x 14.
Initial selling price: £ 19.95

BC-172 ....£ 25.00

Produced by: Westminster Collection **Qty:** 14,950

Issue Notes: 10 x 1st class DS "Union Flag" stamps plus labels. Issued to promote a new Westminster Collection of Business Customised Stamp Sheets. Initially sold at a promotional price of £9.99.

BC-173

250th Anniv. of Birth Of Horatio Nelson

2008 (21 Oct), Litho by Cartor, printed Perf 14½ x 14.
Initial selling price: £ 24.95

BC-173 ....£ 30.00

Produced by: Benham Covers **Qty:** 1758

Issue Notes: 10 x 1st class Flags "White Ensign" stamps plus labels.

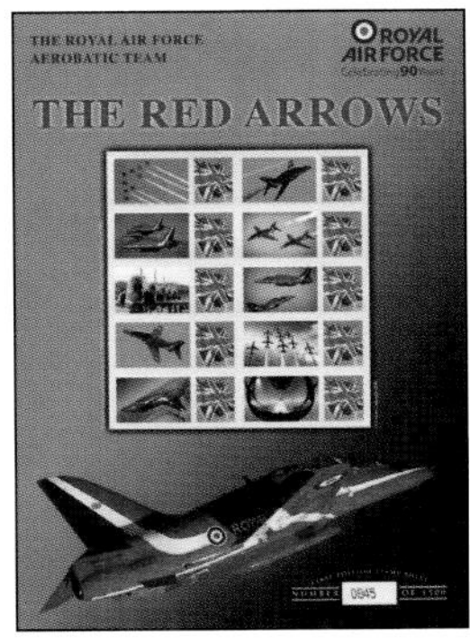

BC-174

Red Arrows - 90 Years of the RAF

2008 (23 Oct), Litho by Cartor, printed on self adhesive paper with elliptical die-cut perfs 15 x 14.
Initial selling price: £ 24.95

BC-174 ....£ 30.00

Produced by: Benham Covers **Qty:** 1500

Issue Notes: 10 x 1st class DS "Union Flag" stamps plus labels. Issued to commemorate the 90th Anniversary of the RAF, the sheet design also features the Red Arrows aerobatic display team, a favourite thematic subject.

BC-175

Lest We Forget - Royal Navy

2008 (23 Oct), Litho by Cartor, printed Perf 14½.
Initial selling price: £ 26.95

BC-175 ....£ 75.00

Produced by: Buckingham Covers **Qty:** 550

Issue Notes: 10 x 1st class Poppy (2006) stamps plus labels. This is sheet 1 of 3 sheets issued by Buckingham Covers to mark Remembrance Day. Sheet 1 remembers the heroes of the Royal Navy.

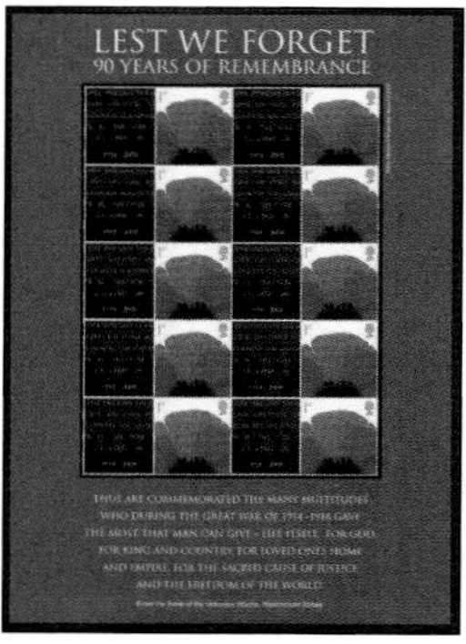

BC-176

Lest We Forget

2008 (25 Oct), Litho by Cartor, printed Perf 14½.
Initial selling price: £ 19.99

BC-176 ....£ 20.00

Produced by: Westminster Collection **Qty:** 14,950

Issue Notes: 10 x 1st class Poppy (2007) stamps plus labels. Initially sold at a promotional price of £9.99. Still available from sheet producer. On the surround of the sheet is the inscription from the tomb of the Unknown Warrior in Westminster Abbey.

BC-177

450th Anniversary Of The Accession Of Queen Elizabeth 1

2008 (25 Oct), Litho by Cartor, printed on self adhesive paper with elliptical die-cut perfs 15 x 14.
Initial selling price: £ 24.95

BC-177 ....£ 35.00

Produced by: Benham Covers **Qty:** 1558

Issue Notes: 10 x 1st class DS "Union Flag" stamps plus labels.

BC-178

Marlin Fishing

2008 (28 Oct), Litho by Cartor, printed on self adhesive paper with elliptical die-cut perfs 15 x 14.
Initial selling price: £ 90.00

BC-178 ....£ 125.00

Produced by: Planet Prints **Qty:** 100

Issue Notes: 10 x 1st class DS "Union Flag" stamps plus labels. Promotional sheet, available in small numbers. Its value is difficult to assess and is largely dependant upon demand, therefore its value may differ significantly from that indicated.

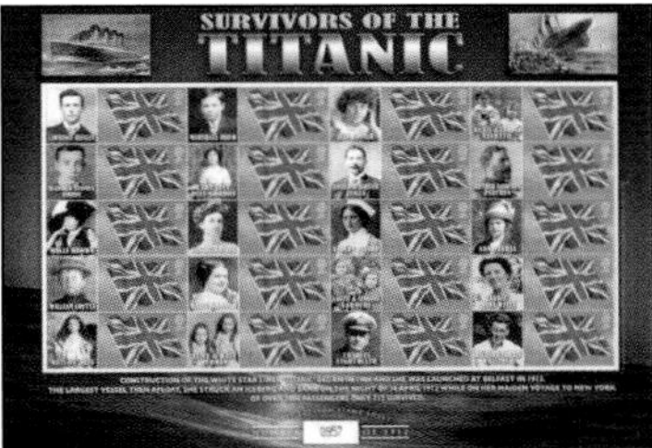

BC-179

Survivors of the Titanic

2008 (6 Nov),), Litho by Cartor, Printed on water-activated gummed paper. Perf 14½.
Initial selling price: £ 24.95

BC-179 ....£ 35.00

Produced by: Benham Covers **Qty:** 1912

Issue Notes: 10 x 1st class Flags "Union Flag" stamps plus labels. An attractive collection of 20 Smilers covers featuring stamps/labels from this sheet and special hand-stamps were also available from Benham Covers.

BC-180

Pantomime

2008 (8 Nov), Litho by Cartor, printed on self adhesive paper with elliptical die-cut perfs 15 x 14.
Initial selling price: £ 30.00

BC-180 ....£ 35.00

Produced by: AG Bradbury **Qty:** 1200

Issue Notes: 10 x 1st class DS "Robin-in-Letterbox" stamps plus labels. Issued to coincide with Royal Mail's Christmas issues, this sheet is a montage of Victorian Pantomime posters and illustrations' and is stamp sheet No. 24 in Bradbury's History of Britain series.

BC-181

The Cross of Sacrifice

2008 (8 Nov),), Litho by Cartor, Printed on water-activated gummed paper. Perf 14½ .
Initial selling price: £ 30.00

BC-181 ....£ 35.00

Produced by: AG Bradbury **Qty:** 1500

Issue Notes: 10 x 1st class Poppy (2008) stamps plus labels. A commemoration of the 90th Anniversary of the end of World War 1, this sheet is No. 25 in Bradbury's History of Britain series.

BC-182

A Victorian Christmas

2008 (8 Nov), Litho by Cartor, Printed on water-activated gummed paper. Perf 14½ .
Initial selling price: £ 24.95

BC-182 ....£ 35.00

Produced by: Benham Covers **Qty:** 1000

Business

Issue Notes: 10 x 1st class Santa + Cracker stamps plus labels. The first Business sheet to use the Santa + Cracker stamp although previously used for Generic Christmas sheets in 2000 and 2001.

BC-183

90th Anniversary of the End of WW1

2008 (11 Nov), Litho by Cartor, Printed on water-activated gummed paper. Perf 14½ .
Initial selling price: £ 24.95

BC-183 ....£ 35.00

Produced by: Benham Covers **Qty:** 1918

Issue Notes: 10 x 1st class Poppy (2008) stamps plus labels. The border design features King George V and his most significant Commanders (Haig, Kitchener etc.,). The labels feature famous battles from World War 1.

BC-184

Lest We Forget - Army

2008 (27 Nov), Litho by Cartor, Printed on water-activated gummed paper. Perf 14½ .
Initial selling price: £ 26.95

BC-184 ....£ 75.00

Produced by: Buckingham Covers **Qty:** 550

Issue Notes: 10 x 1st class Poppy (2007) stamps plus labels. This is sheet No. 2 of 3 sheets, in remembrance of the fallen dead of World War 1. Sheet No. 2 remembers the soldiers who fought during the War. See also BC-175.

BC-185

Lest We Forget - Air Force

2008 (27 Nov), Litho by Cartor, Printed on water-activated gummed paper. Perf 14½ .
Initial selling price: £ 26.95

BC-185 ....£ 100.00

Produced by: Buckingham Covers **Qty:** 1918

Issue Notes: 10 x 1st class Poppy (2008) stamps plus labels. This is sheet No. 3 of 3 sheets, in remembrance of the fallen dead of World War 1. Sheet No. 3 remembers the airman who fought during the War.

Known Varieties: Due to an unfortunate production error which remained undetected until after the sheet went on sale, Buckingham decided to withdraw the sheet after c. 600 sheets had been sold as the captions of the images did not match the label images. The example shown below shows the bottom left-hand label which has captions from the Army Sheet BC-184.

BC-186

Britain's Great Railways (L&NWR)

2008 (28 Nov), Litho by Cartor, printed on self adhesive paper with elliptical die-cut perfs 15 x 14.
Initial selling price: £ 24.95

BC-186 ....£ 35.00

Produced by: Benham Covers **Qty:** 500

Issue Notes: 10 x 1st class DS "Union Flag" stamps plus labels. The first in a series of Railway stamp sheets from Benham Covers, featuring the London and North Western Railway. Benham also released a cover collection bearing these stamps/labels.

BC-187

Wintons Greyhound Winners

2008 (1 Dec), Litho by Cartor, printed on self adhesive paper with elliptical die-cut perfs 15 x 14.
Initial selling price: £ 100.00

BC-187 ....£ 250.00

Produced by: Matthew Christelow **Qty:** 100

Issue Notes: 10 x 1st class DS "Union Flag" stamps plus labels. Produced for a greyhounds enthusiast (a Mr Etherington). Proceeds from the sale of these sheets was donated to caring for retired greyhounds.

BC-188

Gemini Hire and Sales

2008 (15 Dec), Litho by Cartor, printed on self adhesive paper with elliptical die-cut perfs 15 x 14.
Initial selling price: £ 100.00

BC-188 ....£ 250.00

Produced by: Matthew Christelow **Qty:** 100

Issue Notes: 10 x 1st class DS "Big Bang" stamps plus labels. Designed by Ridgewood Designs for Matt Christlow and Gemini Hire & Sales Ltd. A promotional stamp sheet produced in low numbers many of which were split up for promotional postage.

BC-189

90th Anniversary of NARPO

2008 (18 Dec), Litho by Cartor, printed on self adhesive paper with elliptical die-cut perfs 15 x 14.
Initial selling price: £ 95.00

BC-189 ....£ 250.00

Produced by: AG Bradbury **Qty:** 3000 (see Notes)

Issue Notes: 10 x 1st class DS "Union Flag" stamps

plus labels. Designed by Adrian Bradbury for National Association of Retired Police Officers. All except c. 100 were sold to NARPO members for £20 each. Adrian Bradbury secured a supply of 100 sheets for philatelic interest and sold these at £95 a sheet to Smilers sheet collectors. Here is the full story:

In February 2006 the National Association of Retired Police Officers (NARPO) approached Adrian Bradbury to design and produce a customised stamp sheet to help raise funds for police charities and to mark their 90th anniversary in 2009. After almost three years in the planning, the sheet was finally approved and offered to NARPO's 73,000 members through their quarterly journal which was despatched in November 2008.

The sheet, which was limited to 3,000, sold out within a week of the mailing and was massively oversubscribed. Members could only order a maximum of three sheets. The vast majority of orders were for one sheet. This project raised £18,000 for police charities.

Adrian undertook to handle the whole project, from design ideas, to marketing via the journal NARPO NEWS, which included designing the front cover of the journal and the design, print and folding of the leaflet/order form which was stapled inside the journal. Initially, NARPO members were asked for their ideas of what they wanted to see on the sheet and NARPO were to provide images for Adrian's use. However, this was to prove more difficult than originally thought – no images were forthcoming.

The project may not have gone ahead had Adrian not suggested that he get an artist to paint all the images used in the artwork which he eventually did at his cost. The labels feature police transport and the background artwork features police uniforms between 1919 and 2009. Sheets were sold to NARPO members for £20 each, with a maximum order of three sheets per order.

Despite the sell-out, Adrian did manage to pre-order 100 sheets numbered between 2900 and 3000 which were sold to the philatelic community at £95 each in January 2009. The philatelic community first got to hear about this sheet when a sheet appeared on eBay in January 2009 (sheet No. 0328) eventually selling for £320. A few have since appeared on eBay from the non-philatelic stock and appear to be starting at around £220 each.

In what may prove to be a first for Smilers collectors, Adrian Bradbury offered his customers the chance to buy a NARPO sheet with unique numbering 999. The sheet attracted keen interest from collectors, eventually going to the first of two bidders who had offered £500 for the sheet.

BC-190

500th Anniversary of Accession of King Henry VIII

2009 (1 Jan), Litho by Cartor, printed on self adhesive paper with elliptical die-cut perfs 15 x 14.
Initial selling price: £ 19.99

BC-190 ....£ 25.00

Produced by: Westminster Collection **Qty:** Est. 2500

Issue Notes: 10 x 1st class DS "England" stamps plus labels. The issue date has been taken as the date of a souvenir cover bearing these stamps/labels, produced by Westminster and dated 1st January 2009.

BC-191

50th Anniversary of the Mini

2009 (5 Jan), Litho by Cartor, printed on self adhesive paper with elliptical die-cut perfs 15 x 14.
Initial selling price: £ 27.00

BC-191 ....£ 25.00

Produced by: AG Bradbury **Qty:** 1200

Issue Notes: 10 x 1st class DS "Union Flag" stamps plus labels. Issued to coincide with Royal Mail's British Design Classic set of Postage stamps, this is sheet No. 28 in Bradbury's *History of Britain* series.

BC-192

250th Anniv. of the Birth of Robert Burns

2009 (5 Jan), Litho by Cartor, printed on self adhesive paper with elliptical die-cut perfs 15 x 14.
Initial selling price: £ 27.00

BC-192 ....£ 35.00

Produced by: AG Bradbury **Qty:** 1200

Issue Notes: 10 x 1st class DS "Scottish Lion" stamps plus labels. This is sheet No. 29 in Bradbury's *History of Britain* series.

BC-193

50th Anniversary of the Mini (60's Icon)

2009 (13 Jan), Litho by Cartor, printed on self adhesive paper with elliptical die-cut perfs 15 x 14.
Initial selling price: £ 27.00

BC-193 ....£ 35.00

Produced by: Buckingham Covers **Qty:** 2000

Issue Notes: 10 x 1st class DS "Union Flag" stamps plus labels. Sheet produced in association with The Heritage Motor Centre.

BC-194

Concorde - 40th Anniversary of the First Fights

2009 (25 Jan), Litho by Cartor, printed on self adhesive paper with elliptical die-cut perfs 15 x 14.
Initial selling price: £ 26.95

BC-194 ....£ 35.00

Produced by: Buckingham Covers **Qty:** 1969

Issue Notes: 10 x 1st class DS "Big Bang" stamps plus labels.

BC-195

Britain's Great Railways (GWR)

2009 (28 Jan), Litho by Cartor, printed on self adhesive paper with elliptical die-cut perfs 15 x 14.
Initial selling price: £ 24.95

BC-195 ....£ 35.00

Produced by: Benham Covers **Qty:** 500

Issue Notes: 10 x 1st class DS "Union Flag" stamps

plus labels. The second in a series of Railway stamp sheets from Benham Covers, featuring the Great Western Railway. Benham also released a cover collection bearing these stamps/labels.

BC-196

200th Anniversary of the Birth of Charles Darwin

2009(13 Feb), Litho by Cartor, printed on self adhesive paper with elliptical die-cut perfs 15 x 14.
Initial selling price: £ 26.95

BC-196 ....£ 35.00

Produced by: AG Bradbury **Qty:** 1200

Issue Notes: 10 x 1st class DS "Flowers" stamps plus labels. Issued to coincide with Royal Mail's Darwin Bicentenary issue, this is sheet number 30 in Bradbury's *History of Britain* series.

BC-197

The Stamps of Wales

2009 (13 Feb), Litho by Cartor, printed on self adhesive paper with elliptical die-cut perfs 15 x 14.
Initial selling price: £ 26.95

BC-197 ....£ 35.00

Produced by: AG Bradbury **Qty:** 1200

Issue Notes: 10 x 1st class DS "Welsh Dragon" stamps plus labels. A montage of welsh themed GB postage stamps this is sheet number 35 in Bradbury's *History of Britain* series.

BC-198

50th Anniversary of Ivor the Engine

2009 (18 Feb), Litho by Cartor, printed on self adhesive paper with elliptical die-cut perfs 15 x 14.
Initial selling price: £ 26.95

BC-198 ....£ 35.00

Produced by: Buckingham Covers **Qty:** 1959

Issue Notes: 10 x 1st class DS "Welsh Dragon" stamps plus labels. Sheet produced in association with the animal charity - Society for the Protection of Animals Abroad (SPANA). The sheet was issued in a presentation sleeve complete with printed card featuring details of the sheet and the work of SPANA.

BC-199

Great Little Trains of Wales

2009 (18 Feb), Litho by Cartor, printed on self adhesive paper with elliptical die-cut perfs 15 x 14.

Initial selling price: £ 26.95

BC-199 ....£ 35.00

Produced by: Buckingham Covers **Qty:** 2009

Issue Notes: 10 x 1st class DS "Welsh Dragon" stamps plus labels. The main illustration on the sheet is from a painting by railway artist Terence Cuneo. The Ten railways featured on the labels include: Talyllyn, Llanberis, Festiniog, Welsh Highland (Caernarfon), Welshpool and Llanfair, Vale of Rheidol, Brecon Mountain, Bala Lake, Welsh Highland (Porthmadog) and Snowdon Mountain. The sheet was issued in a presentation sleeve complete with printed card featuring details of the featured railways.

BC-200

STAMPEX - Spring 2009

2009 (25 Feb), Litho by Cartor, Printed on water-activated gummed paper. Perf 14½ x 14.
Initial selling price: £ 10.00

BC-200 ....£ 15.00

Produced by: PTS **Qty:** Est. 2000

Issue Notes: 10 x 1st class Hallmarks "Cheers" stamps plus labels. Produced by the Philatelic Traders Society (PTS) on the occasion of the Spring STAMPEX event held at The British Design Centre, Islington, London, 25th-28th February 2008.

BC-201

Pioneers of the Industrial Revolution

2009 (9 Mar), Litho by Cartor, printed on self adhesive paper with elliptical die-cut perfs 15 x 14.
Initial selling price: £ 26.95

BC-201 ....£ 35.00

Produced by: AG Bradbury **Qty:** 1200

Issue Notes: 10 x 1st class DS "Union Flag" stamps plus labels. Issued to coincide with Royal Mail's *Pioneers of the Industrial Revolution* issue on March 10, this is sheet number 31 in Bradbury's *History of Britain* series.

BC-202

Kings and Queens of England The Tudors (1485-1603)

2009 (9 Mar), Litho by Cartor, printed on self adhesive paper with elliptical die-cut perfs 15 x 14.
Initial selling price: £ 26.95

BC-202 ....£ 35.00

Produced by: AG Bradbury **Qty:** 1000

Issue Notes: 10 x 1st class DS "England" stamps

Business

plus labels. Issued to coincide with Royal Mail's *House of Tudor* issue on April 21, this is sheet number 34 in Bradbury's *History of Britain* series.

BC-203

450th Anniversary of the Accession of Queen Elizabeth 1

2009 (18 Mar), Litho by Cartor, printed on self adhesive paper with elliptical die-cut perfs 15 x 14.
Initial selling price: £ 26.95

BC-203 ....£ 35.00

Produced by: AG Bradbury **Qty:** 1000

Issue Notes: 10 x 1st class DS "England" stamps plus labels. This is sheet number 32 in Bradbury's *History of Britain* series.

BC-204

500th Anniversary of the Accession of King Henry VIII

2009 (18 Mar), Litho by Cartor, printed on self adhesive paper with elliptical die-cut perfs 15 x 14.
Initial selling price: £ 26.95

BC-204 ....£ 35.00

Produced by: AG Bradbury **Qty:** 1000

Issue Notes: 10 x 1st class DS "England" stamps plus labels. This is sheet number 33 in Bradbury's *History of Britain* series.

BC-205

100th Anniversary of the Stephenson Locomotive Society

2009 (30 Mar), Litho by Cartor, printed on self adhesive paper with elliptical die-cut perfs 15 x 14.
Initial selling price: £ 26.95

BC-205 ....£ 30.00

Produced by: Buckingham Covers **Qty:** 1909

Issue Notes: 10 x 1st class DS "Big Bang" stamps plus labels. Artwork by John Wigston this sheet also served as a commemoration of the 150th Anniversary of the death of George Stephenson.

BC-206

60th Anniv. First Flight of the Comet

2009 (30 Mar), Litho by Cartor, printed on self adhesive paper with elliptical die-cut perfs 15 x 14.
Initial selling price: £ 26.95

Business

BC-206 ....£ 30.00

Produced by: Buckingham Covers **Qty:** 1949

Issue Notes: 10 x 1st class DS "Union Flag" stamps plus labels. Sheet design based on a painting by John Long (reversed on labels).

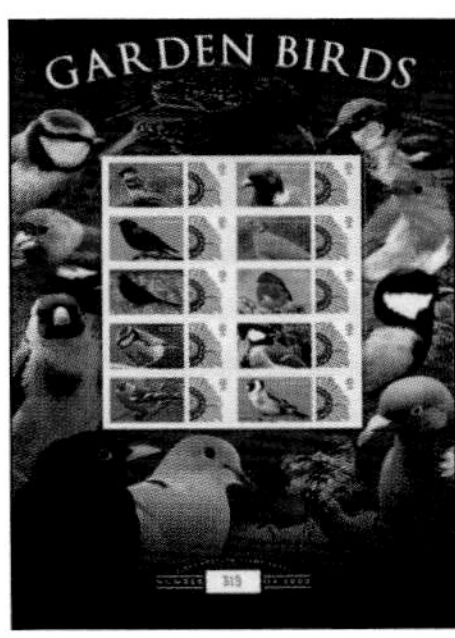

BC-207

Garden Birds

2009 (31 Mar), Litho by Cartor, printed on self adhesive paper with elliptical die-cut perfs 15 x 14.
Initial selling price: £ 24.95

BC-207 ....£ 30.00

Produced by: Benham Covers **Qty:** 1000

Issue Notes: 10 x 1st class DS "Flower" stamps plus labels.

BC-208

Victorian Garden Flowers

2009 (20 Apr), Litho by Cartor, printed on self adhesive paper with elliptical die-cut perfs 15 x 14.
Initial selling price: £ 26.95

BC-208 ....£ 30.00

Produced by: AG Bradbury **Qty:** 1000

Issue Notes: 10 x 1st class DS "Flower" stamps plus labels. This is sheet number 36 in Bradbury's *History of Britain* series.

BC-209

500th Anniversary of the Accession of King Henry VIII

2009 (21 Apr), Litho by Cartor, printed on self adhesive paper with elliptical die-cut perfs 15 x 14.
Initial selling price: £ 24.95

BC-209 ....£ 25.00

Produced by: Benham Covers **Qty:** 1509

Issue Notes: 10 x 1st class DS "England" stamps plus labels.

BC-210

500th Anniversary of The Mary Rose

2009 (21 Apr), Litho by Cartor, Printed on water-activated gummed paper. Perf 14½ x 14.
Initial selling price: £ 26.95

BC-210 ....£ 30.00

Produced by: Buckingham Covers **Qty:** 1509

Issue Notes: 10 x 1st class Flags "White Ensign" stamps plus labels. Produced with the co-operation of the Mary Rose Trust.

BC-211

Garden Birds

2009 (4 May), Litho by Cartor, printed on self adhesive paper with elliptical die-cut perfs 15 x 14.
Initial selling price: £ 225.00

BC-211 ....£ 250.00

Produced by: Planet Prints **Qty:** 100

Issue Notes: 10 x 1st class DS "Union Flag" stamps plus labels. Due to limited availability and supply of this sheet it is difficult to assess a price guide for this sheet. Collectors were contacted by the supplier suggesting an initial price of c. £225.

BC-212

Demolition Company Partnership

2009 (9 May), Litho by Cartor, printed on self adhesive paper with elliptical die-cut perfs 15 x 14.
Initial selling price: £ 200.00

BC-212 ....£ 250.00

Produced by: Matt Christelow **Qty:** 100

Issue Notes: 10 x 1st class DS "Big Bang" stamps plus labels. A promotional business sheet with limited supply and availability to the philatelic community (est. 30 sheets) prices will largely be determined by demand/interest. Sheet designed by Ridgewood Designs.

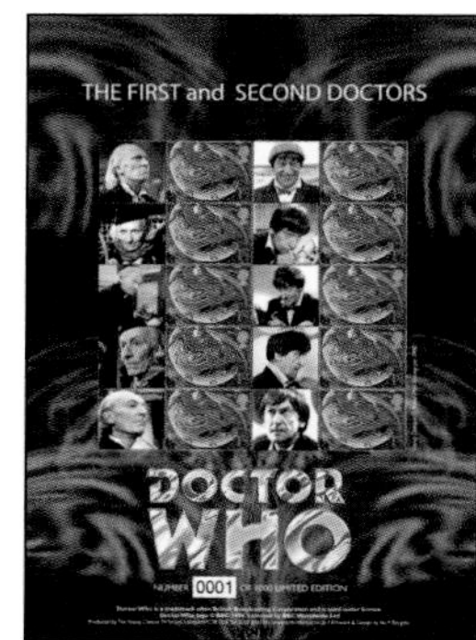

BC-213

Dr. Who - The First and Second Doctors

2009 (11 May), Litho by Cartor, Printed on water-activated gummed paper. Perf 14½ x 14.
Initial selling price: £ 24.95

BC-213 .... £ 25.00

BC-213a Unnumbered .... £ 50.00

Produced by: The Stamp Centre **Qty:** 1000

Issue Notes: 10 x 1st class Smiles "Moon" stamps plus labels. BC-213a are unnumbered sheets which were sheets from an additional batch intended for use on Dr. Who souvenir covers sold by The Stamp Centre.

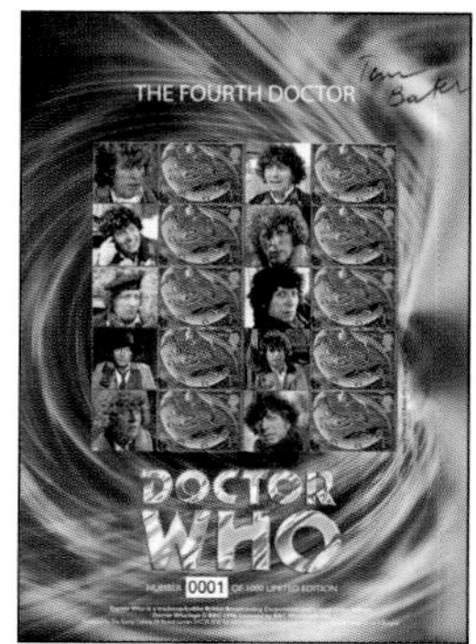

BC-214

Dr. Who - The Fourth Doctor

2009 (11 May), Litho by Cartor, Printed on water-activated gummed paper. Perf 14½ x 14.

Initial selling price: £ 24.95

BC-214 ....£ 25.00

BC-214a Unnumbered ....£ 50.00

Produced by: The Stamp Centre **Qty:** 1000

Issue Notes: 10 x 1st class Smiles "Moon" stamps plus labels. BC-214a are unnumbered sheets which were sheets from an additional batch intended for use on Dr. Who souvenir covers sold by The Stamp Centre. Also available autographed by Tom Baker. This sheet is actually the second "4th Doctor" sheet. Stocks of the original sheet, BC-028, had long been exhausted and coupled with the popularity of Tom Baker in the role of the Doctor a second sheet was commissioned by the Stamp Centre primarily to service their sci-fi cover range.

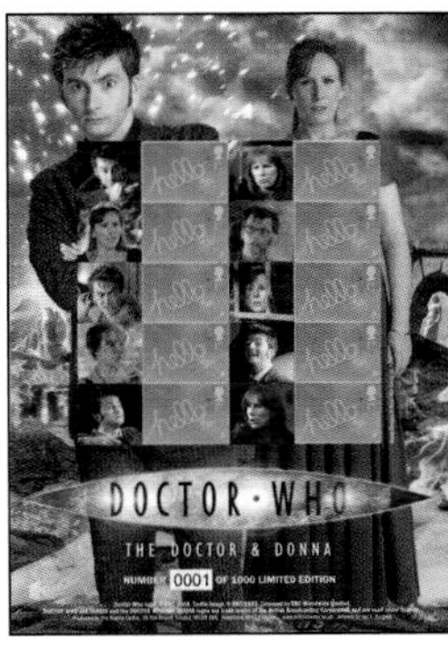

BC-215

Dr Who - The Doctor and Donna

2009 (11 May), Litho by Cartor, Printed on water-activated gummed paper. Perf 14½ x 14.
Initial selling price: £ 24.95

BC-215 ....£ 25.00

BC-215a Unnumbered ....£ 50.00

Produced by: The Stamp Centre **Qty:** 1000

Issue Notes: 10 x 1st class Occasions "Hello" stamps plus labels. BC-214a are unnumbered sheets which were sheets from an additional batch intended for use on Dr. Who souvenir covers sold by The Stamp Centre.

BC-216

Britain's Great Railways (NER)

2009 (11 May), Litho by Cartor, printed on self adhesive paper with elliptical die-cut perfs 15 x 14.
Initial selling price: £ 24.95

BC-216 ....£ 35.00

Produced by: Benham Covers **Qty:** 500

Issue Notes: 10 x 1st class DS "Union Flag" stamps plus labels. The third in a series of Railway stamp sheets from Benham Covers, featuring the North Eastern Railway with Hull and Barnsley. Benham also released a cover collection bearing these stamps/labels.

BC-217

40th Anniv. of the first Moon Landing

2009 (27 May), Litho by Cartor, printed on self adhesive paper with elliptical die-cut perfs 15 x 14.
Initial selling price: £ 26.95

BC-217 ....£ 30.00

Produced by: Buckingham Covers **Qty:** 1969

Issue Notes: 10 x 1st class DS "Big Bang" stamps plus labels. The first in a number of Smilers sheets featuring this iconic event.

BC-218

Great British Prime Ministers

2009 (28 May), Litho by Cartor, printed on self adhesive paper with elliptical die-cut perfs 15 x 14.
Initial selling price: £ 24.95

BC-218 .... £ 25.00

Produced by: Benham Covers **Qty:** 500

Issue Notes: 10 x 1st class DS "Union Flag" stamps plus labels. Issued to coincide with the 250th anniversary of the birth of William Pitt the Younger.

BC-219

British Wildlife

2009 (1 Jun), Litho by Cartor, printed on self adhesive paper with elliptical die-cut perfs 15 x 14.
Initial selling price: £ 49.95

BC-219 .... £ 50.00

Produced by: Ridgewood Stamp Sheets **Qty:** 200

Issue Notes: 10 x 1st class DS "Flowers" stamps plus labels.

BC-220

Mythical Creatures & Heraldry

2009 (1 Jun), Litho by Cartor, printed on self adhesive paper with elliptical die-cut perfs 15 x 14.
Initial selling price: £ 28.99

BC-220 .... £ 27.50

Produced by: AG Bradbury **Qty:** 750

Issue Notes: 10 x 1st class DS "England" stamps plus labels. This is sheet number 37 in Bradbury's *History of Britain* series.

BC-221

British Anniversaries

2009 (15 Jun), Litho by Cartor, printed on self adhesive paper with elliptical die-cut perfs 15 x 14.
Initial selling price: £ 19.99

BC-221 .... £ 20.00

Produced by: Westminster Collection **Qty:** 9,950

Issue Notes: 10 x 1st class DS "Union Flag" stamps plus labels showing various 2009 anniversaries.

BC-222

Mythical Creatures

2009 (17 Jun), Litho by Cartor, printed on self adhesive paper with elliptical die-cut perfs 15 x 14.
Initial selling price: £ 24.95

BC-222 .... £ 35.00

Produced by: Benham Covers **Qty:** 500

Issue Notes: 10 x 1st class DS "Wales" stamps plus labels showing various mythical creatures.

BC-223

125th Anniversary of Greenwich Meridian

2009 (19 Jun), Litho by Cartor, printed on self adhesive paper with elliptical die-cut perfs 15 x 14.
Initial selling price: £ 28.99

BC-223 .... £ 35.00

Produced by: AG Bradbury **Qty:** 750

Issue Notes: 10 x 1st class DS "Union Flag" stamps plus labels. This is sheet number 38 in Bradbury's *History of Britain* series.

BC-224

Duke of Wellington

2009 (30 Jun), Litho by Cartor, printed on self adhesive paper with elliptical die-cut perfs 15 x 14.
Initial selling price: £ 49.99

BC-224 .... £ 125.00

Produced by: AG Bradbury **Qty:** 250

Issue Notes: 10 x 1st class DS "Union Flag" stamps plus labels. The sheet marks the bicentenary of the ennoblement of Arthur Wellesley who was created a Viscount in 1809. He was later created Duke of Wellington in 1815 following the Battle of Waterloo. The sheet was a complete sell out before issue. This is Sheet No. 43 in the *History of Britain* series.

BC-225

Hitachi Class 395

2009 (3 Jul), Litho by Cartor, printed on self adhesive paper with elliptical die-cut perfs 15 x 14.
Initial selling price: £ 26.95

BC-225 .... £ 35.00

Produced by: Buckingham Covers **Qty:** 600

Issue Notes: 10 x 1st class DS "Big Bang" stamps

plus labels. Issued to commemorate the launch of the first Class 395 train from London's St Pancras station to stations in Kent. Produced in conjunction with Hitachi the design borrows from the Art Deco period of the 20's and 30's a "golden age of rail travel". The labels accompanying the stamps have been created by Hitachi's own designer, Michael Ballantine. Originally sold in a presentation pack with an informative presentation card and clear sleeve. All sheets were supplied with a "Carried on Board" cachet.

BC-226

90th Anniv. of First Transatlantic Flights

2009 (3 Jul), Litho by Cartor, printed on self adhesive paper with elliptical die-cut perfs 15 x 14.
Initial selling price: £ 26.95

BC-226 .... £ 35.00

Produced by: Buckingham Covers **Qty:** 600

Issue Notes: 10 x 1st class DS "Union Flag" stamps plus labels. Originally sold in a presentation pack with an informative presentation card and clear sleeve.

BC-227

Delivering the Mail

2009 (3 Jul), Litho by Cartor, printed on self adhesive paper with elliptical die-cut perfs 15 x 14.
Initial selling price: £ 28.99

BC-227 .... £ 35.00

Produced by: AG Bradbury **Qty:** 1000

Issue Notes: 10 x 1st class DS "Union Flag" stamps plus labels. Produced in association with the British Postal Museum & Archive (BPMA), this stamp sheet is a visual interpretation of the early history of the Post Office from the 1635 proclamation by King Charles I through to the issue of the first uniforms supplied to London letter carriers in 1793. It is reportedly the first in a series of stamp sheets to be issued annually in association with the BPMA. This is Sheet No. 39 in the *History of Britain* series.

BC-228

Sir Arthur Conan Doyle - 150th Anniv. of birth

2009 (17 Jul), Litho by Cartor, printed on water activated gummed paper Perf. 14.
Initial selling price: £ 26.95

BC-228 .... £ 30.00

Produced by: Buckingham Covers **Qty:** 1000

Issue Notes: 10 x 1st class Lion and Shield of England stamps plus labels. Originally sold in a presentation pack with an informative presentation card and clear sleeve.

BC-229

100th Anniv. of 1st Cross-Channel Flight

2009 (17 Jul), Litho by Cartor, printed on self adhesive paper with die-cut perfs 15 x 14.
Initial selling price: £ 26.95

BC-229 .... £ 30.00

Produced by: Buckingham Covers **Qty:** 1909

Issue Notes: 10 x 1st class DS "Union Flag" stamps plus labels. This sheet has been issued with regular (i.e. no elliptical) die cut perforations. It would indicate that this sheet has been in production for over a year and is only now being released. The switch to die-cut elliptical perfs occurred roughly mid-2008. Originally sold in a presentation pack with an informative presentation card and clear sleeve.

BC-230

Louis Bleriot Centenary

2009 (24 Jul), Litho by Cartor, printed on self adhesive paper with elliptical die-cut perfs 15 x 14.
Initial selling price: £ 24.95

BC-230 .... £ 35.00

Produced by: Benham Covers **Qty:** 500

Issue Notes: 10 x 1st class DS "Hello" stamps plus labels.

BC-231

300th Anniversary of First Fire Station

2009 (30 Jul), Litho by Cartor, printed on self adhesive paper with elliptical die-cut perfs 15 x 14.
Initial selling price: £ 28.99

BC-231 .... £ 35.00

Produced by: AG Bradbury **Qty:** 750

Issue Notes: 10 x 1st class DS "Union Flag" stamps plus labels. This sheet marks the 300th anniversary of the first purpose built fire station in Chester. The design features a brief pictorial history of the Fire and Rescue Service up to the end of the last century with specially commissioned paintings by Malcolm Greensmith and pictures from a variety of other sources. The sheet also reproduces a special set of stamps issued in 1974 which marked the bicentenary of the first Fire Service legislation. This is Sheet No. 40 in the *History of Britain* Series.

BC-232

Royal Navy Uniforms

2009 (30 Jul), Litho by Cartor, printed on self adhesive paper with elliptical die-cut perfs 15 x 14.
Initial selling price: £ 28.99

BC-232 .... £ 27.50

Produced by: AG Bradbury **Qty:** 750

Issue Notes: 10 x 1st class DS "Union Flag" stamps plus labels. This sheet charts a brief history of British naval uniform from 1250 to 1950. Although England's first navy was established in the 9th century by Alfred the Great, there are no records of naval dress/ uniforms until the mid 13th century. This is Sheet No. 41 in the *History of Britain* Series of Stamp Sheets.

BC-233

London, Brighton & South Coast Railway

2009 (5 Aug), Litho by Cartor, printed on self adhesive paper with elliptical die-cut perfs 15 x 14.
Initial selling price: £ 24.95

BC-233 .... £ 25.00

Produced by: Benham Covers **Qty:** 500

Issue Notes: 10 x 1st class DS "Union Flag" stamps plus labels. Britain's Great Railways - London, Brighton and South Coast Railway. No. 4 in the series.

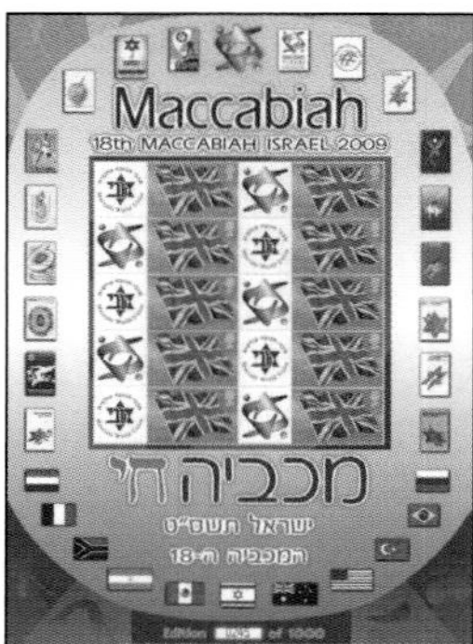

BC-234

Maccabiah - 18th Jewish Games

2009 (5 Aug), Litho by Cartor, printed on water-activated gummed-paper, Perf 14½.
Initial selling price: £ 29.95

BC-234 .... £ 30.00

Produced by: The Stamp Centre **Qty:** 1000

Issue Notes: 10 x 1st class "Union Flag" stamps plus labels. Commemorating the 18th Jewish Games held in Israel this bright and interesting sheet is from the producers of the Dr. Who series of stamp sheets.

BC-235

1969 Moon Landing—40th Anniversary

2009 (18 Aug), Litho by Cartor, printed on self adhesive paper with elliptical die-cut perfs 15 x 14.
Initial selling price: £ 24.95

BC-235 .... £ 30.00

Produced by: Benham Covers **Qty:** 500

Issue Notes: 10 x 1st class DS "Big Bang" stamps plus labels. Commemorating the 40th Anniversary of the first Manned moon landing in 1969.

BC-236

The Pillar Box through the Ages

2009 (26 Aug), Litho by Cartor, printed on self adhesive paper with elliptical die-cut perfs 15 x 14.
Initial selling price: £ 24.95

BC-236 .... £ 25.00

Produced by: Benham Covers **Qty:** 1000

Issue Notes: 10 x 1st class DS “Union Flag” stamps plus labels. Benham's response to the planned Royal Mail Wall Boxes generic Smilers sheet, due in September, was a sheet featuring Pillar Boxes through the Ages.

BC-237

NASA at 50

2009 (28 Aug), Litho by Cartor, printed on self adhesive paper with elliptical die-cut perfs 15 x 14.
Initial selling price: £ 49.95

BC-237 .... £ 50.00

Produced by: Ridgewood Stamp Sheets **Qty:** 200

Issue Notes: 10 x 1st class DS “Big Bang” stamps plus labels. Ridgewood Designs issued three limited edition stamp sheets during 2009 (all 200 each) celebrating the achievements of NASA. The first sheet celebrated the 25th Anniversary of first un-tethered space walk by Bruce McCandless in 1984.

BC-238

40th Anniv. of 1st Manned Moon Landing

2009 (28 Aug), Litho by Cartor, printed on self adhesive paper with elliptical die-cut perfs 15 x 14.
Initial selling price: £ 49.95

BC-238 .... £ 50.00

Produced by: Ridgewood Stamp Sheets **Qty:** 200

Issue Notes: 10 x 1st class DS “Big Bang” stamps plus labels. The second in the mini series of three stamps sheets from Ridgewood Designs celebrating the achievements of NASA. The second sheet celebrates the 40th Anniversary of the first manned moon landing on the Moon in the summer of 1969.

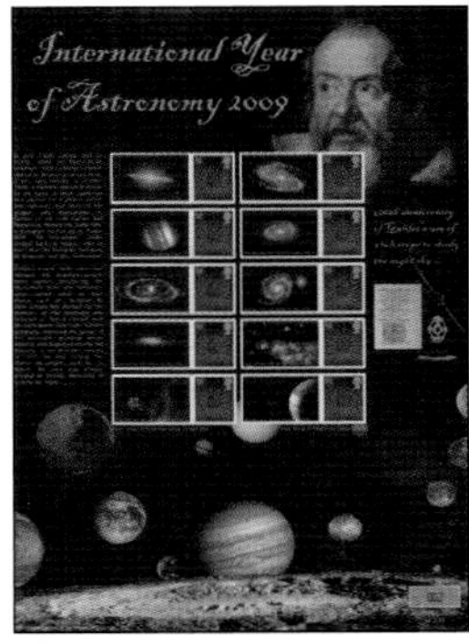

BC-239

International Year of Astronomy

2009 (28 Aug), Litho by Cartor, printed on self adhesive paper with elliptical die-cut perfs 15 x 14.
Initial selling price: £ 49.95

BC-239 .... £ 50.00

Produced by: Ridgewood Stamp Sheets **Qty:** 200

Issue Notes: 10 x 1st class DS "Big Bang" stamps plus labels. The final sheet of three stamp sheets from Ridgewood Designs celebrating the achievements of NASA. This sheet timed to coincide with the International Year of Astronomy features images from the NASA Hubble Telescope.

BC-240

Big Ben (1859-2009)

2009 (28 Aug), Litho by Cartor, printed on self adhesive paper with elliptical die-cut perfs 15 x 14.
Initial selling price: £ 49.95

BC-240 .... £ 50.00

Produced by: Ridgewood Stamp Sheets **Qty:** 200

Issue Notes: 10 x 1st class DS "Union Flag" stamps plus labels. The sheet tells the history of the manufacture and installation of the largest bell in the Clock Tower that has become synonymous with Big Ben, using images that originally appeared in the Illustrated London News.

BC-241

150th Anniv. of the Birth of Sir Arthur Conan Doyle

2009 (3 Sep), Litho by Cartor, printed on self adhesive paper with elliptical die-cut perfs 15 x 14.
Initial selling price: £ 28.95

BC-241 .... £ 35.00

Produced by: AG Bradbury **Qty:** 750

Issue Notes: 10 x 1st class DS "Union Flag" stamps plus labels. This sheet was issued to coincide with Royal Mail's Eminent Britain's special stamp issue and commemorates the 150th anniversary of the Birth of Sir Arthur Conan Doyle. It is sheet No. 42 in Bradbury's *History of Britain* Series.

BC-242

William Ewart Gladstone

2009 (3 Sep), Litho by Cartor, printed on self adhesive paper with elliptical die-cut perfs 15 x 14.
Initial selling price: £ 49.95

BC-242 .... £ 125.00

Produced by: AG Bradbury **Qty:** 250

Issue Notes: 10 x 1st class DS "Union Flag" stamps plus labels. This sheet was issued to coincide with Royal Mail's Eminent Britain's special stamp issue and commemorates the life and times of William Gladstone. The sheet was a complete sell out before issue. This is sheet No. 44 in Bradbury's *History of Britain* Series.

BC-243

Fire and Rescue

2009 (4 Sep), Litho by Cartor, printed on self adhesive paper with elliptical die-cut perfs 15 x 14.
Initial selling price: £ 24.95

BC-243... £ 25.00

Produced by: Benham Covers **Qty:** 1000

Issue Notes: 10 x 1st class DS "Big Bang" stamps plus labels. This sheet was issued to coincide with Royal Mail's Fire and Rescue Service special issue and depicts Fire Engines through the ages on the labels.

BC-244

70th Anniversary of the Auxiliary Fire Service

2009 (7 Sep), Litho by Cartor, printed on self adhesive paper with elliptical die-cut perfs 15 x 14.
Initial selling price: £ 26.95

BC-244 .... £ 27.50

Produced by: Buckingham Covers **Qty:** 1939

Issue Notes: 10 x 1st class DS "Big Bang" stamps plus labels. This sheet was issued to coincide with Royal Mail's Fire and Rescue Service special issue. The labels bear more than a passing resemblance to AG Bradbury's design (BC-231) and depict antique fire fighting appliances.

BC-245

STAMPEX - Autumn 2009

2009 (16 Sep), Litho by Cartor, Printed on water-activated gummed paper. Perf 14½.
Initial selling price: £ 10.00

BC-245...£ 15.00

Produced by: PTS **Qty:** Est. 2000

Issue Notes: 10 x 1st class Flags "White Ensign"

Business

stamps plus labels. Produced by the Philatelic Traders Society (PTS) on the occasion of the Autumn STAMPEX event held at the British Design Centre, Islington, London, 16-19 Sep 2009. Around 500 sheets will have been broken up to service covers and as singles which were sold to collectors at the show priced £1 each.

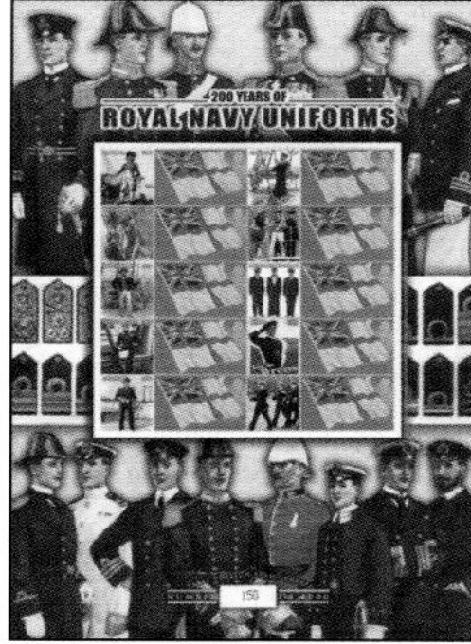

BC-246

Royal Naval Uniforms

2009 (23 Sep), Litho by Cartor, Printed on water-activated gummed paper. Perf 14½.
Initial selling price: £ 24.95

BC-246 .... £ 25.00

Produced by: Benham Covers **Qty:** 1000

Issue Notes: 10 x 1st class Flags "White Ensign" stamps plus labels. This sheet was issued to coincide with Royal Mail's Royal Navy Uniforms special issue which was issued on 17 September 2009.

BC-247

50th Anniversary of the Antarctic Treaty

2009 (28 Sep), Litho by Cartor, printed on self adhesive paper with elliptical die-cut perfs 15 x 14.
Initial selling price: £ 49.95

BC-247 .... £ 50.00

Produced by: Ridgewood Stamp Sheets **Qty:** 200

Issue Notes: 10 x 1st class DS "Union Flag" stamps plus labels. This sheet is a celebration of the work of the British Antarctic Survey (BAS) in this the 50th Anniversary year of the signing of the Antarctic Treaty in Washington DC in 1959. The images on the labels attempt to show the conditions under which the BAS carry out their work in Antarctica.

BC-248

250th Anniversary of Kew Gardens

2009 (28 Sep), Litho by Cartor, printed on self adhesive paper with elliptical die-cut perfs 15 x 14.
Initial selling price: £ 49.95

BC-248 .... £ 50.00

Produced by: Ridgewood Stamp Sheets **Qty:** 200

Issue Notes: 10 x 1st class DS "Flower" stamps plus labels. This sheet depicts the largest Victorian Glasshouse in existence and traces the history of Kew Gardens from its inception as Kew Park in 1759 to the present day.

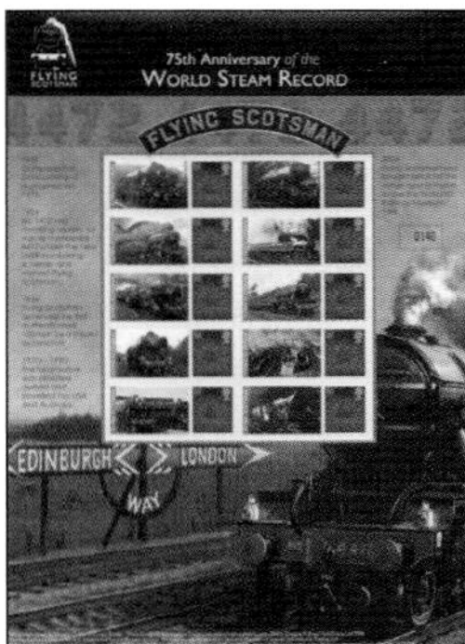

BC-249

70th Anniv. of World Steam Record

2009 (2 Oct), Litho by Cartor, printed on self adhesive paper with die-cut perfs 15 x 14.
Initial selling price: £ 26.95

BC-249 .... £ 27.50

Produced by: Buckingham Covers **Qty:** 1934

Issue Notes: 10 x 1st class DS "Big Bang" stamps plus labels. Commemorates the World speed record for a steam engine set in 1934 by the Flying Scotsman between London and Edinburgh. Originally sold in a presentation pack with information card stiffener and clear sleeve.

BC-250

Uckfield Rugby Club

2009 (10 Oct), Litho by Cartor, printed on self adhesive paper with die-cut perfs 15 x 14.
Initial selling price: See Notes

BC-250 .... £ 150.00

Produced by: Matthew Christelow **Qty:** 100

Issue Notes: 10 x 1st class DS "Union Flag" stamps plus labels. Produced in association with Planet Prints and Uckfield Rugby Club, It is understood from the sheet producer that many sheets were distributed/sold to members or broken up and used as promotional postage. As a result, this sheet is difficult to find as only c. 30 sheets are thought to have been made available/sold to the philatelic community.

BC-251

75th Anniversary of the Olympic Suite

2009 (12 Oct), Litho by Cartor, printed on self adhesive paper with die-cut perfs 15 x 14.
Initial selling price: £ 30.00

BC-251 .... £ 30.00

Produced by: Titanic Heritage Trust **Qty:** 500

Issue Notes: 10 x 1st class DS "Union Flag" stamps plus labels. The White Swan Hotel, is a 300 year old coaching inn, set in the heart of the historic market town of Anlwick. The hotel has experienced many changes over the years, most notably in 1936. The White Star line RMS Olympic was being decommissioned and scrapped at the end of her career. The then owner of the hotel, Algernon Smart who had been a frequent traveller on the liner, bid successfully for the wood panelling, ceiling from the First Class Lounge, also the revolving door from the First Class Restaurant. He returned to Alnwick and built the Olympic Suite with all the oak panelling and fixtures and fittings where it remains today. The sheet depicts an image of RMS Olympic with four interior images together with an image of the White Swan Hotel and four interior Images.

BC-252

130th Anniversary of the Anglo Zulu War

2009 (14 Oct), Litho by Cartor, printed on self adhesive paper with elliptical die-cut perfs 15 x 14.
Initial selling price: £ 49.95

BC-252 .... £ 125.00

Produced by: AG Bradbury **Qty:** 250

Issue Notes: 10 x 1st class DS "Union Flag" stamps plus labels. This sheet was issued to coincide with Royal Mail's eminent Britain's special issue and commemorates the life and times of William Gladstone. The sheet sold out before issue. This is sheet No. 46 in Bradbury's *History of Britain* Series.

BC-253

Supersonic Concorde

2009 (19 Oct), Litho by Cartor, Printed on water-activated gummed paper. Perf 14½.
Initial selling price: £ 19.99

BC-253 .... £ 20.00

Produced by: Westminster Collection **Qty:** 9500

Issue Notes: 10 x 1st Concorde (2009) stamps plus labels. Commemorating the 40th Anniversary of the first flight of Concorde 001 and featuring label images of past Concorde pilots .

BC-254

The Magic of Minerals

2009 (24 Oct), Litho by Cartor, printed on self adhesive paper with elliptical die-cut perfs 15 x 14.
Initial selling price: £ 49.95

BC-254 .... £ 50.00

Produced by: Ridgewood Stamp Sheets **Qty:** 200

Issue Notes: 10 x 1st class DS "Big Bang" stamps plus labels. The International Mineralogical Association (IMA) is an international group of 38 national societies. The most active IMA commission is the Commission on New Minerals and Mineral Names which was founded in 1959 to coordinate the assigning of new mineral names, revision of existing names and discreditation of invalid species. The Commission celebrated its 50th anniversary in 2009.

Business

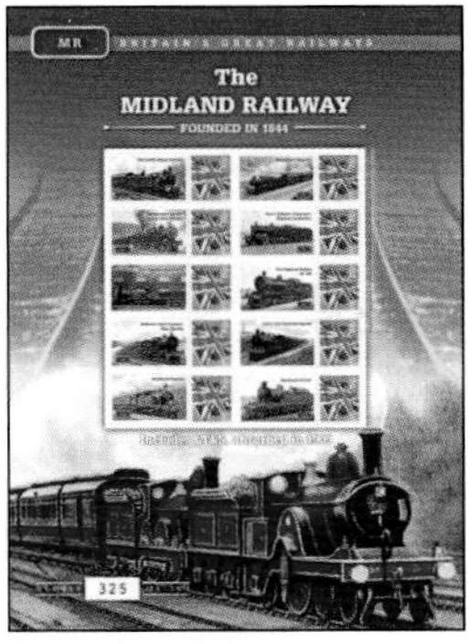

BC-255

The Midland Railway

2009 (27 Oct), Litho by Cartor, printed on self adhesive paper with elliptical die-cut perfs 15 x 14.
Initial selling price: £ 24.95

BC-255 .... £ 25.00

Produced by: Benham Covers **Qty:** 500

Issue Notes: 10 x 1st class DS "Union Flag" stamps plus labels. No.5 in Benham's *Britain's Great Railways* series of limited edition business customised stamp sheets features the Midland - which grew to be the second-largest of the pre-grouping companies serving the Midlands, Manchester and the North West, Merseyside and eventually Scotland. It's distinctive red livery, *Midland Red*, distinguished it from the rest and it built the most impressive of London termini, St Pancras.

BC-256

Cathedrals of England

2009 (6 Nov), Litho by Cartor, printed on self adhesive paper with elliptical die-cut perfs 15 x 14.
Initial selling price: £ 28.99

BC-256 .... £ 30.00

Produced by: AG Bradbury **Qty:** 750

Issue Notes: 10 x 1st class DS "Xmas 09" stamps plus labels. The issue of this sheet coincided with the Royal Mail Christmas 2009 stamp issue featuring stained glass windows. The border design of this sheet features Victorian engravings of fourteen of England's most famous cathedrals, with stained glass images on the stamp labels. This is sheet No. 45 in Bradbury's *History of Britain* Series

BC-257

Christmas 2009

2009 (11 Nov), Litho by Cartor, printed on self adhesive paper with elliptical die-cut perfs 15 x 14.
Initial selling price: £ 24.95

BC-257 .... £ 25.00

Produced by: Benham Covers **Qty:** 500

Issue Notes: 10 x 1st class DS "Xmas 09" stamps plus labels. As with BC-256 this issue coincided with the Royal Mail Christmas 2009 stamp issue featuring stained glass windows. The sheet features labels of stained glass Christmas images framed by soaring vaults and choir stalls.

BC-258

Sinking of the Tirpitz 65th Anniversary

2009 (13 Nov), Litho by Cartor, printed on water activated gummed paper Perf. 14.

Initial selling price: £ 29.95

BC-258 .... £ 30.00

Produced by: Buckingham Covers **Qty:** 617

Issue Notes: 10 x 1st class "Poppy 08" stamps plus labels. Issued to mark the 65th Anniversary of the sinking of the German battleship Tirpitz, on the 12th November 1944. It features the artwork of one of military artist Frank Wooton, and honours 617 Squadron. Originally sold in a presentation pack with an informative presentation card and clear sleeve.

BC-259

Centenary of Death of King Edward VII

2009 (26 Nov), Litho by Cartor, printed on self adhesive paper with elliptical die-cut perfs 15 x 14.
Initial selling price: Sold as a pair for £ 89.99 (see also BC-260)

BC-259 .... £ 50.00

Produced by: AG Bradbury **Qty:** 475

Issue Notes: 10 x 1st class DS "Union Flag" stamps plus labels. One of a pair of Business Customised Stamp Sheets that were issued (some six months early) commemorating the death of King Edward VII and the Accession of King George V. The border features images of Queen Alexandra and King Edward VII with stamp reproductions of the low value definitive's issued 1902-1920. This is sheet No. 47 in Bradbury's *History of Britain* Series.

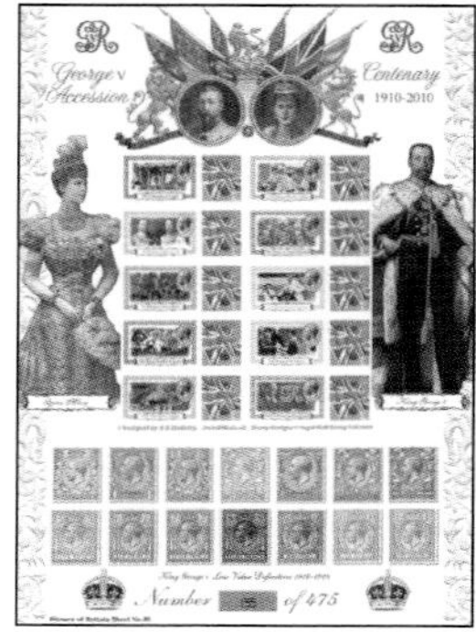

BC-260

Accession of King George V

2009 (26 Nov), Litho by Cartor, printed on self adhesive paper with elliptical die-cut perfs 15 x 14.
Initial selling price: Sold as a pair for £ 89.99 (see also BC-259)

BC-260 .... £ 50.00

Produced by: AG Bradbury **Qty:** 475

Issue Notes: 10 x 1st class DS "Union Flag" stamps plus labels. One of a pair of Business Customised Stamp Sheets that were issued (some six months early) commemorating the death of King Edward VII and the Accession of King George V. The border features images of Queen Mary and King George V with stamp reproductions of the low value definitive's issued 1912-1924. This is sheet No. 48 in Bradbury's *History of Britain* Series.

BC-261

West Kent Shooting Club

2009 (29 Nov), Litho by Cartor, printed on self adhesive paper with elliptical die-cut perfs 15 x 14.
Initial selling price: See Notes

BC-261 .... £ 150.00

Produced by: Matt Christelow **Qty:** 100

Issue Notes: 10 x 1st class DS "Union Flag" stamps plus labels. Produced in association with Planet Prints and West Kent Shooting Club, It is understood from the sheet producer that many sheets were distributed/sold to members or broken up and used as promotional postage. As a result this sheet is difficult to find as only c. 50 sheets are thought to have been made available/sold to the philatelic community. Value is therefore difficult to estimate and will demand on demand/interest.

BC-262

490th Anniversary of the Death of Leonardo Da Vinci - Philatex 2009 Overprint

2009 (1 Dec), Litho by Cartor, printed on water-activated gummed-paper, Perf 14½.
Initial selling price: £115.00

BC-262 .... £ 250.00

Produced by: Rushstamps **Qty:** 100

Issue Notes: 10 x 1st class Occasions "Thanks" stamps plus labels. This sheet is something of an enigma. It is understood from sheet producer Rushstamps that 100 sheets were ordered from Royal Mail but only 35 sheets were pre-sold at Philatex in November 2009. The 35 pre-sold sheets were individually numbered 1-35 in the top left hand corner of the sheet, possibly by overprinting the Royal Mail sheets. The remaining 65 sheets "are being held over for Philatex next year" (2010) accordingly to sources close to the sheet producer. According to Rushstamps the licensing fees and sheet production costs amounted to c. £80 which explains the high initial retail cost.

BC-263

The Great Northern Railway

2009 (2 Dec), Litho by Cartor, printed on self adhesive paper with elliptical die-cut perfs 15 x 14.
Initial selling price: £24.95

BC-263 .... £ 30.00

Produced by: Benham Covers **Qty:** 500

Issue Notes: 10 x 1st class DS "Union Flag" stamps plus labels. No.6 in a series of limited edition business customised stamp sheets featuring Britain's Great Railways. This sheet spotlights The Great Northern Railway (GNR) a British railway company established by the London & York Railway Act of 1846. The main line ran from London via Hitchin, Peterborough, and Grantham, to York, with a loop

Business

line from Peterborough to Bawtry (south of Doncaster) via Boston and Lincoln, and branch lines to Sheffield and Wakefield. The main line became part of the East Coast Main Line and terminated in London at Kings Cross.

BC-264

Portsmouth Historic Naval Dockyard

2009 (3 Dec), Litho by Cartor, printed on water-activated gummed-paper, Perf 14½.
Initial selling price: £29.95

BC-264 .... £ 30.00

Produced by: Buckingham Covers **Qty:** 500

Issue Notes: 10 x 1st class Flag "White Ensign" stamps plus labels. This sheet features the Historic Naval Dockyard at Portsmouth, Hampshire, home to some of the world's most famous historic warships: the Victorian HMS Warrior, Henry VIII's flagship, The Mary Rose and perhaps the most famous of all - Nelson's flagship HMS Victory. Originally sold in a presentation pack with an informative presentation card and clear sleeve.

BC-265

Bagpuss

2009 (21 Dec), Litho by Cartor, printed on water-activated gummed-paper, Perf 14½.
Initial selling price: £29.95

BC-265 .... £ 30.00

BC-265a Unnumbered .... £ 60.00

Produced by: The Stamp Centre **Qty:** 1000

Issue Notes: 10 x 1st class Occasions "Hello" stamps plus labels. This sheet features the children's TV character Bagpuss. BC-264a are unnumbered sheets which were sheets from an additional batch intended for use on souvenir covers sold by The Stamp Centre.

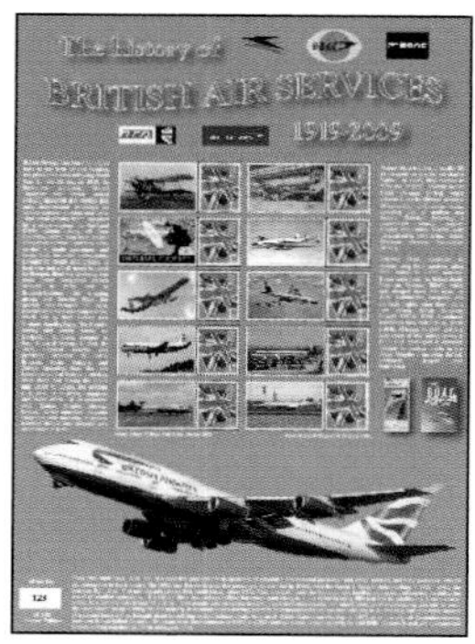

BC-266

The History of British Air Services

2010 (18 Jan), Litho by Cartor, printed on self adhesive paper with elliptical die-cut perfs 15 x 14.
Initial selling price: £29.95

BC-266 .... £ 30.00

Produced by: Ridgewood Stamp Sheets **Qty:** 500

Issue Notes: 10 x 1st class DS "Union Flag" stamps plus labels. Issued to commemorate the 90th Anniversary of British Airways. It tells the story of British Airways from its early days on Hounslow Heath as British Air Services to becoming the "world's favourite airline".

BC-267

Routemaster

2010 (19 Jan), Litho by Cartor, printed on self adhesive paper with elliptical die-cut perfs 15 x 14.
Initial selling price: £49.99

BC-267 .... £ 100.00

Produced by: AG Bradbury **Qty:** 275

Issue Notes: 10 x 1st class DS "Union Flag" stamps plus labels. Issued on the anniversary of the Royal Mail British Design Classic series of stamps. This is sheet No. 49 in Bradbury's *History of Britain* Series.

BC-268

Sir Isaac Newton

2010 (19 Jan), Litho by Cartor, printed on self adhesive paper with elliptical die-cut perfs 15 x 14.
Initial selling price: £35.00

BC-268 .... £ 35.00

Produced by: AG Bradbury **Qty:** 500

Issue Notes: 10 x 1st class DS "Union Flag" stamps plus labels. Sir Isaac Newton was President of the Royal Society from 1703 to 1727. The Royal Society marks its 350th anniversary in 2010. This is sheet No. 50 in Bradbury's *History of Britain* Series.

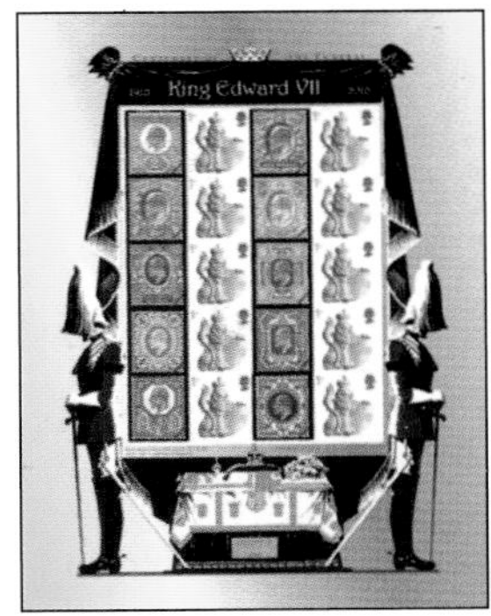

BC-269

Funeral of King Edward VII

2010 (21 Jan), Litho by Cartor, printed on water-activated gummed-paper, Perf 14½.
Initial selling price: £26.95

BC-269 .... £ 27.50

Produced by: Buckingham Covers **Qty:** 1910

Issue Notes: 10 x 1st class Lion and Shield of England stamps plus labels. Originally sold in a presentation pack with an informative presentation card and clear sleeve.

BC-270

Mary Queen of Scots

2010 (26 Jan), Litho by Cartor, printed on self adhesive paper with elliptical die-cut perfs 15 x 14.
Initial selling price: £35.00

BC-270 .... £ 35.00

Produced by: AG Bradbury **Qty:** 275

Issue Notes: 10 x 1st class DS "Scottish Lion" stamps plus labels. This is sheet No. 52 in Bradbury's *History of Britain* Series.

BC-271

Birds of Britain

2010 (31 Jan), Litho by Cartor, printed on self adhesive paper with elliptical die-cut perfs 15 x 14.
Initial selling price: See Notes

BC-271 .... £ 150.00

Produced by: Planet Prints **Qty:** 100

Issue Notes: 10 x 1st class DS "Union Flag" stamps plus labels. It is understood from the sheet producer that some sheets were broken up and used as promotional postage. As a result this sheet may be difficult to find. Value is therefore difficult to estimate and will demand on demand/interest.

Themed Stamp Sheets and Covers

In this Chapter we look at the development of the Themed Customised Stamp Sheets and the souvenir/commemorative covers produced which bear these stamps/labels. They were originally produced by commercial organisations and individuals initially in very small numbers around a specific theme or event. When they first appeared they went almost unnoticed, until a few smilers enthusiasts started to take note and gradually helped increase their popularity amongst Smilers sheet collectors. There popularity increased during 2005/2006 until that interest was effectively killed off by the emergence of too many of the, often over-priced, sheets produced by a few niche sheet producers. They are, in many ways, identical to the Customised Stamp sheets described in Chapter 3, perhaps the only difference is that instead of the usual crop of weddings, dogs and babies, the labels generally feature a design to commemorate an event, theme or other non-personal event.

Aberchirdier and Marnoch Community Association

The first *themed* sheets were produced in 2000 by the Aberchirdier and Marnoch Community Association who commissioned a pair of Christmas customised sheets featuring a stylised view of the New Marnoch Church on labels. The idea was to raise funds for their community by selling souvenir covers. Very few sheets were printed (c. 8-12 of each) of which probably no more than 5 of each survived as whole sheets.

Aberchirdier and Marnoch Community Association souvenir cover

Isle of Pabay

Scotland seems to have pioneered the use of customised stamp sheets because the folks on the Isle of Pabay responsible for the Isle of Pabay carriage labels since the early 1960's also picked up on the idea to use customised stamps and labels on souvenir covers. Just two weeks after the Aberchirdier and Marnoch Community Association souvenir covers were issued, the Isle of Pabay issued a souvenir cover featuring their own version of the customised Christmas stamps. Very few whole sheets are known to have survived as most were used on covers or the sheets broken up to sell singles to collectors.

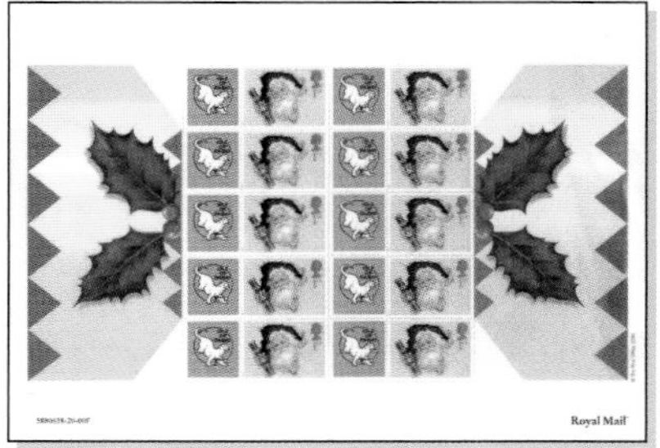

Isle of Pabay Customised Stamp Sheet (TS-003)

Themed

Isle of Pabay Christmas 2000 Cover

British Philatelic Cover Producers Association

In 2001 the British Philatelic Cover Producers Association based in Worthing, Sussex commissioned a number of customised stamp sheets using the Hallmarks issue to commemorate the Australian Ashes Tour of 2001 and used the stamps/labels on commemorative covers dated 5 Jul 2001. At least one whole sheet and one half sheet survived but the majority appear to have been used on commemorative covers.

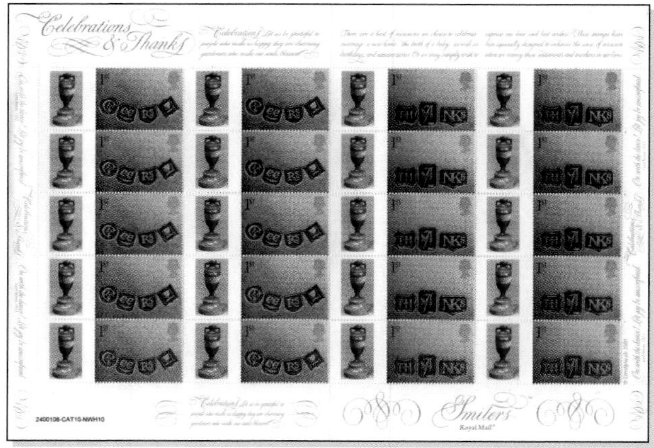

British Philatelic Cover Producers Association - Clashes for the Ashes (TS-004)

Two versions of the sheet were produced to service souvenir covers. Ten sheets of each the *Cheers and Thanks* and *Welcome* Hallmarks sheets were produced as evidenced by the customer order reference number printed in the lower left hand corner of these sheets (2400108-CAT10-NWH10).

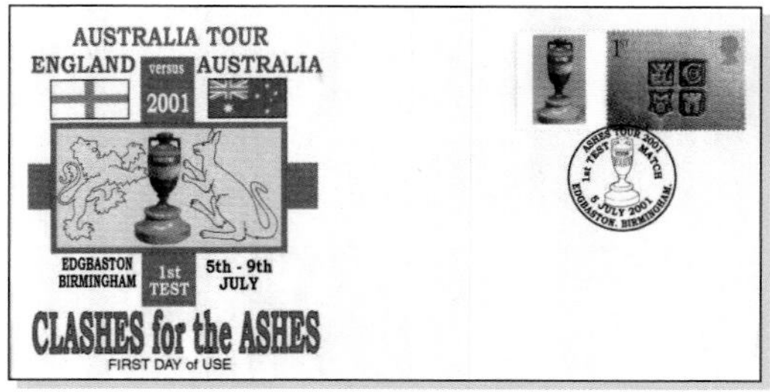

British Philatelic Cover Producers Association - Clashes for the Ashes

Themed

These innovative covers with personalised labels and stamps must have proved popular because the British Philatelic Cover Producers Association produced a further commemorative cover in September 2001 commemorating the Cheltenham and Gloucester Trophy between Somerset CCC and Lancashire CCC held at Lords on 1st September 2001. Five sheets of each the *Cheers and Thanks* and *Welcome* Hallmarks sheets were produced as evidenced by the customer order reference number printed in the lower left hand corner of these sheets (2400101-CAT5-NWH5).

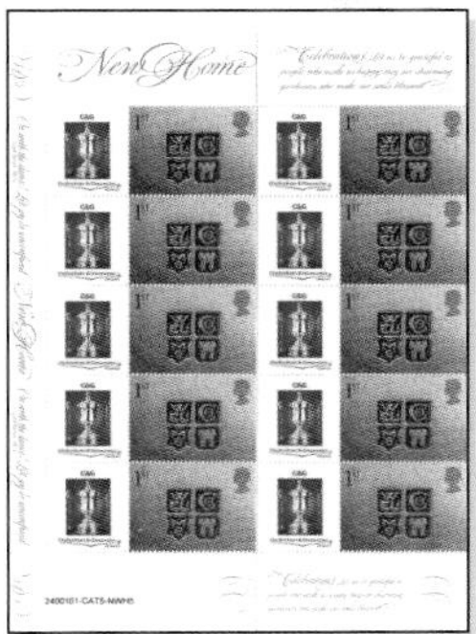

British Philatelic Cover Producers Association - C&G Trophy Souvenirs

We are not aware of any customised stamp sheets produced in 2002 but interest seems to have again picked by again in 2003 with a number of philatelic societies following the lead set by British Philatelic Cover Producers Association. The arrival of more colourful and imaginative stamp sheet designs in 2002/2003 seems to have breathed new life into these collectibles as evidenced by the activity of these Philatelic Societies:

Newlands Road Philatelic Society

Originally formed in 1953 and dissolved in 1967, its main claim-to-fame appears to have been that it was the first all-junior Philatelic Society. To commemorate the 50th Anniversary of its formation, one of the original founding members, Chris Phillips, commissioned four differently designed labels using the customised Flower stamp sheets issue and produced a number of commemorative covers. The only surviving sheets/ half sheets belong to the Society and are not listed, however they are illustrated here for the sake of completeness. The Society appear to have produced two sheets of each with one or more sheets being broken up to service souvenir covers.

Newlands Road Philatelic Society Flowers issue

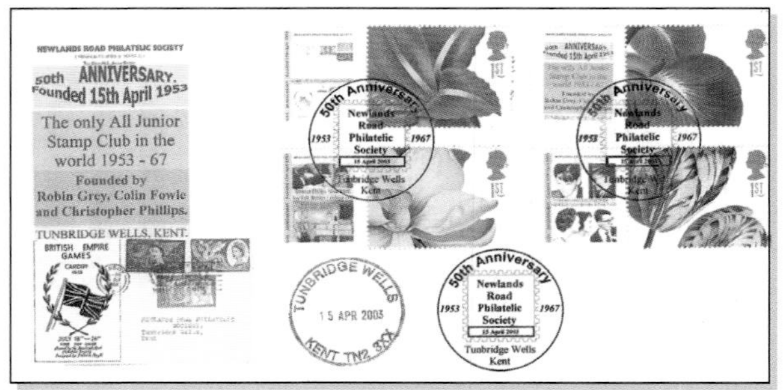

Newlands Road Philatelic Society - Smilers Souvenir dated 15th April 2003

Sudbury Philatelic Society

In May 2003 the Sudbury Philatelic Society produced a numbered limited edition postcard featuring a hand painted view of Sudbury on one side and a customised Flowers Smilers stamp and specially designed label postmarked Sudbury and dated . The stamp/label combination were from a printing of an unknown number of customised Smilers sheets all of which it is understood were broken up for postcards.

Methodist Philatelic Society

In June 2003 the Methodist Philatelic Society commissioned an unknown number of customised stamp sheets featuring the CS-008d Occasions "LOVE" Smilers stamps which they used to produce three commemorative covers. Two covers were dated 17th June 2003 postmarked EPWORTH, DONCASTER, and LINCOLN respectively whilst the third was postmarked LLANDUDNO and dated 28th June on the occasion of the Methodist Conference.

Themed

Methodist Philatelic Society - John Wesley Tercentenary

Bedford Philatelic Society

The Bedford Philatelic Society produced two special covers in April 2004, on their Diamond Anniversary. The society produced a limited quantity of Customised Smilers sheets featuring the Christmas 2003, 2nd class and 1st Class Ice Sculpture designs. The Customised Labels bore a diamond design befitting the occasion.

The East Midlands Philatelic Exhibition was held on the 3rd April 2004 in Bedford which was also the venue for the Railway Philatelic Group annual convention. Two jointly-sponsored covers were produced on the occasion of EMPX 2004 featuring the Xmas stamps and labels produced by the Bedford Philatelic Society. It is understood from the Bedford Philatelic Society that only 10 sheets of each design were produced, of which half were broken up to service covers, 100 of each value were produced.

Bedford Philatelic Society covers and Stamp Sheets

Basildon Philatelic Society

The Basildon Philatelic Society produced two special covers and a presentation pack in November 2004, on the occasion of the 5th National Philatelic Exhibition, organised by the Association of British Philatelic Societies (ABPS). The special covers and presentation pack labels were produced to promote the 5th National Philatelic Exhibition but were also a celebration of the 10th Anniversary of the ABPS, and the 60th Anniversary of the Association of Essex Philatelic Societies ("AEPS"). The event was held on 20th – 21st November 2004 and two special postmarks were available, one on each day of the event.

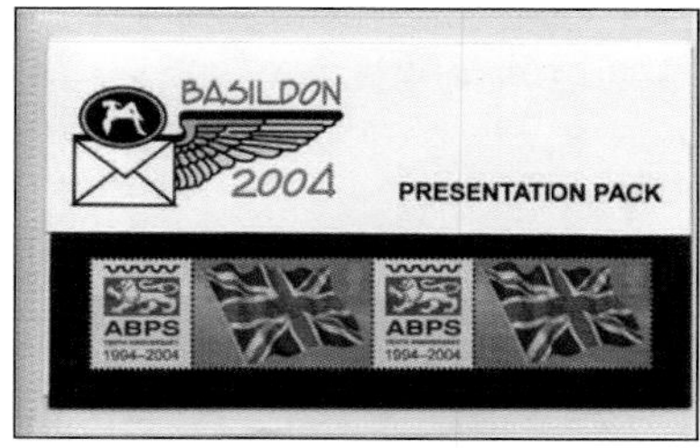

ABPS - 5th National Philatelic Exhibition Covers and Presentation Pack

To service both the covers and presentation packs a number of Customised Rule Britannia Smilers sheet were produced by the society, featuring specially designed labels designed by C. W. Meade. A total of 100 presentation packs and 100+ pairs of covers were produced which sold at the event for £2 each.

The first printing can be identified by the Royal Mail order reference printed in the lower left hand corner of the sheets. The original printing order reference was 32639 and a total of 30 sheets were printed. This print run was used almost exclusively to service the presentation packs and special covers available at the event. A second printing of 20 sheets was commissioned to meet the requirements of members and that order reference was 43713. A third and final printing, reference 56966, was made and a total of ten sheets were printed with that order number in the lower left hand corner. Whilst a total of 60 sheets appear to have been produced, taking into account the number of sheets broken up for covers and presentation packs, the total number of whole sheets surviving is estimated at c. 30.

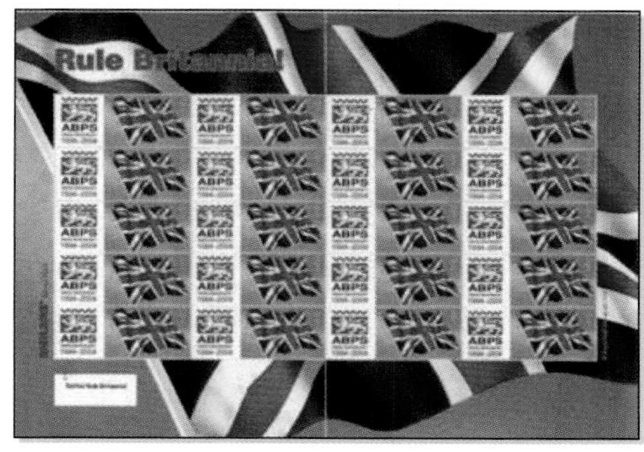

Basingstoke Philatelic Society

The Basingstoke Philatelic Society produced a pair of Customised Smilers sheets in 2005 to mark the 70th Anniversary of the Basingstoke Philatelic Society. Nearly 300 sheets were printed featuring two of the current Customised sheet formats. A total of 240 sheets of the Customised Flowers sheet (CS-013) were printed in four different printings. By comparison the Magic Customised sheet (CS-025) with only 40 sheets printed of which nearly half were broken up to make souvenir booklets sold to members on the day of their show is extremely rare.

CS-013

CS-025

CS-013 exists in four printings identified as follows:

- Original – 25 sheets, no code printed in white code box, Type 1 sheet, label design full height
- First re-print – 15 sheets, code number 9804502, Type 1 sheet, label design squashed
- Second re-print – 75 sheets, code number 0070438, Type 2 sheet, label design squashed
- Third re-print – 125 sheets, code number 0129654, Type 2 sheet, label design squashed

CS-024 exists in two printings, identified as follows:

- Original – 25 sheets, no code printed in white code box, label design full height
- First re-print – 15 sheets, code number 9804502, label design squashed

Approximately 150 souvenir stamp booklets were produced featuring the original printing of the Magic Smilers sheet (full height design on label) featuring either a pair of Smilers stamps and labels or two singles. The later are rarer than the pairs as only 20% of the booklets were made up using singles rather than pairs because of the printing layout of the Smilers sheets.

Derby Philatelic Society

In September 2005, a cover was produced by the Derby Philatelic Society to commemorate their 100th Anniversary since their inaugural meeting held on 11th September 1905. The cover features a King Edward the VII 1d Scarlet and a White Ensign Smilers stamp with special label featuring Derby Cathedral and DERBY PHILATELIC SOCIETY 1905-2005.

The Anniversary itself was marked by a special dinner featuring such delights as The Orange £5 Carrot and Coriander Soup and 1d Black Coffee, the menu for which formed a cover "stiffener"!

The cover is signed on the reverse by the existing and a number of past presidents of the Society together with the Mayor of the City of Derby.

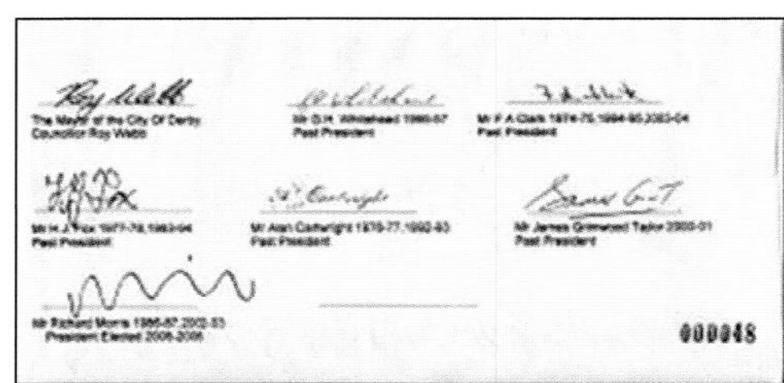

The white ensign flag/tab is from a customised *Smilers* sheet commissioned by Derby Philatelic Society, themed customised Smilers sheet (TS-010) and was designed by Society Secretary, Steven Street. Each stamp is attached to artwork taken from prints done by Mr Harold Macmillan's printers (one of Derby Philatelic Society's most famous philatelists and a Derby businessman) for a visit by members of the society in 1948 and the colour and date restyled to show the centenary period.

The first five sheets printed were proof sheets and rare as the background was a yellow-buff colour, which the Society felt clashed with the rest of the design so it re-coloured the background. The main printing was done with a white background and these were ordered in a bulk of 60 sheets the first 10 sheets of which were broken up and used on the centenary cover for the Society.

Proof sheet

Issued sheet

Sudbury Philatelic Society

Sudbury Philatelic Society again produced a customised stamp sheet and cover in May 2005 to mark their 40th anniversary. Two postcards were produced each featuring a print of a view by a local artist and both bore a Union Flag Smilers stamp and specially designed label. The stamp/label combination were from a printing of 25 customised Smilers sheets of which, it is understood, some 20 sheets were broken up for post-cards, 200 of each design being produced. The five remaining Rule Britannia Customised Smilers Sheets (CS-020) are all thought to be in the hands of private collectors and are thus very rare indeed.

One of a pair of Postcards produced by Sudbury Philatelic Society

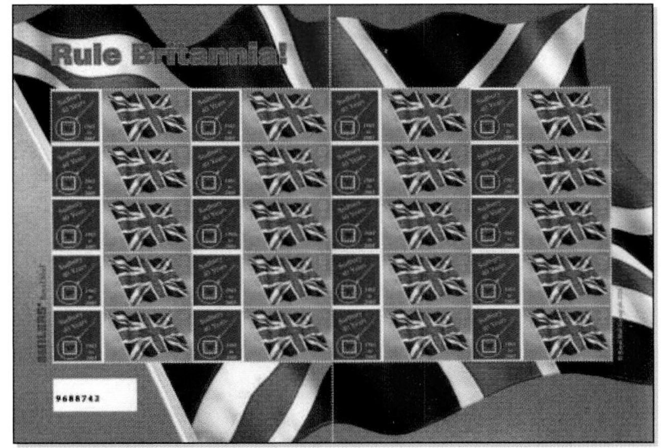

Sudbury Philatelic Society 40th Anniversary 1965-2005

Themed

Britannia Navel College

2005 saw the centenary of Britannia Royal Naval College at Dartmouth and the College decided to commission fifty customised stamp sheets to celebrate the event. The stamps were used by the Commodores and Commanders office to send out mail that included invites to the Centenary celebrations. The Britannia Royal Naval College opened in 1905, in April 2005 college opened its doors to the public with a number of celebrations including a Grand Regatta Ball for 800 people, a Proms in the park on two nights for 3000 people and assorted minor functions such as hosting of US Navy Rugby team from Annapolis. The Commodore / Commander had 5 sheets (for postage use). Something like 25 sheets survived as whole sheets either sold in the college shop or subsequently to collectors by the organisers. The RM Order number of the sheet is 38461/Rule Britannia!

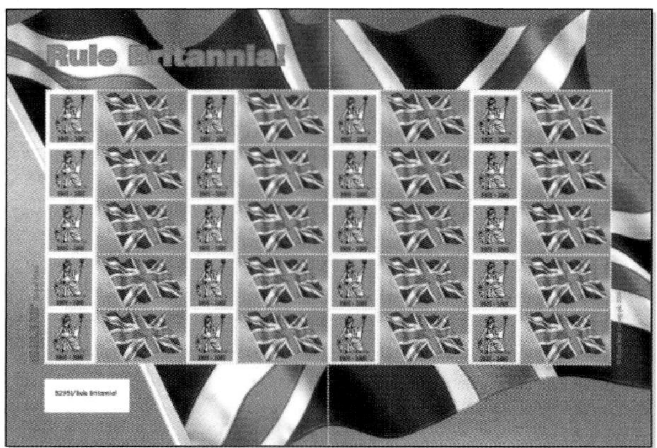

Centenary of the Britannia Royal Naval College, Dartmouth (TS-010)

Self Adhesive Themed Customised Stamp Sheets

The popularity of these customised stamp sheets increased from 2005 following the introduction of the definitive-sized label sheets (DS01-DS06). These new-format stamp sheets provided a larger landscape-sized label and as a result a bigger canvas for *themed* label designs. Some enterprising individuals and companies developed the original idea of Customised Smilers sheets and produced a number of *themed* Customised Smilers sheets using pictorial images rather than personal photographs of individuals to promote topical events and subjects.

Example of early self-adhesive Themed Customised Stamp Sheet

London Boat Show 2006

Perhaps the first of these customised, definitive-sized smilers stamp sheets to really seize the imagination of the Smilers sheet collector was a pair of Customised Smilers sheets produced by Royal Mail and available from an instant Smilers booth at the London Boat Show during January 2006. In addition to the usual instant photo the Instant Smilers booth offered Customised Smilers sheets with the show logo instead of a photo. Whilst it is understood that sheets printed with the show's logo on the labels were never officially sanctioned or approved by Royal Mail, it is probably true to say that the huge increase in interest in this area of Customised Smilers sheets seen in 2006 can be traced back to the excitement generated by the pair of Boat Show Smilers sheets. Whilst not seen it is understood that a much rarer version of these sheets exists with alternate personal photo and show logo on the labels.

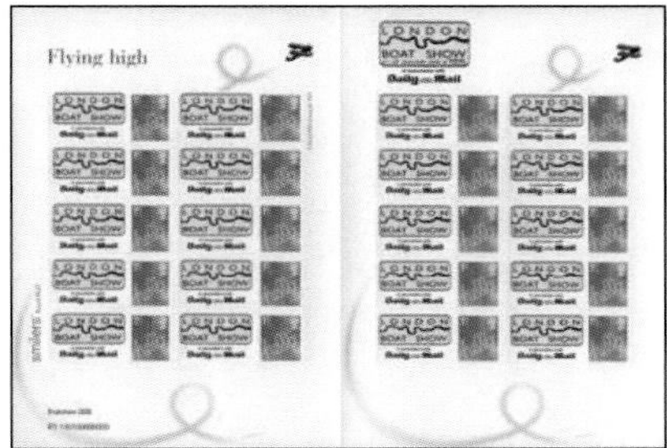

London Boat Show 2006

Honourable Artillery Company

The Honourable Artillery Company is a unit of Britain's Territorial Army. Its origins date back to 1537 when King Henry VIII granted a charter to the Guild of St. George, which subsequently changed its name to the Honourable Artillery Company (HAC). It is the second oldest military unit in the world. The HAC's Company of Pikemen and Musketeers are all former serving soldiers in the HAC and their uniforms date back to the soldiers at the time of the English Civil War (1641). The Company of Pikemen and Musketeers are the official bodyguard of the Lord Mayor of the City of London.

The Company of Pikemen and Musketeers were asked to join the oldest military unit, the Swiss Papal Guard in the celebration of their 500th Anniversary in May 2006. In recognition of this honour and in conjunction with the British Forces Post Office, the HAC decided to mark the 500th Anniversary of the Papal Guard by issuing a number of special covers.

500th Anniversary of the Papal Guard Souvenir Cover

To further mark this event, HAC produced 90 sheets of customised Rule Britannia Smilers stamps and labels featuring the crest of the Honourable Artillery Company coat of arms. Of the 90 sheets printed, the majority of sheets were broken up to service special covers.

There appear to have been four variants of these covers:

- Unsigned, hand-stamped 06 May 2006
- As above, sighed by Colonnello Elmar Th. Maeder, Comandate, Guardia Svizzera Pontifica
- As above, signed by Captain AR O'Hagan TD DL, Company Commander, Company of Pikemen and Musketeers
- As above, signed by Alderman David Brewer CMG, The Rt. Hon Lord Mayor of the City of London

500th Anniversary of the Papal Guard - Signed Souvenir Cover

Of the original 90 sheets printed, around 12 whole sheets are thought to have survived intact and eagerly sought by sheet collectors, changing hands for up to c. £500 late 2006.

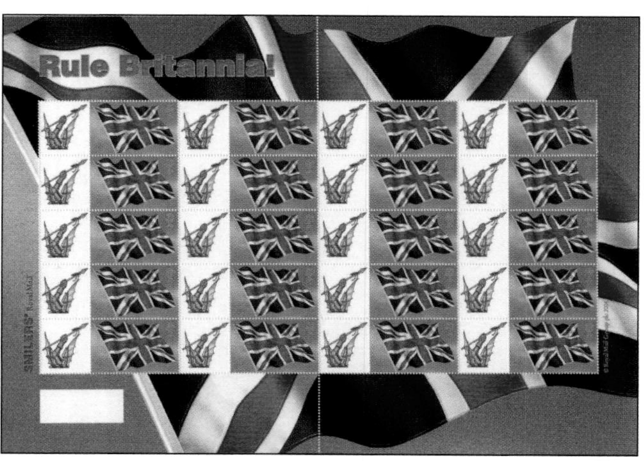

Honourable Artillery Company Smilers Sheet

Newport and Gwent Philatelic Society

To mark its 60th Anniversary in October 2007, the Newport and Gwent Philatelic Society issued a themed Smilers sheet using the Glorious Wales customised Smilers sheet format with the label incorporating the club's logo, originally designed by Vic Sheppard. To celebrate their diamond anniversary the club produced a special "Smilers" sheet and postcard. The postcard was made available in small quantities to club members, with 39 postcards being franked with the special stamp and postmarked at Caldicot Delivery Office (NP26 4VV) on 16 October, the anniversary of the date of the first meeting of the club.

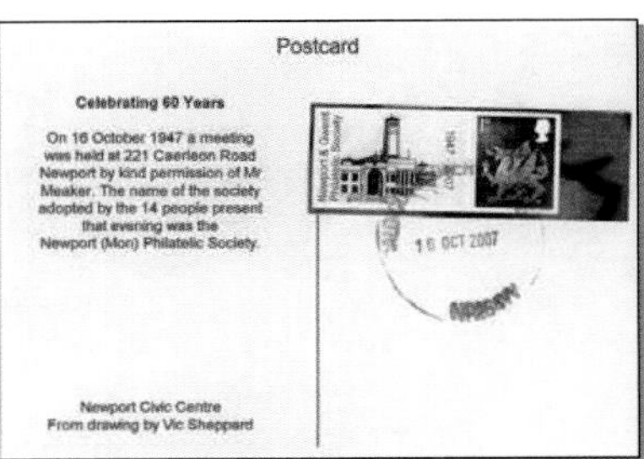

The Original printing of the Newport and Gwent Philatelic Society Smilers Stamp/Label

The original printing was limited to 16 sheets, 2 or which were broken up to service 39 postcards, with the remaining stamp/label being retained as the Society's archive copy. The remaining sheets (14) were issued as whole or part sheets based on pre-orders following the first use on 16 October 2007. The Postcards are franked with a Caldicot Delivery Office hand-stamp which is reserved for occasional use for local deliveries in the area. One final point of interest, the label is based on the logo of the club, designed by Vic Sheppard. It shows the civic centre in Newport, which is the location of the club, with the time on the clock set to 7.15pm, which is when the society

Original and re-print version of the Newport and Gwent Smilers sheet (2007/08)

To meet the somewhat unexpected demand, the sheet was re-printed in January 2008 (RM Order No 213300) with 20 sheets printed using the same customised sheet format and label design. Although they appear different the label design used was exactly the same for both printings. The original printing of these sheets appears to have been printed by Royal Mail using a thermal-ink or laser colour printer. The labels appear sharp, with the background colour a uniform pale bistre. For the re-printed sheets Royal Mail appear to have used a different printer as the labels are far more vibrant with the label background colour a distinct deeper bistre colour and more closely resembling the postcards issued by the society.

A word on the Themed Stamp Sheet listings that follow ....

In the pages that follow we have attempted to identify and list all known *themed Stamp Sheets* that have been made available to collectors through either philatelic societies, mail-order or on-line web-based auction sites such as eBay in reasonable quantities. Since we started recoding these themed sheets we have identified around 500 different designs. Our prefix for these sheets is **TS** which stands for ***Themed Sm****ilers* and in 2007 we introduced a minimum limit to qualify for a listing in the Themed Smilers List of 10 sheets and later increased this to 25 sheets by year end to filter out a worrying but increasing trend in the number of limited sheets produced by individuals who were looking to capitalise on collector interest for very limited editions.

Whilst not wishing to judge these very limited editions we did feel that if they were included these limited availability sheets in a collectibles list collectors would be encouraged to collect them to complete their collection. Since the prices being charged for these sheets were often ten times the production costs (around £15) we felt we could no longer support the inclusion of these sheets since their limited availability meant they were hardly collectible. That said, we also did not want to sit in judgement on these sheets or their producers either! A dilemma! In January 2008 in response to requests from collectors for a listing of these limited availability Themed Smilers we introduced a new list of ***Limited Availability Smilers*** to provide a reference list for those sheets available in limited numbers. The prefix for this list is **TSL** to denote their limited availability status.

Apart form the London Boat Show pair and other *Instant Smilers* produced at Royal Mail booths (e.g. Autumn Stampex 2006), all have been produced by either philatelic societies , stamp dealers or private individuals. Guide prices and quantities are not provided as the quantities associated with these sheets is relatively small, in the range of 10-50 with some being produced in quantities as high as 250, and in some instances unknown. Given the small numbers produced the prices are determined largely by the market demand for these sheets and is variable at best. That said, the Daily Mail Boat Show pair are likely to set you back £250 - £500 for the pair, if you can find them!

The interest in these Themed Smilers seems to have hit a peek around mid 2007, after which they seem to have lost some of their initial collector appeal, perhaps as a consequence of the increasing number (and cost) of the sheets appearing on the collector market. Other factors may also have contributed to their reduced popularity, for example: the increased interest generated by the collecting market in Royal Mail's Business Customised Sheet products, which occurred during 2007, due primarily in the increase in choice and production frequency from various Business Customised Sheet producers.

That said there still seems to be a small market for these overprinted smilers sheets and some of them are quite stunning works of art in their own right. The majority of which are produced by a certain gentlemen who would wish to stay anonymous and we respect that desire. His sheets seem to be sold through limited outlets either via the GB Stamp Centre or Rushstamps and of the 500 or so known sheets this gentlemen who has described himself as a musician and goes by the *nom de timbre* of ARTIZAN (amongst others) is probably responsible for upwards of 25% of this number. However, we have to grant him this - his work is quite superb.

Examples of Limited Availability Smilers sheets produced in smaller quantities (typically 10)

Themed Smilers List	TS-010	TS-020	TS-021	Royal Mail Smilers Reference Code

Sheet	Description	Issued	Royal Mail Smilers Reference Code
TS-001	Christmas 2000 - New Marnoch Church labels on CS-002	2000/01	N/A
TS-002	Christmas 2000 - New Marnoch Church labels on CS-003	2000/01	N/A
TS-003	Christmas 2000 - Isle of Pabay labels on CS-003	2000/01	N/A
TS-004	Ashes Urn labels on CS-004c (New Home/Welcome Labels)	Jul-2001	N/A
TS-005	C&G Trophy labels on CS-004c (New Home/Welcome Labels)	Sep-2001	N/A
TS-006	Winter Robins - Isle of Pabay labels	Dec-2003	SM13
TS-007	Bedford Philatelic Society 60th Anniversary (2nd)	Apr-2004	SM15
TS-008	Bedford Philatelic Society 60th Anniversary (1st)	Apr-2004	SM14
TS-009	Civil Defence Association Logo (Rule Britannia)	Apr-2004	SM19
TS-010	10th Anniversary of ABPS (illustrated)	Nov-2004	SM19
TS-011	Centenary of Britannia Royal Naval College, Dartmouth	Mar-2005	SM19
TS-012	40th Anniversary - Sudbury Philatelic Society	May-2005	SM19
TS-013	Final Voyage of HMS Invincible (Durham City Philatelic Soc.)	Jul-2005	SM24
TS-014	70th Anniversary of Basingstoke Philatelic Society (1)	Jul-2005	SM04
TS-015	70th Anniversary of Basingstoke Philatelic Society (2)	Aug-2005	SM23
TS-016	Enigma Machine (1)	Aug-2005	SM19
TS-017	Civil Defence Association Logo (White Ensign)	Sep-2005	SM24
TS-018	The Ashes Urn (1)	Sep-2005	SM19
TS-019	100th Anniversary Derby Philatelic Society	Sep-2005	SM24
TS-020	Enigma Machine (2) (illustrated)	Sep-2005	SM24
TS-021	Christmas 2005 - Isle of Pabay labels (illustrated)	Dec 2005	SM27
TS-022	Smilers Definitive Sized Issue – First Day of Issue	Oct 2005	DS01
TS-023	Smilers Definitive Sized Issue – First Day of Issue	Oct 2005	DS02
TS-024	Smilers Definitive Sized Issue – First Day of Issue	Oct 2005	DS03
TS-025	Smilers Definitive Sized Issue – First Day of Issue	Oct 2005	DS04
TS-026	Smilers Definitive Sized Issue – First Day of Issue	Oct 2005	DS05
TS-027	Smilers Definitive Sized Issue – First Day of Issue	Oct 2005	DS06
TS-028	Self-Adhesive Small Format Smilers – 1st Issue	Oct 2005	DS01
TS-029	Self-Adhesive Small Format Smilers – 1st Issue	Oct 2005	DS02
TS-030	Self-Adhesive Small Format Smilers – 1st Issue	Oct 2005	DS03

Themed Smilers List

TS-034 TS-058 TS-060

Sheet	Description	Issued	Royal Mail Smilers Reference Code
TS-031	Self-Adhesive Small Format Smilers – 1st Issue	Oct 2005	N/A
TS-032	Self-Adhesive Small Format Smilers – 1st Issue	Oct 2005	N/A
TS-033	Self-Adhesive Small Format Smilers – 1st Issue	Oct 2005	N/A
TS-034	The Ashes Urn (2) (illustrated)	Jan-2006	N/A
TS-035	100th Anniversary of St. Laurence Church, Forres	Jan-2006	N/A
TS-036	London Boat Show (1)	Jan-2006	SM13
TS-037	London Boat Show (2)	Jan-2006	SM15
TS-038	Spring Philatex 2006 - Wrong Dates (23-26 Feb) (1)	Jan-2006	SM14
TS-039	Spring Philatex 2006 - Wrong Dates (23-26 Feb) (2)	Jan-2006	SM19
TS-040	Spring Philatex 2006 - Corrected dates (23-25 Feb) (1)	Jan-2006	SM19
TS-041	Spring Philatex 2006 - Corrected dates (23-25 Feb) (2)	Jan-2006	SM19
TS-042	Spring Philatex 2006 – Correct dates wrong label (23-25 Feb)	Jan-2006	SM19
TS-043	200th Anniversary of Funeral of Lord Nelson	Jan-2006	SM24
TS-044	Paddington Bear - Deepest Darkest Peru	Jan-2006	SM04
TS-045	Fun Fruit & Veg – Speech balloon icon	Jan-2006	SM23
TS-046	Paddington Bear - 80th Birthday of Michael Bond	Mar-2006	SM19
TS-047	Washington Stamp Expo 2006 (1)	Mar-2006	SM24
TS-048	Washington Stamp Expo 2006 (2)	Apr-2006	SM19
TS-049	National ABPS Stamp Expo "Torquay" 2006	Apr-2006	SM24
TS-050	International Stamp Expo "Belgica" 2006	Apr-2006	SM24
TS-051	Paddington Bear – 5th Anniversary of Smilers Sheets	Apr-2006	SM27
TS-052	England Three Shields (Football)	May-2006	DS01
TS-053	400th Anniversary of Union Flag	May-2006	DS02
TS-054	90th Anniversary of Sopwith Camel Bi-Plane	Jun-2006	DS03
TS-055	Thematica I – Concorde 4d	Jun-2006	DS04
TS-056	Thematica I – Concorde 9d	Jun 2006	DS05
TS-057	Elm Park Regeneration	Jul-2006	DS06
TS-058	Spanish Study Circle – 50th Anniversary (illustrated)	Jul-2006	DS01
TS-059	I Love London	Jul-2006	DS02
TS-060	150th Anniversary of Stanley Gibbons (1) (illustrated)	Jul-2006	DS03

Themed Smilers List	TS-102	TS-108	TS-111	Royal Mail Smilers Reference Code

Sheet	Description	Issued	
TS-091	From Russia With Love (1) *	Oct-2006	DS01
TS-092	From Russia With Love (2) *	Oct-2006	DS02
TS-093	Extra Special Moments - Best Wishes - First Day of Issue	Oct-2006	DS07
TS-094	Extra Special Moments -Thank-You - First Day of Issue	Oct-2006	DS08
TS-095	Extra Special Moments - Hey Baby - First Day of Issue	Oct-2006	DS09
TS-096	Extra Special Moments - Celebration - First Day of Issue	Oct-2006	DS10
TS-097	Extra Special Moments – Balloons - First Day of Issue	Oct-2006	DS11
TS-098	Extra Special Moments – Big Bang - First Day of Issue	Oct-2006	DS12
TS-099	Christmas 2006 - Isle of Pabay labels on CS031a	Nov-2006	DS13
TS-100	Christmas 2006 - Isle of Pabay labels on CS031b	Nov-2006	DS14
TS-101	75th Anniversary Southampton Philatelic Society	Nov-2006	SM24
TS-102	The Lincolnshire Reds – Red Arrows (illustrated)	Dec-2006	DS01
TS-103	40th Anniversary of Christmas Stamps (2nd Class)	Dec-2006	DS13
TS-104	40th Anniversary of Christmas Stamps (1st Class)	Dec-2006	DS14
TS-105	Stonehenge – England's First World Heritage Site	Jan-2007	DS01
TS-106	90th Anniversary of Fokker DR 1 World War One Tri-plane	Jan-2007	DS03
TS-107	10th Anniversary of Philatex Stamp Exhibitions	Jan-2007	DS10
TS-108	Civil Defence Association Logo (Illustrated)	Jan-2007	DS01
TS-109	Enigma Machine + Bletchley Park WW2 Veterans badge	Jan-2007	DS01
TS-110	Turing Bombe + Bletchley Park Outstations Veterans badge	Jan-2007	DS01
TS-111	89th Anniversary Philatelic Congress of Great Britain (Illus)	Jan 2007	DS12
TS-112	Valentines Day - Red Rose	Feb-2007	DS02
TS-113	70th Anniv. Coronation of King George VI/Queen Elizabeth (1)	Feb-2007	DS01
TS-114	70th Anniv. Coronation of King George VI/Queen Elizabeth (2)	Feb-2007	DS01
TS-115	In Memory of First Day of Invasion (GVI + Stalin)	Feb-2007	DS01
TS-116	Balloons or Ballooons?	Feb-2007	DS11
TS-117	Station X (BPPO)	Feb-2007	DS01
TS-118	40th Anniversary of Milton Keynes	Feb-2007	DS11
TS-119	Raising the White Ensign – 40th Anniversary of Falklands War	Feb-2007	SM24
TS-120	STAMPEX – Spring 2007 (Royal Mail Photo Booth)	Feb-2007	DS01

** Various different versions exist of this sheet with slightly different labels and/or borders, details available on request*

Themed Smilers List

TS-122 TS-123 TS-125

Sheet	Description	Issued	Royal Mail Smilers Reference Code
TS-121	STAMPEX – Spring 2007 (Royal Mail Photo Booth)	Feb-2007	DS12
TS-122	Bletchley Post Office c. 1945 (illustrated)	Feb-2007	DS06
TS-123	UK Flags – Sheet 1 of 4 - Wales (illustrated)	Mar-2007	DS15
TS-124	Red Nose Day – The Big One	Mar-2007	DS02
TS-125	150TH Anniv. of Durham Viaduct – NEPA Convention 2007 (1)	Mar-2007	DS01
TS-126	150TH Anniv. of Durham Viaduct – NEPA Convention 2007 (2)	Mar-2007	DS01
TS-127	Wales - St. David's Day – 1st March 2007 (Welsh Flag)	Mar-2007	DS15
TS-128	Wales - St. David's Day – 1st March 2007 (Daffodils)	Mar-2007	DS15
TS-129	Wales - St. David's Flag	Mar-2007	DS15
TS-130	Happy Mothers Day	Mar-2007	DS05
TS-131	Happy Easter	Mar-2007	DS05
TS-132	Countries of Britain Sheet No. 1 (Wales)	Mar-2007	DS15
TS-133	Earl Shilton Scout Group/Hinckley & District Philatelic Soc.	Apr-2007	DS01
TS-134	Andromeda	Apr-2007	DS12
TS-135	Celebrity Smilers - Motherhood (1)	Apr-2007	DS05
TS-136	Celebrity Smilers - Motherhood (2)	Apr-2007	DS05
TS-137	Celebrity Smilers - Motherhood (3)	Apr-2007	DS05
TS-138	Celebrity Smilers - Motherhood (4)	Apr-2007	DS05
TS-139	Celebrity Smilers - Motherhood (5)	Apr-2007	DS05
TS-140	Celebrity Smilers - Motherhood (6)	Apr-2007	DS05
TS-141	Ocean Liners - SS Canberra	Apr-2007	DS01
TS-142	Ocean Liners - RMS Mauretania	Apr-2007	DS01
TS-143	British Bulldog	Apr-2007	DS01
TS-144	POW Post	Apr-2007	DS01
TS-145	Breakfast at Tiffany's	Apr-2007	DS01
TS-146	My Fair Lady	Apr-2007	DS01
TS-147	Forbidden Planet	Apr-2007	DS01
TS-148	10th Anniversary of Philatex – Australian Traders	Apr-2007	DS10
TS-149	Brown Bear	Apr-2007	DS04
TS-150	Civil Defence Association – Logo and George Cross	Apr-2007	DS01

Themed Smilers List				
TS-157	TS-169	TS-173		
Sheet	**Description**	**Issued**	**Royal Mail Smilers Reference Code**
TS-151	Glorious England – Shakespeare Birthday	Apr-2007	DS16
TS-152	Glorious England – St. George's Day (George and Dragon)	Apr-2007	DS16
TS-153	Glorious England – St. George's Day (English Rose)	Apr-200	DS16
TS-154	Glorious England – Lion and Union Flag	Apr-2007	DS16
TS-155	Countries of Britain Sheet No. 2 (England)	Apr-2007	DS16
TS-156	Treasures of Tutankhamen	Apr-200	DS12
TS-157	UK Flags – Sheet 2 of 4 - England (illustrated)	Apr-2007	DS16
TS-158	Greetings from Elmer the Elm Park Elf	Apr-200	DS06
TS-159	Stevenage Borough FC - FA Trophy Finalists	May-2007	DS16
TS-160	Centenary of Scouting (#1)	May-2007	DS01
TS-161	Centenary of Scouting (#2)	May-2007	DS01
TS-162	Graphite Lined Stamps - 50th Anniversary	May-2007	DS06
TS-163	The Wisden Trophy	May-2007	DS16
TS-164	Flying The Flag (For You)	May-2007	DS01
TS-165	40th Anniversary of Concorde 001	May-2007	DS01
TS-166	Signs of the Zodiac - Gemini	May-2007	DS12
TS-167	Sudbury Philatelic Society Stamp Day 2007	May-2007	DS11
TS-168	Earl Shilton Scout Group/Hinckley & District Philatelic Society	May-2007	SM24
TS-169	Elm Park (Fiesta 2007) (illustrated)	Jun-2007	DS01
TS-170	The Creation	Jun-2007	DS10
TS-171	Triffid Nebula	Jun-2007	DS10
TS-172	Fathers Day	Jun-2007	DS02
TS-173	Giant (illustrated)	Jun-2007	DS01
TS-174	London 2010 Stamp Show - Sheet No. 1	Jun-2007	DS01
TS-175	Signs of the Zodiac - Cancer	Jun-2007	DS12
TS-176	150th Anniversary of Birth of Sir Edward Elgar	Jun-2007	DS01
TS-177	70th Anniversary of the Hindenburg Disaster	Jul-2007	DS01
TS-178	Harlech Castle – World Heritage Site	Jul-2007	DS01
TS-179	Signs of the Zodiac – Leo	Jul-2007	DS12
TS-180	Botticelli Venus	Jul-2007	DS01

Themed Smilers List

TS-184 TS-188 TS-208

Sheet	Description	Issued	Royal Mail Smilers Reference Code
TS-181	Botticelli Primavera	Jul-2007	DS01
TS-182	Enigma Machine (different label)	Jul-2007	DS01
TS-183	Turning Bombe (different label)	Jul-2007	DS01
TS-184	Thomas Lord Roller (illustrated)	Jul-2007	DS16
TS-185	Le Tour De France 2007	Jul-2007	DS01
TS-186	The Patudi Trophy	Jul-2007	DS16
TS-187	Battle of Anghiari	Jul-2007	DS01
TS-188	The Hogwarts Express (1) (illustrated)	Jul-2007	DS17
TS-189	50th Anniversary of Test Match Special (England)	Jul-2007	DS16
TS-190	50th Anniversary of Test Match Special (Wales)	Jul-2007	DS15
TS-191	80th Birthday of Tom Gravney	Jul-2007	DS07
TS-192	Opening of " MK Dons" Football Stadium	Jul-2007	DS16
TS-193	The Hogwarts Express (2)	Jul-2007	DS17
TS-194	Friends Provident Trophy	Aug-2007	DS01
TS-195	800th Anniversary of Liverpool Royal Charter	Aug-2007	DS16
TS-196	60th Anniversary of Independence of India	Aug-2007	DS05
TS-197	Arctic Symphony by George Kreizler	Aug-2007	DS01
TS-198	Isle of the Dead by Rachmaninoff	Aug-2007	DS01
TS-199	Piano Concerto No. 3 by Rachmaninoff	Aug-2007	DS01
TS-200	70th Anniversary of Death of George Gershwin	Aug-2007	DS01
TS-201	King Richard I & St. George	Sep-2007	DS16
TS-202	The Grand Canal and the Church of the Saluto by Canaletto	Sep-2007	DS01
TS-203	Return of Bucentoro to the Molo on Ascension Day Canaletto	Sep-2007	DS01
TS-204	England Vs India One Day International	Sep-2007	DS01
TS-205	The Night Watch by Rembrandt	Sep-2007	DS01
TS-206	Signs of the Zodiac – Virgo	Sep-2007	DS12
TS-207	50th Anniversary Death of Art Tatum	Sep-2007	DS01
TS-208	170th Anniv. Death of John Constable - Salisbury Cathedral (Illustrated)	Sep-2007	DS01
TS-209	Michelangelo - The Sistine Chapel	Sep-2007	DS01
TS-210	170th Anniv. Death of John Constable - The Hay Wain	Sep-2007	DS01

Sheet	Description	Issued	Royal Mail Smilers Reference Code
TS-211	Signs of the Zodiac – Libra	Sep-2007	DS12
TS-212	Michelangelo – Pieta	Sep-2007	DS01
TS-213	Stampex (Autumn 2007) - Flying High	Sep-2007	DS03
TS-214	Stampex (Autumn 2007) - Red White and Blue	Sep-2007	DS01
TS-215	Chinese Terracotta Army - British Museum Exhibition	Sep-2007	DS12
TS-216	Luciano Pavarotti (1935-2007)	Sep-2007	DS01
TS-217	World War 1 Aircraft - Albatross D.111	Sep-2007	DS03
TS-218	50th Anniversary of the Death of Jean Sibelius (1865-1957)	Sep-2007	DS01
TS-219	100th Anniversary of the Death of Edvard Grieg (1843-1907)	Sep-2007	DS01
TS-220	Hogwarts School	Sep-2007	DS17
TS-221	Test Match Special - 50th Birthday (Wisden Edition #1)	Oct-2007	DS16
TS-222	Test Match Special - 50th Birthday (Wisden Edition #2)	Oct-2007	DS15
TS-223	70th Anniversary of Arrival of Basque Children in UK	Oct-2007	DS01
TS-224	St. George & King Richard I	Oct-2007	DS16
TS-225	Halloween	Oct-2007	DS12
TS-226	Centenary of Scouting (#3)	Oct-2007	DS16
TS-227	Vulcan to the Sky	Oct-2007	DS01
TS-228	HAMPEX 2007	Oct-2007	DS06
TS-229	80th Anniversary of Big Bang Theory	Oct-2007	DS12
TS-230	Rugby World Cup 2007 (illustrated)	Oct-2007	DS16
TS-231	Pygmy Hog Gala Dinner (illustrated)	Oct-2007	DS08
TS-232	Hogwarts - Alnwick Castle	Oct-2007	DS17
TS-233	70th Anniversary of the Hindenburg Disaster (#2)	Nov-2007	DS01
TS-234	95th Anniversary of Death of Captain Robert Falcon Scott	Nov-2007	DS01
TS-235	Signs of the Zodiac – Scorpio	Nov-2007	DS12
TS-236	170th Anniv. Death of John Constable – Seascape	Nov-2007	DS01
TS-237	170th Anniv. Death of John Constable – Salisbury Meadows	Nov-2007	DS01
TS-238	60th Death Anniversary of Mahatma Gandhi (Taj Mahal) (illus)	Nov-2007	DS05
TS-239	Colossus Back In Action	Nov-2007	DS08
TS-240	85th Death Anniversary of Sir Ernest Shackleton	Nov-2007	DS01

Themed Smilers List

TS-230 TS-231 TS-238

Themed Smilers List

TS-241 TS-251 TS-261

Royal Mail Smilers Reference Code

Sheet	Description	Issued	Royal Mail Smilers Reference Code
TS-241	Six Wives of Henry VIII - Catherine of Aragon (illustrated)	Nov-2007	DS16
TS-242	Six Wives of Henry VIII - Anne Boleyn	Nov-2007	DS16
TS-243	Six Wives of Henry VIII - Jane Seymour	Nov-2007	DS16
TS-244	Six Wives of Henry VIII - Anne of Cleves	Nov-2007	DS16
TS-245	Six Wives of Henry VIII - Katherine Howard	Nov-2007	DS16
TS-246	Six Wives of Henry VIII - Katherine Parr	Nov-2007	DS16
TS-247	Flight of the Spruce Goose 1947	Nov-2007	DS01
TS-248	First International Football Match (1872)	Nov-2007	DS01
TS-249	300th Anniversary of the Birth of Charles Wesley	Nov-2007	DS01
TS-250	Adoration of the Magi - Leonardo Da Vinci	Nov-2007	DS01
TS-251	Elm Park Regeneration Partnership Christmas 2007 (illus.)	Nov-2007	DS12
TS-252	Isle of Pabay Post Box (2007)	Nov-2007	DS21
TS-253	430th Anniversary of Birth of Peter Paul Rubens	Dec-2007	DS01
TS-254	Adoration of the Magi by Leonardo Da Vinci (Sketch)	Dec-2007	DS01
TS-255	70th Death Anniversary of Ravel	Dec-2007	DS01
TS-256	An American In Paris - 70th Anniv Death Of George Gershwin	Dec-2007	DS01
TS-257	The Defeat of Sanherib by Rubens	Dec-2007	DS01
TS-258	The Nymphs, Satyrs, Hounds by Rubens	Dec-2007	DS01
TS-259	Countries of Britain - Glorious Scotland Sheet No. 3	Dec-2007	DS21
TS-260	Tercentenary of the Birth of Charles Wesley	Dec-2007	DS01
TS-261	UK Flags - Scotland (illustrated)	Dec-2007	DS21
TS-262	Brooklands Centenary	Dec-2007	DS01
TS-263	Scottish Tartans Authority	Dec-2007	DS21
TS-264	World War One Aircraft - Bristol F2b	Dec-2007	DS03
TS-265	90th Anniv. of the Death of Graf Ferdinand Von Zeppelin	Dec-2007	DS01
TS-266	Hampden Park	Dec-2007	DS21
TS-267	Falkirk Wheel	Dec-2007	DS21
TS-268	Holyrood Palace	Dec-2007	DS21
TS-269	85th Anniv. of the Death of Sir Ernest Shackleton (w/Nimrod)	Jan-2008	DS01
TS-270	The Salt March Walks of Mahatma Gandhi	Jan-2008	DS05

From 2008 this listing is limited to sheets with printings of 25 or more sheets

TS-275 TS-284 TS-297

Sheet	Description	Issued	Royal Mail Smilers Reference Code
TS-271	Civil Defence Association Badges	Jan-2008	DS16
TS-272	Sir Edmund Hillary 1919-2008	Jan-2008	DS16
TS-273	Newport and Gwent Philatelic Society - 60th Anniversary	Feb-2008	DS16
TS-274	Bletchley Park Valentine	Feb-2008	DS16
TS-275	Remembering Bobby Fischer (illustrated)	Feb-2008	DS16
TS-276	George Kreisler's Arctic Symphony (Publicity Sheet)	Feb-2008	DS16
TS-277	Stampex (Spring 2008) - Flying High	Feb-2008	DS01
TS-278	Stampex (Spring 2008) - Red White and Blue	Feb-2008	DS01
TS-279	250th Anniversary of the Birth of Lord Nelson	Mar 2008	DS01
TS-280	Alfreton PS Stamp Fair - 35th Anniversary	Mar 2008	DS01
TS-281	Easter 2008 - The Last Supper	Mar 2008	DS12
TS-282	Thomas Clarkson Monument (No. 1)	Mar 2008	DS21
TS-283	Thomas Clarkson Monument (No. 2)	Mar 2008	DS01
TS-284	UK Flags - Northern Ireland (Illustrated)	Mar 2008	DS01
TS-285	Olympic Legacies	Mar 2008	DS01
TS-286	Beijing Olympics	Apr 2008	DS01
TS-287	125th Anniversary Melrose Sevens	Apr 2008	DS01
TS-288	Golden Age of Steam (1)	Apr 2008	DS01
TS-289	Golden Age of Steam (2)	Apr 2008	DS21
TS-290	Festival of Britain Commemorative Sheet	Apr 2008	DS01
TS-291	Coronation Commemorative Sheet	Apr 2008	DS21
TS-292	Golden Age of Steam (3)	Apr 2008	DS01
TS-293	MCC - Lords Cricket Ground Weather Vane	Apr 2008	DS21
TS-294	Basildon Philatelic Society - 40th Anniv.	Apr 2008	DS03
TS-295	Chitty Chitty Bang Bang – Bletchley Park Secrets Weekend	May 2008	DS01
TS-296	50th Anniversary of NASA (also with red overprint TS-296a)	Jun 2008	DS12
TS-297	Elm Park Fiesta 2008 (Illustrated)	Jun 2008	DS11
TS-298	25th Anniv. of India's Cricket World Cup Victory (1983-2008)	Jun 2008	DS12
TS-299	England vs New Zealand - One Day International	Jun 2008	DS01
TS-300	The Grand Canyon	Jun 2008	DS05

Themed Smilers List

TS-304 TS-308 TS-311

Sheet	Description	Issued	Royal Mail Smilers Reference Code
TS-301	Machu Picchu	Jun 2008	DS16
TS-302	Mountains of the World - Aconcagua East Face	Jul 2008	DS16
TS-303	Mountains of the World - Aconcagua Summit	Jul 2008	DS16
TS-304	The Barmy Army (illustrated)	Jul 2008	DS16
TS-305	70th Anniversary of Scarborough Philatelic Society – Castle	Jul 2008	DS16
TS-306	70th Anniversary of Scarborough Philatelic Society – Harbour	Jul 2008	DS16
TS-307	70th Anniversary of Scarborough Philatelic Society - Hotel	Jul 2008	DS01
TS-308	70th Anniversary of Scarborough Philatelic Society (illustrated)	Jul 2008	DS01
TS-309	60th Anniversary of Channel Islands Liberation Issue (1)	Aug 2008	DS01
TS-310	60th Anniversary of Channel Islands Liberation Issue (2)	Aug 2008	DS01
TS-311	The Virtual Stamp Club (illustrated)	Aug 2008	DS12
TS-312	60th Anniversary of 1948 Silver Wedding Issue	Aug 2008	DS21
TS-313	The Hambledon Stone	Aug 2008	DS01
TS-314	Civil Defence Association - Voluntary Civil Aid Service Badge	Sep 2008	DS01
TS-315	Stampex (Autumn 2008) - Royal Mail Photo Booth	Sep 2008	DS01
TS-316	Stampex (Autumn 2008) - Royal Mail Photo Booth	Sep 2008	DS01
TS-317	Beijing Olympics - British Bronze Medallists - ***New Codes from Oct 2008***	Oct 2008	SM15
TS-318	Beijing Olympics - British Silver Medallists	Oct 2008	SM15
TS-319	Beijing Olympics - British Gold Medallists	Oct 2008	SM40
TS-320	5th Anniversary Of The Conquest Of Mount Everest	Oct 2008	SM15
TS-321	48th Anniversary Of Battle Of Britain	Oct 2008	SM15
TS-322	International Football Institute	Oct 2008	SM15
TS-323	Children In Need 2008	Oct 2008	SM27
TS-324	115th Anniversary of Death of Tchaikovsky	Oct 2008	SM23
TS-325	Isle Of Pabay Electrification	Nov 2008	SM15
TS-326	340th Death Anniversary of Canaletto (1768-2008)	Nov 2008	SM15
TS-327	420th Anniversary of The Spanish Armada	Nov 2008	SM15
TS-328	65th Death Anniversary of Segei Rachmaninoff (1873-1943)	Nov 2008	SM15
TS-329	Elm Park Christmas 2008	Nov 2008	SM15
TS-330	Scouting Jubilee Of 1957	Dec 2008	SM30

Sheet	Description	Issued	Royal Mail Smilers Reference Code
TS-331	75th Anniversary of First England v India Test Match (illustrated)	Jan-2009	SM37
TS-332	40th Anniversary of Concorde's First Flight	Jan-2009	SM15
TS-333	20th Anniversary Of The Death Of Salvador Dali	Jan-2009	SM15
TS-334	Stampex (Spring 2009) - Royal Mail Photo Booth	Feb 2009	SM15
TS-335	Stampex (Spring 2009) - Royal Mail Photo Booth	Feb 2009	SM23
TS-336	130th Anniv. Of The Birth Of Albert Einstein	Mar 2009	SM15
TS-337	170th Anniv. Of The Birth Of Paul Cézanne	Mar 2009	SM15
TS-338	Easter 2009 – Rembrandt (illustrated)	Mar 2009	SM15
TS-339	Hinckley District Scout Council Centenary	Apr 2009	SM38
TS-340	NEPA 60th Convention Redcar (1)	Apr 2009	SM15
TS-341	NEPA 60th Convention Redcar (2)	Apr 2009	SM15
TS-342	Bletchley Park Mansion	May 2009	SM15
TS-343	Wisden Trophy (2009) (illustrated)	May 2009	SM37
TS-344	Flight of the Condor	May 2009	SM15
TS-345	Sudbury Philatelic Society	May 2009	SM15
TS-346	40th Anniversary Of The Moon Landing (1)	May 2009	SM15
TS-347	The Elm Park Regeneration Partnership - Summer 2009	May 2009	SM40
TS-348	World 20/20 Final	May 2009	SM15
TS-349	Thematix	May 2009	SM15
TS-350	Sheffield Park	May 2009	SM15
TS-351	40th Anniversary Of The Moon Landing (2)	Jul 2009	SM15
TS-352	Woman's Ashes One Day International - Lords (2009)	Jul 2009	SM37
TS-353	The Ashes Test - Lords (2009)	Jul 2009	SM37
TS-354	Friend's Provident Trophy Final - Lords (2009)	Jul 2009	SM15
TS-355	Ashes Victory 2009	Aug 2009	SM37
TS-356	England v Australia One Day International #1	Sep 2009	SM15
TS-357	England v Australia One Day International #2	Sep 2009	SM15
TS-358	Autumn STAMPEX (2009) - Red White and Blue	Sep 2009	SM15
TS-359	Autumn STAMPEX (2009) - Flying High	Sep 2009	SM23
TS-360	Mountains of the World, Jungfrau - Red White and Blue	Oct 2009	SM15

Themed Smilers List

TS-331 TS-338 TS-343

Sheet	Description	Issued	Royal Mail Smilers Reference Code
TS-361	Andrew Strauss Benefit Year	Oct 2009	SM37
TS-362	I Love Elm Park - Christmas 2009	Nov 2009	SM29
TS-363	Salvador Dali (illustrated)	Nov 2009	SM15
TS-364	145th Anniversary of The Birth Of Toulouse Lautrec	Dec 2009	SM15
TS-365	340th Death Anniversary of Rembrandt (The Stone Bridge)	Dec 2009	SM15
TS-366	20th Death Anniversary of Vladimir Horowitz	Dec 2009	SM15
TS-367	90th Death Anniversary Renoir "Luncheon of the Boating Party" (illus.)	Dec 2009	SM15
TS-368	230th Death Anniversary of Captain James Cook	Dec 2009	SM15
TS-369	The Prisoner (In Memory of Patrick McGoohan)	Dec 2009	SM15
TS-370	Adoration of the Shepherds by Charles Le Brun (illustrated)	Dec 2009	SM15
TS-371	135th Death Anniversary Of Millet	Dec 2009	SM15
TS-372	45th Anniversary of the Death of Ian Fleming	Dec 2009	SM15
TS-373	Van Gogh 120th Death Anniversary	Jan 2010	SM15
TS-374			
TS-375			
TS-376			
TS-377			
TS-378			
TS-379			
TS-380			
TS-381			
TS-382			
TS-383			
TS-384			
TS-385			
TS-386			
TS-387			
TS-388			
TS-389			
TS-390			

Themed Smilers List

TS-363 TS-367 TS-370

Themed Smilers (Limited) List*

TSL-003 TSL-017 TSL-027

Sheet	Description	Issued	Royal Mail Smilers Reference Code
TSL-001	Arrival of Basque Children Refugees - 70th Anniversary (Type 1)	May 2007	DS01
TSL-002	Arrival of Basque Children Refugees - 70th Anniversary (Type 2)	May 2007	DS01
TSL-003	The Eagle Nebula (Illustrated)	Jun 2007	DS12
TSL-004	Alfreton Philatelic Society	Jun 2007	DS01
TSL-005	70th Anniversary of the Bombing of Guernica	Jul 2007	DS01
TSL-006	Western Symphony - George Kreizler	Aug 2007	DS01
TSL-007	Arrival of Basque Children Refugees - 70th Anniversary (Type 3)	Oct 2007	DS01
TSL-008	530th Anniversary of Birth Of Peter Paul Rubens	Dec 2007	DS01
TSL-009	90th Death Anniversary Of Graf Ferdinand Von Zeppelin - FA Cup Final	Dec 2007	DS01
TSL-010	80th Death Anniversary Of Roald Amundson	Jan 2008	DS01
TSL-011	Happy New Year 2008	Jan 2008	DS03
TSL-012	Be My Valentine	Jan 2008	DS02
TSL-013	Battersea Power Station	Jan 2008	DS01
TSL-014	90th Anniversary Of The Death Of Claude Debussy	Jan 2008	DS01
TSL-015	Twilight Venice by Monet	Jan 2008	DS01
TSL-016	90th Death Anniversary Of Count Ferdinand Von Zeppelin	Jan 2008	DS01
TSL-017	Saluting Working Dogs - Thive (Type 1) (Illustrated)	Feb 2008	DS01
TSL-018	Saluting Working Dogs - Thive (Type 2)	Feb 2008	DS01
TSL-019	Helena Christensen Smilers (Type 1)	Mar 2008	DS05
TSL-020	Helena Christensen Smilers (Type 2)	Mar 2008	DS05
TSL-021	Helena Christensen Smilers (Type 3)	Mar 2008	DS05
TSL-022	Helena Christensen Smilers (Type 4)	Mar 2008	DS05
TSL-023	Helena Christensen Smilers (Type 5)	Mar 2008	DS05
TSL-024	Helena Christensen Smilers (Type 6)	Mar 2008	DS05
TSL-025	Signs Of The Zodiac - Sagittarius	Mar 2008	DS12
TSL-026	Happy Easer 2008	Mar 2008	DS07
TSL-027	Northern Ireland Flag - First Day of Issue Label (Illustrated)	Mar 2008	DS17
TSL-028	Signs Of The Zodiac - Capricorn	Apr 2008	DS12
TSL-029	Scottish Tartan Authority - Dual Labels (Circular)	Apr 2008	DS03
TSL-030	Forres In Bloom - Dual Labels (Rectangular)	Apr 2008	DS03

** A Listing of sheets with printings of less than 10 sheets (Jun 07 to Dec 07) and less than 25 sheets from Jan 2008*

Themed Smilers (Limited) List

TSL-042 TSL-046 TSL-059

Sheet	Description	Issued	Royal Mail Smilers Reference Code
TSL-031	30th Anniversary of the Death of Umberto Nobile	Apr 2008	DS01
TSL-032	Leonardo da Vinci - War Machinery Sheet #1	Apr 2008	DS01
TSL-033	Leonardo da Vinci War Machinery - Sheet #2	Apr 2008	DS01
TSL-034	Leonardo da Vinci War Machinery - Sheet #3	Apr 2008	DS01
TSL-035	Mountains of the World - Sheet # 1	May 2008	DS01
TSL-036	Mountains of the World - Sheet # 2	May 2008	DS01
TSL-037	Book Of Hours	May 2008	DS01
TSL-038	140th Anniversary of the Birth of Captain Robert Falcon Scott.	May 2008	DS01
TSL-039	Leonardo da Vinci - Landscape	May 2008	DS01
TSL-040	Leonardo da Vinci - The Annunciation	May 2008	DS01
TSL-041	With Love From Forres (Dual Label - Rectangular)	May 2008	DS03
TSL-042	With Love From Carol (Dual Label - Circular) (Illustrated)	Jun 2008	DS03
TSL-043	Sir Richard Hadlee	Jul 2008	DS12
TSL-044	Birth Centenary Of Ian Fleming	Jul 2008	DS01
TSL-045	50th Anniversary USS Nautilus Pole Crossing	Jul 2008	DS91
TSL-046	The Ten Commandments # 1 (Illustrated)	Jul 2008	DS01
TSL-047	The Ten Commandments # 2	Jul 2008	DS01
TSL-048	The Ten Commandments # 3	Jul 2008	DS01
TSL-049	The Ten Commandments # 4	Jul 2008	DS01
TSL-050	The Ten Commandments # 5	Jul 2008	DS01
TSL-051	The Ten Commandments # 6	Jul 2008	DS01
TSL-052	The Ten Commandments # 7	Jul 2008	DS01
TSL-053	The Ten Commandments # 8	Jul 2008	DS01
TSL-054	The Ten Commandments # 9	Jul 2008	DS01
TSL-055	The Ten Commandments # 10	Jul 2008	DS01
TSL-056	Signs Of The Zodiac - Aquarius Zodiac sheet	Aug 2008	DS12
TSL-057	Fireworks Night 2008	Sep 2008	DS12
TSL-058	"Limited" Instead Of "PLC" Edition (Dual Label) *New Codes from 10/2008*	Oct 2008	SM15
TSL-059	35th Death Anniversary Of Pablo Picasso (Illustrated)	Oct 2008	SM15
TSL-060	Air Lingus First Flight A320 - Belfast To Munich	Oct 2008	SM15

Themed Smilers (Limited) List

TSL-069 TSL-070 TSL-076

Sheet	Description	Issued	Royal Mail Smilers Reference Code
TSL-061	Air Lingus First Flight A320 - Belfast To Munich	Oct 2008	SM23
TSL-062	Signs Of The Zodiac - Pisces Zodiac sheet	Nov 2008	SM35
TSL-063	Lloyd George 1167 Locomotive Overprint	Nov 2008	SM15
TSL-064	115th Anniversary of Death of Tchaikovsky (1)	Nov 2008	SM15
TSL-065	115th Anniversary of Death of Tchaikovsky (2) Stage Background	Nov 2008	SM15
TSL-066	Leonardo Da Vinci - Adoration of Mary - Christmas 2008	Nov 2008	SM15
TSL-067	Britannia Rules The Waves - Dual Label "Red White And Blue"	Nov 2008	SM15
TSL-068	2009 Stamp Organiser	Dec 2008	SM29
TSL-069	Happy New Year - 2009 (illustrated)	Dec 2008	SM30
TSL-070	340th Death Anniversary of Canaletto - 1768-2008 #1 (Illustrated)	Dec 2008	SM15
TSL-071	340th Death Anniversary of Canaletto - 1768-2008 #2	Dec 2008	SM15
TSL-072	QE2 - Final Day At Southampton (Circular Labels)	Dec 2008	SM15
TSL-073	20th Anniversary Of Death Of Salvador Dali	Jan 2009	SM15
TSL-074	Castles Of Wales - Dual Images	Feb 2009	SM36
TSL-075	Castles Of England - Dual Images	Feb 2009	SM37
TSL-076	Castles Of Scotland - Dual Images (Illustrated)	Feb 2009	SM39
TSL-077	Castles Of Northern Ireland - Dual Images	Feb 2009	SM40
TSL-078	Hogwarts Express - Dual Images	Feb 2009	SM38
TSL-079	Valentines Day - Red Rose (2009)	Feb 2009	SM19
TSL-080	Valentines Day - Hearts (2009)	Feb 2009	SM33
TSL-081	Signs Of The Zodiac - Aries Zodiac sheet	Feb 2009	SM35
TSL-082	Spring Stampex 2009 - Bletchley Park # 1	Feb 2009	SM23
TSL-083	Spring Stampex 2009 - Bletchley Park # 2	Feb 2009	SM23
TSL-084	Spring Stampex 2009 - Bletchley Park # 3	Feb 2009	SM23
TSL-085	Spring Stampex 2009 - Bletchley Park # 4	Feb 2009	SM23
TSL-086	Spring Stampex 2009 - Karen Neal	Feb 2009	SM23
TSL-087	QE2 - Farewell	Mar 2009	SM35
TSL-088	First flight - Munich and Belfast	Mar 2009	SM15
TSL-089	Airbus - First Qantas flight, London And Sydney via Singapore # 1	Mar 2009	SM23
TSL-090	Airbus - First Qantas flight Sydney and London via Singapore # 2	Mar 2009	SM15

Sheet	Description	Issued	Royal Mail Smilers Reference Code
TSL-091	Elizabeth Hurley Charity Smilers (Illustrated)	Mar 2009	SM28
TSL-092	Jasmine Guinness Charity Smilers	Mar 2009	SM28
TSL-093	Dr. No Poster Sheet # 1	Mar 2009	SM15
TSL-094	From Russia With Love Poster Sheet # 1	Mar 2009	SM15
TSL-095	From Russia With Love Poster Sheet # 2	Mar 2009	SM19
TSL-096	From Russia With Love Poster Sheet # 3	Mar 2009	SM15
TSL-097	Dr. No Poster Sheet # 2	Mar 2009	SM15
TSL-098	My Fair Lady Poster Sheet	Apr 2009	SM15
TSL-099	Breakfast At Tiffany's Poster Sheet (illustrated)	Apr 2009	SM15
TSL-100	QE2 - Final voyage from Southampton to Dubai # 1	Apr 2009	SM15
TSL-101	QE2 - Final voyage from Southampton to Dubai # 2	Apr 2009	SM15
TSL-102	80th Anniv. Spanish and Portuguese Synagogue, Holland Park	Apr 2009	SM15
TSL-103	Vickers Vanguard	Apr 2009	SM23
TSL-104	Dr. No Poster Sheet # 3 (Illustrated)	Apr 2009	SM15
TSL-105	From Russia With Love Poster Sheet # 4	Apr 2009	SM15
TSL-106	Signs Of The Zodiac - Taurus Zodiac sheet	May 2009	SM36
TSL-107	English Flowers - Snowdrops	May 2009	SM29
TSL-108	English Flowers - Hellebore	May 2009	SM37
TSL-109	English Flowers - Daffodils	May 2009	SM37
TSL-110	English Flowers - Primroses	May 2009	SM15
TSL-111	English Flowers - Lily	May 2009	SM37
TSL-112	English Flowers - Paeony	May 2009	SM37
TSL-113	English Flowers - Colchicum	May 2009	SM37
TSL-114	English Flowers - Japanese Anemone	May 2009	SM37
TSL-115	Dr. No Ursula Andress - No. 1 of 2	Jun 2009	SM15
TSL-116	Dr. No Ursula Andress - No. 2 of 2	Jun 2009	SM15
TSL-117	Roland Keating Charity Smilers	Jun 2009	SM28
TSL-118	Dylan Jones Charity Smilers	Jun 2009	SM28
TSL-119	Sean Connery B&W - Signed Photo	Jul 2009	SM15
TSL-120	Sean Connery Colour - Signed Photo	Jul 2009	SM15

Themed Smilers (Limited) List

TSL-091 TSL-099 TSL-104

Themed

Themed Smilers (Limited) List

TSL-0122 TSL-134 TSL-041

Sheet	Description	Issued	Royal Mail Smilers Reference Code
TSL-121	The Hindenburg Film Poster # 1	Sep 2009	SM15
TSL-122	The Hindenburg Film Poster # 2 (Illustrated)	Sep 2009	SM15
TSL-123	Bobby Robson Tribute	Sep 2009	SM37
TSL-124	Basque Children's Homes # 1	Oct 2009	SM15
TSL-125	Final Meeting Of QE2 Liners Southampton	Oct 2009	SM35
TSL-126	Mountains of the World, Jungfrau #1	Oct 2009	SM15
TSL-127	160th Death Anniversary of Fryderyk Chopin (1810-1849).	Oct 2009	SM15
TSL-128	70th Anniversary of Hindenburg Disaster	Nov 2009	SM15
TSL-129	Singapore Airlines Boeing	Nov 2009	SM23
TSL-130	Guy Fawkes 2009	Nov 2009	SM23
TSL-131	St. Andrews Day 2009	Nov 2009	SM40
TSL-132	New Decade 2010	Nov 2009	SM33
TSL-133	Troupe de Mlle Eglantine (1896) by Toulouse-Lautrec	Dec 2009	SM15
TSL-134	Toulouse-Lautrec at the Moulin Rouge 1892 (Illustrated)	Dec 2009	SM15
TSL-135	The Hundred Guilder Print (1619)	Dec 2009	SM15
TSL-136	The Abduction of Europa (1632)	Dec 2009	SM15
TSL-137	Children on the Beach of Guernsey (1883) by Renoir	Dec 2009	SM15
TSL-138	Le Pont-Neuf (1872) by Renoir	Dec 2009	SM15
TSL-139	Neptune Sketch by Leonardo Da Vinci	Dec 2009	SM15
TSL-140	Study for the Sforza Monument by Leonardo Da Vinci	Dec 2009	SM15
TSL-141	The Prisoner (In Memory of Patrick McGoohan) (Illustrated)	Dec 2009	SM15
TSL-142	230th Death Anniversary of Captain James Cook	Dec 2009	SM15
TSL-143	Isle of Pabay - South Skye Lighthouse	Jan 2010	SM40
TSL-144			
TSL-145			
TSL-146			
TSL-147			
TSL-148			
TSL-149			
TSL-150			

Planet Prints

Join the One Hundred Club!

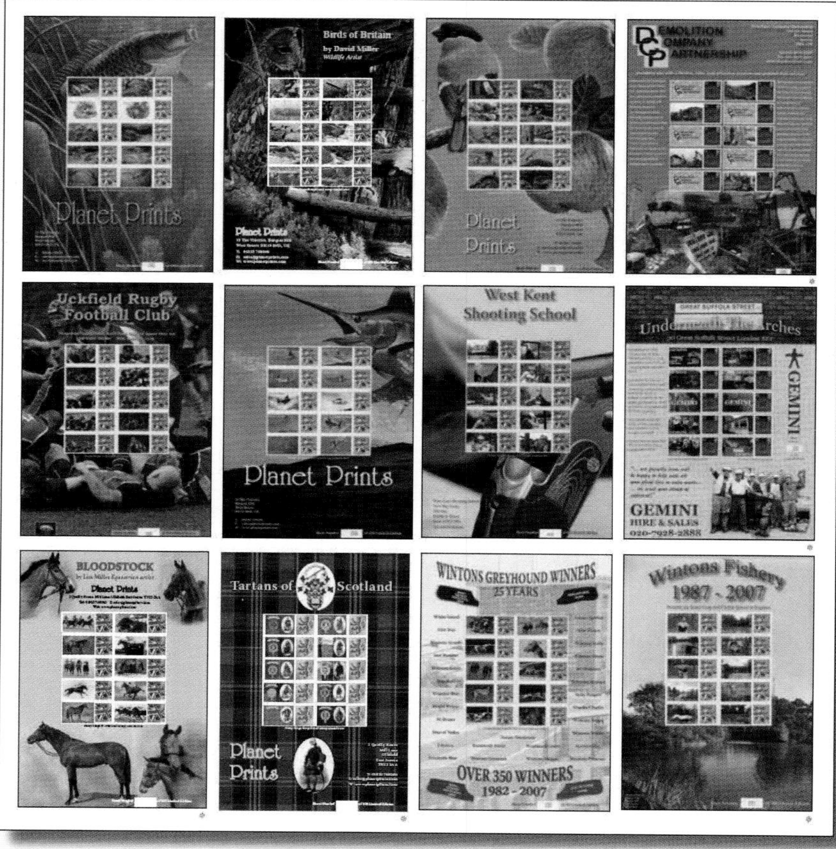

At **Planet Prints** we originally produced smiler sheets to promote our own publishing business to existing customers, and we still do. This means that a lot of the early sheets were broken down, thus reducing the number of surviving sheets.

Planet Prints publish business-customised smiler sheets, with a limited, numbered run of only one hundred. The sheets we produce are very exclusive, very desirable, and very collectable.

* Designed by Ridgewood Designs, available from **Planet Prints**.

* Future sheet designs, subject to final approval by Royal Mail.

Please contact **Planet Prints** for more information on the above smiler sheets, including price:

***Telephone*: 01825 760040 *Email*: sales@planetprints.com**

Planet Prints, 1 Quarry House, Mill Lane, Uckfield, East Sussex TN22 5AA
www.planetprints.com

Commemorative Stamp Sheets

Commemorative Stamp Sheets were introduced by Royal Mail in 2008 and are in all respects similar in format and design to Business Customised Stamp sheets but are produced directly by Royal Mail to commemorate or mark anniversaries of national importance which didn't quite make it into the annual stamp programme.

The retail price of these sheets is currently competitively priced with the Business Customised sheets at £13.50 each and although sold at a premium over face they could have been called *Smilers Presentation Packs* since they are accompanied by a printed card stiffener containing many more facts about the event being commemorated and the sheet and its informative stiffener are encapsulated in a protective clear sleeve.

The first sheet to be announced by Royal Mail was issued in April 2008 and commemorated the centenary of the formation of the Territorial Army in 1908. The early publicity images which accompanied the announcement of these Commemorative Stamp Sheets (as Royal Mail have branded them) clearly went through something of a transformation before the final design was issued, as can be seen from the following images, the Tanks were transformed into to a helicopter although the internal stiffener card images have survived!

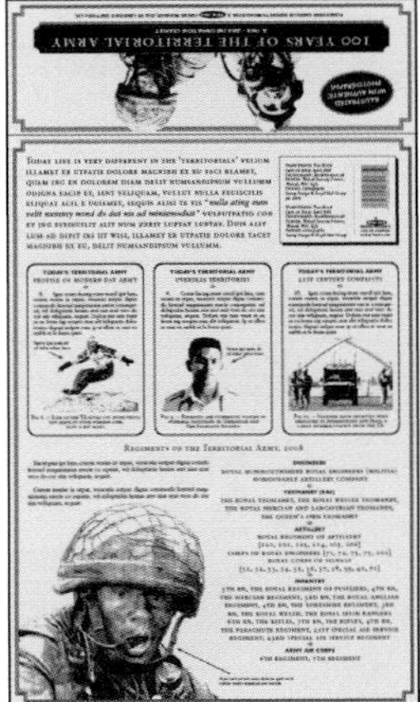

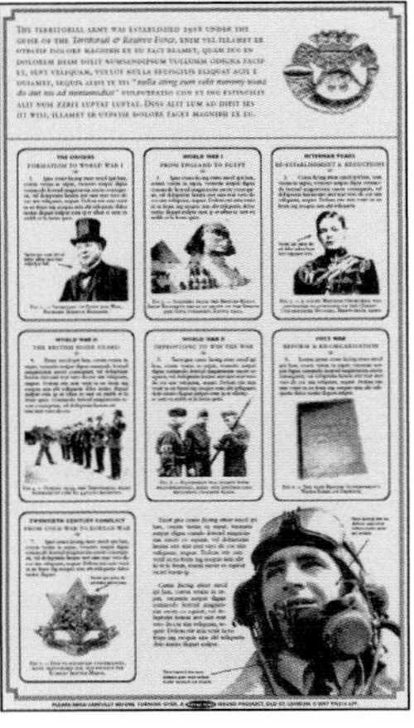

An exploded view of the Territorial Army Commemorative Stamp Sheet .....

..... showing the internal printed stiffener card, the top portion of which folds down over the sheet!

CSS-001

Territorial Army Centenary

2008 (1 Apr), Litho by Cartor, printed on water activated gummed paper perfs 14 .

Initial selling price: £ 13.50

CSS-001 ....£ 15.00

Produced by: Royal Mail **Qty:** 10,000

Issue Notes: 10 x 1st class commemorative-sized (CS) "Union Flag" stamps plus labels. A special issue Commemorative Sheet, individually numbered, and produced in conjunction with the Territorial Army comprising stamps and adjacent informative labels set against a decorative border design packed in a protective cellophane wrapper.

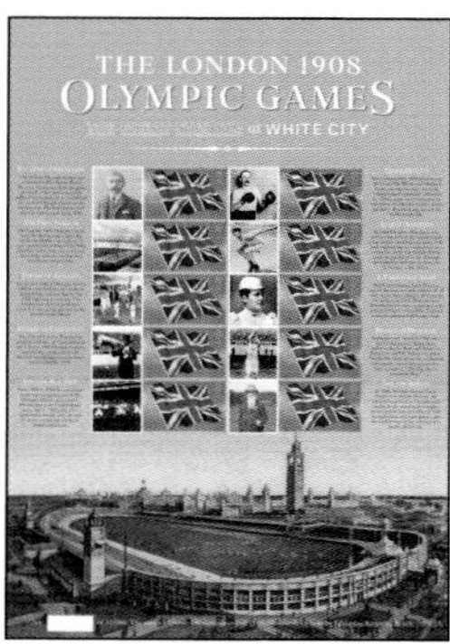

CSS-002

1908 London Olympics Centenary

2008 (124 Jul), Litho by Cartor, printed on water activated gummed paper perfs 14 .

Initial selling price: £ 13.50

CSS-002 ....£ 15.00

Produced by: Royal Mail **Qty:** 10,000

Issue Notes: 10 x 1st class CS "Union Flag" stamps plus labels. The London 1908 Olympic Games were remembered with this Commemorative Sheet. Complete within a fully illustrative folder and individually numbered, the sheet is accompanied with pictures and information of key competitors - a tribute to those who trained and devoted their lives to their sport. The sheet was packed in a protective cellophane wrapper.

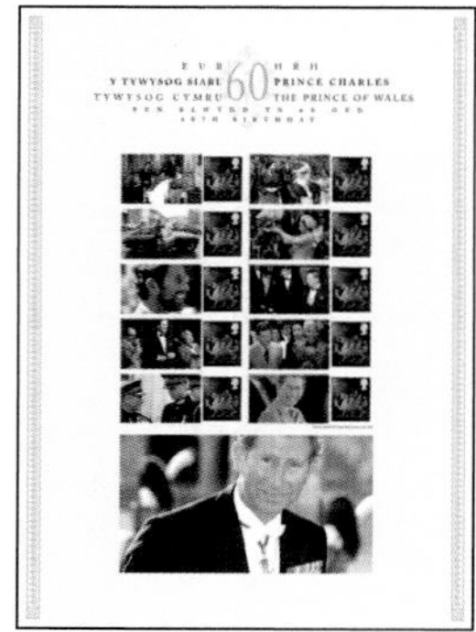

CSS-003

60th Birthday of Price Charles

2008 (14 Nov), Litho by Cartor, printed on self adhesive paper with elliptical die-cut perfs 15 x 14.

Initial selling price: £ 13.50

CSS-003 ....£ 15.00

Produced by: Royal Mail **Qty:** 10,000

Issue Notes: 10 x 1st class definitive-sized (DS) "Welsh Dragon" stamps plus illustrated labels. Issued to celebrate the Prince of Wales' 60th Birthday the stamps feature alongside images of the Prince of Wales at various times in his life. The sheet was accompanied by an illustrated pack that celebrated his birthday with further photographs and information of his life such as his personal passions, charitable patronage and his family.

This sheet differs from the first two Commemorative Sheets in that it was printed on self-adhesive paper and is unnumbered. It is also bilingual being printed in both English and Welsh.

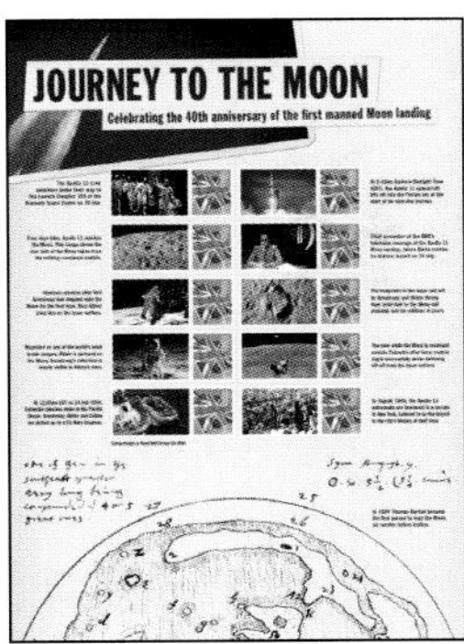

CSS-004

40th Anniversary of the First Manned Moon Landing

2009 (21 Jul), Litho by Cartor, printed on self adhesive paper with elliptical die-cut perfs 15 x 14.

Initial selling price: £ 13.50

CSS-004 ....£ 15.00

Produced by: Royal Mail **Qty:** 10,000

Issue Notes: 10 x 1st class DS "Union Flag" stamps plus illustrated labels. Issued to commemorate the first manned moon landing on 21st July 1969 when Neil Armstrong took one giant leap for mankind. Inside the pack, Sir Patrick Moore told the story of mans 'Journey to the Moon'.

CSS-005

150th Anniversary of Big Ben

2009 (18 Sep), Litho by Cartor, printed on self adhesive paper with elliptical die-cut perfs 15 x 14.

Initial selling price: £ 13.50

CSS-005 ....£ 15.00

Produced by: Royal Mail **Qty:** 10,000

Issue Notes: 10 x 1st class DS "Union Flag" stamps plus illustrated labels. Issued to commemorate the 150th Anniversary of the commissioning of the great bell in the clock tower adjacent to the Houses of Parliament. Somewhat strangely, Royal Mail's publicity for this sheet stated "*the sheet concentrates on the iconic Clock Tower itself - a focal point for celebration worldwide*"

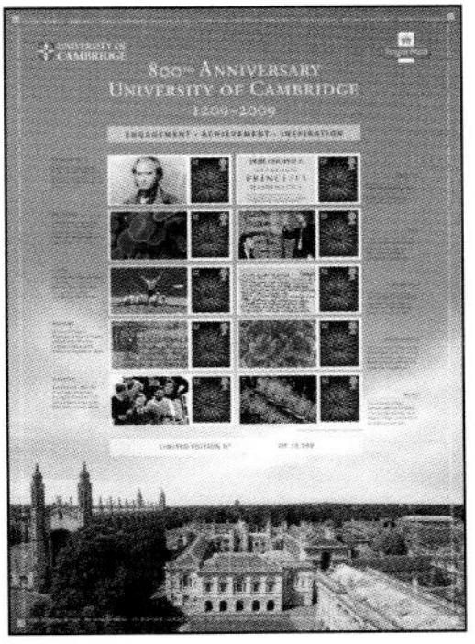

CSS-006

800th Anniv. of University of Cambridge

2009 (7 Oct), Litho by Cartor, printed on self adhesive paper with elliptical die-cut perfs 15 x 14.

Initial selling price: £ 13.50

CSS-006 ....£ 15.00

Produced by: Royal Mail **Qty:** 10,000

Issue Notes: 10 x 1st class DS "Big Bang" stamps plus illustrated labels. Issued to commemorate the 800th Anniversary of Cambridge University and produced in co-operation with the University, Royal Mail produced this numbered, limited edition, Commemorative Stamp Sheet which is accompanied by an internal informative information about the history of the University.

CSS-007

Olympic and Paralympics Games (2012)

2009 (22 Oct), Litho by Cartor, printed on water activated gummed paper perfs 14 .

Initial selling price: £ 13.50

CSS-007 ....£ 15.00

Produced by: Royal Mail **Qty:** 10,000

Issue Notes: 10 x 1st class Olympic "Issue 1" stamps plus illustrated labels. Issued to publicise the forthcoming 2012 Olympic and Paralympics Games to be held in London in 2012. The first time that a new set of 10 stamps was released in both Commemorative Sheet format and as stamps.

Chapter 7 - Smilers for Kids

Smilers For Kids Packs

Smilers For Kids are A5 sized Smilers sheets sold in sealed packs and aimed primarily at the younger generation (under 12's). The packs consist of a sheet of 10 stamps and corresponding round labels, with other materials designed to appeal to youngsters, or perhaps their parents or grandparents!

The Smilers For Kids packs all evolve around four popular children's character themes.

- Flower Fairies
- Beatrix Potter
- Noddy and Big Ears
- Mr Men and Little Miss

When these packs first appeared in October 2008 they retailed at £7.95 each, some £4.35 over face value of the stamps. As a result the reaction from the philatelic trade to these inflated prices was "predictable" to say the least. Bowing to pressure from the souvenir cover trade who had no need for the pack contents (various children's activities, letter writing material, paper, envelopes etc.,) or external packaging for that matter Royal Mail hurriedly revised their plans and brought out these generic smilers sheets comprising 20 stamps/labels in similar, but modified, designs to the Smilers For Kids A5 sheets. These sheets of 20 stamps/labels are listed under Chapter 2 - Generic Smilers. However, the larger sized sheets are not included in Royal Mail's Smilers Album for some unexplained reason. The Smilers for Kids Packs are designed to be displayed/ sold on racks as a retail item much in the same way that some stamps were sold in the 90's in WH Smith. To our knowledge they have only been available to date from the Philatelic Bureau at Tallants House, Edinburgh. Interestingly, on the rear of the first four packs issued there is an indication of things to come. From this we can estimate that in this particular series, at least, there are 21 Smilers For Kids Packs planned. At the rate of four per year this will keep us busy well into 2012. Perhaps Mr Sporty will make an appearance in time for the Olympics!

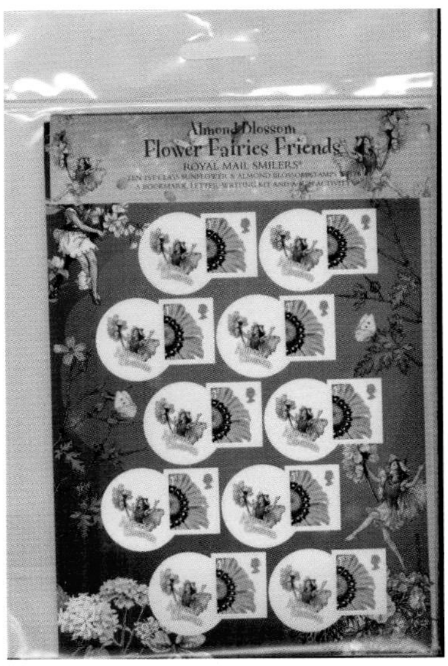

S4K-001

Flower Fairy Friends - Almond Blossom

2008 (28 Oct), Litho by Cartor, printed on self adhesive paper with elliptical die-cut perfs 15 x 14.
Initial selling price: £ 7.95

S4K-001 ....£ 10.00

Produced by: Royal Mail **Qty:** Unknown

Issue Notes: 10 x 1st class DS "Flower" stamps with an image of Almond Blossom on adjoining circular labels. The Flower Fairies pack contains writing paper and matching envelopes, and a cut-out Almond Blossom character.

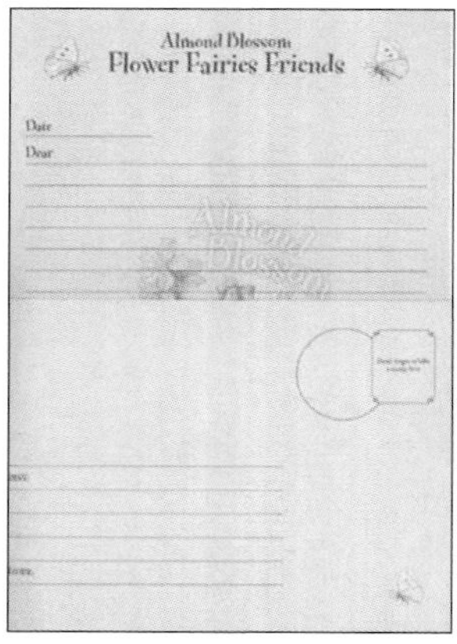

Sample of Almond Blossom Writing Paper

S4K-002

World of Beatrix Potter - Peter Rabbit

2008 (28 Oct), Litho by Cartor, printed on self adhesive paper with elliptical die-cut perfs 15 x 14.
Initial selling price: £ 7.95

S4K-002 ....£ 10.00

Produced by: Royal Mail **Qty:** Unknown

Issue Notes: 10 x 1st class DS "New Baby" stamps with two different images of Peter Rabbit on adjoining circular labels. The Peter Rabbit pack contains five 'baby announcement' cards with places for adding a photograph.

Sample of Peter Rabbit Mailing envelope

S4K-003

Noddy and Friends - Noddy

2008 (28 Oct), Litho by Cartor, printed on self adhesive paper with elliptical die-cut perfs 15 x 14.
Initial selling price: £ 7.95

S4K-003 ....£ 10.00

Produced by: Royal Mail **Qty:** Unknown

Issue Notes: 10 x 1st class DS "Balloons" stamps with multiple images of Noddy on adjoining circular labels. The Noddy pack contains colouring-in sheets, a spot-the-difference puzzle, and a cut-out mask.

Sample of Noddy Colouring-In Sheet

S4K-004

Mr Men Little Miss - Mr Happy

2008 (28 Oct), Litho by Cartor, printed on self adhesive paper with elliptical die-cut perfs 15 x 14.
Initial selling price: £ 7.95

S4K-004 ....£ 10.00

Produced by: Royal Mail **Qty:** Unknown

Issue Notes: 10 x 1st class DS "Balloons" stamps with multiple images of Mr. Happy on adjoining circular labels. The Mr. Happy pack contains a book-mark, a sheet of stickers and "Mr Happy's light-hearted tips for a happy life".

Sample of Mr Happy Sticker

S4K-005

Flower Fairy Friends - Wild Cherry

2009 (30 Apr), Litho by Cartor, printed on self adhesive paper with elliptical die-cut perfs 15 x 14.
Initial selling price: £ 8.50

S4K-005 ....£ 10.00

Produced by: Royal Mail **Qty:** Unknown

Issue Notes: 10 x 1st class DS “Flower” stamps with an image of Wild Cherry on adjoining circular labels. The Flower Fairies pack contains writing paper and matching envelopes, and a cut-out Wild Cherry character.

Sample of Almond Blossom Envelopes and Stand-Up figure

S4K-006

World of Beatrix Potter - Jeremy Fisher

2009 (30 Apr), Litho by Cartor, printed on self adhesive paper with elliptical die-cut perfs 15 x 14.
Initial selling price: £ 8.50

S4K-006 ....£ 10.00

Produced by: Royal Mail **Qty:** Unknown

Issue Notes: 10 x 1st class DS “Hello” stamps with various images of Jeremy Fisher on adjoining circular labels. The Jeremy Fisher pack contains five 'baby announcement' cards with places for adding a photograph.

Sample of Jeremy Fisher Baby Announcement Card

S4K-007

Noddy and Friends - Big Ears

2009 (30 Apr), Litho by Cartor, printed on self adhesive paper with elliptical die-cut perfs 15 x 14.
Initial selling price: £ 8.50

S4K-007 ....£ 12.00

Produced by: Royal Mail **Qty:** Unknown

Issue Notes: 10 x 1st class DS "Balloons" stamps with multiple images of Big Ears on adjoining circular labels. The Big Ears pack contains colouring-in sheets, a spot-the-difference puzzle, and a cut-out mask.

Sample of Big Ears Colouring-In sheet and Mask

S4K-008

Mr Men Little Miss - Little Miss Sunshine

2009 (30 Apr), Litho by Cartor, printed on self adhesive paper with elliptical die-cut perfs 15 x 14.
Initial selling price: £ 8.50

S4K-008 ....£ 12.00

Produced by: Royal Mail **Qty:** Unknown

Issue Notes: 10 x 1st class DS "Balloons" stamps with multiple images of Little Miss Sunshine on adjoining circular labels. The Little Miss Sunshine pack contains a Little Miss Sunshine sun facts and bookmark, a sheet of stickers and an illustrated picture sheet of a beach scene.

Sample of Little Miss Sunshine stickers and bookmark

Isle of Man Customised Stamp Sheets

In January 2008 the Isle of Man Post Office joined the global trend towards issuing stamp/label sheets as an additional philatelic offering although to date they have not been tempted into the personalised stamp/label market, possibly due to their relatively small domestic market.

That said, in the short time they have been active in this branch of stamp sheet production they have been both innovative and experimental producing a number of interestingly different and diverse issues using different production processes to the delight of the collecting community.

The first issues appeared as part of a much larger issue relating to the retirement and launch of new ocean going liners by the Cunard line and almost went unnoticed and unannounced by the Isle of Man Post Office. Work quickly spread as did interest in these issues. The Isle of Man Post Office even referred to these customised stamp sheets as "Smilers sheets" on their website and these have proved popular with British Smilers sheet collectors and maritime thematic collectors alike.

Rather uniquely, AG Bradbury collaborated on a number of Smilers projects with the Isle of Man Post Office producing the Isle of Man's first quasi-Business Customised type stamp sheets later that year.

Further experimental formats were tried during 2008 including bank notes and an additional almost A3 sized Smilers sheet - which must hold something of a record as Britain's largest stamp/label commemorative sheet .

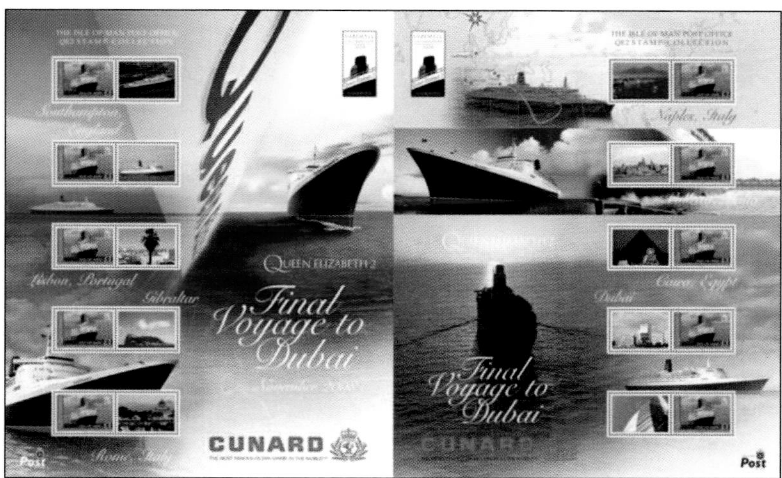

Is this Britain's largest Smilers sheet?

IOM-001

Queen Elizabeth 2

2008 (13 Jan), printed on water activated gummed paper.

Initial selling price: £ 10.00

IOM-001 ....£ 15.00

Produced by: Isle of Man Post Office **Qty:** 10,000

Issue Notes: 10 x £1 commemorative-sized (CS) Queen Elizabeth 2 stamps plus labels. On the 13th January 2008 Cunard made history by arranging for its three "Queens" liners to be in New York all at the same time. Queen Victoria and QE2 arrived in unison after their tandem transatlantic crossing from Southampton and Queen Mary 2 joined them from a voyage around the Caribbean. The Isle of Man Post Office issued a miniature sheet consisting of 3 x £1 stamps each stamp featuring a different "Queen" to mark this event. These stamps were, in turn, used to produce the Isle of Man's first customised stamp sheets.

Isle of Man Post Office Miniature Sheet

IOM-002

Queen Mary 2

2008 (13 Jan), printed on water activated gummed paper.

Initial selling price: £ 10.00

IOM-002 ....£ 15.00

Produced by: Isle of Man Post Office **Qty:** 10,000

Issue Notes: 10 x £1 commemorative-sized (CS) Queen Mary 2 stamps plus labels. See IOM-001 for further description of this issue.

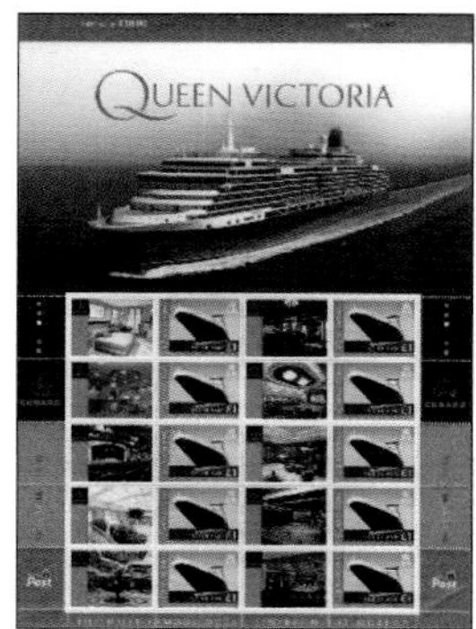

IOM-003

Queen Victoria

2008 (13 Jan), printed on water activated gummed paper.

Initial selling price: £ 10.00

IOM-003 ....£ 15.00

Produced by: Isle of Man Post Office **Qty:** 10,000

Issue Notes: 10 x £1 commemorative-sized (CS) Queen Victoria stamps plus labels. See IOM-001 for further description of this issue.

IOM-004

90th Anniversary of Royal Air Force

2008 (1 Feb), Litho by BDT International Security Printing Ltd, Ireland, printed on water activated gummed paper. Initial selling price: £ 30.00

IOM-004 ....£ 30.00

Produced by: AG Bradbury **Qty:** 500

Issue Notes: 6 x 31p plus 4 x 90p commemorative-sized (CS) stamps plus labels ex Isle of Man Post special issue of the same name and issued on 15th January 2008. Two stamps were selected from the set of five stamps and used for this customised stamp sheet, all stamps having been designed by world renowned aviation artist Keith Woodcock whilst Adrian Bradbury designed the background and labels. Both stamps are genuinely valid for postage from the Isle of Man but not from mainland UK, Surprisingly this sheet was not marketed by the Isle of Man Post Office, being only available from AG Bradbury.

IOM-005

The Manx Bank

2008 (1 Jun), Litho by BDT International Security Printing Ltd, Ireland, printed on water activated gummed paper. Initial selling price: £ 30.00

IOM-005 ....£ 30.00

Produced by: AG Bradbury **Qty:** 500

Issue Notes: 2 x 30p, 2 x 31p, 2 x 44p, 2 x 56p, 1 85p and 1 x 114p CS stamps plus illustrated labels ex Isle of Man Post special issue of the same name issued on 7th April 2008. Adrian Bradbury collaborated again with the Isle Of Man Post Office to produce a stunning Customised Stamp Sheet featuring all of the new stamps released by the Isle of Man Post Office to celebrate Manx Banking, a mainstay of the Isle of Man economy of the Isle of Man. Unlike the earlier collaboration, this sheet was marketed indirectly by the Isle of Man Post Office who provided brief details and a link to Adrian Bradbury's website from the Isle of Man Post website thus acknowledging the collaboration however, like its forerunner it was only available from AG Bradbury. The background image and labels depict various aspects of Manx currency, past and present.

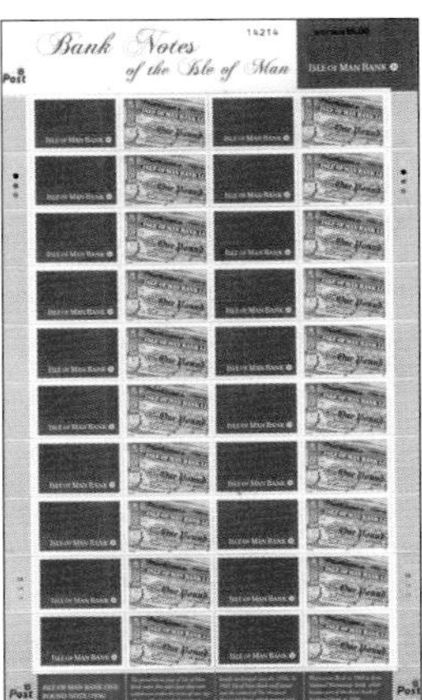

IOM-006

Bank Notes of the Isle of Man (30p)

2008 (30 Jun), Litho by BDT International Security Printing Ltd, Ireland, printed on water activated gummed paper. Initial selling price: £ 6.00

IOM-006 ....£ 9.00

Produced by: Isle of Man Post Office **Qty:** Unknown

Issue Notes: 20 x 30p CS Manx Banks stamps plus tab labels (Isle of Man Bank). The stamps were first released as a special issue in set and presentation

Isle of Man

pack form on 7th April 2008. The sheets of stamps are similar to Generic Smilers due to presence of associated tab labels. Although not highly decorated the tabs were clearly separate from the stamp and not to be used for postage on their own.

This special issue of stamps had been prepared in conjunction with Manx National Heritage who provided the research material and visuals. The issue features images of both bank notes and such items as promissory notes and internment camp monetary tokens.

There were six different values in this series all issued in sheets of 20 (Values 30p, 31p, 44p, 56p, 85p and 114p) incorporating illustrated gutters and featuring the logos of a selection of the Island's prominent banks. The series of six sheets were sponsored by two private businesses, the Royal Bank of Scotland International Group and Habib Bank. Sheet 1 of 6 features the 30p stamp showing the Isle of Man Bank One Pound note of 1956, the penultimate issue of Isle of Man Bank notes, five years later they were withdrawn under the terms of new legislation. The design had remained largely unchanged since the 1930s.

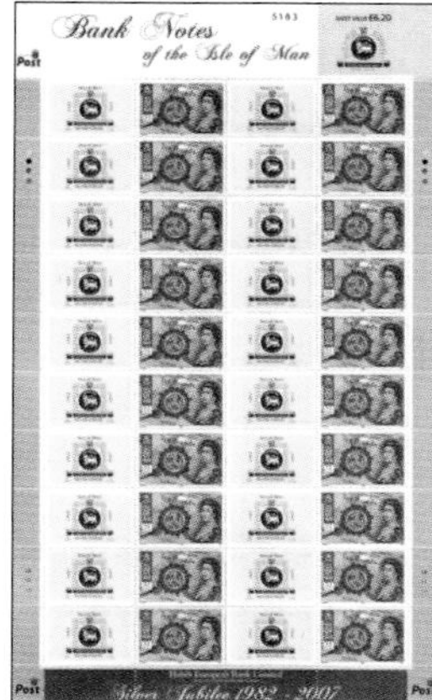

IOM-007

Bank Notes of the Isle of Man (31p)

2008 (30 Jun), Litho by BDT International Security Printing Ltd, Ireland, printed on water activated gummed paper. Initial selling price: £ 6.20

IOM-007 ....£ 9.50

Produced by: Isle of Man Post Office **Qty:** Unknown

Issue Notes: 20 x 31p CS Manx Banks stamps plus tab labels (Habib Bank) The labels commemorate the Silver Jubilee of the Habib European Bank Limited (1982-2007). Sheet No. 2 of 6 features the 31p stamp showing the 1972 Isle of Man Government Ten Pound note, the first to feature the new Anthony Buckley portrait of HM The Queen, this early issue ten pound note is broadly similar to that in use today with the same colour and reverse design (Peel Castle) but differs in detail, notably the signature of P.H.G. Stallard.

See IOM-006 for further notes on this issue.

IOM-008

Bank Notes of the Isle of Man (44p)

2008 (30 Jun), Litho by BDT International Security Printing Ltd, Ireland, printed on water activated gummed paper . Initial selling price: £ 8.80

IOM-008 ....£ 13.00

Produced by: Isle of Man Post Office **Qty:** Unknown

Issue Notes: 20 x 44p CS Manx Banks stamps plus tab labels (Nat West Bank). This is sheet No. 3 of 6 issued by the Isle of Man Post Office in this series. Sheet No 3 features the 44p stamp which shows a Manx Bank note. The Manx Bank commenced business in 1882 at its head office, 57 Victoria Street, Douglas. It was bought out by the Mercantile Bank of Lancashire in December 1900.

See IOM-006 for further notes on this issue.

IOM-009

Bank Notes of the Isle of Man (56p)

2008 (30 Jun), Litho by BDT International Security Printing Ltd, Ireland, printed on water activated gummed paper. Initial selling price: £ 11.20

IOM-009 ....£ 17.00

Produced by: Isle of Man Post Office **Qty:** Unknown

Issue Notes: 20 x 56p CS Manx Banks stamps plus tab labels (RBS International - 1982-2007) This is sheet No. 4 features the 56p stamp showing a 1969 Isle of Man Government Fifty New Pence decimal note. Under plans for decimalisation, the Isle of Man Government decided to retain a note instead of using a coin for fifty new pence.

See IOM-006 for further notes on this issue.

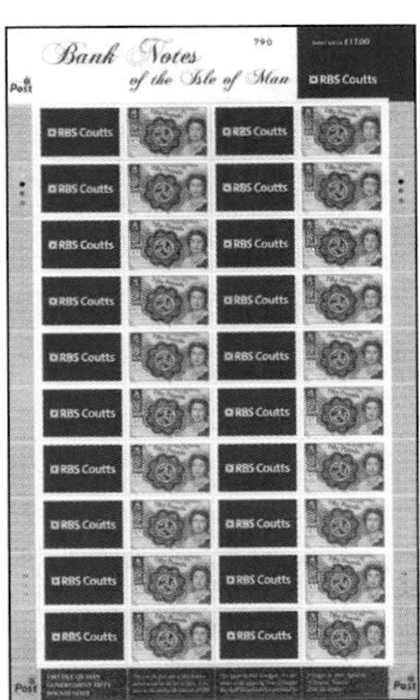

IOM-010

Bank Notes of the Isle of Man (85p)

2008 (30 Jun), Litho by BDT International Security Printing Ltd, Ireland, printed on water activated gummed paper. Initial selling price: £ 17.00

IOM-010 ....£ 25.00

Produced by: Isle of Man Post Office **Qty:** Unknown

Issue Notes: 20 x 854p CS Manx Banks stamps plus tab labels (RBS Coutts, 1982-2007) This is sheet No. 5 and features the 85p stamp showing a 1983 Isle of Man Government Fifty Pound note. This was the first note of this denomination issued on the Isle of Man. It features on the obverse the portrait of HM The Queen by Peter Grudgeon and Douglas Baya.

See IOM-006 for further notes on this issue.

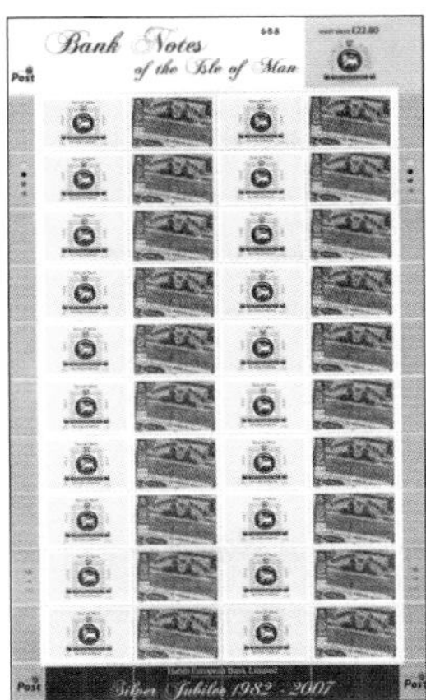

IOM-011

Bank Notes of the Isle of Man (114p)

2008 (30 Jun), Litho by BDT International Security Printing Ltd, Ireland, printed on water activated gummed paper. Initial selling price: £ 22.50

IOM-011 ....£ 32.50

Produced by: Isle of Man Post Office **Qty:** Unknown

Issue Notes: 20 x 114p CS Manx Banks stamps plus tab labels. The label commemorates the Silver Jubilee of the Habib European Bank Limited (1982-2007). This is final sheet in the series of six sheets and features the 114p stamp showing Parr's Bank note 1918. After the Dumbell's bank crash in February 1900, Parr's (an English bank) purchased the wreckage, including the licence to issue notes. This they did until 1918, when they in turn were taken over by the Westminster Bank and ultimately became part of the NatWest group.

See IOM-006 for further notes on this issue.

IOM-012

Queen Elizabeth 2— Final Voyage

2008 (11 Nov), printed on water activated gummed paper. Initial selling price: £ 10.00

IOM-012 ....£ 15.00

Produced by: Isle of Man Post Office **Qty:** 10,000

Issue Notes: 10 x £1 commemorative-sized (CS) Queen Elizabeth 2 stamps plus labels. Available as a single folded large sheet of stamps/labels or as part of a 216 pp book "QE2 Book - Britain's Greatest Liner" priced £35. Three leading ship historians joined forces to produce the definitive history of Cunard's Queen Elizabeth 2. The luxurious hardback book with 216 large format colour pages has a foreword by HRH Duke of Edinburgh.

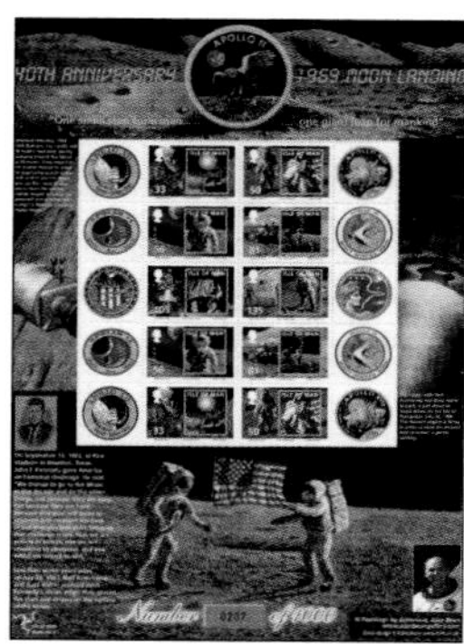

IOM-013

40th Anniversary of 1969 Moon Landing

2009 (1 May), Litho The Lowe-Martin Group, Canada, printed on water activated gummed paper .

Initial selling price: £ 28.99

IOM-013 ....£ 30.00

Produced by: AG Bradbury **Qty:** 1000

Issue Notes: 2 x 33p, 2 x 50p, 2 x 56p, 2 x 81p, 1 x 105p and 1 x 135p commemorative-sized (CS) stamps plus labels. The sheet features the special issue stamps ex-Isle of Man Post issued on 12th April 2009. The artwork for the stamps is that of former USA astronaut Alan Bean who also provided the images for Adrian Bradbury's sheet, produced in collaboration with the Isle of Man Post Office.

Universal Mail Generic and Personalised Stamps

Universal Mail United Kingdom Limited (UMUKL) was established through the deregulation of the UK postal industry in 2006. UMUKL produces generic and personalised postage stamps in the UK which may be used to prepay postage to send postcards or letters to any destination worldwide. An agreement between UMUKL and Royal Mail enables any postcard or envelope bearing a UMUKL postage stamp to be mailed through the extensive network of Royal Mail's post boxes located throughout the UK. All UMUKL postage stamps are also accepted over the counter at Post Office's throughout UK.

UMUKL is owned by Universal Mail New Zealand Limited (UMNZL). UMNZL was formed in 2001 as a consequence of deregulation of the Postal Industry in New Zealand. It specialises in producing personalised $1.50 and $2.00 postage stamps as well as postcards for the international tourist market. UMNZL is the largest producer of personalised postage stamps in New Zealand.

Mail Holdings Limited is the New Zealand based holding company of UMNZL. It is also the holding company for New Zealand Mail Limited, a registered postal operator in New Zealand that specialises in promoting a company brands through the use of personalised postal products. Through an agreement with New Zealand Post, all stamps bearing their registered postal identifier may be posted into any New Zealand Post street mailing boxes or mail centres.

Chapter 9 - Universal Mail Customised Stamps

Universal Mail Generic and Personalised Stamps

UMUKL stamps are currently supplied in self adhesive strips of five stamps, either as a strip of five complementary designs or a single stamp design, generally with a location theme for focused marketing. UMUKL's market for these stamps is primarily the tourist operators, regional tourist offices (information centres), hotels, general retailers and souvenir shops through which they sell their products.

Front and rear view of Universal Mail's Customised Stamps

In addition to marketing customised stamps for the tourist market they also provide a personalised stamps service, the minimum order is for 10,000 stamps but to date it is understood that no personalised postage stamps have been commissioned. Judging by their New Zealand affiliates, and subject to the postal deregulation laws here in the UK, it is perhaps only a matter of time before we see company branded postage stamps available from Universal Mail for use in the UK.

UM-001

UM001a

UM-002

UM002a

London Day

2008 (Oct), Litho by Joh. Enschede, printed on self adhesive paper with simulated die-cut perforations.

Initial selling price: £ 2.80 (£3.25 after 1 April 2009)

UM-001 ....£ 10.00

UM-001a (May 2009) ....£ 5.00

Produced by: Universal Mail **Qty:** 10,000 (each)

Issue Notes: 5 x international postcard rate, depicting tourist scenes of London by day. The stamps were valid for postcards up to 10g in weight sent to any destination in the world excluding UK and the Channel Islands. London tourists were the first target for Universal Mail who issued their 1st Edition as a set of ten strips of five postage stamps in October 2008 (UM-001). The strip is numbered UK0001 10/08.

The strip was reprinted in 2009 (UM-001a) and sold for £3.25 a strip. UM-001a is similar to UM-001 with modified header, a different scene in the second stamp (Buckingham Palace replaced the London Eye) and a slightly wider white band between the flag and depicted scene. This strip is numbered UK0001 05/09.

London Night

2008 (Oct), Litho by Joh. Enschede, printed on self adhesive paper with simulated die-cut perforations.

Initial selling price: £ 2.80 (£3.25 after 1 April 2009)

UM-002 ....£ 10.00

UM-002a (May 2009) ....£ 5.00

Produced by: Universal Mail **Qty:** 10,000 (each)

Issue Notes: 5 x international postcard rate, depicting tourist scenes of London by night. The stamps were valid for postcards up to 10g in weight sent to any destination in the world excluding UK and the Channel Islands. London tourists were the first target for Universal Mail who issued their 1st Edition as a set of ten strips of five postage stamps in October 2008 (UM-002). The strip is numbered UK0002 10/08.

The strip was reprinted in 2009 (UM-002a) and sold for £3.25 a strip. UM-002a is similar to UM-002 with modified header, a different scene in the fifth stamp (Trafalgar Circus replaced Westminster Abbey) and a slightly wider white band between the flag and depicted scene. This strip is numbered UK0001 05/09.

UM-003 UM003a

UM-004 UM004a

London Icons

2008 (Oct), Litho by Joh. Enschede, printed on self adhesive paper with simulated die-cut perforations.

Initial selling price: £ 2.80 (£3.25 after 1 April 2009)

UM-003 .... £ 10.00

UM-003a (English Icons - May 2009) .... £ 5.00

Produced by: Universal Mail **Qty:** 10,000 (each)

Issue Notes: 5 x international postcard rate, depicting tourist scenes of London icons. The stamps were valid for postcards up to 10g in weight sent to any destination in the world excluding UK and the Channel Islands. London tourists were the first target for Universal Mail who issued their 1st Edition as a set of ten strips of five postage stamps in October 2008 (UM-003). This strip is numbered UK0003 10/08.

The strip was reprinted in 2009 (UM-003a) and sold for £3.25 a strip. UM-003a is similar to UM-003 and has a modified header and title (English Icons replaced London Icons) and a slightly wider white band between the flag and depicted scene. The strip is numbered UK0003 05/09.

Tower Bridge

2008 (Oct), Litho by Joh. Enschede, printed on self adhesive paper with simulated die-cut perforations.

Initial selling price: £ 2.80 (£3.25 after 1 April 2009)

UM-004 .... £ 10.00

UM-004a (May 2009) .... £ 5.00

Produced by: Universal Mail **Qty:** 10,000 (each)

Issue Notes: 5 x international postcard rate, depicting Tower Bridge at dusk. The stamps were valid for postcards up to 10g in weight sent to any destination in the world excluding UK and the Channel Islands. London tourists were the first target for Universal Mail who issued their 1st Edition as a set of ten strips of five postage stamps in October 2008 (UM-004). This strip is numbered UK0004 10/08.

The strip was reprinted in 2009 (UM-004a) and sold for £3.25 a strip. UM-004a is similar to UM-004 and has a modified header and a slightly wider white band between the flag and depicted scene. The strip is numbered UK0004 05/09.

UM-005

Palaces and Castles

2008 (Oct), Litho by Joh. Enschede, printed on self adhesive paper with simulated die-cut perforations.

Initial selling price: £ 2.80 (£3.25 after 1 April 2009)

UM-005... £ 10.00

Produced by: Universal Mail **Qty:** 10,000

Issue Notes: 5 x international postcard rate, depicting various Palaces and Castles of London. The stamps were valid for postcards up to 10g in weight sent to any destination in the world excluding UK and the Channel Islands. London tourists were the first target for Universal Mail who issued their 1st Edition as a set of ten strips of five postage stamps in October 2008 (UM-005). This strip is numbered UK0005 10/08.

UM-006

Piccadilly and Trafalgar

2008 (Oct), Litho by Joh. Enschede, printed on self adhesive paper with simulated die-cut perforations.

Initial selling price: £ 2.80 (£3.25 after 1 April 2009)

UM-006... £ 10.00

Produced by: Universal Mail **Qty:** 10,000

Issue Notes: 5 x international postcard rate, depicting various tourist scenes in Piccadilly and Trafalgar. The stamps were valid for postcards up to 10g in weight sent to any destination in the world excluding UK and the Channel Islands. London tourists were the first target for Universal Mail who issued their 1st Edition as a set of ten strips of five postage stamps in October 2008 (UM-006). This strip is numbered UK0006 10/08.

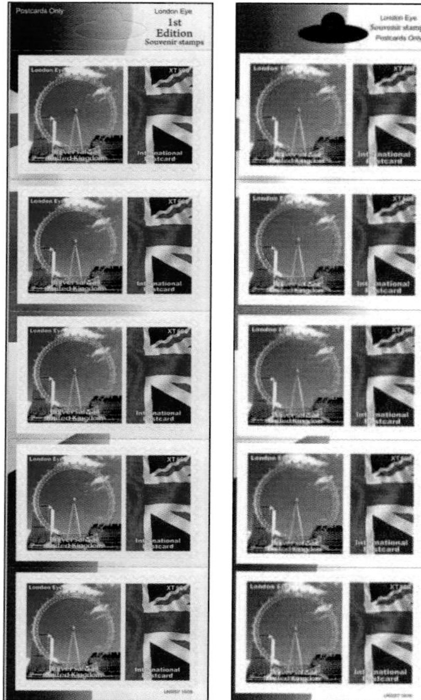

UM-007 UM007a UM-008

London Eye

2008 (Oct), Litho by Joh. Enschede, printed on self adhesive paper with simulated die-cut perforations.

Initial selling price: £ 2.80 (£3.25 after 1 April 2009)

UM-007 .... £ 10.00

UM-007a (May 2009) .... £ 5.00

Produced by: Universal Mail **Qty:** 10,000 (each)

Issue Notes: 5 x international postcard rate, depicting the London Eye. The stamps were valid for postcards up to 10g in weight sent to any destination in the world excluding UK and the Channel Islands. London tourists were the first target for Universal Mail who issued their 1st Edition as a set of ten strips of five postage stamps in October 2008 (UM-007). This strip is numbered UK0007 10/08.

The strip was reprinted in 2009 (UM-007a) and sold for £3.25 a strip. UM-007a is similar to UM-007 with modified header and a slightly wider white band between the flag and depicted scene. The strip is numbered UK0007 05/09.

Big Ben

2008 (Oct), Litho by Joh. Enschede, printed on self adhesive paper with simulated die-cut perforations.

Initial selling price: £ 2.80 (£3.25 after 1 April 2009)

UM-008 .... £ 10.00

Produced by: Universal Mail **Qty:** 10,000

Issue Notes: 5 x international postcard rate, depicting the clock tower of the Houses of Parliament. The stamps were valid for postcards up to 10g in weight sent to any destination in the world excluding UK and the Channel Islands. London tourists were the first target for Universal Mail who issued their 1st Edition as a set of ten strips of five postage stamps in October 2008 (UM-008). This strip is numbered UK0008 10/08.

UM-009

UM-010

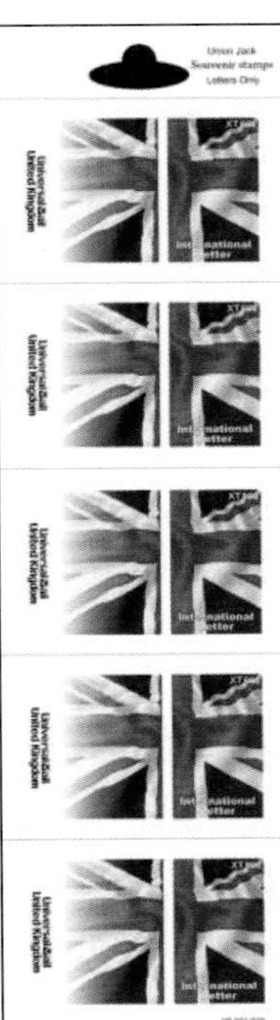

UM010a

Buckingham Palace

2008 (Oct), Litho by Joh. Enschede, printed on self adhesive paper with simulated die-cut perforations.

Initial selling price: £ 2.80 (£3.25 after 1 April 2009)

UM-009 .... £ 10.00

Produced by: Universal Mail **Qty:** 10,000

Issue Notes: 5 x international postcard rate, depicting a view of Buckingham Palace from the Pall. The stamps were valid for postcards up to 10g in weight sent to any destination in the world excluding UK and the Channel Islands. London tourists were the first target for Universal Mail who issued their 1st Edition as a set of ten strips of five postage stamps in October 2008 (UM-009). This strip is numbered UK0009 10/08.

Union Jack

2008 (Oct), Litho by Joh. Enschede, printed on self adhesive paper with simulated die-cut perforations.

Initial selling price: £ 4.05 (£4.25 after 1 April 2009)

UM-010 .... £ 10.00

UM-010a (May 2009) .... £ 5.00

Produced by: Universal Mail **Qty:** 10,000

Issue Notes: 5 x international letter rate, depicting the Union Flag. The stamps were valid for letters up to 10g in weight (standard size and thickness) sent to any destination in the world excluding UK and the Channel Islands. London tourists were the first target for Universal Mail who issued their 1st Edition as a set of ten strips of five postage stamps in October 2008 (UM-009). This strip is numbered UKL0001 10/08.

The strip was reprinted in 2009 (UM-010a) and sold for £4.25 a strip. UM-010a is similar to UM-010 with modified header and a slightly wider white band between the flag and depicted scene. The strip is numbered UKL0001 05/09.

UM-11

London Landmarks

2009 (May), Litho by Joh. Enschede, printed on self adhesive paper with simulated die-cut perforations.

Initial selling price: £ 3.25

UM-011 .... £ 5.00

Produced by: Universal Mail **Qty:** 10,000

Issue Notes: 5 x international postcard rate, depicting views of famous London landmarks. The stamps were valid for postcards up to 10g in weight sent to any destination in the world excluding UK and the Channel Islands. Universal Mail issued their 2nd edition of stamp strips in May 2009 comprising a mix of London tourist scenes and regional tourist destinations. This strip is numbered UK0010 05/09.

UM-12

South East England

2009 (May), Litho by Joh. Enschede, printed on self adhesive paper with simulated die-cut perforations.

Initial selling price: £ 3.25

UM-012 .... £ 5.00

Produced by: Universal Mail **Qty:** 10,000

Issue Notes: 5 x international postcard rate, depicting views of famous regional landmarks. The stamps were valid for postcards up to 10g in weight sent to any destination in the world excluding UK and the Channel Islands. Universal Mail issued their 2nd edition of stamp strips in May 2009 comprising a mix of London tourist scenes and regional tourist destinations. This strip is numbered UK0011 05/09.

UM-13

East Midlands

2009 (May), Litho by Joh. Enschede, printed on self adhesive paper with simulated die-cut perforations.

Initial selling price: £ 3.25

UM-013 .... £ 5.00

Produced by: Universal Mail **Qty:** 10,000

Issue Notes: 5 x international postcard rate, depicting views of famous regional landmarks. The stamps were valid for postcards up to 10g in weight sent to any destination in the world excluding UK and the Channel Islands. Universal Mail issued their 2nd edition of stamp strips in May 2009 comprising a mix of London tourist scenes and regional tourist destinations. This strip is numbered UK0012 05/09.

UM-14

Yorkshire & the Humber

2009 (May), Litho by Joh. Enschede, printed on self adhesive paper with simulated die-cut perforations.

Initial selling price: £ 3.25

UM-014 .... £ 5.00

Produced by: Universal Mail **Qty:** 10,000

Issue Notes: 5 x international postcard rate, depicting views of famous regional landmarks. The stamps were valid for postcards up to 10g in weight sent to any destination in the world excluding UK and the Channel Islands. Universal Mail issued their 2nd edition of stamp strips in May 2009 comprising a mix of London tourist scenes and regional tourist destinations. This strip is numbered UK0013 05/09.

UM-15

East England

2009 (May), Litho by Joh. Enschede, printed on self adhesive paper with simulated die-cut perforations.

Initial selling price: £ 3.25

UM-015 .... £ 5.00

Produced by: Universal Mail **Qty:** 10,000

Issue Notes: 5 x international postcard rate, depicting views of famous regional landmarks. The stamps were valid for postcards up to 10g in weight sent to any destination in the world excluding UK and the Channel Islands. Universal Mail issued their 2nd edition of stamp strips in May 2009 comprising a mix of London tourist scenes and regional tourist destinations. This strip is numbered UK0014 05/09.

UM-16

West Midlands

2009 (May), Litho by Joh. Enschede, printed on self adhesive paper with simulated die-cut perforations.

Initial selling price: £ 3.25

UM-016 .... £ 5.00

Produced by: Universal Mail **Qty:** 10,000

Issue Notes: 5 x international postcard rate, depicting views of famous regional landmarks. The stamps were valid for postcards up to 10g in weight sent to any destination in the world excluding UK and the Channel Islands. Universal Mail issued their 2nd edition of stamp strips in May 2009 comprising a mix of London tourist scenes and regional tourist destinations. This strip is numbered UK0015 05/09.

UM-17

North West England

2009 (May), Litho by Joh. Enschede, printed on self adhesive paper with simulated die-cut perforations.

Initial selling price: £ 3.25

UM-017 .... £ 5.00

Produced by: Universal Mail **Qty:** 10,000

Issue Notes: 5 x international postcard rate, depicting views of famous regional landmarks. The stamps were valid for postcards up to 10g in weight sent to any destination in the world excluding UK and the Channel Islands. Universal Mail issued their 2nd edition of stamp strips in May 2009 comprising a mix of London tourist scenes and regional tourist destinations. This strip is numbered UK0016 05/09.

UM-18

North East England

2009 (May), Litho by Joh. Enschede, printed on self adhesive paper with simulated die-cut perforations.

Initial selling price: £ 3.25

UM-018 .... £ 5.00

Produced by: Universal Mail **Qty:** 10,000

Issue Notes: 5 x international postcard rate, depicting views of famous regional landmarks. The stamps were valid for postcards up to 10g in weight sent to any destination in the world excluding UK and the Channel Islands. Universal Mail issued their 2nd edition of stamp strips in May 2009 comprising a mix of London tourist scenes and regional tourist destinations. This strip is numbered UK0017 05/09.

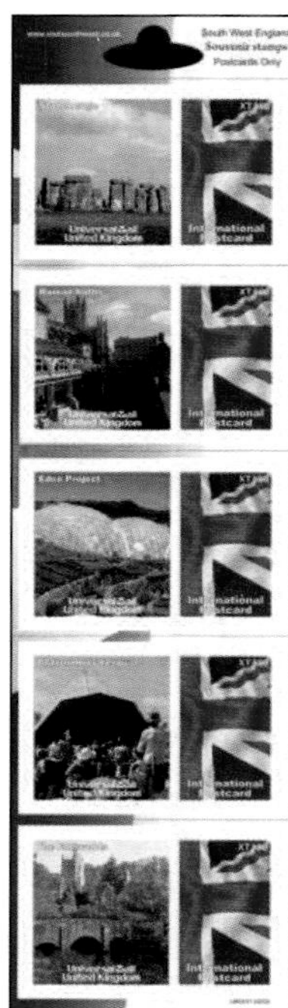

UM-19

South West England

2009 (May), Litho by Joh. Enschede, printed on self adhesive paper with simulated die-cut perforations.

Initial selling price: £ 3.25

UM-019 .... £ 5.00

Produced by: Universal Mail **Qty:** 10,000

Issue Notes: 5 x international postcard rate, depicting views of famous regional landmarks. The stamps were valid for postcards up to 10g in weight sent to any destination in the world excluding UK and the Channel Islands. Universal Mail issued their 2nd edition of stamp strips in May 2009 comprising a mix of London tourist scenes and regional tourist destinations. This strip is numbered UK0018 05/09.

UM-20

Wales

2009 (May), Litho by Joh. Enschede, printed on self adhesive paper with simulated die-cut perforations.

Initial selling price: £ 3.25

UM-020 .... £ 5.00

Produced by: Universal Mail **Qty:** 10,000

Issue Notes: 5 x international postcard rate, depicting views of famous regional landmarks. The stamps were valid for postcards up to 10g in weight sent to any destination in the world excluding UK and the Channel Islands. Universal Mail issued their 2nd edition of stamp strips in May 2009 comprising a mix of London tourist scenes and regional tourist destinations. This strip is numbered UK0019 05/09.

UM-21

UM-22

Edinburgh

2009 (May), Litho by Joh. Enschede, printed on self adhesive paper with simulated die-cut perforations.

Initial selling price: £ 3.25

UM-021 .... £ 5.00

Produced by: Universal Mail **Qty:** 10,000

Issue Notes: 5 x international postcard rate, depicting views of famous regional landmarks. The stamps were valid for postcards up to 10g in weight sent to any destination in the world excluding UK and the Channel Islands. Universal Mail issued their 2nd edition of stamp strips in May 2009 comprising a mix of London tourist scenes and regional tourist destinations. This strip is numbered UK0020 05/09.

Scotland

2009 (May), Litho by Joh. Enschede, printed on self adhesive paper with simulated die-cut perforations.

Initial selling price: £ 3.25

UM-022 .... £ 5.00

Produced by: Universal Mail **Qty:** 10,000

Issue Notes: 5 x international postcard rate, depicting views of famous regional landmarks. The stamps were valid for postcards up to 10g in weight sent to any destination in the world excluding UK and the Channel Islands. Universal Mail issued their 2nd edition of stamp strips in May 2009 comprising a mix of London tourist scenes and regional tourist destinations. This strip is numbered UK0021 05/09.

UM-23

Northern Ireland

2009 (May), Litho by Joh. Enschede, printed on self adhesive paper with simulated die-cut perforations.

Initial selling price: £ 3.25

UM-023 .... £ 5.00

Produced by: Universal Mail **Qty:** 10,000

Issue Notes: 5 x international postcard rate, depicting views of famous regional landmarks. The stamps were valid for postcards up to 10g in weight sent to any destination in the world excluding UK and the Channel Islands. Universal Mail issued their 2nd edition of stamp strips in May 2009 comprising a mix of London tourist scenes and regional tourist destinations. This strip is numbered UK0022 05/09.

Appendix A - Smilers Dealers

Company	Generic Smilers	Customised Smilers	Business Sheets	Smilers Covers
B. Alan (Stamps) Limited 2 Pinewood Avenue Sevenoaks, Kent TN14 5AF Tel: 01732 743387 info@balanstamps.co.uk	Yes	Yes	No	Yes
Benham Covers Limited Unit K, Concept Court Shearway Business Park Folkestone, Kent, CT19 4RG Tel: 08708 500654 www.benham.co.uk	Yes	No	Yes	Yes
A.G. Bradbury (BFDC) 3 Link Road Stoneygate, Leicester LE2 3RA www.smilers.co.uk	Yes	No	Own	Yes
Buckingham Covers Warren House Shearway Road Folkestone, Kent CT19 4BF Tel: 01303 278137 www.buckinghamcovers.com	Yes	No	Own	Yes
Chapman & Mitchell Covers Ltd Bletchley Park Post Office The Mansion, Bletchley Park Milton Keynes, MK3 6EB Tel: 01908 631797 www.bletchleycovers.co.uk	No	Own	No	Yes
Dauwalders Limited 42 Fishton Street Salisbury, Wiltshire SP2 7RB Tel: 01722 412100 www.worldstamps.co.uk	Yes	No	Yes	No

Company	Generic Smilers	Customised Smilers	Business Sheets	Smilers Covers
Mark Sargent PO Box 4167, Hornchurch, Essex RM11 1ZP Tel: 01708 440173 www.stampsforsale.co.uk	Yes	No	Yes	No
Mike Holt PO Box 177, Stourbridge West Midlands DY8 3DE Tel: 01384 443317 www.mikeholt-britishstamps.com	Yes	No	No	No
Norvic Philatelics PO Box 119, Dereham, NR20 3YN Tel: 08450 090939 www.norphil.co.uk	Yes	No	No	Yes
Phil Stamp Covers PO Box 178 Dartford, Kent, DA2 7YE Tel: 01322 278674 http://www.philstampcovers.co.uk	No	Yes (on covers)	No	Yes
Planet Prints 1 Quarry House Mill Lane Uckfield, East Sussex TN22 5AA www.plantprints.com	No	No	Own	No
Rushstamps (Retail) Limited PO Box One Lyndhurst, Hampshire SO43 7PP Tel: 02380 282044 www.rushstamps.co.uk	Yes	Own	Yes	No

Appendix A - Smilers Dealers

Company	Generic Smilers	Customised Smilers	Business Sheets	Smilers Covers
Ridgewood Stamp Sheets 50 Basingbourne Road, Fleet, Hampshire, GU52 6TH Tel: 07795 265546 www.smilers-info.com	Yes	Yes	Yes	Yes
Stanley Gibbons 399 The Strand, London WC2R 0LX, Tel: 020 7836 8444 www.stanleygibbons.com	Yes	No	Yes	No
The GB Stamp Centre 18 Greenside, Pudsey Leeds, West Yorkshire LS28 8PU Tel: 0800 542 0781 www.smilers-sheets.co.uk	No	Yes	Few	No
The Stamp Centre 79 The Strand, London, WC2R 0DE Tel: 0207 240 3778 www.stamp-centre.co.uk	Yes	No	Yes	Yes
The Westminster Collection PO Box 30, Broadsword House, Brixton Road, Watford, WD24 4ZY. Tel: 08708 500505 www.westminstercollection.com	No	No	Yes	Yes
Stuart Woodhouse (STU1967) 'Hafod Heddwch' Glyncynwal Road Upper Cwmtwrch Swansea, SA9 2UN www.stu1967.co.uk	Yes	No	Few Only (Stampex)	No

Smilers Stamps ..

... so-called because they have appeared in Customised Smilers sheets and have been designated as such by Royal Mail. In truth, these are stamps selected from various special issues and intended to be used on mail with adjacent, specially printed, personalised labels bearing a picture of Aunt Dot, the dog or the latest member of the family. Until 2002 these were referenced by name e.g. TEDDY but with the introduction of the 2002 Occasions sheet (which duplicated some of the earlier named stamps e.g. LOVE, each was been given a Royal Mail reference number in Smilers publicity material. The following reference guide will assist the reader in interpreting the reference information provided in the listing of Themed Customised Smilers Sheets in Chapter 5. Where sheets had multiple stamp designs the stamp design used by Royal Mail in their publicity material, is illustrated.

SM01 SM02 SM03 SM04 (10 stamps)

SM05 SM06 SM07 SM08

SM09 (5 Stamps) SM10 (5 stamps) SM11 SM12 (10 stamps)

SM13 (CS-015) SM14 SM15 SM16 (2 stamps)

SM17 (3 stamps) SM18 SM19 SM20

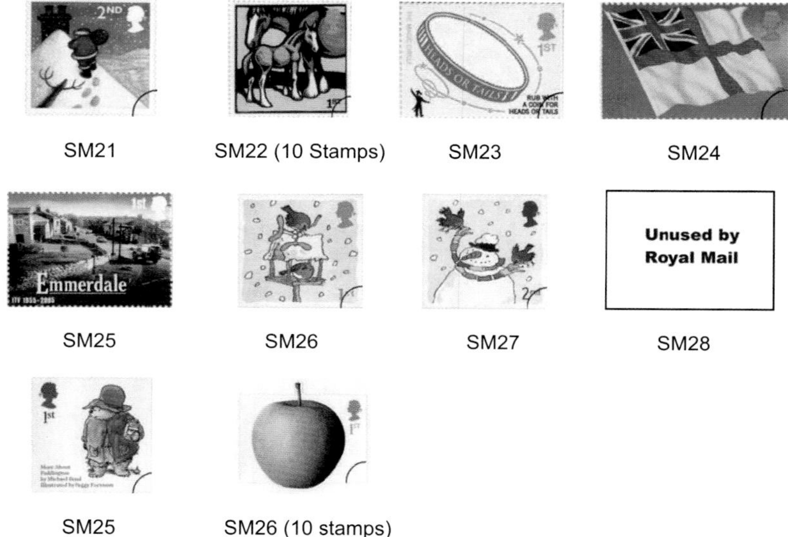

SM21 SM22 (10 Stamps) SM23 SM24

SM25 SM26 SM27 SM28

SM25 SM26 (10 stamps)

Definitive Sized Smilers Stamps (DS Series)

DS01* DS02 DS03 DS04 DS05 DS06

DS07 DS08 DS09 DS10 DS11 DS12

DS13 DS14 DS15 DS16 DS17 DS18

* Codes DS01 to DS17 were revised in 2008 (see Appendix B, page B-34, leaflet RMJ117DL) to reflect Royal Mail's revised Smilers pricing policy and to distinguish orders placed after the introduction of the new coding system using revised codes ending in N, in the form DSXXN

Appendix B - Smilers Stamps

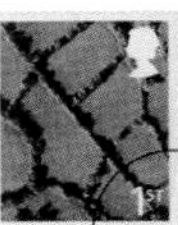

DS19 DS20 DS21 DS22

Introduction of New Pricing and Production Policy (October 2007)

From about October 2007 Royal Mail introduced a new pricing and production policy for Smilers sheets making Smilers more affordable and available in smaller quantities. Prior to that date customised Smilers sheets could be ordered by the public at a cost of £14.95 per sheet of 20 stamps/photo tabs, £13.95 for 2-4 sheets of 20 stamps/photo tabs or £11.95 per sheet for 5 or more sheets. Smilers sheets could be ordered on-line at the Royal Mail web site or by post using a downloadable form.

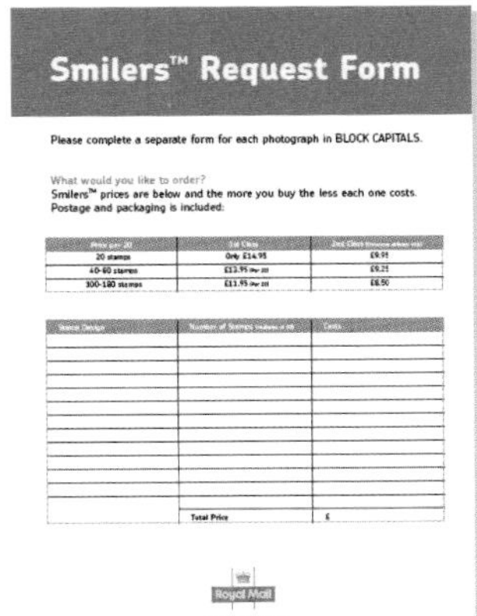

Smilers™ Request Form

Please complete a separate form for each photograph in BLOCK CAPITALS.

What would you like to order?
Smilers™ prices are below and the more you buy the less each one costs.
Postage and packaging is included:

Price per 20	1st Class	2nd Class [illegible]
20 stamps	Only £14.95	£9.95
40-60 stamps	£13.95 per 20	£9.25
100-180 stamps	£11.95 per 20	£8.50

Stamp Design	Number of Stamps [illegible]	Costs
	Total Price	£

Royal Mail

with us it's personal™

Smilers™ Request Form

How would you like to pay?
Please complete the appropriate boxes, sign and return this order form to the freepost address below, with your photograph and cheque if applicable.

I enclose a cheque made payable to Smilers stamps for: £ ☐
Maestro/Switch ☐ MasterCard ☐ Visa ☐
Card No ☐☐☐☐☐☐☐☐☐☐☐☐☐☐☐☐☐☐☐
Issue no ☐ Valid from ☐ Expiry date ☐

Title Mr ☐ Mrs ☐ Miss ☐ Ms ☐
First Name(s) Surname
Address

Postcode
Daytime Telephone Number: Email:

Where did you first hear about Smilers™?

You must sign this form for it to be valid.
I authorise usage of the photograph enclosed for Smilers™ and I have read and agree to the Terms and Conditions (sign below).

Signature Date
☐ Please tick if your order is for business purposes.

Please return this form with your photograph to:
Smilers™
Freepost SCO5817
Edinburgh
EH12 9PH
UNITED KINGDOM

Smilers™ helpline 0845 600 2557

Data Protection
The information you provide will be held under the Data Protection Act 1998 and will be used by Royal Mail Group plc, including Parcelforce Worldwide and Post Office Ltd. We may want to contact you from time to time with details of other products and services available from us. If you do not want this, tick here ☐

We will return your original photograph but will retain it in digital form, for six months from the date of this order or any subsequent re-order. If you do not want your image to be retained, tick here ☐

03JAM

Smilers-by-post Order Form

Royal Mail's pricing and production policies appear to have been modified over a period of 3-6 months. Firstly, the introduction of a revised pricing policy occurred around October 2007, in time for the Christmas issues, which were subsequently made available at £13.50 for a single sheet of 20 x 1st class stamps/photo tabs or £12.50 for two or more sheets. The 2nd class sheet price was revised to £8.50 for a sheet of 20 stamps/photo tabs or £8 for two or more sheets. From January 2008 production policy was also revised making it possible for the first time for the public to order half-sheets of 10 x 1st stamps/labels at a reduced cost of £7.50. With this new pricing policy Royal Mail adopted a new smilers stamp coding system which was first evident in the Christmas 2008 Smilers publicity leaflet: RM Ref. RM116 (see page C - 35) which reverted to using stamp names rather than codes, e.g. Big Bang, New Baby etc.,

This revised pricing policy was perhaps intended to simplify the order processing. However, the opportunity to use two different photo images on a single sheet of 20 stamps/photo-tabs had not previously been available to Smilers collectors before January 2008. From this date it was possible to order a sheet of 20 stamps/photo tabs with two different photo images.

Appendix B - Smilers Stamps

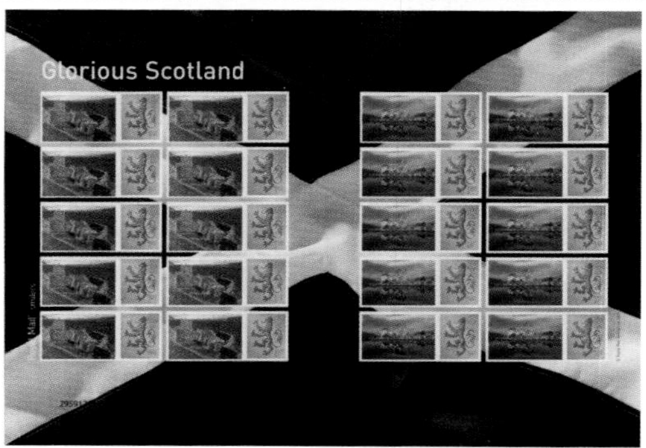

Example of a dual-photo-image Smilers sheet

To facilitate the ordering of half/full sheets of stamps/photo-tabs, Royal Mail changed the Smilers Stamp coding system around January 2008. Using the previous codes DS01 to DS22, the letter N was added to signify the applicability of the New pricing policy from 1st January 2008. To distinguish between full sheets and half sheets the number 10 was added to the Smilers reference code.

DS01 became DS01N for full sheets of 20 stamps/photo-tabs whilst DS01N10 was used to order a half sheet of 10 stamps/photo-tabs. Whilst this served a purpose for the first few months of 2008 to distinguish orders made prior to and after January 1st , it was rather cumbersome and meaningless as the year progressed.

By October 2008 Royal Mail had introduced a modified coding system reminiscent of the original Smilers coding system, in the format SMXX-YYYYYYY where XX referred to the sheet type (stamp design/10 or 20 stamps/rectangular/circular photo-tabs) and YYYYYYY was the customer order reference number. Royal Mail released an updated list of Smilers codes which covered their entire range of the then available Smilers sheets which was intended to make consumer ordering easier. It soon became apparent however that the system was not in universal use by Royal Mail as different order reference systems were apparently in use. The SM prefix has also been seen as a suffix i.e. YYYYYY -SMXX.

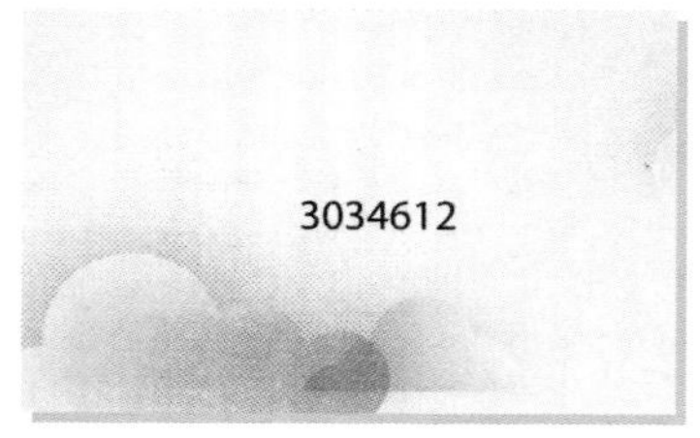

Examples of Smilers Customer Order reference numbering

Smilers sheets with the SM prefix were printed by Royal Mail sub-contract printer, *St. Ives Print*, who had been Royal Mail's sole print supplier for posters, advertising and other business related materials i.e. everything except stamps. Please refer to the following Smilers Coding List as supplied by Royal Mail for a full list of these codes on the pages that follow, originally issued in October 2008 and updated to end of 2009 to include the 2009 Xmas Stained Glass Smilers sheets.

Appendix B - Smilers Stamps

CODE	Sheet Design
SM01	Teddy Standard x 10
SM02	Flower x 10
SM03	Robin x 10
SM04	Best Wishes x 10
SM05	Thank You x 10
SM06	New Baby x 10
SM07	Celebrations x 10
SM08	Balloons x 10
SM09	Big Bang x 10
SM10	Glorious Wales x 10
SM11	Glorious England x 10
SM12	Harry Potter x 10
SM13	Glorious Scotland x 10
SM14	Glorious Northern Ireland x 10
SM15	Rule Britannia Standard x 20
SM16	Rule Britannia Circluar x 20
SM17	Rule Britannia Circluar x 10
SM18	Rule Britannia Standard x 10
SM19	Love Standard x 20
SM20	Love Circular x 20
SM21	Love Circular x 10
SM22	Love Standard x 10
SM23	Hello Standard x 20
SM24	Hello Circular x 20
SM25	Hello Circular x 10
SM26	Hello Standard x 10
SM27	Teddy Standard x 20
SM28	Flower x 20
SM29	Robin x 20
SM30	Best Wishes x 20

Appendix B - Smilers Stamps

CODE	Sheet Design
SM31	Thank You x 20
SM32	New Baby x 20
SM33	Celebrations x 20
SM34	Balloons x 20
SM35	Big Bang x 20
SM36	Glorious Wales x 20
SM37	Glorious England x 20
SM38	Harry Potter x 20
SM39	Glorious Scotland x 20
SM40	Glorious Northern Ireland x 20
SM41	Genie Standard x 20
SM42	Genie Circular x 20
SM43	Genie Circular x 10
SM44	Genie Standard x 10
SM45	Ugly Sisters Standard x 20
SM46	Ugly Sisters Circular x 20
SM47	Wicked Queen Standard x 10
SM48	Angel Standard x 20
SM49	Angel Standard x 10
SM50	Angel Standard 2nd x 20
SM51	Santa Standard x 20
SM52	Santa Standard x 10
SM53	Snowman Standard 2nd x 20
SM54	1st Stained Glass x 20
SM55	1st Stained Glass x 10
SM56	2nd Stained Glass x 20
SM57	56p Stained Glass x 10
SM58	90p Stained Glass x 10
SM59	To be announced

ROYAL MAIL SMILERS PUBLICITY

In this section we take a look at the evolving nature of the Smilers related publicity material that has been issued by Royal Mail following the introduction of the Smilers range of customised products in 2000.

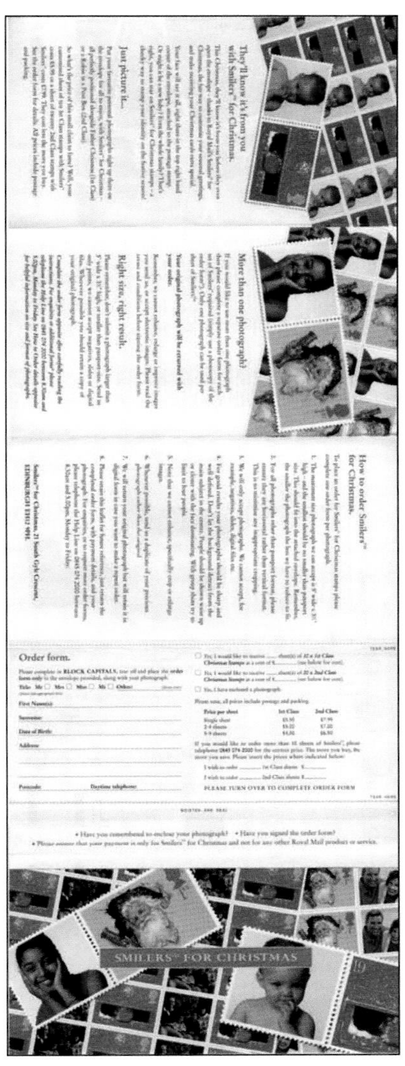

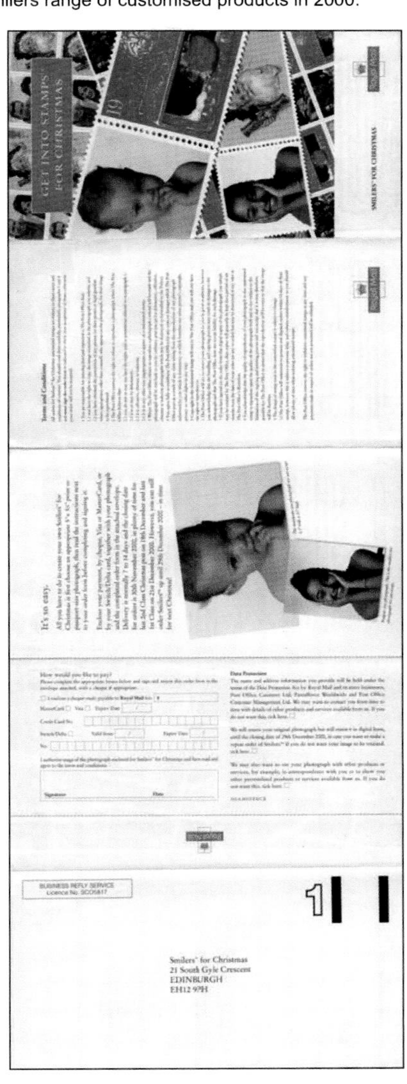

"GET INTO STAMPS FOR CHRISTMAS"

Post Office leaflet and reply paid envelope, Christmas 2000 Smilers RM Ref: 01CA HGFEDCB

Smilers™ for Christmas- 2000

Description of items **00ZYA**	Value	Code	Qty	£	p
10 x 1st class sheet of Smilers for Christmas	£2.95	XA012			
20 x 2nd class sheet of Smilers for Christmas	£3.99	XA013			
Handling Charge - UK and Europe 18p					
Rest of the World 34p					
TOTAL COST OF COMPLETE ORDER					

My personal reference number is: ☐☐☐☐☐☐☐☐

My title is : Mr☐ Mrs☐ Miss☐ Ms☐ Other:Please specify............

First Name................Surname.................................

Address...

....

....

Postcode............. Telephone number..........................

Please tick this box if you have recently changed address ☐

My payment of £.............. is made by:

- ☐ **Cheque / Money order** made payable to the British Philatelic Bureau
- ☐ **Debit** from my Bureau account
- ☐ **Debit** from my Bureau account (includes by VDD or CCCC)
- ☐ **By MasterCard / Visa** Expiry Date ☐☐☐☐

My Card No. is: ☐☐☐☐ ☐☐☐☐ ☐☐☐☐ ☐☐☐☐

Signature.................................... Date...........

Please write your personal reference number on the back of your payment, I understand any overpayment will be left in my account.

If you do not wish to receive further mailings from the BPB please tick this box ☐

All artwork remains copyright of Royal Mail. Stamp visuals may change slightly on issue. Please allow 21 days for delivery of your order items. All items subject to availability.

UK TELEPHONE ORDER AND ENQUIRY LINE
08457 641 641
Monday to Friday 8.30am to 5pm

FAX US ON:
Monday to Friday
0131 316 7337

British Philatelic Bureau
FREEPOST
EH3647
21 South Gyle Crescent
EDINBURGH
EH12 9PE

WWW
Visit us at the Royal Mail Website
www.royalmail.co.uk

British Philatelic Bureau

A Royal Mail Service

News for collectors from Royal Mail's British Philatelic Bureau

December 2000 Supplement

Stamp Preview

Ho! Ho! Ho!

Santa Claus is coming to town! This Christmas, Royal Mail is giving you an ever greater choice of Special Stamps for your Christmas mail than in past years. Building on the success of Smilers™ stamps at Stamp Show 2000, sheets of Smilers™ for Christmas, shown right, are now available.

Festive First

You may have already heard about the Smilers™ for Christmas stamps that can be produced with your picture next to a festive First or Second class stamp. Well these stamps are also available with a charming yuletide label attached. As you can see, these sheets come in either sheets of twenty Second class (19p) costing £3.99 or ten First class (27p) at £2.95.

It's a cracker!

The 1st class stamp, designed by John Gorham, was originally issued as part of the 1997 Christmas Cracker issue. This issue was one of Royal Mail's most popular secular designs for Christmas and as part of Royal Mail's policy of getting more Special Stamps on mail and promoting philately to a wider audience, this superlative Santa was selected for the Smilers™ for Christmas sheet.Both 1st class and 2nd class sheets are printed by The House of Questa and will only be available by mail order or from Postshops.

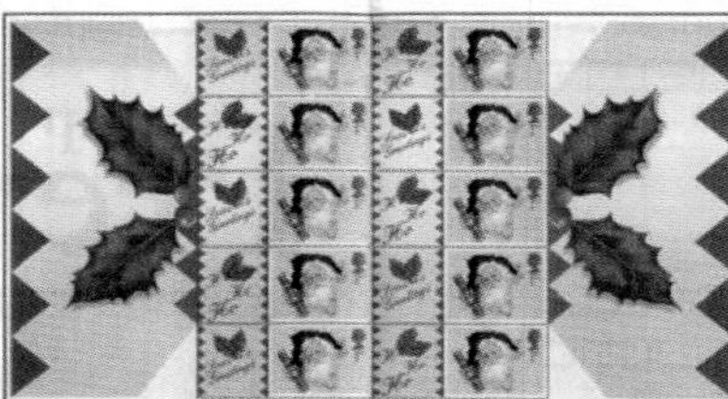

Above: Smilers™ for Christmas A4 sheet of ten First class Santa stamps.
Below: Smilers™ for Christmas A4 sheet of twenty Second class Robin stamps.

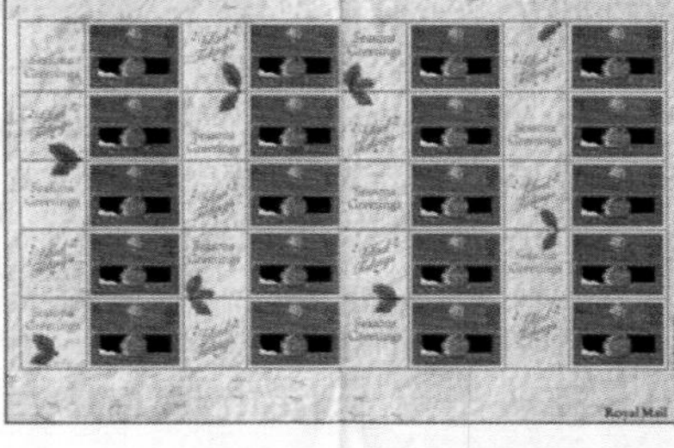

When the Red Red Robin...

The 2nd Class stamp featuring a Robin first appeared in the 1995 Christmas Special Stamp issue. This stamp is reproduced for Smilers™ for Christmas in a sheet of twenty stamps. Attached to these stamps are charming labels which carry either a Glad Tidings or Seasons Greetings text message. Both this item and the First class sheet can be ordered overleaf. As both these stamps have previously been available, there will be no Presentation Packs or Postcards associated with this issue.

Want to know more?

If you want to know more about getting your photograph on Smilers™ for Christmas, please call our telephone helpline on:

0845 074 2000
between 8.30am and 5.00pm, Monday to Friday.

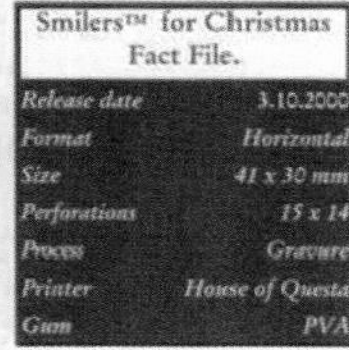

Smilers™ for Christmas Fact File.	
Release date	3.10.2000
Format	*Horizontal*
Size	*41 x 30 mm*
Perforations	*15 x 14*
Process	*Gravure*
Printer	*House of Questa*
Gum	*PVA*

Royal Mail Stamp Preview (December 2000)

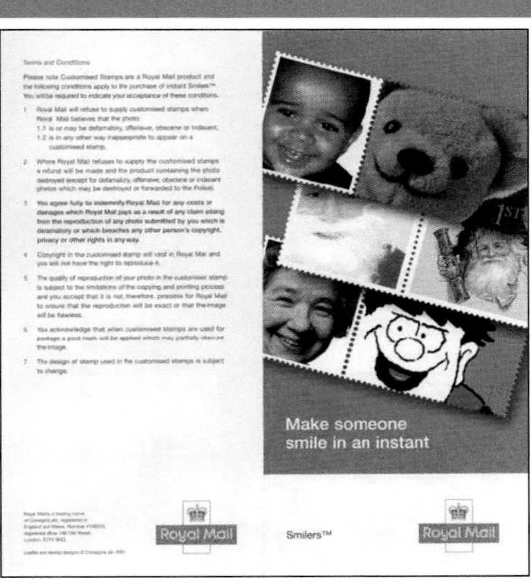

"Make someone smile in an instant" ....

.... a Royal Mail Instant Smilers Promotion.

Royal Mail Instant Smilers Leaflet Depicting current range of Customised Smilers sheets c. 2001

Instant Smilers booth

Go on, make someone's day.

With instant Smilers™ your letters and cards will be the pick of the pile.

Using the Snap Digital photo booth available on site you can have your image printed alongside your chosen set of stamps – all in an instant! Simply follow the instructions in the booth. Select your preferred image from the four taken then take your receipt up to the counter to collect your stamps.

Royal Mail's instant Smilers™ range of First Class stamps include Father Christmas or a mixture of non-seasonal 'smile' designs including Teddy Bear, Laughing Policeman, Punch and Clown.

For £7.50 you'll get a sheet of 10 First Class stamps of either Father Christmas or the 'smile' selection alongside your image.

Instant Smilers™ are available until 31 January 2002 in a small number of Post Office™ branches*. However Father Christmas Smilers™ will only be available until 24 December 2001.

Smilers™ also work as great gifts as well as souvenirs, so make sure you get enough done now.

It's easy. Just smile!

Smilers™ are also available by mail order. Ask one of our staff for a leaflet and application form or visit Royal Mail's website at www.royalmail.com/smilers.

A RM banner card used in Safeway's supermarkets, where the Instant Smilers booths were located c. 2002

Appendix C

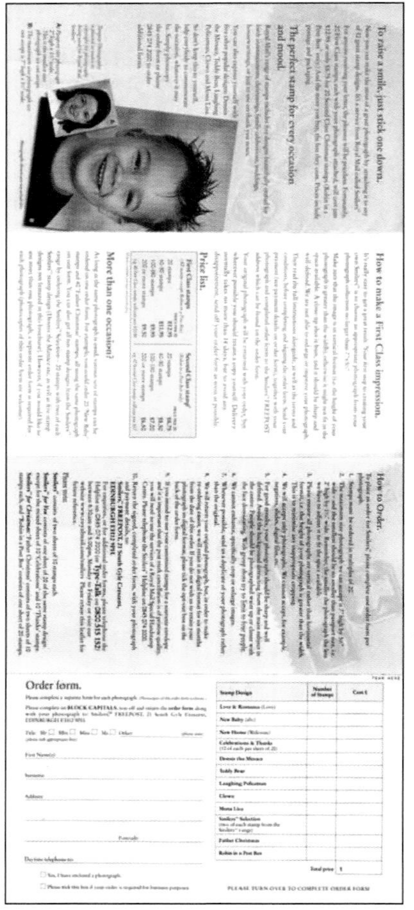

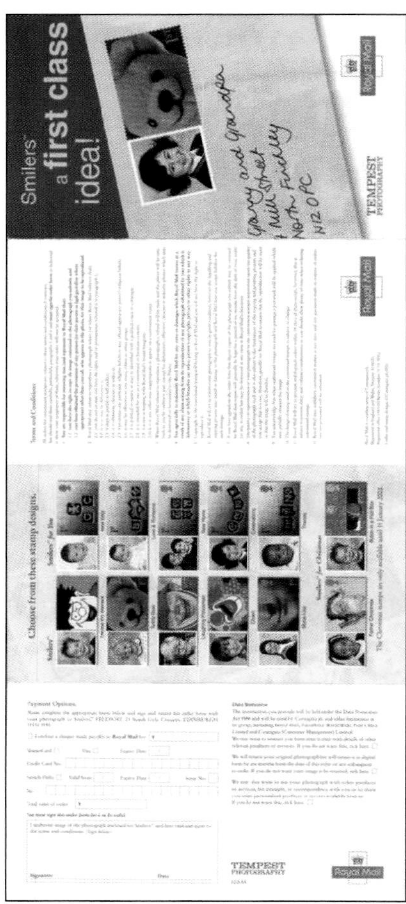

"SMILERS FIRST CLASS IDEA"

Tempest Photography/Royal Mail leaflet and Order Form

Features Smiles issues, Hallmarks issues and Christmas 2001 Customised Sheets

RM Ref: 02AAE c. 2001

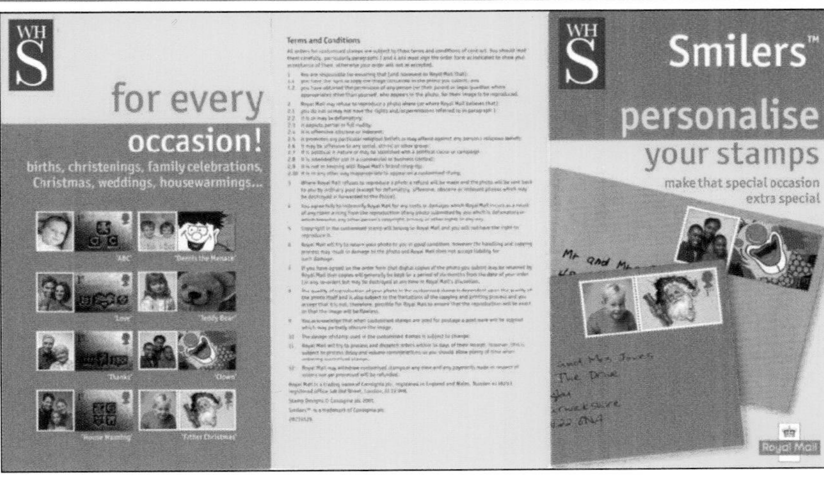

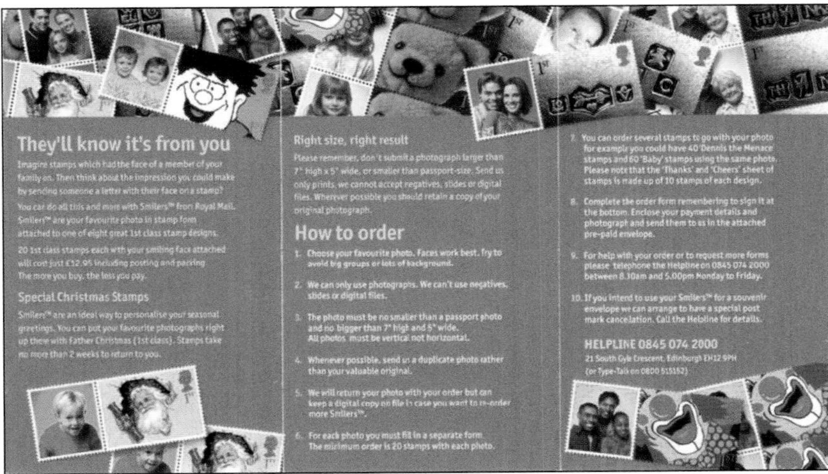

"SMILERS FOR EVERY OCASSION"

WH Smith/Royal Mail Smilers publicity leaflet

Features Smiles issues, Hallmarks issues and Christmas 2001 Customised Sheets

c. 2001

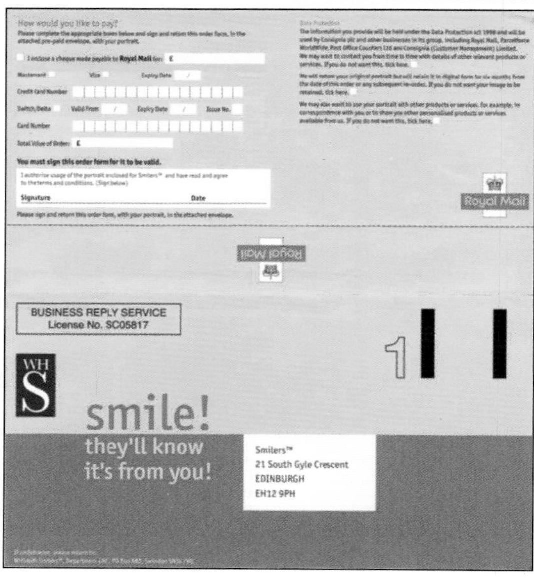

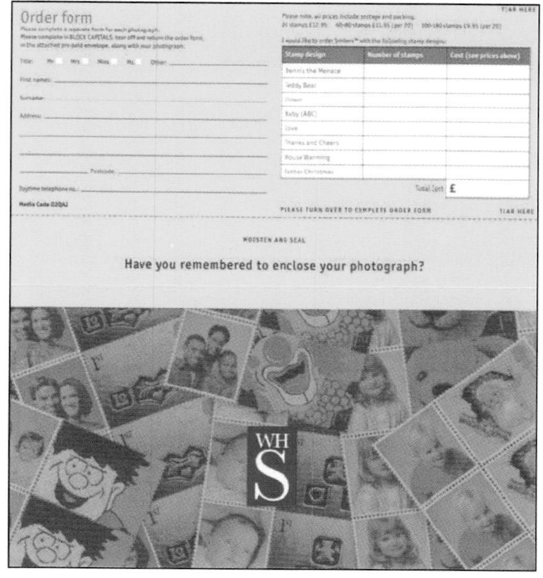

Smilers-By-Post

WH Smith/Royal Mail Promotion

Pre-Paid Business Reply

Envelope and Order Form

c. 2001

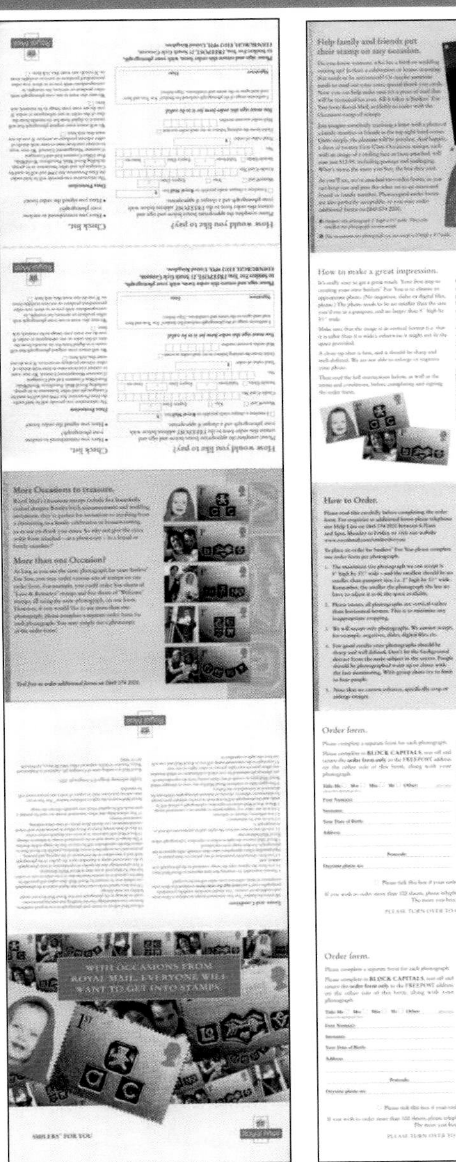

Help family and friends put their stamp on any occasion.

How to make a great impression.

How to Order.

Order form.

Order form.

Hallmarks 2001

Consignia plc and
Post Office Counters Ltd.

Smilers Publicity Leaflet and Order Forms (2) !

RM Ref: 02CAA c. May 2001

"WITH OCCASIONS FROM ROYAL MAIL, EVERYONE WILL WANT TO GET INTO STAMPS"

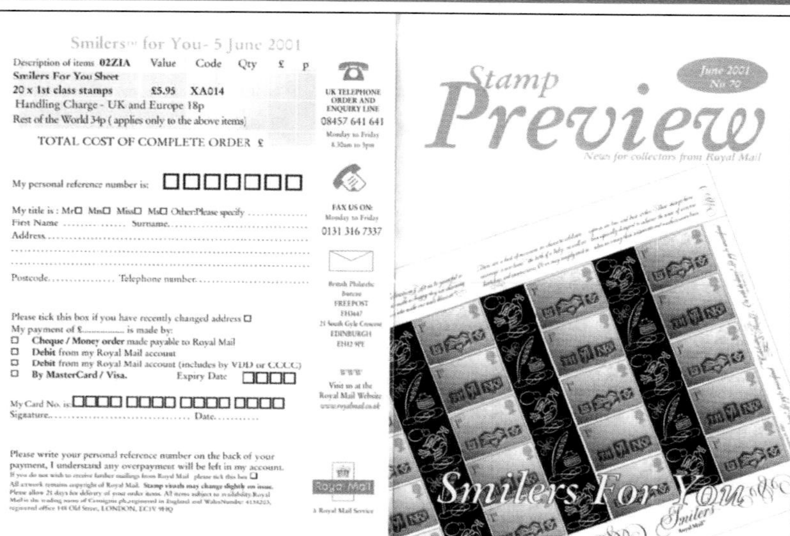

Smilers™ for You - 5 June 2001

Description of items 02ZIA	Value	Code	Qty	£	p
Smilers For You Sheet					
20 x 1st class stamps	**£5.95**	**XA014**			
Handling Charge - UK and Europe 18p					
Rest of the World 34p (applies only to the above items)					

TOTAL COST OF COMPLETE ORDER £

My personal reference number is: □□□□□□□□

My title is : Mr□ Mrs□ Miss□ Ms□ Other:Please specify ....
First Name .... Surname.................................
Address..
....
....
Postcode............... Telephone number..........................

Please tick this box if you have recently changed address □
My payment of £.............. is made by:
□ **Cheque / Money order** made payable to Royal Mail
□ **Debit** from my Royal Mail account
□ **Debit** from my Royal Mail account (includes by VDD or CCCC)
□ **By MasterCard / Visa.** Expiry Date □□□□

My Card No. is:□□□□ □□□□ □□□□ □□□□
Signature................................. Date...........

Please write your personal reference number on the back of your payment, I understand any overpayment will be left in my account.

UK TELEPHONE ORDER AND ENQUIRY LINE
08457 641 641
Monday to Friday 8.30am to 5pm

FAX US ON:
Monday to Friday
0131 316 7337

British Philatelic Bureau
FREEPOST
EH3447
21 South Gyle Crescent
EDINBURGH
EH12 9PE

WWW
Visit us at the Royal Mail Website
www.royalmail.co.uk

Royal Mail
A Royal Mail Service

It's For You!

Following the incredible success of both the Smilers™ for Christmas sheets and the recent Occasions stamp issue, Royal Mail has been inspired to integrate both these innovative ideas into a delightful new sheet entitled **Smilers For You.** Released on 5 June 2001, this stunning sheet contains twenty First Class Non-Value Indicator (NVI) stamps. The sheet is made up with four of each of the original five Occasions stamps, each one with a lavish label attached, all held securely in an attractive A4 sized sheet.

When You're smiling...

These Smilers™ For You sheets are printed by the House of Questa in Litho. As these stamps have previously been available, there will be no Presentation Pack or Postcards associated with this issue. Smilers™ products are not currently dispatched on a regular order so these items can only be bought by mail order from this Preview, or from your local Postshop.

Hallmark of quality

Royal Mail and the British Hallmarking Council wish to make it clear that the Occasions Stamp issue of 6 February bearing specially created "Hallmarks" symbols was not intended to represent in any way official hallmarks placed on precious metal articles by the four Assay Offices and by certain recognised independent offices in other countries. Royal Mail acknowledges the importance of authorised hallmarks as a guarantee to the consumer of the standard of fineness of the precious metal content in articles of jewellery or silver.

Move on up!

February's Occasions stamps were truly a work of art. They were originally photographed by Julian Deghy from models made by Model Solutions and designed by Springpoint Limited. The topical themes chosen for this stamp issue reflect some of the good news you can receive through the post, from heralding a new baby to a simple thank you, from a romantic message to news of a house move coming up.

Stamp collecting

This issue was one of Royal Mail's most popular with the public and was part of Royal Mail's policy of getting more Special Stamps on mail and promoting stamp collecting to a wider audience. These charming stamps have been especially popular with women who are regular letter writers. The original Stamps, Packs and Stampcards are still available.

Above: Smilers™ For You A4 sheet of twenty First class Occasions stamps.

Smilers™ For You - Generic Sheet - Fact File.

Availability date	5.06.2001
Format	Horizontal
Stamp Size	40.6mm x 29.8mm
Process	Litho
Paper	OBA-free
Printer	House of Questa
Gum	PVA
Perfs	14.8 x 14.1

There is no handstamp for this sheet although a first day of availability has been set for 5 June 2001.

Want to know more?

If you wish to have sheets of twenty identical Occasions stamps personalised with your photograph on the label, these items are also available from Royal Mail. The sheets we can offer with your image attached are either twenty stamps of: Love and Romance, New Baby or New Home or one sheet with ten Celebration Stamps and ten Thank You stamps. If you want to know more about getting your photograph on Smilers™ For You, please call our telephone helpline on:

0845 074 2000

8.30am and 5pm Monday to Friday.

Royal Mail Stamp Preview No. 70 (June 2001)

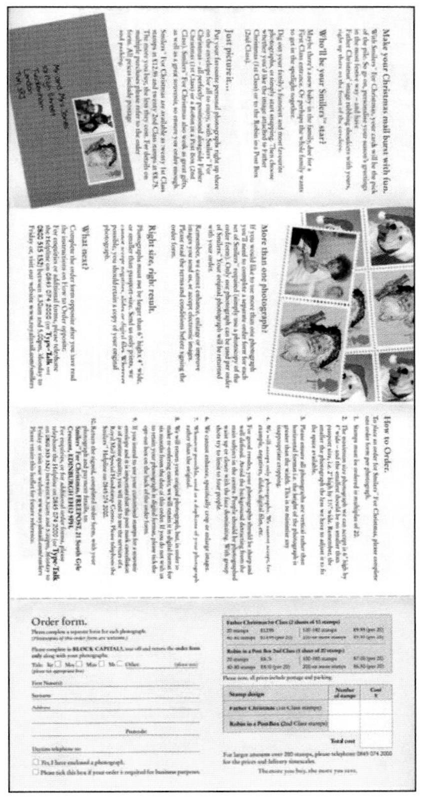

Make your Christmas mail burst with fun.

Who'll be your Smilers™ star?

Just picture it...

More than one photograph?

Right size, right result.

What next?

How to Order.

Order form.

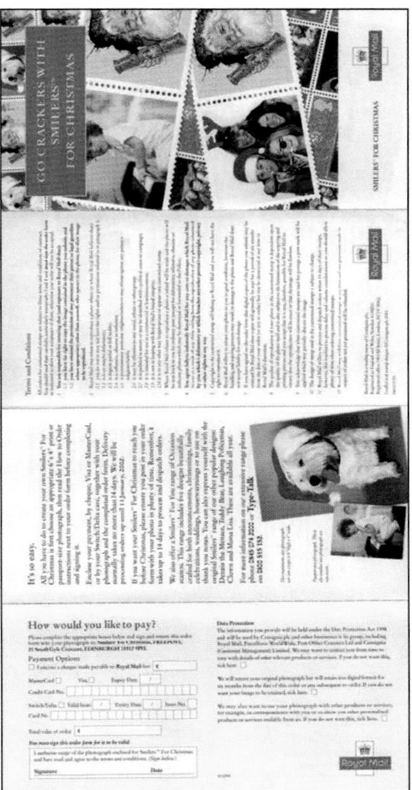

GO CRACKERS WITH SMILERS™ FOR CHRISTMAS

Royal Mail

Terms and Conditions

It's so easy.

How would you like to pay?

"GO CRACKERS WITH SMILERS™ FOR CHRISTMAS"

Consignia plc/PO counter leaflet and order form

Christmas 2001 Smilers RM Ref: 02 QVA

Smilers™ for You- 5 June 2001

Description of items 02ZIA	Value	Code	Qty	£	p
Smilers For You Sheet					
20 x 1st class stamps	**£5.95**	**XA014**			
Handling Charge - UK and Europe 18p					
Rest of the World 34p (applies only to the above items)					
TOTAL COST OF COMPLETE ORDER £					

My personal reference number is: ☐☐☐☐☐☐☐

My title is : Mr☐ Mrs☐ Miss☐ Ms☐ Other:Please specify ....
First Name .... Surname..................................
Address...
....
....
Postcode............... Telephone number...........................

Please tick this box if you have recently changed address ☐
My payment of £.................. is made by:

- ☐ **Cheque / Money order** made payable to Royal Mail
- ☐ **Debit** from my Royal Mail account
- ☐ **Debit** from my Royal Mail account (includes by VDD or CCCC)
- ☐ **By MasterCard / Visa.** Expiry Date ☐☐☐☐

My Card No. is: ☐☐☐☐ ☐☐☐☐ ☐☐☐☐ ☐☐☐☐
Signature.................................. Date...........

Please write your personal reference number on the back of your payment, I understand any overpayment will be left in my account.
If you do not wish to receive further mailings from Royal Mail please tick this box ☐

UK TELEPHONE ORDER AND ENQUIRY LINE
08457 641 641
Monday to Friday
8.30am to 5pm

FAX US ON:
Monday to Friday
0131 316 7337

British Philatelic Bureau
FREEPOST
EH3647
21 South Gyle Crescent
EDINBURGH
EH12 9PE

WWW
Visit us at the Royal Mail Website
www.royalmail.co.uk

Royal Mail
A Royal Mail Service

Stamp Preview
June 2001 No 70
News for collectors from Royal Mail

Smilers For You

It's For You!

Following the incredible success of both the Smilers™ for Christmas sheets and the recent Occasions stamp issue, Royal Mail has been inspired to integrate both these innovative ideas into a delightful new sheet entitled **Smilers For You**. Released on 5 June 2001, this stunning sheet contains twenty First Class Non-Value Indicator (NVI) stamps. The sheet is made up with four of each of the original five Occasions stamps, each one with a lavish label attached, all held securely in an attractive A4 sized sheet.

When You're smiling...

These Smilers™ For You sheets are printed by the House of Questa in Litho. As these stamps have previously been available, there will be no Presentation Pack or Postcards associated with this issue. Smilers™ products are not currently dispatched on a regular order so these items can only be bought by mail order from this Preview, or from your local Postshop.

Hallmark of quality

Royal Mail and the British Hallmarking Council wish to make it clear that the Occasions Stamp issue of 6 February bearing specially created "Hallmarks" symbols was not intended to represent in any way official hallmarks placed on precious metal articles by the four Assay Offices and by certain recognised independent offices in other countries. Royal Mail acknowledges the importance of authorised hallmarks as a guarantee to the consumer of the standard of fineness of the precious metal content in articles of jewellery or silver.

Move on up!

February's Occasions stamps were truly a work of art. They were originally photographed by Julian Deghy from models made by Model Solutions and designed by Springpoint Limited. The topical themes chosen for this stamp issue reflect some of the good news you can receive through the post, from heralding a new baby to a simple thank you, from a romantic message to news of a house move coming up.

Stamp collecting

This issue was one of Royal Mail's most popular with the public and was part of Royal Mail's policy of getting more Special Stamps on mail and promoting stamp collecting to a wider audience. These charming stamps have been especially popular with women who are regular letter writers. The original Stamps, Packs and Stampcards are still available.

Celebration & Thanks

Above: Smilers™ For You A4 sheet of twenty First class Occasions stamps.

Smilers™ For You - Generic Sheet - Fact File.

Availability date	5.06.2001
Format	Horizontal
Stamp Size	40.6mm x 29.8mm
Process	Litho
Paper	OBA-free
Printer	House of Questa
Gum	PVA
Perfs	14.8 x 14.1

There is no handstamp for this sheet, although a first day of availability has been set for 5 June 2001.

Want to know more!

If you wish to have sheets of twenty identical Occasions stamps personalised with your photograph on the label, these items are also available from Royal Mail. The sheets we can offer with your image attached are either twenty stamps of: Love and Romance, New Baby or New Home or one sheet with ten Celebration Stamps and ten Thank You stamps. If you want to know more about getting your photograph on Smilers™ For You, please call our telephone helpline on:

0845 074 2000

8.30am and 5pm Monday to Friday.

Royal Mail Stamp Preview No. 70 (June 2001)

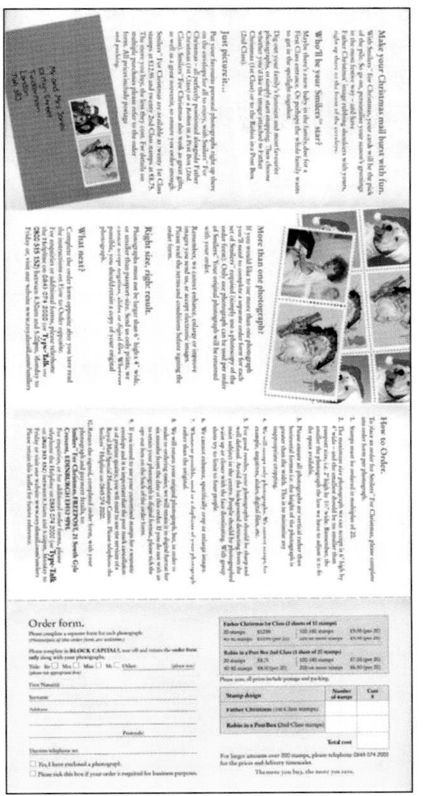

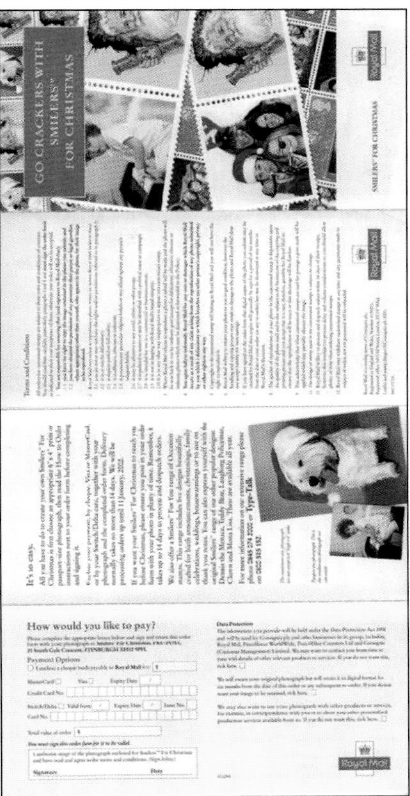

"GO CRACKERS WITH SMILERSTM FOR CHRISTMAS"

Consignia plc/PO counter leaflet and order form

Christmas 2001 Smilers RM Ref: 02 QVA

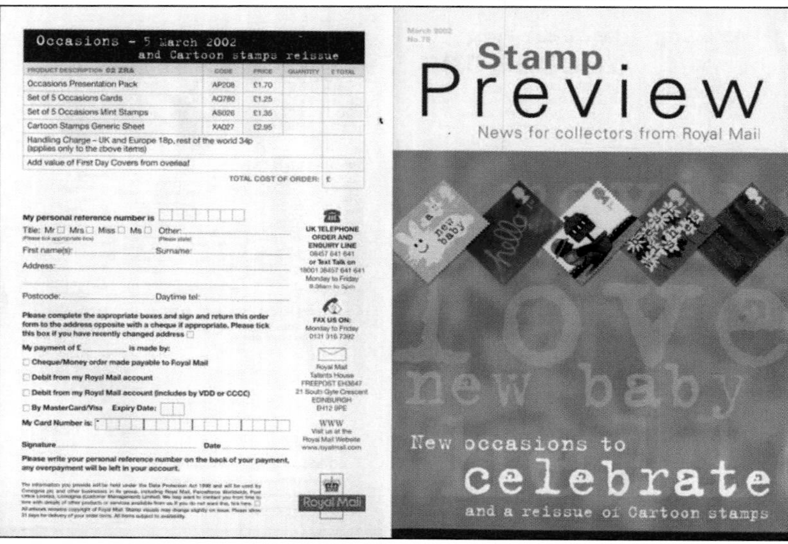

Occasions - 5 March 2002
and Cartoon stamps reissue

PRODUCT DESCRIPTION 02 ZRA	CODE	PRICE	QUANTITY	£ TOTAL
Occasions Presentation Pack	AP208	£1.70		
Set of 5 Occasions Cards	AQ780	£1.25		
Set of 5 Occasions Mint Stamps	AS026	£1.35		
Cartoon Stamps Generic Sheet	XA027	£2.95		
Handling Charge – UK and Europe 18p, rest of the world 34p (applies only to the above items)				
Add value of First Day Covers from overleaf				
			TOTAL COST OF ORDER:	£

My personal reference number is

Title: Mr ☐ Mrs ☐ Miss ☐ Ms ☐ Other: (Please state)
(Please tick appropriate box)

First name(s): Surname:

Address:

Postcode: Daytime tel:

Please complete the appropriate boxes and sign and return this order form to the address opposite with a cheque if appropriate. Please tick this box if you have recently changed address ☐

My payment of £ is made by:

- ☐ **Cheque/Money order made payable to Royal Mail**
- ☐ **Debit from my Royal Mail account**
- ☐ **Debit from my Royal Mail account (includes by VDD or CCCC)**
- ☐ **By MasterCard/Visa Expiry Date:**

My Card Number is:

Signature **Date**

Please write your personal reference number on the back of your payment, any overpayment will be left in your account.

UK TELEPHONE ORDER AND ENQUIRY LINE
08457 641 641
or Text Talk on
18001 08457 641 641
Monday to Friday

FAX US ON:
Monday to Friday
0131 316 7392

Royal Mail
Tallents House
FREEPOST EH3847
21 South Gyle Crescent
EDINBURGH
EH12 9PE

WWW
Visit us at the
Royal Mail Website
www.royalmail.com

Royal Mail

March 2002
No.79

Stamp Preview

News for collectors from Royal Mail

New occasions to
celebrate
and a reissue of Cartoon stamps

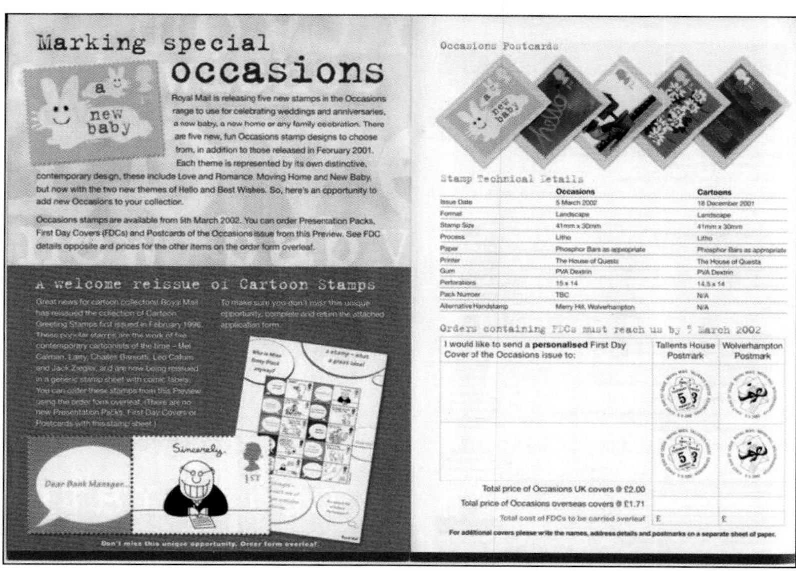

Marking special occasions

Royal Mail is releasing five new stamps in the Occasions range to use for celebrating weddings and anniversaries, a new baby, a new home or any family celebration. There are five new, fun Occasions stamp designs to choose from, in addition to those released in February 2001. Each theme is represented by its own distinctive, contemporary design, these include Love and Romance, Moving Home and New Baby, but now with the two new themes of Hello and Best Wishes. So, here's an opportunity to add new Occasions to your collection.

Occasions stamps are available from 5th March 2002. You can order Presentation Packs, First Day Covers (FDCs) and Postcards of the Occasions issue from this Preview. See FDC details opposite and prices for the other items on the order form overleaf.

A welcome reissue of Cartoon Stamps

Great news for cartoon collectors! Royal Mail has reissued the collection of Cartoon Greeting Stamps first issued in February 1996. These popular stamps are the work of five contemporary cartoonists of the time – Mel Calman, Larry, Charles Barsotti, Leo Cullum and Jack Ziegler, and are now being reissued in a generic stamp sheet with comic labels. You can order these stamps from this Preview using the order form overleaf. (There are no new Presentation Packs, First Day Covers or Postcards with this stamp sheet.)

To make sure you don't miss this unique opportunity, complete and return the attached application form.

Don't miss this unique opportunity. Order form overleaf.

Occasions Postcards

Stamp Technical Details

	Occasions	Cartoons
Issue Date	5 March 2002	18 December 2001
Format	Landscape	Landscape
Stamp Size	41mm x 30mm	41mm x 30mm
Process	Litho	Litho
Paper	Phosphor Bars as appropriate	Phosphor Bars as appropriate
Printer	The House of Questa	The House of Questa
Gum	PVA Dextrin	PVA Dextrin
Perforations	15 x 14	14.5 x 14
Pack Number	TBC	N/A
Alternative Handstamp	Merry Hill, Wolverhampton	N/A

Orders containing FDCs must reach us by 5 March 2002

I would like to send a **personalised** First Day Cover of the Occasions issue to:	Tallents House Postmark	Wolverhampton Postmark
Total price of Occasions UK covers @ £2.00		
Total price of Occasions overseas covers @ £1.71		
Total cost of FDCs to be carried overleaf	£	£

For additional covers please write the names, address details and postmarks on a separate sheet of paper.

Royal Mail Stamp Preview No. 79 (March 2002) featuring the Cartoons Sheet

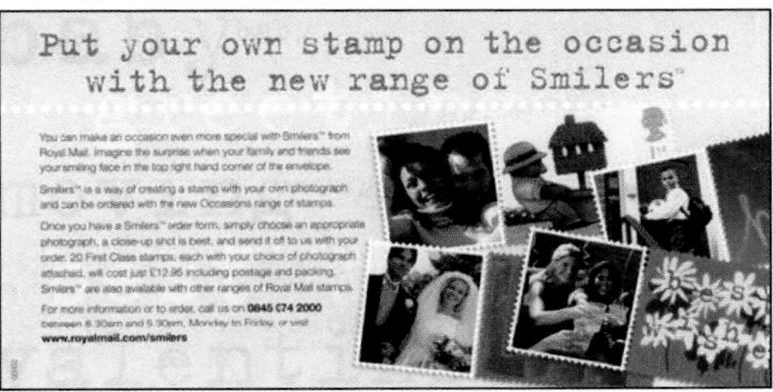

03/02 ex-Occasions Presentation Pack issued 23rd April 2002

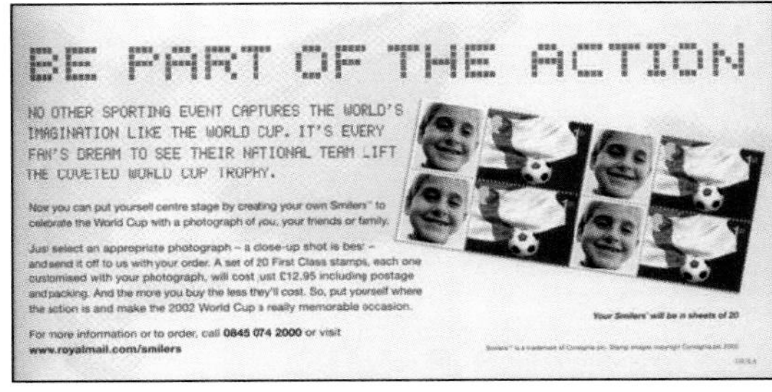

03UEA/05/02 ex-World Cup 2002 Presentation Pack issued 21st May 2002

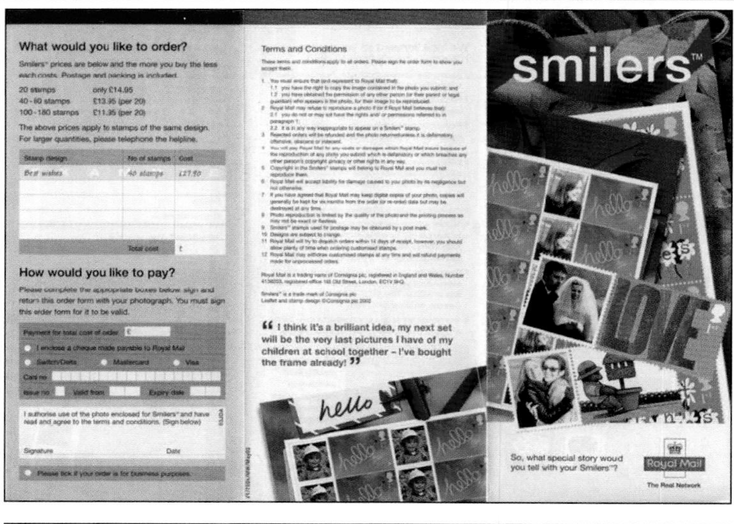

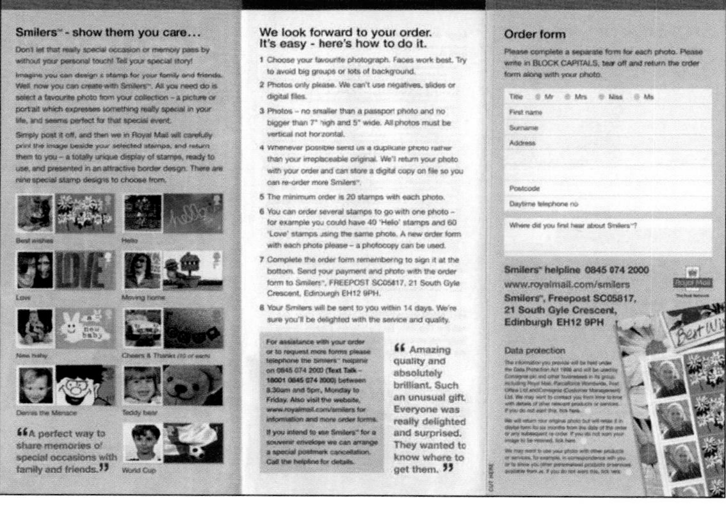

RM Ref: V1/750k/MW/May02/03JDA

Also exists in (apparently) identical format with revised code: V1/750k/MW/May02 S&C172DL with 03JCA in box

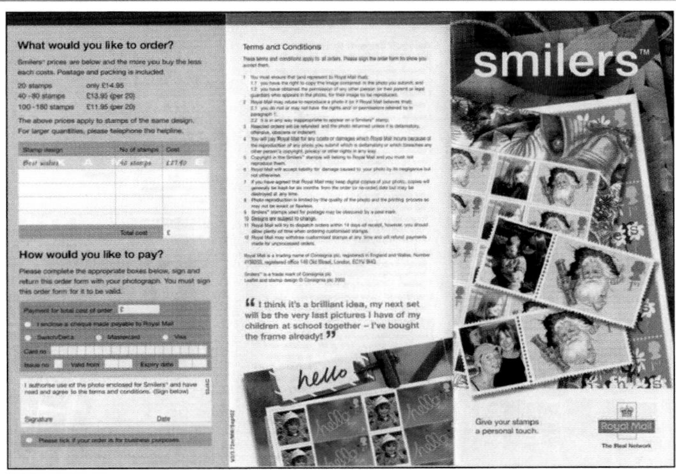

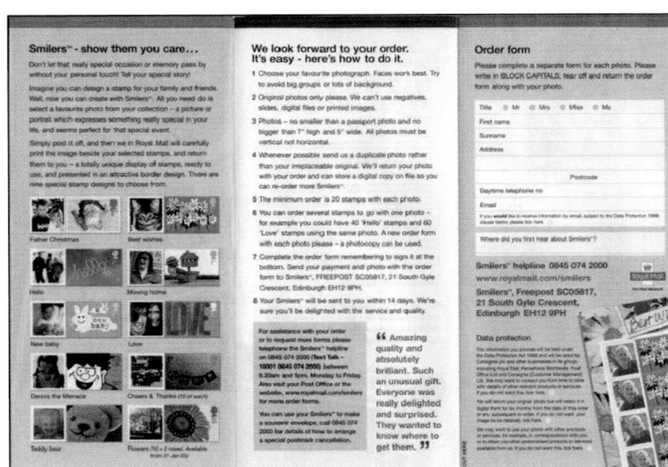

RM Ref. V2/3.72m/MW/Sept02/03JAC

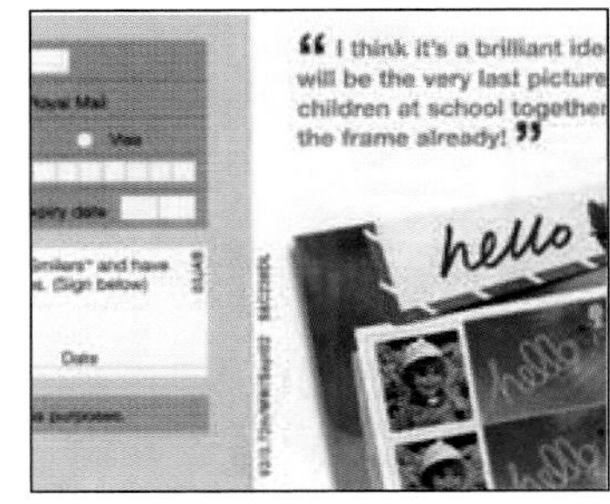

Also exists in (apparently) identical format with revised code: V2/3.72m/MW/Sept02, S&C238DL with 03JAB in box

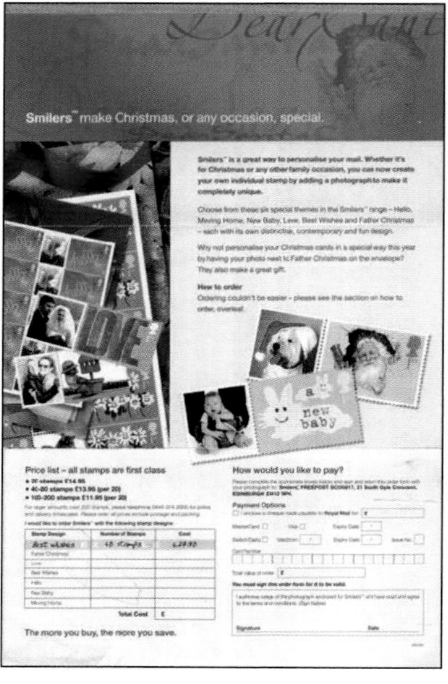

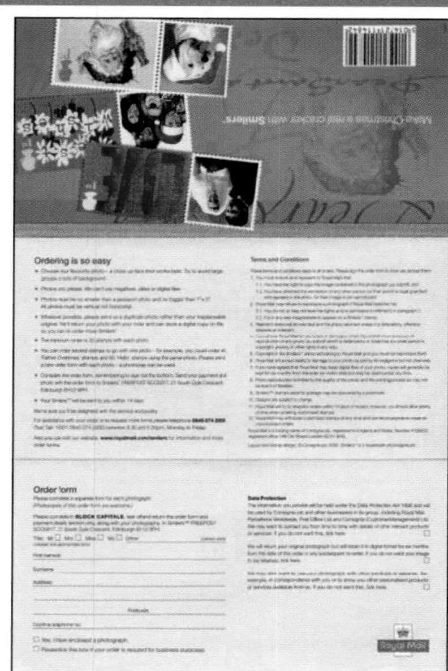

"Smilers™ make Christmas, or any occasion, special. "
Consignia plc/Post Office Counters
Early Smilers leaflet and order form
Christmas 2002 Smilers

RM Ref: 03UMA 10/02

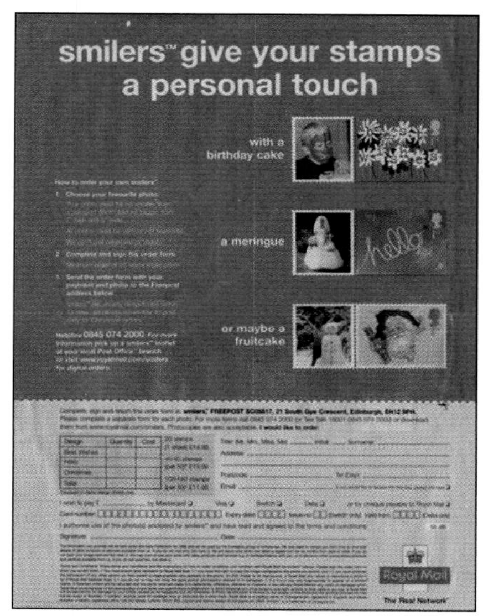

"Smilers™ give your stamps a personal touch"
A magazine advertisement for Smilers c. 2002

Appendix C

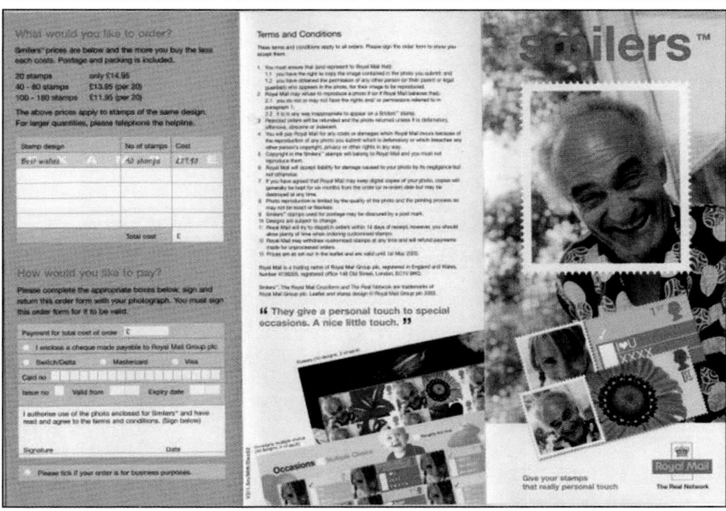

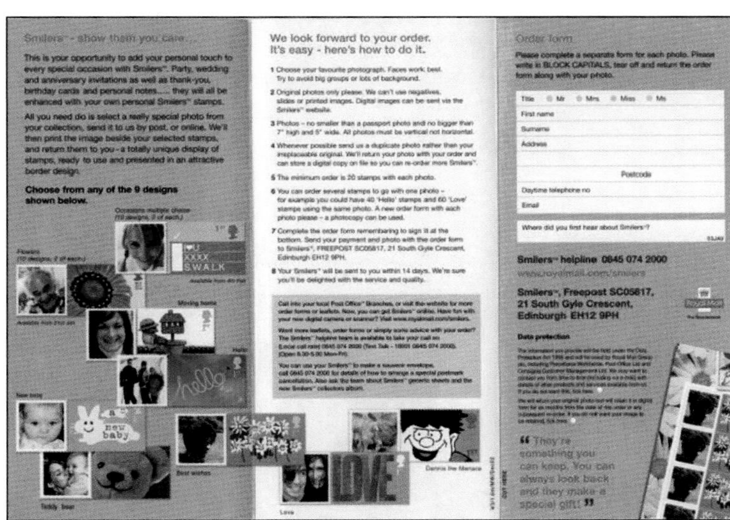

RM Ref: V3/1.6m/MW/Dec02 /03JAV

Also exists in (apparently) identical formats with revised coding:

V3/1.6m/MW/Dec02 /03JAU in box, and

V3/1.6m/MW/Dec02, S&C252DL with 03JAN in box

Appendix C

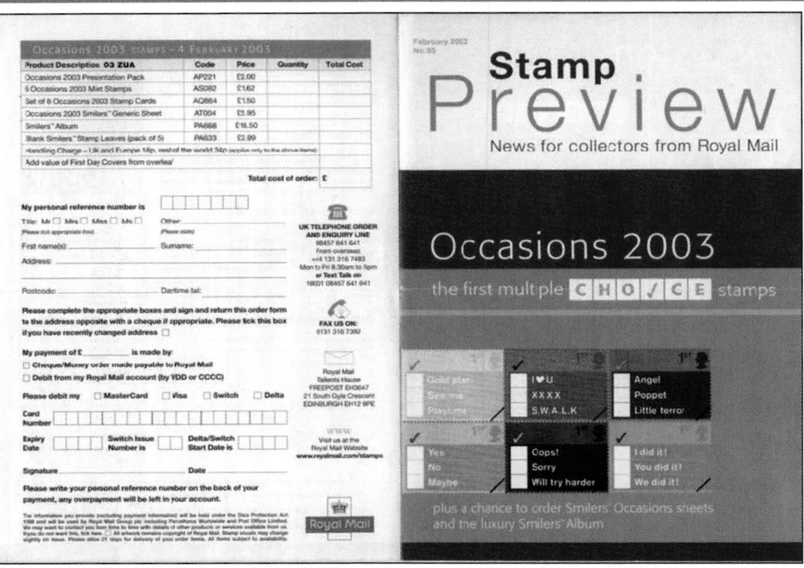

Occasions 2003 STAMPS – 4 FEBRUARY 2003

Product Description 03 ZUA	Code	Price	Quantity	Total Cost
Occasions 2003 Presentation Pack	AP221	£2.00		
6 Occasions 2003 Mint Stamps	AS082	£1.62		
Set of 6 Occasions 2003 Stamp Cards	AQ864	£1.50		
Occasions 2003 Smilers™ Generic Sheet	AT004	£5.95		
Smilers™ Album	PA668	£16.50		
Blank Smilers™ Stamp Leaves (pack of 5)	PA633	£2.99		
Handling Charge – UK and Europe 18p, rest of the world 34p (applies only to the above items)				
Add value of First Day Covers from overleaf				
			Total cost of order:	£

My personal reference number is

Title: Mr ☐ Mrs ☐ Miss ☐ Ms ☐ (Please tick appropriate box) Other: ______ (Please state)

First name(s): ______ Surname: ______

Address: ______

Postcode: ______ Daytime tel: ______

Please complete the appropriate boxes and sign and return this order form to the address opposite with a cheque if appropriate. Please tick this box if you have recently changed address ☐

My payment of £ ______ is made by:

☐ Cheque/Money order made payable to Royal Mail

☐ Debit from my Royal Mail account (by VDD or CCCC)

Please debit my ☐ MasterCard ☐ Visa ☐ Switch ☐ Delta

Card Number

Expiry Date / Switch Issue Number is / Delta/Switch Start Date is

Signature ______ Date ______

Please write your personal reference number on the back of your payment, any overpayment will be left in your account.

The information you provide (including payment information) will be held under the Data Protection Act 1998 and will be used by Royal Mail Group plc including Parcelforce Worldwide and Post Office Limited. We may want to contact you from time to time with details of other products or services available from us. If you do not want this, tick here. ☐ All artwork remains copyright of Royal Mail. Stamp visuals may change slightly on issue. Please allow 21 days for delivery of your order items. All items subject to availability.

UK TELEPHONE ORDER AND ENQUIRY LINE
08457 641 641
From overseas
+44 131 316 7483
Mon to Fri 8.30am to 5pm
or Text Talk on
18001 08457 641 641

FAX US ON:
0131 316 7392

Royal Mail
Tallents House
FREEPOST EH3647
21 South Gyle Crescent
EDINBURGH EH12 9PE

WWW
Visit us at the Royal Mail Website
www.royalmail.com/stamps

Royal Mail

February 2003
No.95

Stamp Preview

News for collectors from Royal Mail

Occasions 2003

the first multiple CHO✓CE stamps

plus a chance to order Smilers™ Occasions sheets and the luxury Smilers™ Album

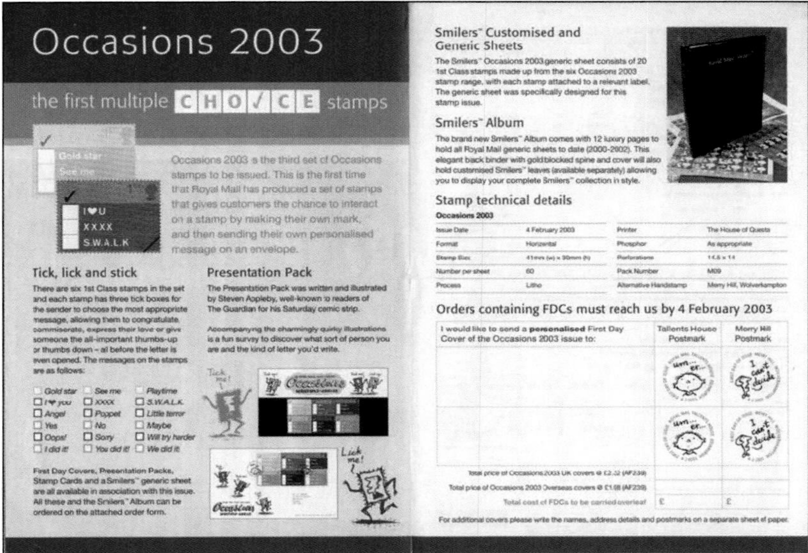

Occasions 2003

the first multiple CHO✓CE stamps

Occasions 2003 is the third set of Occasions stamps to be issued. This is the first time that Royal Mail has produced a set of stamps that gives customers the chance to interact on a stamp by making their own mark, and then sending their own personalised message on an envelope.

Tick, lick and stick

There are six 1st Class stamps in the set and each stamp has three tick boxes for the sender to choose the most appropriate message, allowing them to congratulate, commiserate, express their love or give someone the all-important thumbs-up or thumbs down – all before the letter is even opened. The messages on the stamps are as follows:

☐ Gold star	☐ See me	☐ Playtime
☐ I ♥ you	☐ XXXX	☐ S.W.A.L.K.
☐ Angel	☐ Poppet	☐ Little terror
☐ Yes	☐ No	☐ Maybe
☐ Oops!	☐ Sorry	☐ Will try harder
☐ I did it!	☐ You did it!	☐ We did it!

First Day Covers, Presentation Packs, Stamp Cards and a Smilers™ generic sheet are all available in association with this issue. All these and the Smilers™ Album can be ordered on the attached order form.

Presentation Pack

The Presentation Pack was written and illustrated by Steven Appleby, well-known to readers of The Guardian for his Saturday comic strip.

Accompanying the charmingly quirky illustrations is a fun survey to discover what sort of person you are and the kind of letter you'd write.

Smilers™ Customised and Generic Sheets

The Smilers™ Occasions 2003 generic sheet consists of 20 1st Class stamps made up from the six Occasions 2003 stamp range, with each stamp attached to a relevant label. The generic sheet was specifically designed for this stamp issue.

Smilers™ Album

The brand new Smilers™ Album comes with 12 luxury pages to hold all Royal Mail generic sheets to date (2000-2002). This elegant black binder with gold blocked spine and cover will also hold customised Smilers™ leaves (available separately) allowing you to display your complete Smilers™ collection in style.

Stamp technical details

Occasions 2003

Issue Date	4 February 2003	Printer	The House of Questa
Format	Horizontal	Phosphor	As appropriate
Stamp Size	41mm (w) x 30mm (h)	Perforations	14.5 x 14
Number per sheet	60	Pack Number	M09
Process	Litho	Alternative Handstamp	Merry Hill, Wolverhampton

Orders containing FDCs must reach us by 4 February 2003

I would like to send a **personalised** First Day Cover of the Occasions 2003 issue to:	Tallents House Postmark	Merry Hill Postmark
Total price of Occasions 2003 UK covers @ £2.32 (AF238)		
Total price of Occasions 2003 Overseas covers @ £1.98 (AF238)		
Total cost of FDCs to be carried overleaf	£	£

For additional covers please write the names, address details and postmarks on a separate sheet of paper.

Royal Mail Stamp Preview No. 95 (February 2003) featuring 2003 Occasions Issue

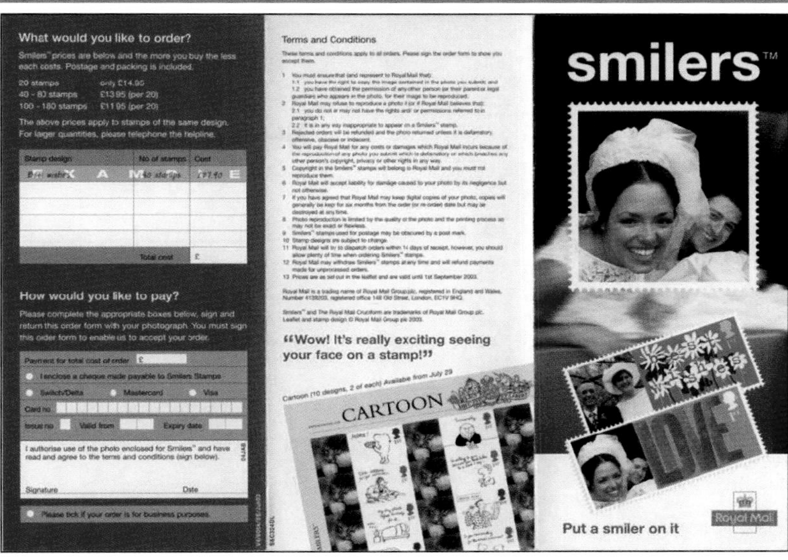

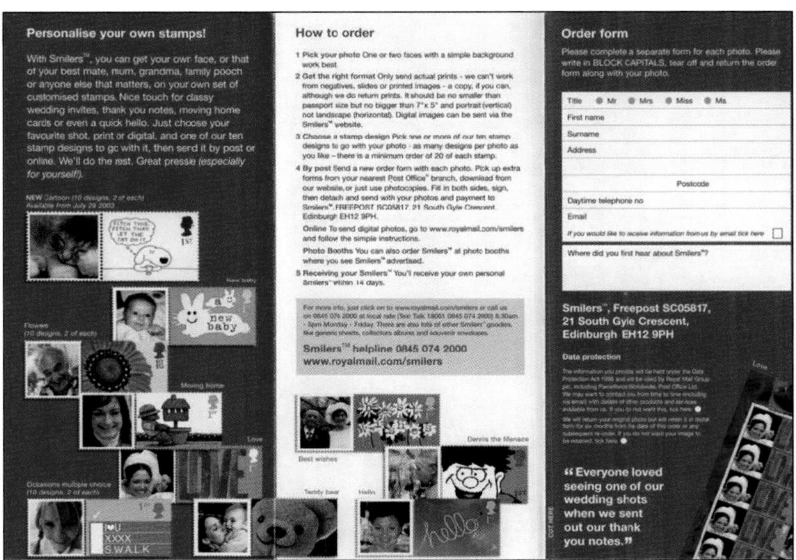

RM Ref: V4/605k/SE/Jun03, S&C324DL

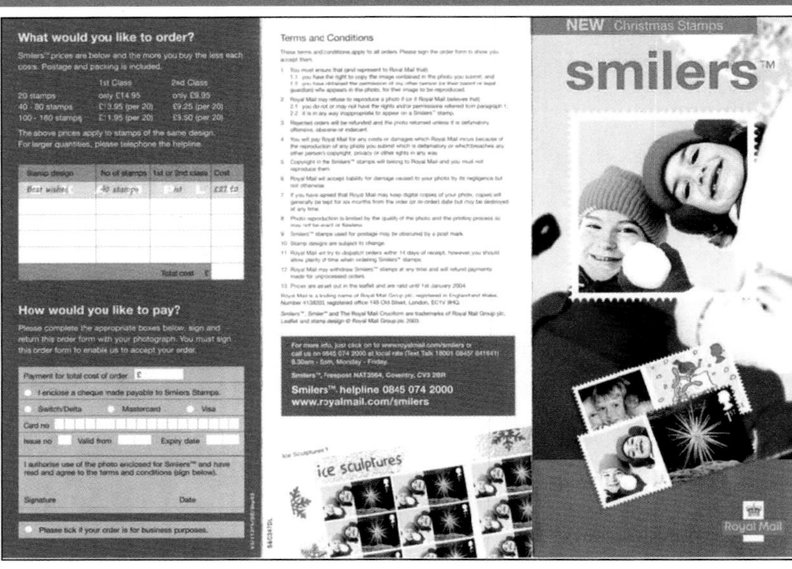

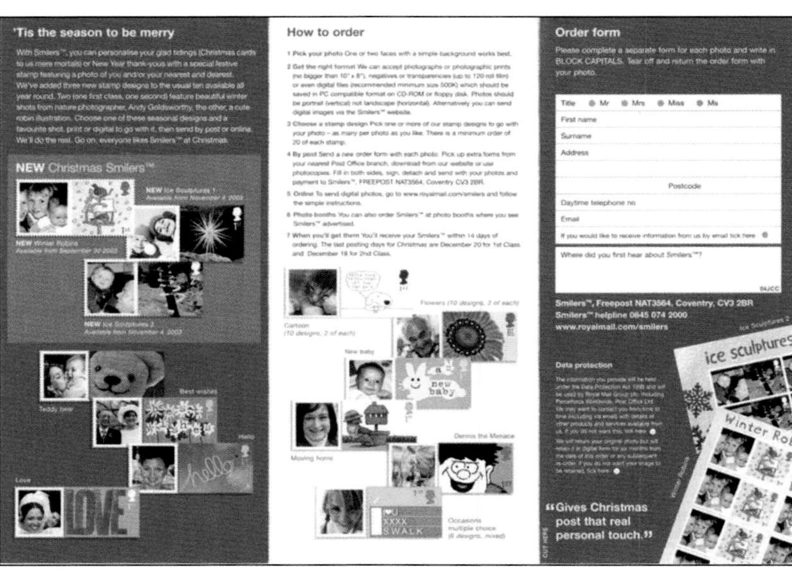

RM Ref: V5/1137k/SE/Sep03, S&C347DL

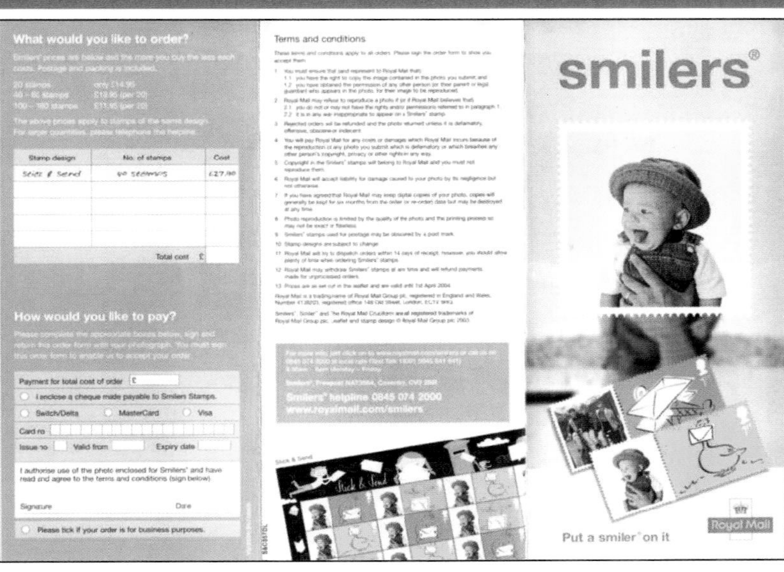

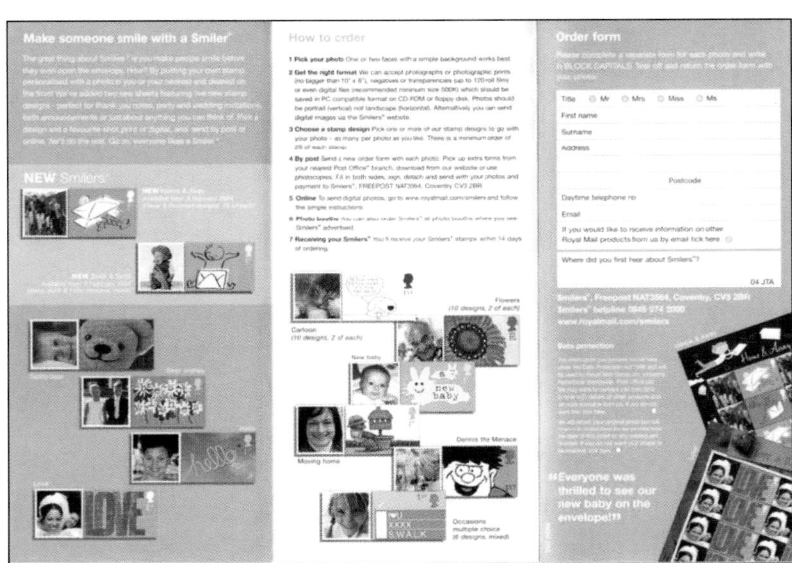

RM ref: V5/950k/SE/Jan04, S&C357DL

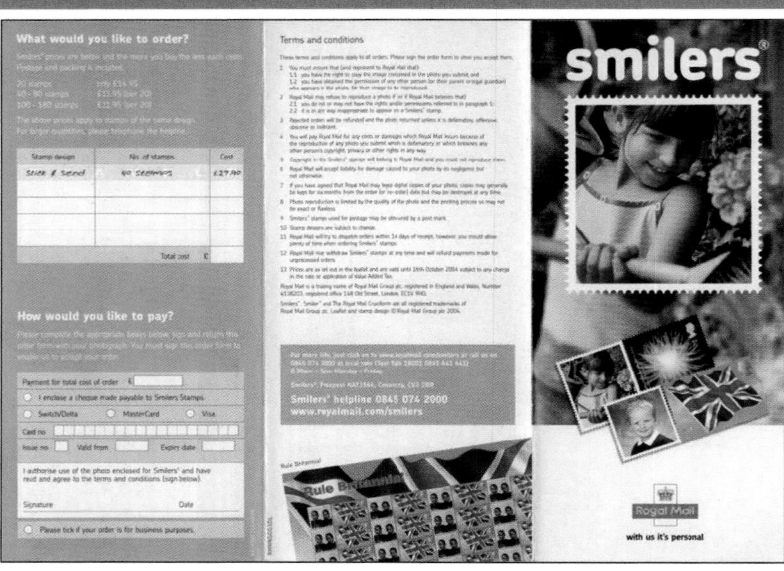

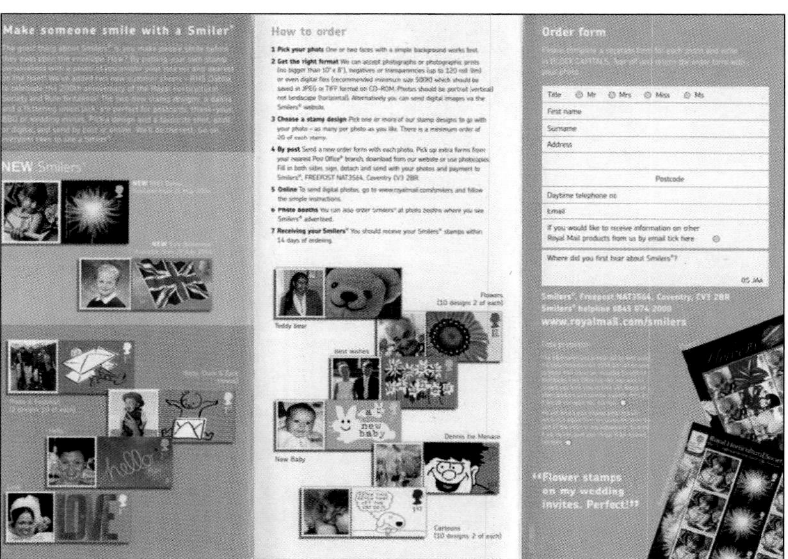

RM Ref: V6/950/TL/Jun04, RMMKG003DL

Place your order

Smilers® prices are below and the more you buy the less each costs. Postage and packing is included. For larger quantities please call 0845 074 2000.

20 stamps	only £14.95
40-80 stamps	£13.95 (per 20)
100-180 stamps	£11.95 (per 20)

2nd class (available on Christmas Delivery Ref SM21 only)

20 stamps	only £9.95
40-80 stamps	£9.25 (per 20)
100-180 stamps	£8.50 (per 20)

The above prices apply to stamps of the same design

Stamp Design/Ref No.	No. of stamps	Cost
Love SM8	40 stamps	£27.90
	Total Cost £	

How would you like to pay?

You must sign this order form to enable us to accept your order.

Payment for total cost of order £

☐ I enclose a cheque made payable to Smilers® Stamps.

☐ Maestro/Switch ☐ MasterCard ☐ Visa

Card No

Issue no Valid from Expiry date

I authorise use of photo enclosed for Smilers® and have read and agree to the terms and conditions (sign below)

Signature date

☐ Please tick if your order is for business purposes.

to help you...

Royal Mail can arrange for alternative formats of this booklet to be sent to you.

To obtain a free copy call Customer Services on 08457 740 740. If you are deaf or hard of hearing we offer a textphone service on 08457 640 640

Alternatively please visit our website www.royalmail.com which has been designed with all of our customers in mind.

Terms and conditions

New Christmas stamps

smilers®

your image, your stamp

1 Choose a photo & a stamp design

2 Send your order by post or online

3 We'll do the rest!

Royal Mail

with us it's personal™

Plenty to choose from

There are 20 different Smilers® designs to choose from, some of which are shown below. When ordering please write down the name and the reference number of the stamp style(s) you have chosen on the order form. For the complete range visit www.royalmail.com/smilers

*This is the only 2nd class stamp available

What are Smilers®?

Smilers® are stamps you can customise with an image of your choice. All you need to do is send in the image you want to use whether it be a son or daughter, grandchild, wedding image or just about anything else you fancy and we'll do the rest!

Ordering Smilers® couldn't be simpler

> **Pick your photo**
One or two faces with a simple background works best.

> **Get the right format**
We can accept photographs or photographic prints (no bigger than 10x8"), negatives or transparencies (up to 120 roll film) or even digital images (recommended minimum size 500k) which should be saved as a JPEG or TIFF format on CD-ROM. Photos should be portrait (vertical) not landscape (horizontal). Alternatively you can send digital images via the Smilers® website.

> **Choose a stamp design**
Pick one or more of our stamp designs to go with your photo from those shown opposite or on the web. There is a minimum order of 20 of each stamp.

> **Send to us**
By post: Send a new order form with each photo. Pick up extra forms from your nearest Post Office® branch, download some from our website or use photocopies. Fill in both sides, sign, detach and send with your photos and payment to Smilers®, FREEPOST NAT3564, Coventry CV3 2BR.
Online: To send digital photos go to www.royalmail.com/smilers where you will find a simple instruction on how to create your Smilers®.
Photo booths: You can also order Smilers® at photo booths where you see Smilers® advertised.

> **Receive your Smilers®!**
You should receive your Smilers® stamps within 14 days of ordering.

Remember the last posting days for Christmas are 21st December for 1st class, and 18th December for 2nd class.

Please refer to our website for further details: www.royalmail.com/smilers

Order Form

Please complete a separate form for each photo and write in BLOCK CAPITALS. Tear off and return this order form with your photo.

Title Mr ☐ Mrs ☐ Miss ☐ Ms ☐

First Name

Surname

Address

Postcode

Daytime Telephone no

Email

If you would like to receive information on other Royal Mail products by email please tick here ☐

Where did you first hear about Smilers®?

05 JGA

Smilers®, Freepost NAT3564, Coventry CV3 2BR

Smilers® helpline 0845 074 2000
www.royalmail.com/smilers

Data Protection
The information you provide will be held under the Data Protection Act 1998 and will be used by Royal Mail Group plc, including Parcelforce Worldwide and Post Office Ltd. We may want to contact you from time to time with details of other products and services available from us. If you do not wish this, tick here ☐

We will return your original photo but will retain it in digital form for six months from the date of this order or any subsequent reorder. If you do not want your image to be retained, tick here ☐

Each sheet contains 20 stamps and an attractive border design – ideal for framing

RM Ref: 945/TL/September04, RMMKG020DL

Appendix C - Smilers Publicity

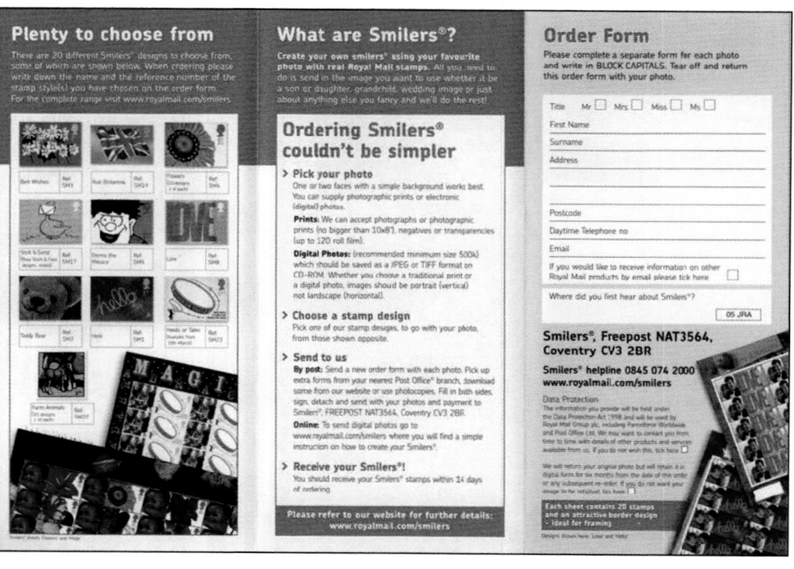

RM Ref: 100/TL/March05, RMMKG074DL

Place your order

Smilers® prices are shown below and the more you buy the less each costs. Postage and packing is included. For larger quantities please call 0845 074 2000.

20 stamps (one sheet)	only £14.95
40-80 stamps (2-4 sheets)	£13.95 (per 20)
100-180 stamps (5-9 sheets)	£11.95 (per 20)

The above prices apply to stamps of the same design

Stamp Design/Ref No	No. of stamps	Cost
Love Smg	40 stamps	£27.90
	Total Cost £	

How would you like to pay?

You must sign this order form to enable us to accept your order.

Payment for total cost of order £

☐ I enclose a cheque made payable to Smilers® Stamps.

☐ Maestro/Switch ☐ MasterCard ☐ Visa

Card No

Issue no Valid from Expiry date

I authorise use of photo enclosed for Smilers® and have read and agree to the terms and conditions (sign below).

Signature date

☐ Please tick if your order is for business purposes.

to help you...

Royal Mail can arrange for alternative formats of this booklet to be sent to you.

To obtain a free copy call Customer Services on **08457 740 740**. If you are deaf or hard of hearing we offer a textphone service on **08457 640 640**

Alternatively please visit our website **www.royalmail.com** which has been designed with all of our customers in mind.

Terms and conditions

smilers®

Your favourite photo with real Royal Mail stamps

Miss C Davies
1F Imagen Street
ALTRINCHAM
Cheshire
WA20 9JW

Royal Mail

with us it's personal™

Plenty to choose from

With a wide range of different Smilers® designs to choose from, some of which are shown below. When ordering please write down the name and the reference number of the stamp style(s) you have chosen on the order form. For the complete range visit www.royalmail.com/smilers

What are Smilers®?

Create your own smilers® using your favourite photo with real Royal Mail stamps. All you need to do is send in the image you want to use whether it be a son or daughter, grandchild, wedding image or just about anything else you fancy and we'll do the rest!

Ordering Smilers® couldn't be simpler

> Pick your photo

One or two faces with a simple background works best. You can supply photographic prints or electronic (digital) photos.

Prints: We can accept photographs or photographic prints (no bigger than 10x8"). If only part of the image on the photo is required please indicate this accordingly.

Digital Photos: (recommended minimum size 500k) which should be saved as a JPEG or TIFF format on CD-ROM. Whether you choose a traditional print or a digital photo, images should be portrait (vertical) not landscape (horizontal).

> Choose a stamp design

Pick one of our stamp designs, to go with your photo, from those shown opposite

> Send to us

By post: Send a new order form with each photo. Pick up extra forms from your nearest Post Office® branch, download some from our website or use photocopies. Fill in both sides, sign, detach and send with your photos and payment to Smilers®, Royal Mail, Freepost SCO 5817, EDINBURGH, EH12 9PH.

Online: To send digital photos go to www.royalmail.com/smilers where you will find a simple instruction on how to create your Smilers®.

> Receive your Smilers®!

You should receive your Smilers® stamps within 14 days of ordering.

Please refer to our website for further details: www.royalmail.com/smilers

Order Form

Please complete a separate form for each photo and write in BLOCK CAPITALS. Tear off and return this order form with your photo.

Title Mr ☐ Mrs ☐ Miss ☐ Ms ☐

First Name

Surname

Address

Postcode

Daytime Telephone no

Email

If you would like to receive information on other Royal Mail products by email please tick here ☐

Where did you first hear about Smilers®?

Smilers®, Royal Mail, Freepost SCO 5817, EDINBURGH, EH12 9PH

Smilers® helpline 0845 074 2000
www.royalmail.com/smilers

Data Protection

Each sheet contains 20 stamps and an attractive border design – ideal for framing

RM Ref: 560/PJM/June05, RMMKH001DL – see also Welsh language version, page C –39

Appendix C - Smilers Publicity

ex-MAGIC Presentation Pack issued 15th March 2005

after the watershed

Make sure you order your Classic ITV stamps today. They won't be repeated. **Available until 14 September 2006.**

Our six Classic ITV Special Stamps celebrated the 50th anniversary of Independent Television broadcasting in 2005. The issue features some of Britain's favourite programmes, including cult classic The Avengers, high-brow drama Inspector Morse, and the unforgettable 70s comedy Rising Damp. The First Class stamp features Emmerdale, voted as Britain's favourite ITV soap opera by the public. Each stamp shows an image from the programme's opening sequence.

Presentation Pack

Royal Mail "Preview" Sept/October 2005 - shows ITV Cartor printing

Appendix C - Smilers Publicity

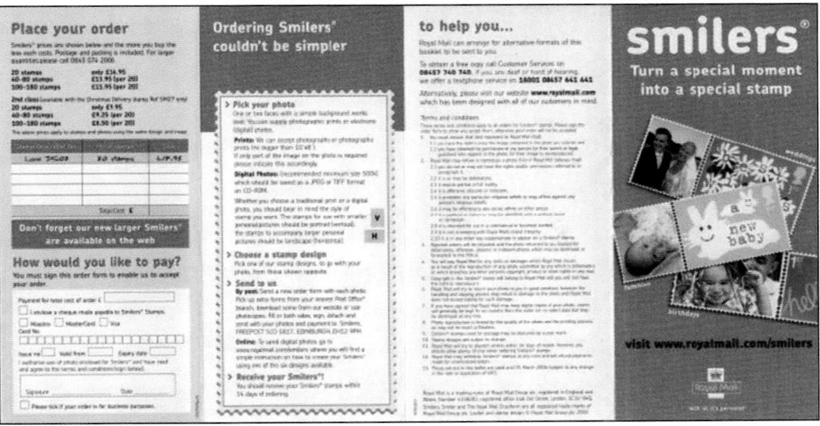

RM Ref: 924/PM/Nov05, RMMH053

Seen with either 06 GMA or 06 GJA in the code box against the question "Where did you hear about Smilers?" These codes are believed to be regional marketing identifiers. Other codes may exist.

Welsh language version

A dual English/Welsh language version of this pamphlet was also issued. It is a double sized pamphlet with English text in the lower half and Welsh text in the upper half. Some of the panels have been repositioned in the Welsh version although the basic content is the same. See page C - 40

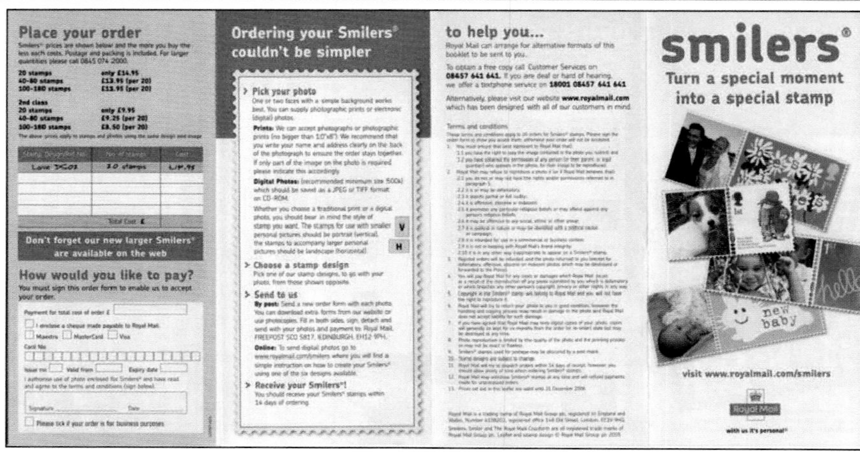

RM Ref: 62/PM/Feb06

Seen with either 06 JIA, 06 JJA or 06 JKA in the code box against the question "Where did you hear about Smilers?" These codes are believed to be regional marketing identifiers. Other codes may exist.

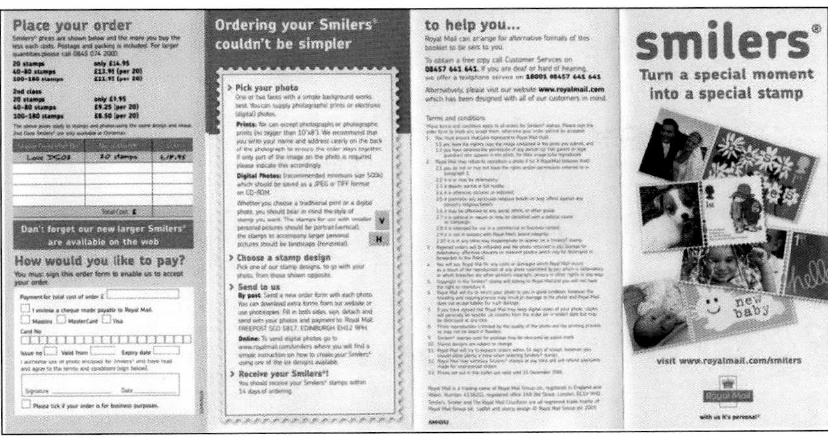

RM Ref: 150/PM/May06, RMH092

Identical to the Feb 06 issue with the addition of the Robin in Pillarbox stamp which was previously omitted in error. Seen with 07 JCA in the code box against the question "Where did you hear about Smilers?" This code is believed to be a regional marketing identifier. Other codes may exist.

Welsh language version

A dual English/Welsh language version of this pamphlet was also issued and referenced RMH093 in the bottom right hand corner of the pamphlet. See page C–39 for further information of the Welsh Language versions. The dual language, double-sized pamphlet had English text in the lower half and Welsh text in the upper half. Some of the panels have been repositioned in the Welsh version although the basic content is the same.

Appendix C - Smilers Publicity

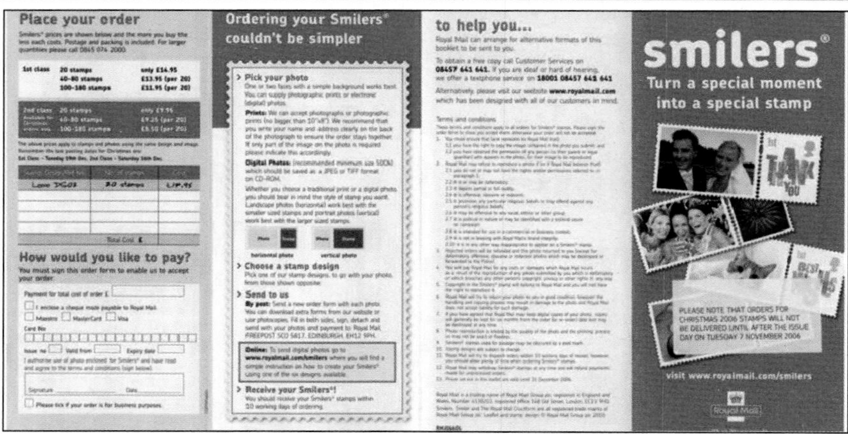

RM Ref: 150/PM/Sept06, RMJ046DL

Seen with either 07 JLA or 07 JNA in the code box against the question "Where did you hear about Smilers?" These codes are believed to be regional marketing identifiers. Other codes may exist.

Welsh language version

A dual English/Welsh language version of this pamphlet was also issued and referenced RMH093 in the bottom right hand corner of the pamphlet. See page C–39 for further information of the Welsh Language versions. The dual language, double-sized pamphlet had English text in the lower half and Welsh text in the upper half. Some of the panels have been repositioned in the Welsh version although the basic content is the same.

smile!

Put your face on a sheet of Smilers® Customised Stamps to add some sparkling personality to your Christmas mail. In addition to the new Smilers® stamps **issued on 17 October 2006**, the following stamps designs are also available.

Rule Britannia Ref: DS01 · **Love** Ref: DS02 · **Hello** Ref: DS03 · **Teddy** Ref: DS04 · **Flower** Ref: DS05 · **Robin** Ref: DS06 · **Christmas 2006** Ref: DS14, Ref: DS13

Smilers® Customised Stamps are great for personalising your post no matter what the occasion, they're excellent for baby photos and wedding pictures too. And there's no better time to make your friends and family feel special than at Christmas. The self adhesive stamps are suitable for any landscape photo, so why not be creative and add some festive fun to your post. Plus, once you've chosen a personal photo to use, you can then choose from our selection of Smilers® designs to get the right message across with your picture. Go on, have some fun with your post and put your face next to a stamp.

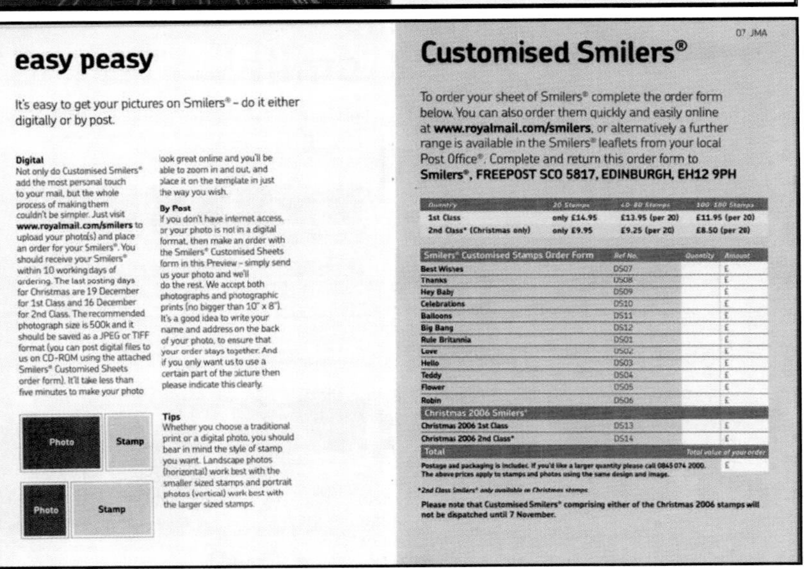

easy peasy

It's easy to get your pictures on Smilers® – do it either digitally or by post.

Digital
Not only do Customised Smilers® add the most personal touch to your mail, but the whole process of making them couldn't be simpler. Just visit **www.royalmail.com/smilers** to upload your photo(s) and place an order for your Smilers®. You should receive your Smilers® within 10 working days of ordering. The last posting days for Christmas are 19 December for 1st Class and 16 December for 2nd Class. The recommended photograph size is 500k and it should be saved as a JPEG or TIFF format (you can post digital files to us on CD-ROM using the attached Smilers® Customised Sheets order form). It'll take less than five minutes to make your photo look great online and you'll be able to zoom in and out, and place it on the template in just the way you wish.

By Post
If you don't have internet access, or your photo is not in a digital format, then make an order with the Smilers® Customised Sheets form in this Preview – simply send us your photo and we'll do the rest. We accept both photographs and photographic prints (no bigger than 10" x 8"). It's a good idea to write your name and address on the back of your photo, to ensure that your order stays together. And if you only want us to use a certain part of the picture then please indicate this clearly.

Tips
Whether you choose a traditional print or a digital photo, you should bear in mind the style of stamp you want. Landscape photos (horizontal) work best with the smaller sized stamps and portrait photos (vertical) work best with the larger sized stamps.

07 JMA

Customised Smilers®

To order your sheet of Smilers® complete the order form below. You can also order them quickly and easily online at **www.royalmail.com/smilers**, or alternatively a further range is available in the Smilers® leaflets from your local Post Office®. Complete and return this order form to **Smilers®, FREEPOST SCO 5817, EDINBURGH, EH12 9PH**

Quantity	20 Stamps	40–80 Stamps	100–180 Stamps
1st Class	only £14.95	£13.95 (per 20)	£11.95 (per 20)
2nd Class* (Christmas only)	only £9.95	£9.25 (per 20)	£8.50 (per 20)

Smilers® Customised Stamps Order Form	Ref No.	Quantity	Amount
Best Wishes	DS07		£
Thanks	DS08		£
Hey Baby	DS09		£
Celebrations	DS10		£
Balloons	DS11		£
Big Bang	DS12		£
Rule Britannia	DS01		£
Love	DS02		£
Hello	DS03		£
Teddy	DS04		£
Flower	DS05		£
Robin	DS06		£
Christmas 2006 Smilers®			
Christmas 2006 1st Class	DS13		£
Christmas 2006 2nd Class*	DS14		£
Total			Total value of your order
Postage and packaging is included. If you'd like a larger quantity please call 0845 074 2000. The above prices apply to stamps and photos using the same design and image.			£

*2nd Class Smilers® only available on Christmas stamps

Please note that Customised Smilers® comprising either of the Christmas 2006 stamps will not be dispatched until 7 November.

Royal Mail Stamp Preview No. 153 (October 2006)

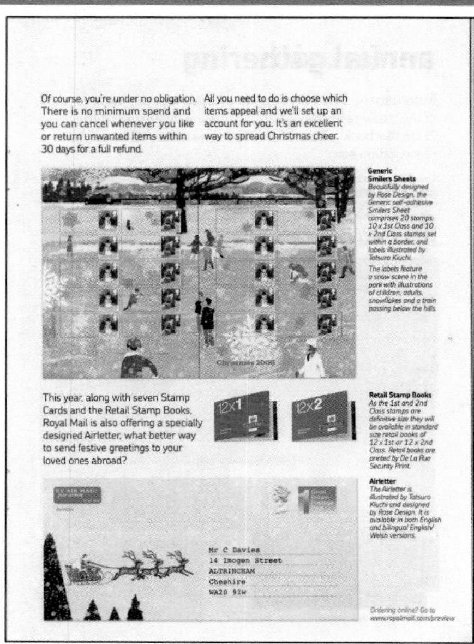

Of course, you're under no obligation. There is no minimum spend and you can cancel whenever you like or return unwanted items within 30 days for a full refund. All you need to do is choose which items appeal and we'll set up an account for you. It's an excellent way to spread Christmas cheer.

Generic Smilers Sheets
Beautifully designed by Rose Design, the Generic self-adhesive Smilers Sheet comprises 20 stamps. 10 x 1st Class and 10 x 2nd Class stamps set within a border, and labels illustrated by Tatsuro Kiuchi.

The labels feature a snow scene in the park with illustrations of children, adults, snowflakes and a train passing below the hills.

This year, along with seven Stamp Cards and the Retail Stamp Books, Royal Mail is also offering a specially designed Airletter, what better way to send festive greetings to your loved ones abroad?

Retail Stamp Books
As the 1st and 2nd Class stamps are definitive size they will be available in standard size retail books of 12 x 1st or 12 x 2nd Class. Retail books are printed by De La Rue Security Print.

Airletter
The Airletter is illustrated by Tatsuro Kiuchi and designed by Rose Design. It is available in both English and bilingual English/Welsh versions.

Mr C Davies
14 Imogen Street
ALTRINCHAM
Cheshire
WA20 9IW

Ordering online? Go to www.royalmail.com/preview

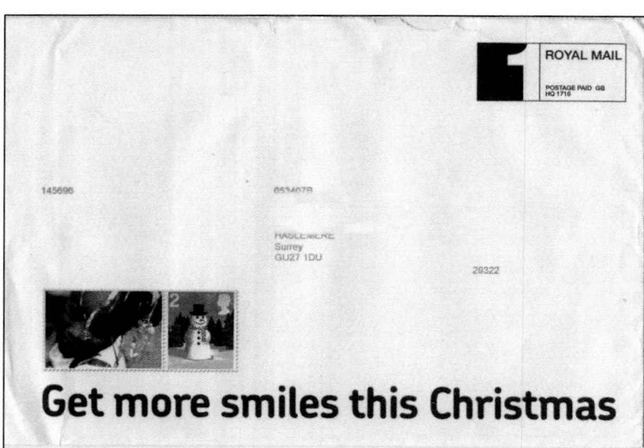

Royal Mail Preview November 2006

This included a feature on Christmas Smilers including an illustration on the envelope. Interestingly no mention is made of the customised versions featured on the envelope!

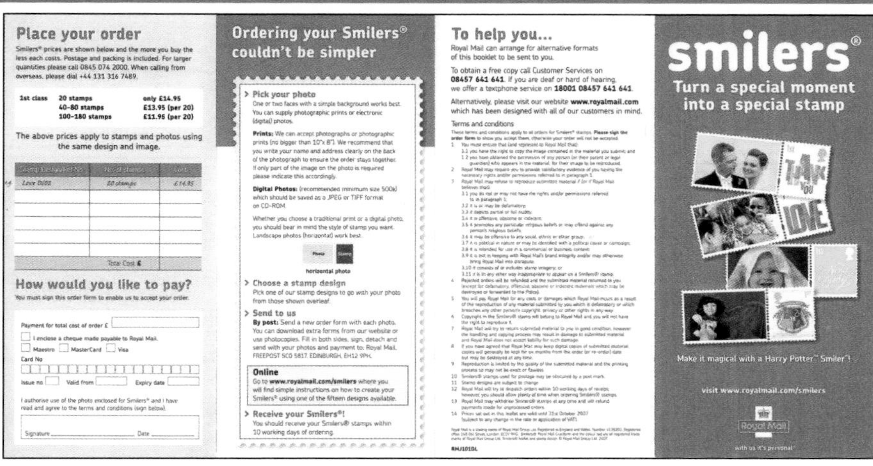

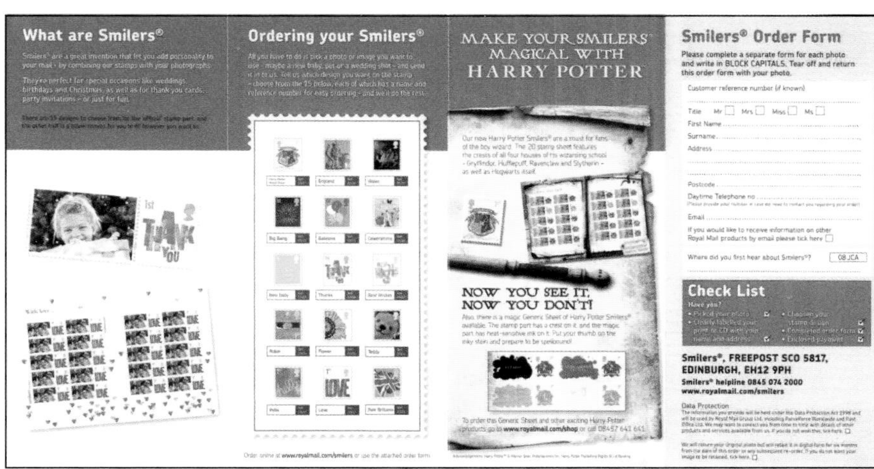

RM Ref: RMJ101DL May 2007

Seen with 08 JCA in the code box against the question “Where did you hear about Smilers?” This codes is believed to be a regional marketing identifier. Other codes may exist.

Welsh language version

A Welsh language version of this pamphlet also exists in similar format to this version. See page C - 42

Appendix C

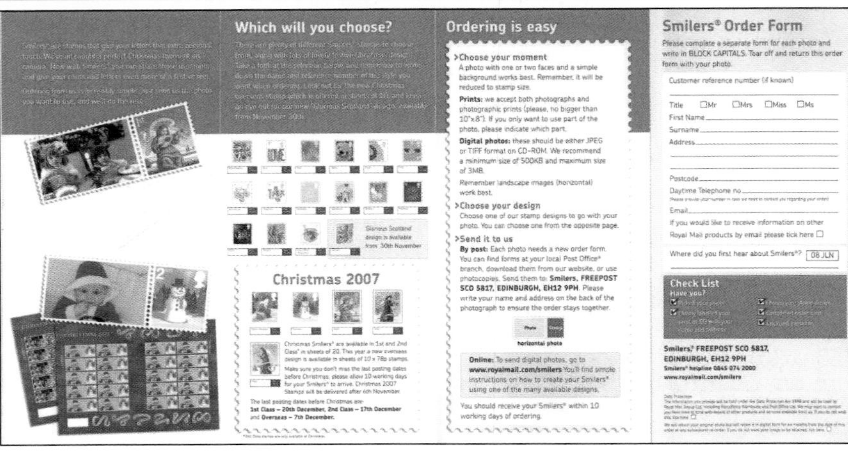

RM Ref: RMJ117DL (Oct 2007)

Seen with 08 JLN in the code box against the question "Where did you hear about Smilers?" This codes is believed to be a regional marketing identifier. Other codes may exist. This leaflet had a cut-out on the front panel which when closed showed the location of a photo image where the label would be. Coding of the Smilers stamps shown in this leaflet were revised to reflect Royal Mail's revised Smilers pricing policy and to distinguish orders placed after the introduction of the new coding system using revised codes ending in N, in the form DSXXN

Welsh language version

A Welsh language version of this pamphlet also exists in similar format to above, RM Ref: RMJ118DL. See page C - 43.

Appendix C

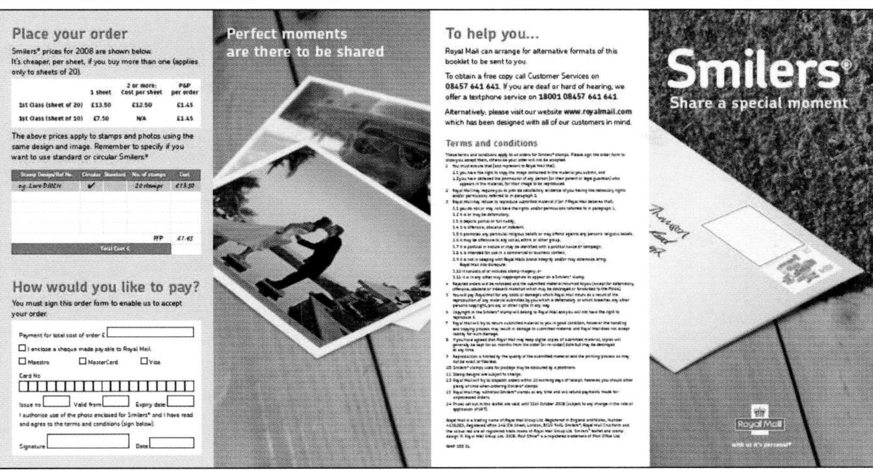

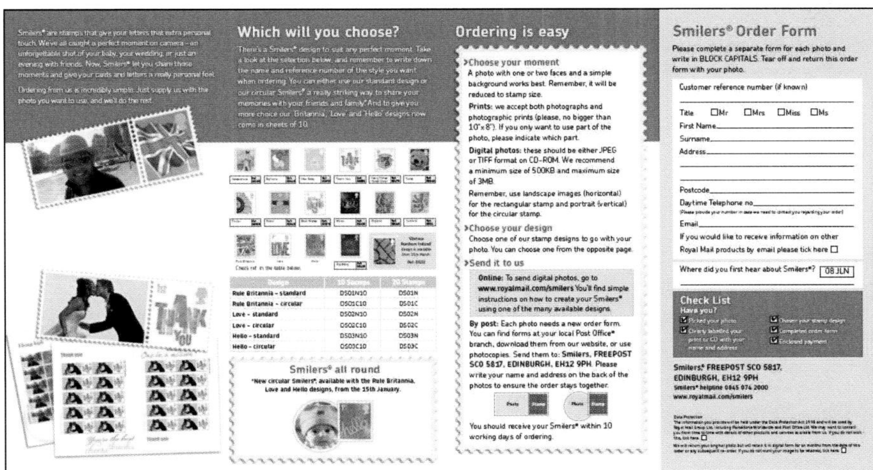

RM Ref: RMP 005 DL (June 2008)

Seen with 08 JLN in the code box against the question "Where did you hear about Smilers?" This code is believed to be a regional marketing identifier. Other codes may exist. This leaflet had a cut-out on the front panel which when closed showed the location of a photo image where the label would be.

Appendix C - Smilers Publicity

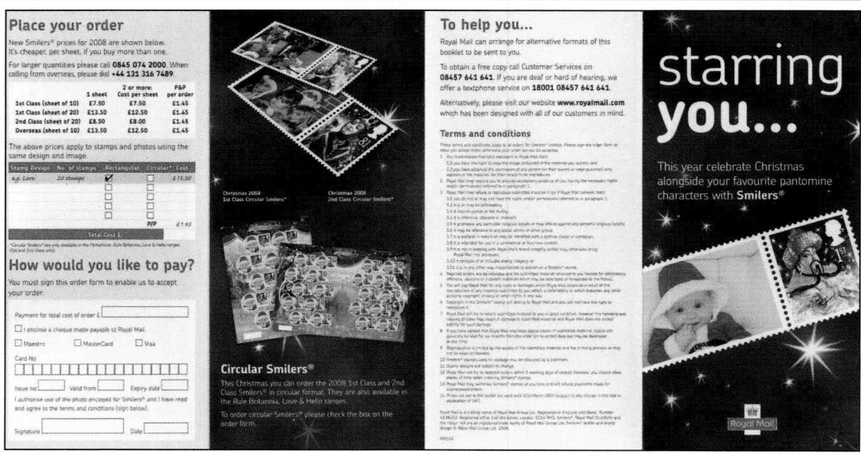

RM Ref: RM116 (Oct 2008)

Seen with 09 JAB in the code box against the question "Where did you hear about Smilers?" This code is believed to be a regional marketing identifier. Other codes may exist. This leaflet had a cut-out on the front panel which when closed showed the location of a photo image where the label would be.

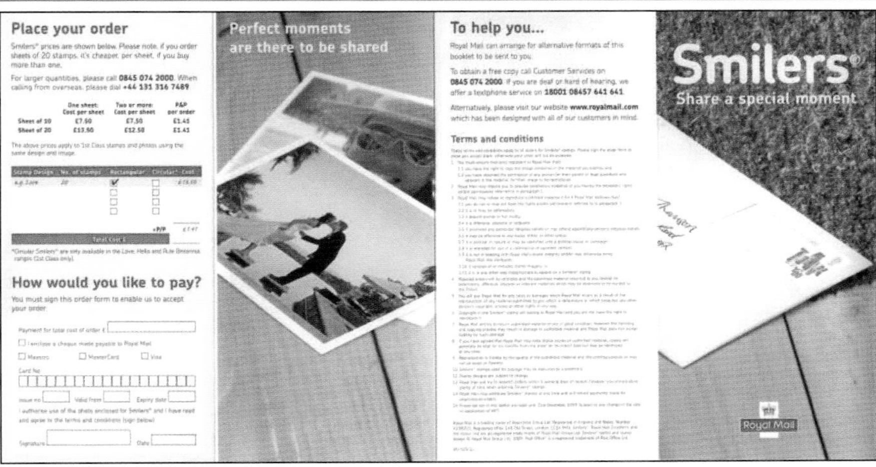

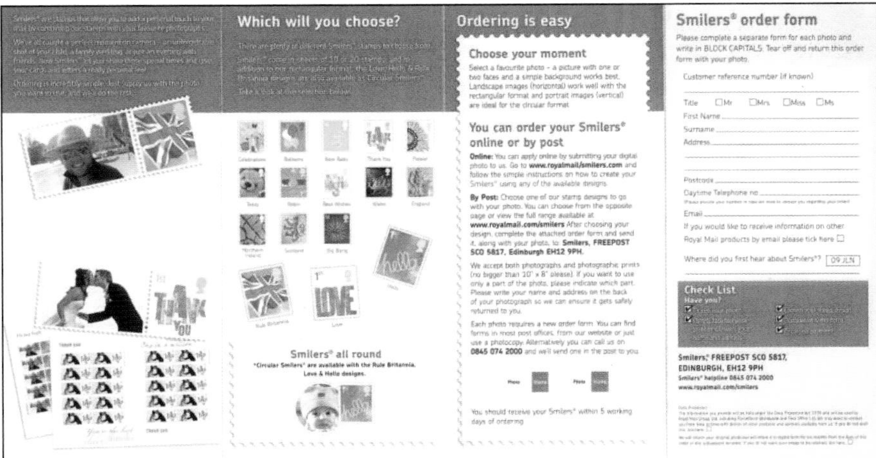

RM Ref: RM 509 DL (June 2009)

Similar to RMP 005 DL (June 2008) but without the Smilers stamp reference number table printed underneath the images of the smilers stamps. Seen with 09 JLN in the code box against the question "Where did you hear about Smilers?" This code is believed to be a regional marketing identifier. Other codes may exist. This leaflet had a cut-out on the front panel which when closed showed a photo image where the label would be.

Welsh language version

A Welsh language version of this pamphlet exists in similar format to this version. RM Ref: RM 510 DL, see page C - 44.

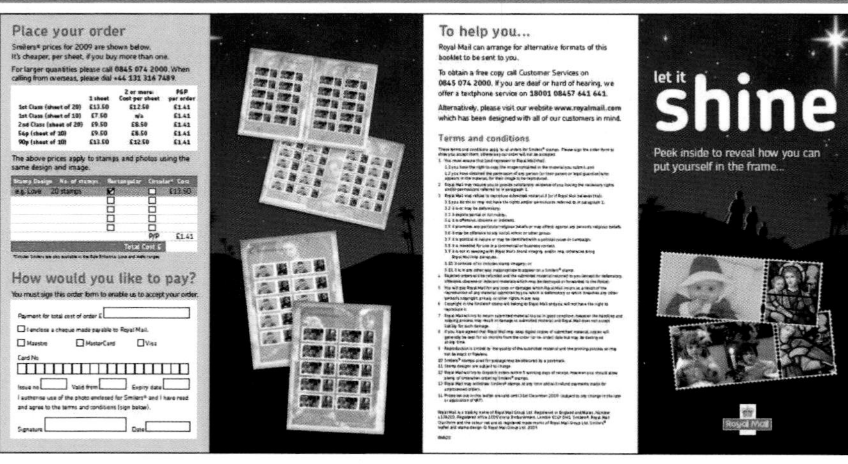

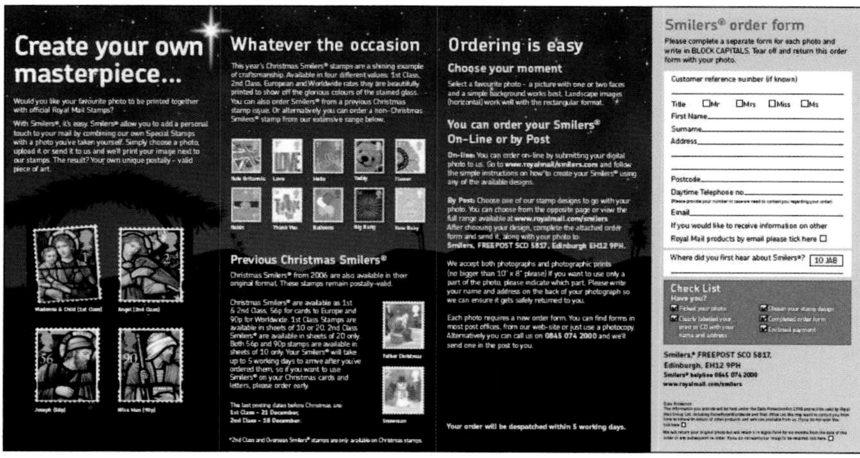

RM Ref: RMX20 (Oct 09)

Seen with 10 JAB in the code box against the question “Where did you hear about Smilers?” This codes is believed to be a regional marketing identifier. Other codes may exist.

Welsh language version

A Welsh language version of this pamphlet exists in similar format to this version. RM Ref: RMX21, see page C - 45.

560/PJM/June05, RMMKH002DL

Note incorrect SM reference to the Farm Animals and Teddy Bear stamps, should be reversed. i.e. Teddy = SM2. Seen with Code 06 JBA, others may exist. See also equivalent English language version, page C - 25.

English/Welsh Dual Language Smilers Publicity Leaflet

Available from June 2005 in dual languages. Generally, they are double sized pamphlets with English text in the lower half and Welsh text in the upper half, depending upon your point of view! Some of the panels have been repositioned in the Welsh versions although the basic content is the same. In this pamphlet, the Welsh language and English language sections were separated by a perforated fold which could be easily separated.

In the subsequent four-panel pamphlets the whole is un-perforated and folded inwards, concertina fashion, and then folded over and down like a conventional map. Given that the English pamphlet already existed, it is somewhat puzzling as to why both languages were printed on a double sized sheet when perhaps only one language at any one time would be read. However, the introduction of dual language Smilers pamphlets is an interesting development by Royal Mail, but probably owes more to their legal obligation to reflect other national languages within UK rather than any specific Welsh marketing effort.

Appendix C - Smilers Publicity

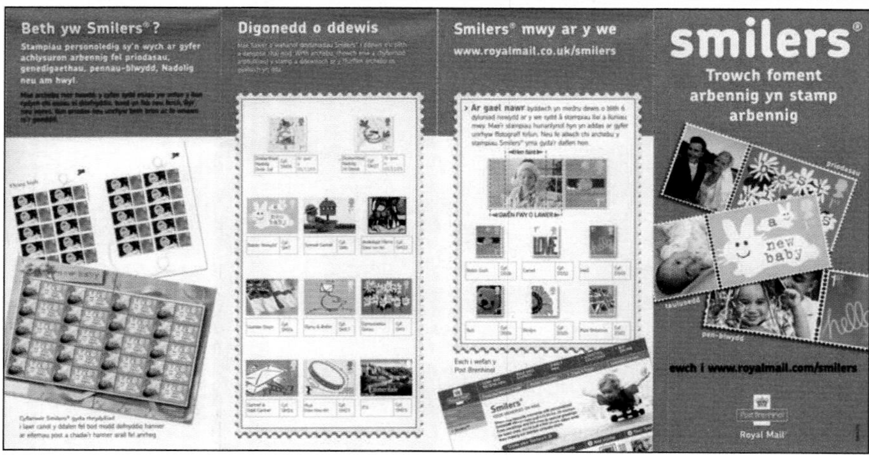

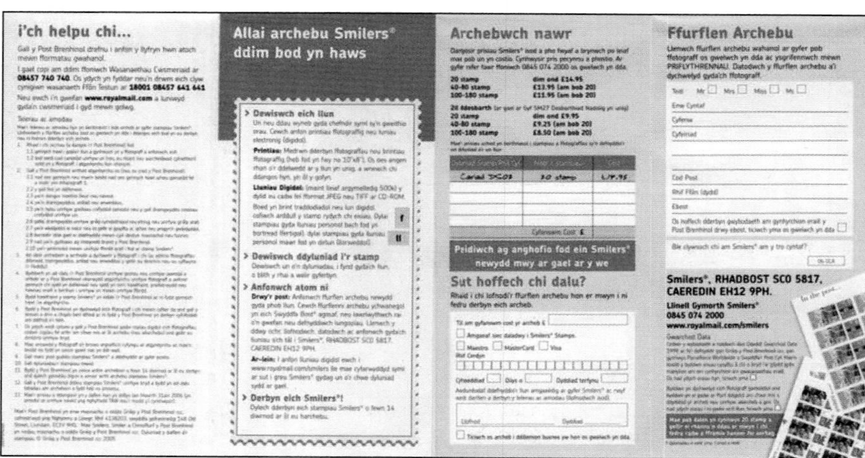

100/PM/Nov05, RMH054

Dual English/Welsh language version of Smilers pamphlet also issued in English (924/PM/Nov05, RMMH053). This version is referenced RMH054 in the bottom right hand corner of the pamphlet cover.

The pamphlet is a double sized double sided with the English text in the lower half and Welsh text in the upper half. Some of the panels have been repositioned in the Welsh version although the basic content is the same. See page C - 27 for equivalent English Language version.

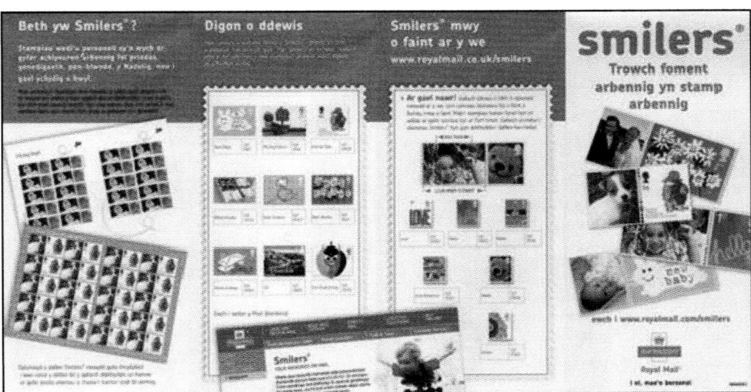

150/PM/May06, RMH093 (Welsh)

Dual English/Welsh language version of Smilers pamphlet also issued in English (RM Ref: 62/PM/Feb06). This version is referenced RMH093 in the bottom right hand corner of the pamphlet cover.

The pamphlet is a double sized double sided with the English text in the lower half and Welsh text in the upper half.

Some of the panels have been repositioned in the Welsh version although the basic content is the same. See page C - 28 for equivalent English Language version.

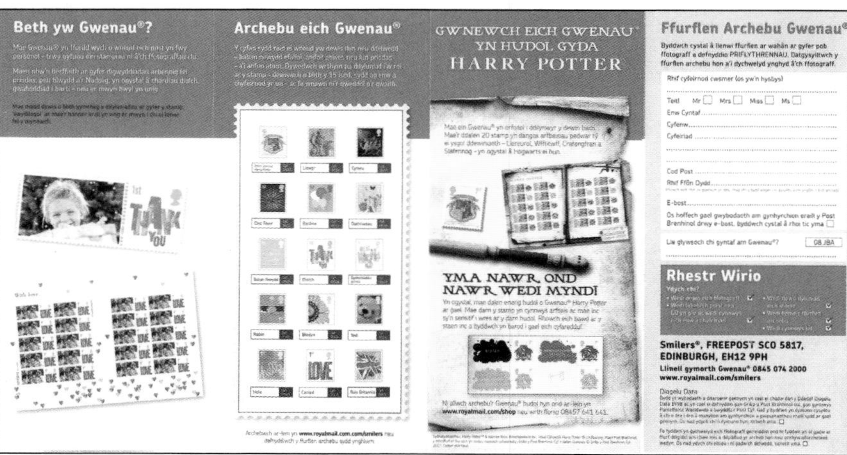

RM Ref: RMJ102DL May 2007 (Welsh)

Seen with 08 JBA in the code box against the question "Lie glywsoch chi gyntaf am Gwenau?" This codes is believed to be a regional marketing identifier. Other codes may exist.

See page C - 33 for equivalent English Language version.

Appendix C

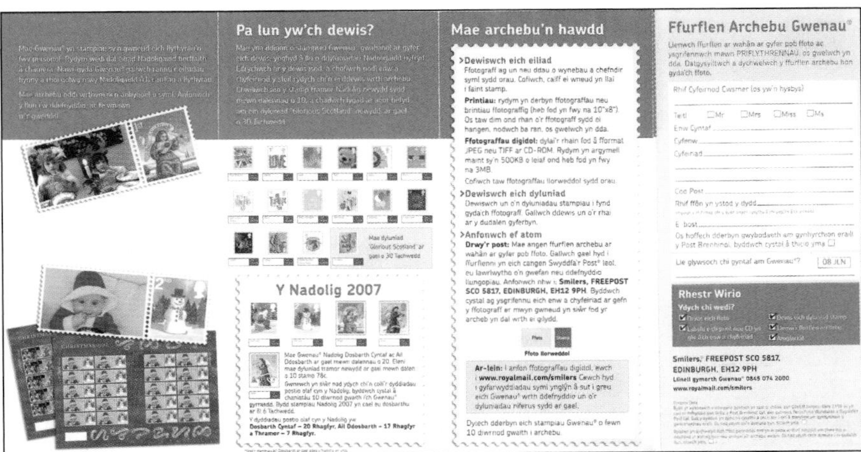

RM Ref: RMJ118DL Oct 2007 (Welsh)

Seen with 08 JLN in the code box against the question ""Lie glywsoch chi gyntaf am Gwenau?" Other codes may exist. This leaflet had a cut-out on the front panel which when closed showed the location of a photo image where the label would be. Coding of the Smilers stamps shown in this leaflet were revised to reflect Royal Mail's revised Smilers pricing policy and to distinguish orders placed after the introduction of the new coding system using revised codes ending in N, in the form DSXXN.

See also English language version of this pamphlet: RM Ref: RMJ117DL (Oct 2007), page C - 34.

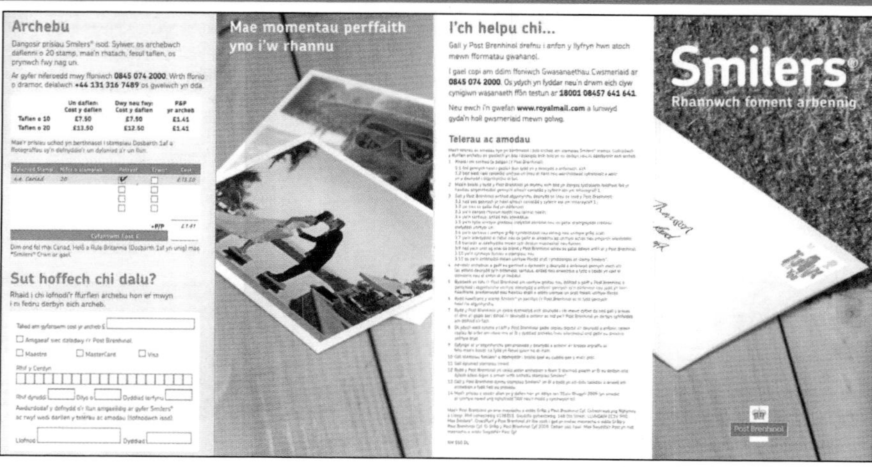

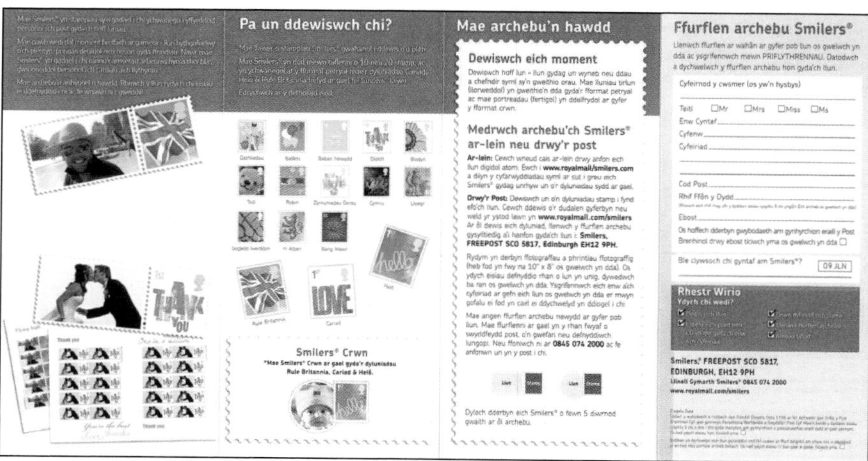

RM Ref: RM 510 DL Jun 2009 (Welsh)

Seen with 09 JLN in the code box against the question “Ble clywsoch chi gyntaf am Smilers?” This code is believed to be a regional marketing identifier. Other codes may exist. This leaflet had a cut-out on the front panel which when closed showed a photo image where the label would be. There was also an English Language version of this pamphlet - RM Ref: RM 509DL, see page C - 37.

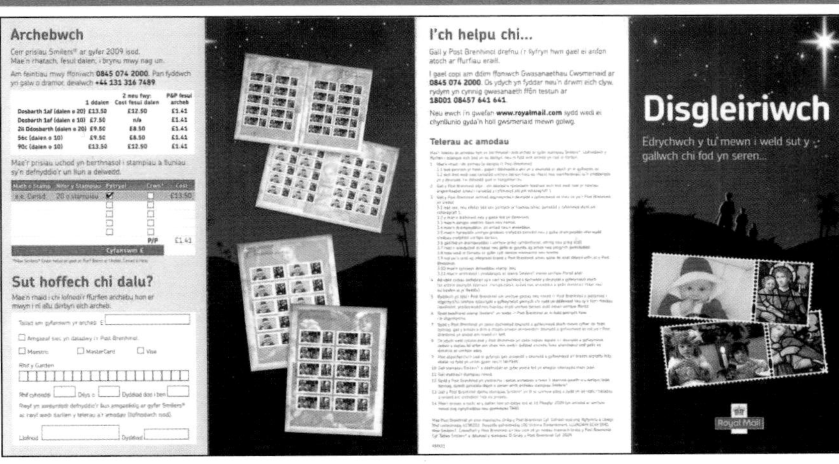

RM Ref: RMX21 Oct 2009 (Welsh)

Seen with 10 JAB in the code box against the question “O Ble y clywsoch chi am Smilers gyntaf ?” This code is believed to be a regional marketing identifier. Other codes may exist. There was also an English Language version of this pamphlet - RM Ref: RMX20, see page C - 38.

FIAT GRANDE PUNTO

Fiat Auto UK: In September 2006 FIAT Auto UK released a Business Customised Stamp sheet to celebrate the sales success of its Grande Punto supermini. To publicise these stamp sheets FIAT Auto UK also produced a pop-up desktop advert which could be found on most dealers counters at the time of the release of these stamp sheets. The sheet designed and released by Fiat Auto UK can claim to be the first true non-philatelic inspired Business Customised Stamp Sheet as it was released in large numbers (6000) targeting a non-philatelic consumer.

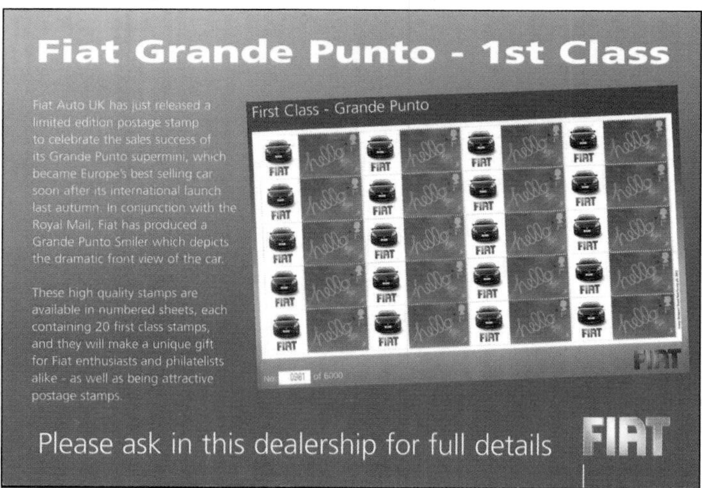

Fiat Grande Punto Business Customised Stamp Sheet "Stand-Up" advert

TRUPRINT

Truprint Film Processing: Royal Mail joined forces with Truprint, one of the UK's largest mail-order film processing companies and using the medium of their film processing envelopes, supplied with a variety of magazines and mail-shots, invited the public to turn their cherished photos into Customised Smilers sheets.

They were also available from dispensers at railway stations and Post Offices branches, having been folded down vertically by machine in advance to make them one-third A4 size (DL) to fit in the racks. Here is a selection of some of those mailing envelopes.

S&C242 DL

SC248 DL

S&C373 DL

S&C211 DL

S&C211 DL (Dispenser)

RMMKG095 DL

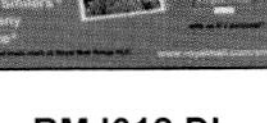

RMJ012 DL

RMJ0093 DL

Smilers Retail Packs

In 2006 Royal Mail considered introducing a new marketing concept for Smilers through retail outlets such as WH Smith & Sons. The *Smilers Retail Pack* was proposed as a neat, straight-off-the-shelf product designed to make life simple for both the retailer and customer. It was proposed that retailers would purchase the Packs, which were specifically designed for easy hook and hang display, at discounted prices to sell direct to customers. The Retail Packs did not contain any stamps, instead they contained a Smilers information and ordering leaflet with a unique ID number that identified the product as a retail purchase. Customers would simply purchase the pack - which includes the cost of processing – fill out the order form, sending it back with the selected image. The cost of packs was proposed at £14.95 per pack, the then cost of a Customised Smilers sheet. Despite going as far as manufacturing some mock-ups and holding discussions with some retail outlets we are not aware that this scheme was ever implemented by Royal Mail.

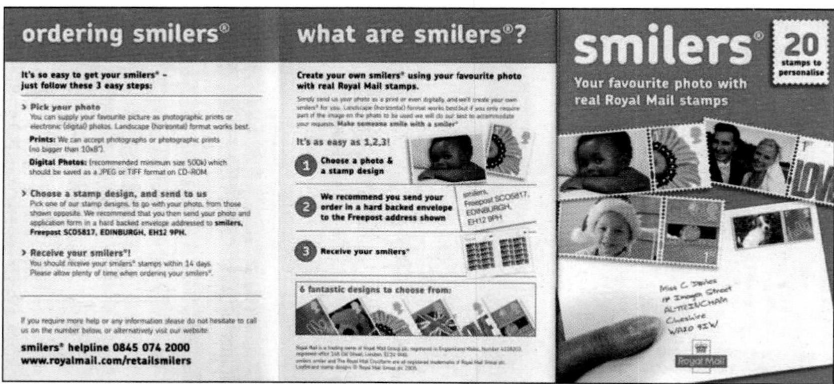

Enclosed leaflet explaining ordering process

Retail Pack - front

Retail Pack - rear